Judaism, History, and the Environment

Judaism, History, and the Environment

Climate Change and Natural Disasters

Dean Phillip Bell

BLOOMSBURY ACADEMIC
LONDON • NEW YORK • OXFORD • NEW DELHI • SYDNEY

BLOOMSBURY ACADEMIC
Bloomsbury Publishing Plc, 50 Bedford Square, London, WC1B 3DP, UK
Bloomsbury Publishing Inc, 1385 Broadway, New York, NY 10018, USA
Bloomsbury Publishing Ireland, 29 Earlsfort Terrace, Dublin 2, D02 AY28, Ireland

BLOOMSBURY, BLOOMSBURY ACADEMIC and the Diana logo are trademarks of
Bloomsbury Publishing Plc

First published in Great Britain 2026

Cover design: Jade Barnett
Cover image © Matt Hardy on Unsplash

Bloomsbury Publishing Plc does not have any control over, or responsibility for, any third-
party websites referred to or in this book. All internet addresses given in this book were
correct at the time of going to press. The author and publisher regret any inconvenience
caused if addresses have changed or sites have ceased to exist, but can accept no
responsibility for any such changes.

A catalogue record for this book is available from the British Library.

A catalog record for this book is available from the Library of Congress.

ISBN: HB: 978-1-3504-6320-2
PB: 978-1-3504-6321-9
ePDF: 978-1-3504-6323-3
eBook: 978-1-3504-6322-6

Typeset by Deanta Global Publishing Services, Chennai, India
Printed and bound in Great Britain

For product safety related questions contact productsafety@bloomsbury.com.

To find out more about our authors and books visit www.bloomsbury.com
and sign up for our newsletters.

Contents

Acknowledgments   vi

Introduction   1

PART I   Historical Cases: Toward a Jewish Environmental History

1   Earthquakes: Understanding Nature and Natural Disasters   11
2   Plague as Natural Disaster   29
3   Floods: From Theology to Technology—Understanding, Mitigation, and
    Prevention   45
4   Learning with Fire   59
5   Comparative Perspectives: Natural Disasters, Jews, and Islam   75

PART II   Disaster, History, and Religion: Tradition and Innovation

6   Beyond History: Disasters and Crises in the Anthropocene   91
7   History, Narratives, and Temporality   107
8   Religion and the Environment: Some Traditional Assessments and
    Applications   121
9   Religion: New Conceptions and Opportunities   137

PART III   New Approaches in the Anthropocene

10   Complexity, Polarization, and Resilience   155
11   From Conceptual Challenges to Practical Applications   169

Notes   185
Bibliography   228
Index   245

Acknowledgments

Work on this book has spanned most of my academic career: from the early days of reading late medieval and early modern German chronicles for my dissertation and noticing the frequent references to what I would learn was "the little ice age" to many conference presentations and articles on aspects of natural disaster and environmental history and the more recent opportunities to explore the application of Jewish texts, thoughts, and experiences to complex and thorny contemporary issues such as climate change throughout my work at the Spertus Institute for Jewish Learning and Leadership.

As a result of that expanse of time and topics, I have both dabbled with and dug into a very broad range of materials. In some cases, this has afforded me the chance to read and interpret historical sources from my own primary field of study. In other cases, it has enticed me to read broadly in areas of history removed from my own, as well as in a diverse range of studies in religion, philosophy, and ecology. In still other cases, it has encouraged me to examine contemporary studies in areas of resilience, psychology, and even artificial intelligence that I would once have imagined to be far from my thoughts.

While I once hoped to make a contribution to what I think of as Jewish environmental history—and the first part of this book aims to do precisely that—I have increasingly come to hope to add to and advance the work of addressing how we think about and counter environmental degradation (which I attempt to consider in the last part of the book). Connecting these two goals (i.e., the first and last parts of this book), I realized that there is much of great significance in the study of history and religion (and especially Jewish history and Judaism) that is helpful and that there is also a need to think differently and more deeply within (and beyond) these fields if we are to make substantive progress for the future.

One of the results of this broad-reaching work is the accumulation of many significant debts of gratitude: for my family—Malkaya, Chanan, Roni, and Yair—who each engaged with different ideas in this volume in their own ways and who always offered different perspectives shaped by their own experiences and their read of the present and the future, and Juli, who over many years has heard a lot about the themes in the volume and who read the manuscript closely in its earliest form and offered feedback and questions; for all the readers of various articles that formed the first part of the book; for Seb Claas, Emily Wootton, and Lalle Pursglove at Bloomsbury, who extracted from me a proposal and helped me to shape it into what would become this book; for Camille Brown, who tracked down many, and often obscure, books and articles; for Harold Israel, for his leadership, support, and friendship as Spertus' Board Chair; for Sharon Silverman, my friend and partner in the important work at Spertus Institute who, as always, read the manuscript with the careful eye of someone who knows just what questions to ask; for Nigel Savage, who shared generously from his pioneering work and insights in Jewish environmentalism to improve many parts of this book; and for Robert Jütte, a dear and long-time friend, whose expertise in a most enviable range of historical, scientific, and medical topics helped me to add depth and nuance throughout this work.

I am especially grateful to Mike Hogue, who has been a leading scholar in many of the fields I have attempted to tackle in this book. Anyone familiar with his seminal works will see the deep influence that he and his scholarship have had (and continue to have) on me. I have had the privilege to work with and learn from Mike for many years now. His impressive scholarship and deep thinking are matched only by his friendship and humanity.

To Keren Fraiman, I extend my most profound appreciation for her constant thought partnership, friendship, and fiery intellect. Keren always challenges me to think more deeply, to ask better questions, and to find ways to engage with students and readers more effectively and with greater impact. She was the first one with whom I discussed this book, and it was her significant insights that gave it its initial shape and it has been our frequent conversations and her regular reflections and suggestions that have made it far better than it would otherwise ever have been.

Finally, I extend my appreciation to the publishers of several of my previous articles and my book on plague in the early modern world, who gave me permission to include parts of and ideas from those works. Thanks for permission from:

- Berghahn Books: "The Great Fire of 1711: Re-Conceptualizing the Jewish Ghetto and Jewish-Christian Relations in Early Modern Frankfurt am Main," in *Archaeologies of Confession: Writing the German Reformation 1517–2017,* ed. Carina Johnson, David Luebke, and Jesse Spohnholz (2017), 193–218.
- Indiana University Press: "Learning from Disasters Past: The Case of an Early Seventeenth-Century Plague in Northern Italy and Beyond," *Jewish Social Studies* 26:1 (Fall 2020): 55–66.
- Oxford University Press: "Navigating the Flood Waters: Perspectives on Jewish Life in Early Modern Germany," *Leo Baeck Institute Yearbook* 56 (2011): 29–52.
- Purdue University Press: "Environmental History and Jewish Studies: Methodological Intersections and Opportunities," *Casden Annual* (2022): 187–204.
- Routledge: *Plague in the Early Modern World: A Documentary History* (2019).
- Vandenhoeck and Ruprecht: "Vulnerability in Judaism: Anthropological and Divine Dimensions," in *Exploring Vulnerability,* ed. Heike Springhart and Günter Thomas (2017), 93–106.

Introduction

The Problem

We have entered a new age, termed the Anthropocene by some, in which human activity has had a significant impact on the climate and the environment. While there are still some people who deny that humans have had a(n) (overly) negative effect on the environment, most scientists and most people today have come to the conclusion that human-induced climate change has had significant impact reflected in increasing temperatures (with corresponding changes to landmasses, oceans, and the atmosphere), along with dramatic storms (including strong hurricanes), severe floods in some places and equally severe droughts in others, raging wildfires, earthquakes, and even the spread of infectious diseases.

While there has been a good deal of discussion on these issues in scholarship, media, public discourse, and governmental policy, the earth continues to heat at alarming rates and with potentially disastrous implications for the future of human and animal life, the environment, and even the planet itself. As a species, humans seem challenged to appreciate the very real implications of climate change for the future as well as for today. It has been difficult to alter our behavior to mitigate climate change, especially when the impact of this change can feel far away from the daily life of many people and when we have the (mistaken) perception that it is largely the "problem" of others far removed from our own communities and realities—such distancing is increasingly less possible. Even as the impact of climate change is increasingly being felt across the globe (including in the availability of resources, the cost of goods, and the frequency of more severe and unpredictable weather patterns, etc.), we do not seem to be motivated to make a great deal of change. There have been some initiatives, of course—and these are important—including commitments from governments related to carbon dioxide emissions and individuals around consumption and the use of alternative energy. But overall, the problem of global warming (described by Timothy Morton as a "hyperobject," meaning that it may be too large and existential for us to believe we can reverse or affect) is one that feels unsolvable (a wicked problem or a wicked predicament). What is more, there are many associated societal challenges in contemporary life that feel equally impossible to solve. This is expressed well in the growing polarization in politics and religion, but also in economic crises—a different form of "heating."

Scientists have regularly sounded alarm bells about the rising temperatures on earth and the significant implications this may have. They have also offered some ways to respond to climate change. But science—which is increasingly deemed to be subjective and changeable and which is often unable to stir people's emotions or move them to make changes that are needed to avoid the dramatic transformations that it has warned are coming—cannot solve the problem on its own.

The Argument

Are there other ways to mobilize people to address climate change and stem the tide of the associated natural (and societal) disasters? On the surface, history seems like it could be helpful in providing examples of the challenges that natural disasters have caused in the past. And there are many, quite dramatic examples. Perhaps such examples would give people a small insight into the difficulties that emerge from such disasters and encourage them to think about ways to avoid them and to understand and perhaps mitigate or respond to them when avoidance is impossible. In fact, history is often valuable in identifying and elevating issues (from the past and from the present (even if decanted through the past)). We can learn valuable lessons about how other people in different settings and at different times understood the challenges around them and tried to respond to them.

In exploring what history can offer, I have chosen examples from Jewish history and premodern (largely medieval and early modern Jewish) history. I selected Jewish history because Jews occupied a liminal position in European society and so offer an opportunity for comparative study, sitting as they did at the intersection of diverse cultures and absorbing a range of ideas and behaviors. Jews themselves discussed natural disasters as well as weather and climate.[1] They did so by drawing on biblical and rabbinic writing and thinking, but also the insights of ancient and non-Jewish sources as well as their own experiences. I selected premodern historical examples for two reasons. First, we have an increasing number and diverse range of source materials in the early modern period. Second, since much of the discussion of the Anthropocene ascribes current climate and environmental issues to modernity (especially since industrialization), it is helpful to compare and contrast premodern worldviews and experiences with more modern ones in order to assess what has changed and what continuities there may have been.[2]

On the surface, religion could provide another valuable way to approach climate change and environmental degradation. On one hand, religion has at times been viewed as part of the problem, since religion, especially the Judeo-Christian tradition, has often been seen to advocate for human exceptionalism and human domination of nature. Nevertheless, religion has also been useful for discussions of stewardship and social and environmental justice. Religion has and continues to provide important insights about the relationship that humans have with each other and with nature (as well as the divine). It provides frameworks for understanding the world and the scope and impact of change. It also gives us powerful narratives and messages that can instill emotion and mobilize and motivate people for change. Related to the Jewish historical cases in Part I (Chapters 1–5) that emphasize communal and social concerns and developments are discussions about Judaism, since premodern Jewish life did not make strict distinctions between religion and other aspects of life. Premodern Jewish life was guided by insights from the Hebrew Bible and the corpus of rabbinic writings that informed the way Jews saw the world around them and how they responded to everyday occurrences as well as intellectual advances, political events, and natural disasters. I focus on Judaism obviously because that is the religion of our historical protagonists in Part I. However, there are other reasons as well. First, Judaism could draw from an extensive reservoir of writing, ideas, and practices that were formative for Jews but that also impacted Christians and Muslims. Second, premodern Judaism— even after the canonization of the Bible, the closing of the Talmud, and the codification of Jewish law—allowed for a great deal of flexibility and adaptability in ways that helped Jews navigate challenging social and political situations and natural disasters. Finally, Judaism has engaged with modernity in complex and important ways. The transformation of Jewish traditions, thinking, and observance can be helpful as an example of ways to shift to address new needs, while emphasizing moral and ethical values.

Part I of this book surfaces some of the lessons we can draw from Jewish history and Judaism, which remain quite important. Disaster management identifies key stages in emergency response, including mitigation, preparedness, response, and recovery. The Jewish historical cases provide examples of ways that premodern people learned from their experiences and developed practices and policies to help respond to and recover from disasters and to prevent or mitigate the impact of future disasters. This could include directives about construction materials, urban planning, quarantine, and even social distancing. Examples of action might include the heroic acts of individuals or groups (for example, rushing to the aid of victims or people in crisis). Inherent in the historical cases was an appreciation for social, communal, and political structures that were valuable in advance of, during, and after disaster struck. Premodern Jews (and others) recognized the need for social relationships as well as political connections and collaboration across and beyond their own communities. Often such collaboration was short-lived and regnant norms of social separation returned after an immediate threat passed. On other occasions, disasters stirred latent tensions and animosities and exploded into marginalization and even physical attacks against outgroups (including Jews and foreigners, for example). The cases in Part I reveal that disasters could challenge the status quo and force new ways of thinking, even as they reinforced power structures and identity (especially through memorialization of events). Natural disasters called on premodern people to seek explanations, which sometimes led to serious grappling with causality and agency, though usually mono-causality and often agency displaced onto an angry God or nefarious others. While premoderns could display awareness of larger, sometimes even regional impact, they rarely had a global perspective and largely saw and understood the world through local conditions and experiences.

The premodern Judaism that emerges in Part I was far less compartmentalized than we once imagined, however. Jews interacted with non-Jews and Jewish ideas fermented in a larger non-Jewish context that also absorbed the flavor of ancient and contemporary scientific thinking and experiences. Religion and science did not have to be, and often were not, at odds in the premodern world. Premodern Judaism provided Jews with a multivalent and meaningful framework for understanding the world and the challenges that they might face. It could also remind Jews of the need to pay attention to their behavior, their religious observance, and their moral and ethical principles. Judaism, and religion more generally, could offer solace in times of despair and uncertainty. It could provide strength to individuals as well as create common cause and a sense of common destiny within Jewish communities and at times beyond in the cities or regions in which Jews lived. Premodern Judaism gave Jews practical tools too, such as restrictions on wasteful destruction, the need to rest the land, and the need to adjust to changing conditions.

The natural disasters of the premodern period could be quite significant, and while they could force new ways of behaving, they could generally be subsumed under traditional intellectual models and frameworks of response. Some exceptional events, such as massive plagues, could upend traditional and inherited ways of thinking, but premoderns managed to navigate through what in hindsight appear to have been difficult circumstances, though not the kind of paradigm-shifting event that climate change represents in the twenty-first century. A model of attitudes advanced by work in Social Psychology suggests that attitudes can be separated into affect (feelings), behavior (actions), and cognition (thought). Premodern Jews grappled with the feelings and emotions evoked by natural disasters; they also developed many helpful practical ways to respond to, mitigate, and prevent future disasters. Yet the cognitive model that premoderns possessed, despite their possibly more direct and organic connection to nature and the absence of rampant modern consumption, is not entirely sufficient for the accelerated multi-scalar change of climate and associated disasters that have emerged and will continue to challenge humans today and into the future.

Judaism, History, and the Environment argues that Jewish history (in its specific context and as part of more general history) and Judaism (as well as religion, and especially the Judeo-Christian tradition more specifically) have a great deal to offer as we face climate change and natural disaster today. Of course, we should not expect that the lessons from the past should be sufficient, whether from history, religion, or any other discipline. But I believe that in addition to some of the benefits that we can harvest from Jewish history and Judaism, there are additional opportunities that are available to us even in the face of the unprecedented and ever-accelerating changes of the Anthropocene. New areas of focus and approaches that we will see in Part II in the field of Jewish history and in the study and practice of Judaism will reveal additional lessons and perspectives that will equip us to respond to the environmental crises around us in valuable and novel ways.

What are these new areas of focus and approaches? In order to provide context for this discussion, Part II opens (in Chapter 6) with a discussion of disasters generally in history and today as a segue to a review of the Anthropocene and its primary features and challenges—including special attention to the debate over the universal and the particular, the idea of the self, notions of progress, globalization, science and technology, the acceleration of time, and complexity. I discuss new trends in history (Chapter 7) that can help us to think about climate change and natural disaster in a contemporary context. Discussions of learning processes and cycles that have emerged in history, especially in environmental history, move history beyond observation and analysis to the realm of practice and performance—that is, history can help us identify ways that people responded to disasters in the past but also uncover the processes by which they learned and adapted and how such processing and adaptation can be useful in other, including contemporary and future, contexts. In a related way, the exploration of "deep history," which extends beyond individual time periods and looks for very long-term changes provides possible ways to understand historical and contemporary developments that are highly contextual as well as connected. Contextualizing and connection are important framing techniques for engaging with complexity and uncertainty, some of the hallmarks of the current climate and environmental crises. "Deep history" affords us insights into broad historical trajectories as well as information about various models and experiences in the past, which sometimes coexisted at the same time. In the rejection of the many binaries that have animated modernity—such as object and subject and human and nature—new approaches to history allow us to engage in perspective shifting and so to understand the experiences and needs of others during the current climate crisis, even when we have not had the same experiences that they have had. It also encourages us to dispel the artificial separation that has kept people from seeing themselves as part, as opposed to above or outside, of nature. Such positioning can help us to invest in environmental work more personally, directly, and emotionally.

In a similar way, Part II digs deeper into the benefits of religion, and Judaism in particular, in understanding and responding to natural disasters and environmental challenges (Chapter 8), as noted above. However, it then outlines new ways of thinking about and engaging with religion that can help encourage new approaches (intellectual and activist) to climate change and environmental crises. Judaism, and religion more generally, provides moral guidance through traditional texts and in response to contemporary issues. Here the emphasis on perennial, ongoing revelation means that people must continually adapt and find and make meaning. As with history, religion offers opportunities for learning. We will see that tradition is an active process that engages with the past and with religious texts but also applies these to new situations to create new meaning and to maintain or discard certain ideas in changed circumstances. In the realm of religious practice, new rituals, liturgies, and stories can mobilize people to take more activist roles, to change their own behavior, or simply raise their own level of consciousness. All of these are important. As the discussion of changing tradition reveals, the call to question traditions, traditional ways of doing things, and handed-down wisdoms more generally is a powerful stance as we explore the reasons for and the ways to combat climate change.

Judaism, History, and the Environment highlights the ways that Jewish history and Judaism have been useful in thinking about and responding to natural disasters in the past and how new inflections in the study of history and religion, especially in a Jewish context, can provide tools even for engaging with climate change and environmental crises now. These contemporary challenges are made all the more difficult, however, because of the acceleration of change, the greater interconnection of people, the complexity of human and environmental systems, and the polarization that is dividing the world and making collaboration and the advancement of shared concerns and values more difficult.

Part III unpacks these issues. If complexity involves self-organization and emergence, a Jewish history that is open to multiple causalities and diverse and indirect impacts can provide resources to understand and respond to new forms of agency and different ideas of causation. Such a Jewish history that can grapple with and hold multiple pasts and multiple narratives also offers resources to imagine multiple futures and examine a variety of possible scenarios for which we can plan. If navigating complexity means we need to move beyond simplicity and binaries, then a Judaism that is used to examining and elevating competing positions and a Jewish history that takes contextualization and change seriously can be valuable. If complexity requires understanding and being able to adapt to change, then Jewish history that focuses on learning processes and a Judaism that understands tradition as an ongoing process of engagement and application that remains relevant throughout time positions us well to navigate whatever changes we may encounter. If complexity demands richer and more deeply connected relationships, then a Judaism that recognizes the importance of engaging with one's own vulnerability and seeing the needs and perspectives of others and a Jewish history that finds community and meaning in diversity of experiences can create connections that will be strong and help forge networks that survive change but that also provide the structure for meaningful adaptation. Part III and the book conclude with some brief reflections on why these observations about history, religion, education, complexity, responsibility, and change matter.

This book does not argue that Jewish history and Judaism—or for that matter, history and religion more generally—hold all the solutions for us to mitigate and respond to climate change and environmental degradation. It does argue, however, that they have always offered important resources and that even today, amid the unprecedented changes we are experiencing, they are valuable. Combined with other ways of understanding the challenges we face, helping us to change our behavior, and providing ways to ameliorate the fear and uncertainty that is rampant, they are essential.

The Audience

This book is for anyone interested in Jewish history, especially medieval and early modern Jewish history, and what has become an emerging field of Jewish environmental history. It is also for those interested in what Judaism has to offer in framing and providing ways to think about and respond to natural disasters and contemporary climate change. But this book is also for anyone who is interested in thinking about how Jewish history and Judaism might be relevant to and offer significant insights about central issues for us today and into the future. I sometimes refer to this as applied Jewish learning—the application of Jewish texts, thoughts, and experiences to the most pressing issues that we face today and are likely to confront tomorrow.

For those less interested in the Jewish inflection of this book, the exploration of how history—which has often been seen as related primarily to the past and, on occasion, to the present (in which the discipline is conducted)—may be helpful in thinking about the future may also resonate. The book also argues that although there is plenty in Judaism and in all religions and faith traditions that can lead to negative developments (witness the conflict that religion often seems to spark or exacerbate), there is an equal, if not greater, measure of wisdom to help us make sense of and adapt to a radically changing world—to reimagine the world and to innovate in ways that will help enrich and perhaps even ensure human life well into the future. This book is about learning and questioning and about making connections across time periods and disciplines. As such, I hope it will be of interest to an engaged adult learning audience, the broader public, and students and scholars in a wide range of academic disciplines who want to see the fruitful way that scholarship today can advance our thinking and make possible connections we may never have imagined.

Historical Cases

Toward a Jewish Environmental History

1

Earthquakes

Understanding Nature and Natural Disasters

Introduction

We experience many different natural disasters. While the nature and intensity of some of these disasters have changed over time or can have different impacts in specific contexts, the experiences of people in the past provide us with important lessons on how to understand and respond to disasters when they happen and how to prepare for them before they occur.

History provides a valuable set of tools and frameworks for this work, even when older ways of thinking have changed or been superseded by new understanding. Part I of this book considers several different natural disasters in Jewish history in order to identify some of the lessons we may learn from previous grappling with disasters and to understand ways that we might need to adjust our thinking and actions in response to contemporary and future events.

The cases in these chapters are from medieval and early modern Jewish history—that is, purposefully from the premodern period. In part, the reason for this is that it allows for the study of natural disasters and views of nature in a relatively delimited historical period (and geography). The focus on premodern events is also valuable because much of the recent discussion of natural disasters and climate change has ascribed the degradation of the environment by humans to modernity, with the result that the premodern experience of humans is often contrasted (positively) with the consumerist and exploitative behavior of modern people. While there is some truth to this assertion, the distinctions between modern and premodern are not always so clear. The cases considered in the chapters in Part I, therefore, allow us to evaluate this argument and to pull out themes that may be helpful today as well as to see connections and disconnections throughout history. Each of these chapters places specific events within a broader context that includes the intellectual sources—biblical, rabbinic, and scientific and philosophical—that helped premodern Jews (and others) attempt to make sense of the disasters that they experienced and heard about. I begin here with a discussion of earthquakes, which models this approach and also uncovers some key observations that will be useful in Parts II and III of this book.

Earthquakes can be devastating, reorganizing ecologies, destroying houses, buildings, and infrastructure, and claiming a significant number of lives. As I write these pages, major earthquakes have claimed thousands of lives in Turkey, Morocco, and Afghanistan. Among my formative experiences in graduate school at the University of California, Berkeley, was the 6.9 magnitude Loma Prieta earthquake in the San Francisco Bay Area in 1989, which caused 63 deaths, 3,757 injuries, and $6 billion in damage, including through collapsed freeways, bridges, and homes. Despite being of generally brief duration, earthquakes can have ongoing impact with subsequent tremors. Earthquakes have plagued humans throughout history, and some regions are particularly noted for seismic activity. While earthquakes are typically caused by natural processes, such as the movement of tectonic plates or the eruption of volcanoes, they can also be caused by human activity, most recently as a result of fracking, which in some places has led to thousands of quakes, for example in Oklahoma.[1]

In this chapter, I will examine Jewish responses to earthquakes in mid-eighteenth-century England. These responses will be placed into a broader context of medieval and early modern experiences with and accounts of earthquakes. Responses to earthquakes throughout history, like responses to other natural disasters (mass events), drew from a range of scientific knowledge, religious texts and theology, social and cultural lenses, and personal experiences. As with all "narratives," accounts of earthquakes were more than "objective" reports; rather they served particular purposes that could be political and polemical.

Sources for Understanding Earthquakes: Bible, Rabbinics, and Classical Philosophy and Science

Individuals reporting on earthquakes in the eighteenth century, like their predecessors, were informed by ideas that streamed to them through religious texts—in the case of Jews, especially from the Bible and the corpus of rabbinic texts, which often interpreted biblical texts and tales—and the scientific knowledge of the day, which often borrowed from Greco-Roman philosophical schools and contemporary scientific knowledge. When it came to the Bible, there were several well-known passages that could be levied to describe and understand earthquakes. At times, the Bible associated the quaking of the earth with God's anger (and the use of God's power against Israel's enemies or in response to human sins). In the book of Ezekiel, for example, the shaking of the land was depicted as punishment due to God's anger. As Ezek. 38:18-23 relates,

On that day, when Gog sets foot on the soil of Israel—declares the Sovereign GOD—My raging anger shall flare up.

For I have decreed in My indignation and in My blazing wrath: On that day, a terrible earthquake shall befall the land of Israel.

The fish of the sea, the birds of the sky, the beasts of the field, all creeping things that move on the ground, and every human being on earth shall quake before Me.

Mountains shall be overthrown, cliffs shall topple, and every wall shall crumble to the ground.

I will then summon the sword against him throughout My mountains—declares the Sovereign GOD—and every man's sword shall be turned against his kin.

I will punish him with pestilence and with bloodshed; and I will pour torrential rain, hailstones, and sulfurous fire upon him and his hordes and the many peoples with him.

Thus will I manifest My greatness and My holiness, and make Myself known in the sight of many nations. And they shall know that I am GOD.

In this case, God's anger is stirred against the Israelites' enemy, Gog. While the biblical passage refers to a particular figure, Gog, from the land of Magog, later interpretations and translations (including the Septuagint) referred to Gog and Magog as two enemies to be defeated by the messiah at the end of days. Regardless of who Gog may have been or where he came from—possibly in central Anatolia in the seventh century BCE—the biblical figure of Gog serves as a powerful symbol of an evil enemy of God and the Israelites that drew a range of biblical texts together to further describe him. In the next chapter of Ezek. (39:1-8), God dictates to the prophet:

And you, O mortal, prophesy against Gog and say: Thus said the Sovereign GOD: I am going to deal with you, O Gog, chief prince of Meshech and Tubal!

I will turn you around and drive you on, and I will take you from the far north and lead you toward the mountains of Israel.

I will strike your bow from your left hand and I will loosen the arrows from your right hand.

You shall fall on the mountains of Israel, you and all your battalions and the peoples who are with you; and I will give you as food to carrion birds of every sort and to the beasts of the field, as you lie in the open field. For I have spoken—declares the Sovereign GOD.

And I will send a fire against Magog and against those who dwell secure in the coastlands. And they shall know that I am GOD.

I will make My holy name known among My people Israel, and never again will I let My holy name be profaned. And the nations shall know that I, GOD, am holy in Israel.

Ah! it has come, it has happened—declares the Sovereign GOD: this is that day that I decreed.

The text connects God's anger and blazing wrath with the terrible earthquake, though the question of cause and effect is complex. It appears that God allows or causes an earthquake (*ra'ash gadol*) because of anger. The effect quite literally is the quaking (*romash*) of all creatures—trembling before God, as the mountains and cliffs crumble and fall down. While the earthquake is in response to Gog and his armies, it is curiously the land of Israel that is afflicted. The passage continues with a range of punishments that God brings against Gog, including pestilence, bloodshed, heavy rain, hail, and sulfurous fire; that is, the earthquake is one of a range of disasters that God sends down upon Gog. Again, it is unclear what the connection of these various punishments might be. What is clear is that the range of disasters has some connection and that together they doom Gog and his minions. The end goal of the earthquake, as noted at the end of this passage, is the manifestation of God's power and, in the succeeding text, also the destruction of Gog and the devastation of his lands. In the text, therefore, earthquakes are controlled by God and serve particular and destructive purposes.

Similarly, in Ps. 18:8, the earth shook and trembled, and the foundations of the mountains moved because God was angry:

> Then the earth rocked and quaked;
> the foundations of the mountains shook,
> rocked by His indignation;

In this psalm, David expresses his thanks for being saved from his enemies. At the same time, God's devastating actions are reported:

> The ocean bed was exposed;
> the foundations of the world were laid bare
> by Your mighty roaring, O LORD,
> at the blast of the breath of Your nostrils. (18:16)

As in many biblical passages, earthquakes were accompanied by other natural (and at times supernatural) events, such as lightning, hail, and fiery coals falling from the sky.

God's anger could be directed not only at Israel's enemies but also at the Israelites themselves when their behavior was unacceptable, and they spurned the word of God. According to Isa. 5:25, for example, the shaking of the earth denoted that God's anger had been kindled:

> That is why
> GOD's anger was roused
> Against this covenanted people,
> Why God's arm was stretched out against it
> And struck it,
> So that the mountains quaked,
> And its corpses lay
> Like refuse in the streets.
> Yet God's anger has not turned back,
> And a divine arm is outstretched still.

The medieval exegete Rashi here connects the mountains with the kings and princes of Israel, who were quaking at God's wrath. In this case, as the text notes, God's arm struck the people such that the mountains quaked, with the effect that people died in the streets. Though the text does not specify subsequent earthquakes, the people have not repented, and so God's anger is still outstretched. It is tempting to imagine the aftershocks continuing while the Israelites had not returned to God.

At times, the quaking of the earth signals something momentous—not necessarily destructive fury. The Exodus narrative related to the revelation, for example, describes God's thundering voice that accompanied direct revelation ("there was thunder, and lightning, and a very loud blast of the horn" (Exod. 19:16)), perceived by some as an earthquake.

The rabbis similarly associated earthquakes with God and, in particular, with God's power or displeasure. Consider, for example, the Babylonian Talmud Tractate Berakhot 59a:

> And over earthquakes. What are earthquakes? R. Kattina said: A rumbling of the earth. R. Kattina was once going along the road, and when he came to the door of the house of a certain necromancer, there was a rumbling of the earth. He said: Does the necromancer know what this rumbling is? He called after him, Kattina, Kattina, why should I not know? When the Holy One Blessed be He, calls to mind His Children, who are plunged in suffering among the nations of the world. He lets fall two tears into the ocean, and the sound is heard from one end of the world to the other, and that is the rumbling. Said Kattina: The necromancer and his words are false. If it was as he says, there should be one rumbling after another! He did not really mean this, however. There really was rumbling after another, and the reason why he did not admit it was so that people would not go astray after him. R. Kattina, for his own part, said: [God] clasps His hands, as it says: I will also smite my hands together, and I will satisfy my fury. R. Nathan said: [God] emits a sigh, as it is said: I will satisfy my fury upon them and I will be eased. And the Rabbis said: He treads upon the firmament, as it says: He giveth a noise as they that tread grapes against all the inhabitants of the earth. R. Aha b. Jacob says: He presses his feet together beneath the throne of glory, as it says: Thus saith the Lord, the heaven is my throne and the earth is my foot-stool.

As with the biblical texts, this rabbinic text offers a number of explanations for the quaking of the earth. These range from God's sadness at the persecution of the Chosen People—in this scenario, it is the heaviness of God's tears pounding into the ocean that causes the rumbling—to the expression of pent-up fury against people, presumably for their poor behavior. It is unclear if this is a punishment for the persecutors of the Jews, as would follow from the trajectory of the passage, or for the Jews themselves. Indeed, as would be true in later historical periods as well, the rabbis might leverage stories of earthquakes as a form of moral upbraiding. In some rabbinic writing, such as the midrash to the Book of Samuel, earthquakes are understood as a tool to awaken people from sins such as divisiveness, idleness, and idolatry.[2]

In addition to traditional Jewish sources of knowledge, premodern Jews, like their Christian and Muslim neighbors, also read and reflected upon a wide range of classical philosophical and scientific sources. When it came to the natural sciences, the authority of Aristotle (fourth century BCE) and Pliny the Elder (23–79 CE) were frequently cited, if not always completely accepted, in the medieval and early modern periods.

Aristotle treated the topic of earthquakes in his *Meteorologica* II chapter VII. He discussed various views (e.g., those of the ancient Greek philosophers Anaxagoras, Democritus, and Anaximenes) on the cause of earthquakes.[3] But he rejected these views and, instead, posited that the cause of earthquakes and earth tremors was akin to that of wind. Aristotle maintained that

> Now it is clear, as we have already said, that there must be exhalation both from moist and dry, and earthquakes are a necessary result of the existence of these exhalations . . . So the cause of earth tremors is neither water nor earth but wind, which causes them when the external exhalation flows inwards . . . This is why the majority of earthquakes and the greatest occur in calm weather.[4]

Aristotle observed that earthquakes are less violent when the wind is blowing, that most major earthquakes occur at night, and that those that occur during the day tend to occur at midday, this being, as a rule the calmest time of the day.[5] He continued that "for the same reason earthquakes occur most often in spring and autumn and during rains and droughts, since these periods produce most wind. For summer and winter, both bring calm weather, the one because of its frosts, the other because of its warmth, the one thus being too cold, the other too dry to produce winds."[6] The wind is the cause of subterranean noises known to proceed earthquakes,[7] and while water sometimes bursts forth during an earthquake, it is not the cause (the cause is the wind).[8] Aristotle also discussed signs for coming earthquakes, and he described the ongoing reverberations after an earthquake.[9]

Other classical writers addressed the phenomenon of earthquakes as well.[10] Pliny the Elder, for example, in his *Natural History* offered several observations that would continue to be cited for centuries. He noted, "I think it indubitable that their cause is to be attributed to the winds; for the tremors of the earth never occur except when the sea is calm and the sky so still that birds are unable to soar because all the breath that carried them has been withdrawn."[11] Earthquakes, he noted, are preceded or accompanied by a terrible sound and they are more frequent in autumn and spring and more frequent at night than in the daytime. Pliny also noted that the sudden wave on the sea is a forecast of an earthquake, just as a thin streak of cloud over a wide space is. Another sign of earthquakes is muddy and foul-smelling water in the wells and certain inundations of the sea. As for Aristotle, wind also played a role in Pliny's explanation and he argued that earthquakes stopped when the wind had found an outlet. For Pliny, it was not only the earthquake itself that was a problem. The earthquake served as a portent of other natural events about to happen.[12]

Understanding Earthquakes in the Middle Ages

Biblical and rabbinic sources provided a foundation for how premodern Jews could understand earthquakes. Intellectually, such disasters could be ascribed to divine warning or anger, and they forced reflection and repentance. That is, in a certain sense, this approach removed some human agency and simultaneously provided a path for humans to take action in order to prevent or end the quaking of the earth. Biblical and rabbinic sources also provided language and metaphors that helped to make experiences like earthquakes relatable and part of daily life, domesticating them. These discussions also placed disasters like earthquakes on a much larger stage, related to core theological ideas and religious beliefs. To deepen this analysis, let's consider responses to specific earthquakes in history in order to see how this intellectual apparatus was utilized and how it related (or not) to more practical responses.

We have records of many earthquakes throughout Antiquity and into the Middle Ages. While we tend to associate the year 1348 with the outbreak of devastating plague, the year also witnessed massive earthquakes. Those events help us to identify some key issues associated with premodern experiences of earthquakes. One of the best-known examples from this period is from Italy and Austria. An initial event may have occurred in January of 1348. The massive tremor of March 5 had an epicenter in Villach, destroying houses and entire villages. It also led to massive flooding in some villages in Carinthia, which were underwater for days. In response, some governing authorities called for special recitations of psalms.[13]

The events of 1348 were further intensified by the conditions of the previous decade, which included harsh winters, flooding, plague, and scarce food supplies.[14] A tinderbox of social tensions led to riots and anti-Jewish violence in many places.[15] Various natural and divine explanations were rallied to explain the earthquake, often referencing or reinforcing political conditions[16] and spawning later historical accounts for a variety of purposes.[17] As could often be the case, one disaster could follow another—less than a decade later, in 1356, another major earthquake struck Basel. Drawing from biblical precedents, most historical accounts in the Middle Ages explained natural disasters and social calamities as proof of God's sovereignty over the world and as God's revenge for human pride and sin. The events of this world were not random; rather, they were ordered, and most people believed that Divine omnipotence was still reflected in daily happenings.[18]

For medieval Jews, the investigation of nature was generally linked to a philosophical or theological system.[19] Some medieval Jews were involved in the translation and discussion of classical philosophical and scientific works. They elevated the quest for understanding of God and the act of creation to the ultimate ideal of Jewish religiosity. While the great medieval Jewish thinker Bahya ibn Pakuda (second half of the eleventh century), for example, argued that it was wrong to predict and calculate the forces of nature, he nevertheless believed that it was the highest form of divine worship to contemplate the wondrous activities of nature and thereby to praise God.[20]

When it came to understanding nature, medieval Jews also drew from a well of rabbinic attitudes, characterized by the historian David Ruderman as unsystematized, chaotic, and at times even contradictory.[21] That rabbinic view included a few common elements, however: openness to most forms of spiritual and physical healing; more than passing knowledge of ancient cosmological schemes, astronomy, and natural philosophy; an appreciation for astral forces that helped to determine the fate of those living on earth; and an enthusiastic belief in the power of magic to transform and manipulate the physical world.[22]

A helpful example of the medieval Jewish approach to earthquakes can be gleaned from a fifteenth-century anonymous chronicle from Gerona, in Catalonia (northeast Spain).[23] The situation for Jews there was complicated, as it was in other parts of Spain after the forced conversions of 1391. Jews maintained some privileges, but in 1442 the area of the Jewish quarter was reduced. In the midst of complicated political and social conditions, a severe earthquake struck the city in 1427.

The author of the anonymous chronicle began the account by providing a clear description of the date and time of the quake, connecting it with biblical passages suggesting punishments for sin and transgression of the Torah. Indeed, permeating the entire presentation were many biblical quotes, which were often strung together in long succession. Consider, for example, section two, which utilized several biblical passages to describe the details of the event:

> *Then the earth rocked and quaked* (2 Sam 22:8), the fifth day in the night, the third hour after midnight. And the entire day was not silent (Isa 62:6), voices of alarm were heard in the air like the raging voice of the bull and *[there was a] great and mighty wind* (1 Kgs 19:11) coming from the west over the entire earth and that rose from below the earth like the rim of the earth, sidelong eastward and spanned the earth and the walls and the rims sidelong westward. And all the oscillations that were on the earth were sidelong westward. See this, wonders of God.[24]

The structure of the account is more akin to a biblical commentary than a chronicle, memoir, or scientific observation.

The account described the destruction wrought by the earthquake, in terms of general alarm and degree of destruction, and narrated the evacuation of the city. The author drew from biblical texts and precedents but also inserted numerous observations taken from contemporary chronicles.[25] The author called the earthquake a wonder of God and also noted that no Jews died in the event. In fact, the account could be construed as obliquely polemical, as it juxtaposed the fact that no Jews died in the quake with descriptions of the destruction of Christian sites and the death of some Christians.[26] In section three, the author noted, regarding destruction in an area near a synagogue, that "And not one among the men and women and the children died because it all was a miracle; they built tents in which to dwell in the fields and vineyards according to voice of the earthquake." Or, consider section nine, where the author wrote:

> And the sages of Israel say that [the quaking of the earth] alludes to the creation of the kingdoms, and they bring [the] witness of the prophecy of Jeremiah, *see, I am arousing a destructive wind against Babylon etc.* (Jer 51:1), and there is no doubt that the sign of this is great and this terrible earthquake is a sign and a miracle, because this did not bring calamity upon the community, although this great storm is a terrible quaking, so *that they reeled and staggered like a drunken man* (Ps 107:27).

The author associated the earthquake, as did classical scholars such as Pliny, with a variety of natural conditions, including rising water levels, vapors and smells emanating from the earth, rain and clouds, as well as wind inside the earth. In section nine, the author related that "It is written in philosophy that the wind gathered and was detained in the belly of the earth, and the unfortunate vapors there caused the earthquake." Here, the author balanced traditional classical thinking about the relation of wind and earthquakes with rabbinic discussions about earthquakes as signs and miracles, as well as punishment for sins. Indeed, the author suggested that the earthquake should be a sign to turn to God, and he observed that the tremors themselves ceased upon repentance.[27]

Throughout the account, it was God who was the agent directing the earthquake,[28] as the author cited Isa. 24, "and behold the Lord will strip the earth bare."[29] Ultimately, earthquakes were presented as mysteries of God that were beyond human understanding and that should allow us to see the power of God and increase our estimation of Him.[30] The account followed a broader historical outline as well. Following Davidic prophecy, it helped to signal the end of the Babylonian reign. The author ended the account with a review of some significant earthquakes in history, placing the events in Gerona within both a historical and theological context.

Early Modern Earthquake Narratives

Early modern Jews also narrated earthquakes, drawing from the same Jewish and classical sources. They simultaneously placed their narratives into other intellectual and political contexts, often leveraging them for religious or polemical purposes. While they drew from much of the same intellectual stock that medieval Jews leveraged, they also signaled some intellectual shifts related to changing religious ideas and scientific advances.

Azaria de Rossi, who lived between approximately 1511 and 1578, was one of the greatest Jewish scholars of the early modern period.[31] Born in Mantua, he spent time in various locations throughout Italy, settling for a second time in Ferrara in 1569, after the expulsion of the Jews from the Papal States. His major work, *Me'or Enayim* (Enlightenment to the Eyes), 1573–75, showcased de Rossi's broad erudition and familiarity with Jewish and non-Jewish sources.[32] Spurned by some rabbinic authorities, the book nevertheless continued to exercise important influence well into the modern period.

The first chapter of *Me'or Enyaim* is entitled "Kol Elohim" (The Voice of God), and it described an earthquake that de Rossi experienced in Ferrara in 1571. De Rossi's account contained recognizable features of other contemporary accounts,[33] but he also utilized classical philosophical (regarding the ideal conditions for earthquakes, air turbulence, etc.) as well as Jewish sources. De Rossi provided a lengthy quotation from Plutarch that gathered together in summary fashion the views of the great philosophers on earthquakes.[34] Citing the "philosophers" generally, for example, de Rossi noted that the works of the natural philosophers contain expressions to denote seven kinds of earthquakes.[35] He pointed out that "men of science" explained the cause of earthquakes by the movements of the celestial bodies,[36] and he wrote that "According to scholars, and as we ourselves know from our own experience, the earthquake occurs most often and with the greatest virulence during the night and from midnight onwards when people are sound asleep."[37] But de Rossi also engaged a wide range of rabbinic sources, including discussions from the Talmud (especially in tractate Berakhot), midrashic works, the *Zohar*, as well as contemporary rabbinic writings.[38] Throughout, his method resembled biblical exegesis, as he unpacked various biblical passages and interspersed observations from various rabbinic *midrashim* and *aggadot* in his discussion.

The early part of de Rossi's account was highly descriptive. He provided a vivid portrayal of the general terror (shattering sounds and reverberations), ensuing destruction (collapsing buildings, pestilence, and fires, for example), and the widespread distribution of charity. For de Rossi, the earthquake was a major and unusual event: he wrote, for example, of the shattering and resounding noise,

> We had never heard the likes of it before, and as for our ancestors, it was hundreds of years since they had reported such a happening. Quite apart from the tumultuous noises and threatening sounds emitted from the skies, there was the clanging of the tiles and drains of the roofs as they collided against each other and rolled around. The ears of anyone who heard it rang—and who was so deaf not to hear it? Their hearts quivered with fear lest the earth be annihilated and the world and its inhabitants left desolate.[39]

De Rossi also provided details about the timing and date of events, as well as of his family's escape and his wife's illness and recovery. He noted that in their rush to find a haven, people left their possessions behind and ran for open spaces:

> How could God not forgive the iniquities of His people at a time like this? It was by then the Lord's Sabbath, but in order to save life and deliver from death those who were prepared to serve Him in perpetuity, many persons took their children on their shoulders, their clothes and other belongings on their backs, with a light or torch to illuminate their path. The difference between holy and profane was now obliterated; it was as though God had forgotten the appointed time and Sabbath.[40]

De Rossi wrote that ten synagogues remained miraculously intact and that no able-bodied Jews died: "Yet miraculously, not one of the ten prayer houses and synagogues devoted to God here in Ferrara fell into disuse. It is true they were damaged and suffered from cracks and fissures, which had to be prepared, but this did not deter people from using them for prayer day and night."[41] Despite the emphasis on the impact on the Jewish community, his account, nevertheless, evinced a certain patriotic fervor for the city in which he was living.[42]

Throughout his exposition, de Rossi posited an inextricable link between terrestrial and celestial worlds. He presented earthquakes as portents of changing times and a means that God utilized to admonish the wicked to repent, suggesting that

> But as for us, to God alone do we attribute such events, who also employs natural causes as a vehicle [for His actions]. Thus, with penitence and the performance of pious acts do we react to such events in the hope of deflecting His anger away

from us and ensuring that we appear righteous in His eyes. Or at least we should steer a middle path.[43]

De Rossi was scornful of astrological predictions of occurrences of unnatural phenomena.[44] He also rejected the idea that any rabbinic notion of earthquakes as punishment for impious behavior should be taken as categorical. De Rossi pointed out that earthquakes do not always occur by means of divine intervention. There were natural causes and consequences, and they should not be attributed to God or nature consistently.[45] For de Rossi, then, earthquakes were not miracles per se, since they have happened many times in the world. They did, however, have the appearance of miracles, in part because humans were more affected by the stimulation of the senses than by the dictates of the intellect, and they were unaffected by things that occur regularly and constantly.[46]

While de Rossi pointed out here, as in other places, that the writings of the rabbis should not always be taken literally, he did note that the rabbis basically agreed that earthquakes were initiated by divine decree. De Rossi highlighted the arguments that earthquakes demonstrated God's wonders and were intended to instill awe and fear. He concluded that such disasters served an important purpose in bringing people to repent, supplicate God, and thank and praise God upon salvation.[47]

David Gans was born in 1541 and died in 1613. He was a chronicler, astronomer, and mathematician. He also studied Talmud at Bonn and Frankfurt, and he was a student of many of the leading rabbis of the age. At the same time, Gans was familiar with and utilized a wide variety of German and Czech chronicles, and he was in contact with leading non-Jewish intellectuals and the eclectic court of Rudolph II in Prague.[48]

His chronicle *Zemah David* (Seed of David) was in the format of a universal chronicle that was in fashion among many late sixteenth-century central European Protestants.[49] The chronicle was divided into two sections. The first focused on Jewish history, especially the famous Jewish sages. Part two, however, presented broader world history, though still focused in large measure on the Jews.

Gans was criticized by some for combining Jewish and non-Jewish source materials, though he defended his approach, arguing that he utilized non-Jewish sources only when their authors had nothing particular to gain in writing and where they could help fill in the historical picture.[50] Nonetheless, Gans clearly imbibed much of the intellectual culture that surrounded him, and his work shared an emphasis on various portents and wonders so popularly narrated in the sixteenth and early seventeenth centuries, while often recasting them for a Jewish audience. The retelling of history, Gans argued, served many purposes. The narration of earthquakes and other natural events provided evidence of Divine Providence; knowledge that God's justice punishes the wicked even in this world; and encouragement to pray to God "to restore our judges as of old and to bring about the messianic redemption."[51]

Often, Gans' accounts were of a historical nature, discussing incidents from the past; though Gans also narrated a number of more contemporary earthquakes from the late sixteenth century. In general, his descriptions were neutral, and he discussed the general devastation wrought by such quakes. To give one example, for the year 188 CE, he wrote:

> Signs appeared in the great, awe-inspiring and wondrous heavens in the city of Rome
> in the year 948, 188 according to the Christians, that in [that] year fire fell from the
> skies and the palaces and houses of worship that were in the city of Rome were set on
> fire, and the rest of the wondrous buildings along with the collection houses and all
> the books that were there were consumed, as was in Alexandria in Egypt. And after
> the fire there was a great earthquake in Rome, and after the dreadful earthquake fire
> fell from the sky twice and consumed many parts of the city of Rome. And after this
> there was a great hunger, and after the hunger plague, Casius mark 17.[52]

Gans' depiction of earthquakes and other natural disasters combined general
descriptions of devastation with contemporary penchants for finding signs and portents
in events in the world. As with other natural disasters narrated in the chronicle, Gans
saw such events as following various signs (eclipses, new stars or comets, multiple suns
in the sky, etc.) of God's anger or displeasure.[53] At other times, Gans simply detailed the
damage caused by earthquakes, drawing from Christian sources, without placing the
events themselves into a broader theological mold. Regarding the powerful earthquake
in Lisbon in 1531, for example, he wrote:

> Also, in this year there was a great and terrible earthquake in the large city of
> Lisbon, which is in the land of Portugal. And all the towers and high buildings
> fell to the ground because of the earthquake, including 1,500 houses. And the
> earthquake killed many people, and the trembling did not cease for eight days.[54]

Gans' accounts may have responded to popular tastes for such information, but they
also paralleled discussions in many non-Jewish accounts and, in a sense, allowed Gans
to co-opt historical and natural events in the service of presenting Jews as central in
history. While Gans did not engage directly with the philosophical authorities cited by
de Rossi, he did clearly read and draw from a range of Jewish and Christian chronicles
for much of his information. Although the resulting account was more a synthesis of
various events and historical personalities, the ways in which Gans selected material
and the general goals he addressed in so doing make his chronicle a helpful text in
understanding contemporary approaches to earthquakes and a range of natural
disasters, environmental conditions, and cosmic portents. How Gans understood
such events affords us an opportunity to evaluate an important late sixteenth-century
thinker, steeped in a rich intellectual world at a time of great environmental turmoil.
Many of Gans' descriptions are brief and fairly "neutral." Within the scope of his
purpose in writing the second book of *Zemah David*, however, the events he narrated
had great meaning.

Earthquake Accounts at the Edge of Modernity

During the early modern period, a variety of scientific advances, together labeled as
the scientific revolution, occurred. Distinctions between objective knowledge and

subjective understanding or feeling were introduced, and nature frequently came to be seen as an abstract existence apart from humanity (consider the work and figure of Galileo).[55] In some cases, the workings of nature became mere movements stripped of any larger purpose or connections. Although this new orientation could be anti-supernaturalist, it was never entirely antagonistic to religious belief. There was a growing feeling among some by the sixteenth century that miracles had ceased, but since the world was governed by divine providence, God could still produce earthquakes, floods, and other natural signs if God so chose. Although the potential for divine disempowerment was latent in these scientific advances, the idea that God designed and operated the world remained central, especially in popular and theological discourse.[56]

With the Enlightenment at the end of the eighteenth century, some have seen the beginning of human subjugation of nature. The modern scientific study of nature was informed by experimentation, and the full range of natural phenomena was considered an area of legitimate study. Some scholars question whether the idea of a scientific "revolution" is the correct way to think about the intellectual developments of the period. In any event, even during the eighteenth century, explanations of unnatural events and natural disasters were not completely "secular." For many, the idea of a *deus absconditus*, who abandoned creation to its own devices, was still problematic. Some argued that natural disasters were not affected by God in immediate response to some piece of human evildoing, but that they were instead inserted by God into the original scheme of creation, because God had foreseen the moral choices humans would make. Many eighteenth-century theologians continued to preach that the experiences of trouble and adversity directed man's attention to religion (whereas worldly success was the greatest enemy to piety). When stricken, individuals were afforded the opportunity for introspection to help them to discover the moral defect that had provoked God's wrath. Divine providence had a certain self-confirming quality, and some suffering was almost taken as essential proof that God retained an interest in the person or in humankind more generally.

Early modern Jews, even in the eighteenth century, were not growing skeptical of religious arguments; they continued to be guided by theological principles and ideas. At the same time, they were not closed off from the scientific theories inherited from the classical world, nor were they unaffected by the observations and discussions of contemporary non-Jews. To that extent, early modern responses were remarkably complex and prove the early modern period to be one that defies simple categorization as merely a transition from medieval to modern mindsets.

In 1750, a large earthquake hit London. On November 1, 1755, an even more massive quake rocked Lisbon. The Lisbon earthquake was among the most devastating that ever hit Europe. It may have killed 10,000 people, with two to three times that number injured, and many of those dying in the ensuing weeks.[57] At least 20,000 homes were swallowed by the quake, whose magnitude was possibly as high as 8.5. Much of the city's cultural heritage was damaged or destroyed.[58]

The response to these earthquakes among European writers, scientists, and theologians varied greatly.[59] Some used the event to leverage political control and reduce the influence of the church, especially the Jesuits.[60] Some even saw the quakes as an expression of God's anger with the Inquisition. Many people cast the quake as a divine warning for human sins and a call for repentance. The Lisbon earthquake recast the social and intellectual foundations of the city, the country, and many other places as well. As was the case with other earthquakes, the Lisbon earthquake was cast as divine punishment for a variety of sins, including what some saw as both Portuguese and Jesuit imperialism.[61]

Public discussions of earthquakes in the eighteenth century frequently followed scientific explanations of the causes, especially associations with chemical subterranean explosions or associations with weather conditions, especially lightning. Still, natural explanations were often relegated to secondary causes, and many writers continued to see God as the prime mover and responsible for the disaster. This distinction between primary and secondary causes, in fact, allowed Europeans to entertain natural explanations without dismissing God or religion.[62]

Indeed, the boundaries between religion and science remained permeable throughout the early modern period. Even in the middle of the eighteenth century, the acceptance of Newtonian natural philosophy did not necessarily dictate a rejection of the idea that God had an active hand in the events of the world.[63] Some saw the quakes as divine warnings for political or military defeats.[64] Many sermons of the period combined calls for religious and moral reform with stark nationalism.[65]

Rabbi Isaac Nieto (1687–1773), who was born in Leghorn and moved to London with his family in 1701, succeeded his father as *haham* (rabbi) from 1732 until 1741. Between 1751 and 1757, he was the *av bet din* (head of the court) of the community. Nieto did not have an easy career and was frequently at odds with the communal leadership—he resigned as *av bet din* in protest of the appointment of a member of the *bet din*.[66] Nieto published several sermons in Spanish and Portuguese. One, on the occasion of another earthquake in London in 1756, was translated into English and published that same year, the first Jewish sermon to be published in English.[67] In the sermon, Nieto stressed the important role of the preacher in helping to introduce a reformation of life and manners. "It is Actions, not Words alone, that make an Impression on the Heart; and Reformation of Manners, is more indebted to Example, than to the greatest Eloquence of Rhetorick," he wrote.[68] Nieto placed his remark within both the context of Jewish tradition and the call to observe the proclamation of the King of England:

> Our most gracious sovereign the King, has issued out a Proclamation to observe this Day as a solemn Fast, and to implore the Mercy of the King of Kings, who out of his great Clemency was pleased to shew that he was incensed against us, in order to prepare us to Contrition and Repentance. And His Majesty, knowing the Dissoluteness of the Age, with Reason judged, that the Anger of Heaven might have been raised against us; and directed, with a devout Heart, that we should examine our Actions, and with a sincere Penitence and Sorrow, endeavour to divert the Punishment that the Hand of Divine Justice seems to threaten us with. And at the same Time His Majesty also commanded us to implore the Divine Assistance to his Armies, in case our Neighbours should oblige him to declare War.[69]

Sincere repentance, Nieto argued, appeases God's anger. As a proof text, Nieto reviewed the biblical story of Jonah and the city of Nineveh.[70] He wrote that "But oh, dear Brethren, reflect that the divine Clemency calls us to Penitence; consider that the Mercy of Heaven invites us to Repentance; *behold the Sword of divine Justice drawn against all the World*," referring the latter statement to passages in the Talmudic tractate Yoma and the biblical book 1 Chronicles.[71]

The situation of the time, according to Nieto, was bleak. Jews puffed themselves up with the vain belief that their merits diverted the rigor of divine justice, and they deceived themselves by thinking that they were better than their neighbors. Religion among the Jews, more generally, however, was never more neglected or less practiced. Fidelity and brotherly love were lacking, Nieto rued, just as envy, vengeance, and hatred proliferated. After castigating his audience for self-deception and vanity in the form of pursuing pleasure and entertainments, Nieto fired,

Tell me, oh dear Brethren, When was *Religion* more neglected? When were the *Laws* of Almighty, and Eternal God, less observed? When were his divine *Commandments* less obeyed? When were his sacred *Precepts* more foreign to our Thoughts? When was *Devotion* less practiced? When was *Wisdom* held more in Derision? And, in short, When was even *God* himself, less the Subject of our Contemplation?[72]

According to Nieto, there may be natural causes for earthquakes. He noted, "I do not deny that there may be natural Causes for Earthquakes, proceeding either from the Compression of the Air, Rarification of the Waters, or Eruption of Volcanos; or, perhaps, from all three, or by any other Causes of which I am ignorant, and may be unknown even to Philosophers."[73] It is God, however, who makes the earth tremble. "But what I affirm," he wrote, "is, that he who guides, rules, orders, and governs these Causes, is the Omnipotent and Infinite Being, who created them; and to him alone should be attributed their Effects, and to no other, since he is the effective Cause of all Causes."[74] In this light, only sincere repentance and reform can divert and annul the sentence already passed in heaven.

Nieto ended the sermon with a prayer for the king, who he presented as pious and whose actions were most gracious, and who was not vain in his ambition to extend his dominions.[75] The king was engaged in just war, Nieto wrote, not to enrich his subjects with the spoils of his enemies, but rather to protect his subjects' rights and liberties. Nieto, therefore, requested blessings and happiness for the king.

Accused by some of Deism early in his career, Nieto appears rather "traditional" in his earthquake sermon. He recognized the role of nature and scientific interpretations, and we know from his earlier writings that he was familiar with a wide range of scientific works,[76] even if he appears generally to have favored the opinions of the rabbis over those of the philosophers.[77] Nieto attributed earthquakes to God as a warning to repent, and he took full advantage of the situation to call for a stirring reformation of morals and actions. While the text is brimming with biblical and rabbinic citations, Nieto's sermon is similar in some respects to Christian sermons of the period. What is more, Nieto constructed the sermon within the context of the national fast day called for by the king, and he added an extensive prayer for the king that was quite national in sentiment.

Conclusions

Religion remained central in early modern accounts of earthquakes, even amid scientific advances and political turmoil. Unique contexts, however, helped to dictate the balance between science or natural causes, politics, and religion. Well into the eighteenth century, earthquakes were seen as signs and warnings from God, calling people to repentance, or as punishment for sins and lack of repentance. But discussions of earthquakes could have social as well as religious dimensions. The accounts we have examined indicate that the early modern period was not simply one of transition, with separate and neat categories of "religion" and "science." In the end, critical engagement with the environment and natural disasters does not have to pit science against religion. Each of the accounts we have examined briefly operated fairly comfortably with scientific and natural explanations, while also subsuming the observations drawn from these fields into broader discourse in the service of religion. This raises intriguing questions for today, when we often create silos between religion and science and insist on singular perspectives in understanding our experiences and identifying ways to respond in times of crisis. Religion could provide valuable tools for self-reflection as well as for developing a sense of common cause and need; it could also devolve into scapegoating and polemic. How do we pull out the most constructive parts of this tradition for the most effective and positive responses?

Depictions of premodern earthquakes reveal Jews as members of broader society, for example, in the discussion of general damages that at times affected everyone. More specifically, the accounts we have reviewed here also supply evidence of significant Jewish engagement with non-Jewish society and non-Jewish thinkers and texts. Surprisingly, perhaps, our earliest account from the fifteenth century engaged non-Jewish accounts and science just as heavily as the writings from the middle of the eighteenth century. While Jews drank from these external stimuli, they also molded what they read and heard into uniquely Jewish contexts and for a variety of Jewish purposes. In this sense, Jews did not assimilate non-Jewish ideas, but rather acculturated them to Judaism. The premodern earthquake narratives reveal that we are almost never completely separate from other communities and cultures or removed from other intellectual traditions. How do we find ways to engage beyond our own perspectives in constructive ways and recognize the mutual influence that we have on others?

Jewish responses to earthquakes were quite similar to those of Christians and to their responses to natural disasters more generally, and in specific contexts they can tell us a great deal about Jewish history, Jewish society, and Jewish interactions with non-Jews and the non-Jewish world. They point to the intersection and amplification of disasters and to the range of ways that people could understand (and change their understanding) of disasters based on experience and new knowledge. These responses to earthquakes reveal current conditions as well as opportunities and needs for new ways of thinking and behaving (including through policies and planning of responses).

They also highlight the ways in which disasters serve to reinforce and challenge social and communal norms and structures, especially in the short run. In reinforcing and upending traditional views and sensibilities, we, like our premodern ancestors, have an opportunity to assess ways to prepare more fully for other disasters and to learn from the past and others and their experiences.

Plague as Natural Disaster

Introduction

What exactly we mean by a "natural disaster" has been open to discussion. How do we categorize disasters that appear to be more human-induced? Should diseases be considered "natural" disasters? In this book, I have chosen to take a rather broad approach. Many natural disasters throughout history are related to human actions, and often they have led to conflicts between humans. Famine and disease, for example, could be related to military conflict; drought and floods could lead to political instability. The scope and impact of diseases are related to changes in nature, but the transmission and virulence of diseases are also related to human settlement and interaction.

The discussion in Chapter 1 revealed the fluid and permeable relationship between religion and science in how we understand and respond to natural disasters; this chapter finds a similar relationship, especially between religion and medicine. The chapter highlights even more directly the ways that we might better prepare for and mitigate the impact of a disaster, especially through policies and regulations. The examination of plague also elevates the opportunities for collaborative work as well as the latent tensions within communities and societies that could erupt into violence against and the blaming of others. As in the previous chapter, I begin with a similar review of some of the religious and scientific strands that helped premodern people understand plague, before considering some of the practical responses that emerged and evolved over time as they confronted regular and, at times, dramatic epidemics.

Diseases have affected human society before and even after the advances of modern medicine, as the recent pandemic of Covid-19 demonstrated. This chapter examines the experience of disease, with a special case related to plague in seventeenth-century Italy. While there were many explanations for plague, the historical experiences presented in this chapter highlight the various scientific, cultural, communal, and religious ways of understanding plague. I give special attention to the nature and challenges of the "economy of sin" (in which God punishes for sinful behavior) model that often animates religious discussions of disasters. Plagues could be local or regional, crossing a variety of geographical and political boundaries and with a wide range of impacts. There were significant discussions about how to prevent and contain plagues, which led to a proliferation of regulations and policies (some of which we still follow today!). This chapter asks us to consider what tools we have at our disposal for adaptation in periods of crisis and change, such as plague, and how we might understand and engage with both human vulnerability and resilience. Disasters such as plague can lead to moralizing on one hand and scapegoating on the other, and our historical vignettes demonstrate both—do they also suggest ways to advance beyond both (especially in the long run)?

The study of disease has a long history. And, of course, there have been many quite devastating epidemics over the centuries that we could examine. Aside from the impact that they have on humans and human communities, diseases can also affect animals and larger environmental systems as well. What is more, the role of human actions in unleashing, spreading, and amplifying disease has become much clearer in recent years. Climate change caused by humans has released some diseases that had been long dormant, literally frozen away. Human experiments gone awry and the mass of human settlements can impact the generation and spread of disease. When combined with other disasters and crises—including floods, famines, and droughts, for example—that always seem just at hand, plagues can have an even more dramatic impact. Beyond the actual outbreak of diseases, the ways that people understand and respond to diseases can determine what kind of impact (medical as well as social) those diseases might have and what courses they may run.

These preliminary reflections were dramatically on display in the recent experience of Covid-19. Throughout history, however, there have been many disease epidemics (and the metaphor of the epidemic has reflected a whole host of social, religious, and political movements and events)—from smallpox to diphtheria, typhus, cholera, influenza, and syphilis. Perhaps bubonic plague—in its three major historical waves—has received the most sustained attention, especially since the early twentieth century, even as its grip on the world human population has shrunk from the enormous impact it had from the fourteenth through the nineteenth century across Europe and parts of Asia. Increasingly, we have evidence for outbreaks in other places as well, including Africa and the Americas.

In Latin, the word *plaga* denoted a "blow" or "wound," and it did not need, by definition, to refer to a disease. What is more, it might not always be clear when a specific disease was in fact plague, as many diseases had similar symptoms. There is some debate among historians about how well people of the past could distinguish between various diseases.[1]

Biblical, Rabbinic, and Classical Understanding
of and Approaches to Plague

Religious worldviews and narratives of plague deeply affected how people have understood and responded to plague well into modernity. They still color some approaches to and reflections on disease. Both the Hebrews and the Greeks saw plagues, as well as diseases more generally, alternately as either a punishment or a test from God.[2] As a result, the appropriate response to the outbreak of plague could vary, but very frequently involved repentance and prayers to God (or the gods).

The term plague occurs frequently in the Hebrew Scriptures. The biblical passages in which it was detailed served as prooftexts and fodder for much of the early modern (and a good deal of modern) discussion about plague in Jewish, Christian, and Islamic societies. The Hebrew Bible addressed plague in a variety of contexts. Like its Latin equivalent, the Hebrew word "maggefah" (as well as other forms, including *negef, nega, makkah*), denoted "striking" or "smiting." It was associated with the plagues that God famously inflicted upon the Egyptians (as described in the book of Exodus), the punishment of the spies who reconnoitered in the Holy Land,[3] as well as a variety of rebellions,[4] idolatrous practices,[5] and various other transgressive behaviors.[6] Plague might also be associated in biblical texts with other diseases, such as leprosy.[7] The multivalency and multi-dimensionality of plagues are significant and reflect many human experiences throughout history when various natural disasters emerge together or in close proximity, increasing the impact of each. Biblical plagues, like those of the early modern period, it should also be pointed out, could affect people as well as animals.

Leviticus twenty-six is a key biblical text for the consideration of plague and natural disasters more generally. This pivotal text (and associated ones) is often examined in the context of calamities that befall people, as part of what some scholars have termed the "economy of sin." As we will see, the economy of sin could be complicated and, in many cases, apparently more metaphorical than literal. In this case, the punishment of plague is embedded in a much larger discussion of punishments, and the biblical passage is constructed around a much more complicated theological structure. Some scholars place the chapter into a broader context of discussions about covenant, for example, within the Hebrew Bible and in later biblical and rabbinic writings and Ancient Near Eastern political documents.

Let's unpack the text a bit. The chapter begins with the prohibition of making idols to worship and the admonition to observe the Sabbath and venerate the divine sanctuary. For following God's laws and commandments, the Israelites are rewarded with a range of natural and agricultural benefits—rain in its season, produce and fruit, and food stability. They will also be blessed with peace and physical security. They will be fertile and multiply and God will abide in their midst. However, should the Israelites disobey God's commandments, rejecting the laws and breaking the covenant, they are presented with a range of curses—from consumption and fever to lack of food and defeat by their enemies.

At this point, God appears to provide an opportunity for repentance. Should the Israelites nonetheless continue in their disobedience, their fields will not yield produce nor their trees fruit. Again, there appears to be a chance to return . . . but should they not, then God will smite them for their sins with attacks by wild beasts, swords against them, pestilence, and hunger. Should they continue to persist in their waywardness, God will turn them to cannibals and destroy their cultic sites, make the land desolate, and scatter them (in agricultural language, dispersion is related to the winnowing process)[8] among the nations. At that point, at this most precarious stage, the text notes that the land will rest and make up for its Sabbath years—"it shall observe the rest that it did not observe in your sabbath years while you were dwelling upon it." On the other hand, the land of their enemies will consume them. But all is not lost, for verse 39 declares that those who survive will confess their iniquity and that of their fathers. They will atone and God will "remember My covenant" with

Abraham, Isaac, and Jacob and, importantly, with the land. God asserts that God will not (finally) reject or spurn them so as to destroy them, but rather God will remember the covenant.

While it is true that there are many punishments meted out for human transgressions, the underlying covenant also builds in opportunities for repentance and return and, in the end, does not seem to allow for the final destruction of the Israelites. That is, pestilence and other afflictions are punishments, but also tools to bring humans back to repentance and better behavior. In an interesting additional layer, the land plays a significant role in this drama and is impacted by human behavior and remains in a covenantal relationship with God. As one modern biblical commentator notes: "The expulsion of Israel was necessitated by their defilement of the land. Leviticus focuses on Israel's unholy and impure condition as the primary factor leading to her ultimate collapse and deportation. Leviticus shares this viewpoint with Deuteronomy, Jeremiah, and Ezekiel."[9]

Other biblical passages offer additional nuance in the discussion of plague (and other disasters). God might, alternately, end a plague because of some "virtuous" action, as, for example, depicted in the book of Numbers (25),

> And when Phinehas, son of Eleazar, the son of Aaron the priest, saw this, he rose up from the midst of the congregation, and took a spear in his hand. And he followed the Israelite into the chamber and stabbed both of them, the man of Israel and the woman through her belly. Then the plague against the Israelites was stopped. Those who died in the plague numbered 24,000.

Similarly, prayer and penitence were presented in the Hebrew Bible as possible ways to end plague and other catastrophes. In an approach that would find an echo in many early modern narratives, 2 Chron. 6:28–31 recorded that

> If there is famine in the land, if there is pestilence, blight, mildew, locusts, or caterpillars, or if their enemies oppress them in any of the settlements of their land. In any plague and in any disease, any prayer or supplication offered by any person among all Your people Israel—each of whom knows his affliction and his pain—when he spreads forth his hands toward this House, may You hear in Your heavenly abode, and pardon.

It was trust in God, which, at the end of the day, was most effective in addressing and protecting one from plague.

Psalm 91, a frequently quoted text, with imagery that would be repeated throughout the centuries, concluded that

> Whoever sits in the refuge of the most High, he will dwell in the shadow of the Almighty. I will say of the Lord, He is my refuge and my fortress, my God, I will trust in him. For he will deliver you from the ensnaring trap, from the devastating pestilence. With His pinions He will cover you, and beneath His wings you will be protected; shield and armor are His truth. You need not fear the terror of night;

nor the arrow that flies by day; nor the pestilence that walks in the dark; nor the destruction that lays waste at noon.

The rabbis also discussed plague on occasion, defining the scope of an epidemic and suggesting remedies for it. In the Babylonian Talmud, tractate Ta'anit,[10] for example, the rabbinic writers explored ways to define a plague:

What constitutes a plague? If in a city that can supply five hundred foot-soldiers three deaths take place on three consecutive days, this constitutes a plague; less than this is no plague. The alarm is sounded everywhere on account of the following [visitations]: blast, mildew, locust, cricket, wild beasts, and the sword, as they are all plagues likely to spread

Plague here was defined by the number of deaths within a specific period of time. Plague was also utilized as a term for the spread of a variety of devastations from animals (locusts, crickets, wild beasts) to mildew and military attack. In the gloss on this passage, the rabbis took the opportunity to discuss the merits of individuals who could keep the plague (and other disasters) away or cure the victims:

Once a plague broke out in Sura but it did not affect the locality in which Rab resided. People thought that this was on account of Rab's great merit but in a dream it was made clear to them that this was far too small a matter to need Rab's great merit, but that it was on account of the merit of a certain man who made it a practice to lend shovel and spade for burials.

Fighting plague, therefore, could involve pious behavior, especially of particularly holy people. The rabbinic approach to plague reflected both the complex and layered nature of plague itself. It also traded in the economy of sin that aligned human sin with punishment in the form of plagues; and human virtue with overcoming the devastation of plague.

Like the Israelites and the rabbis, the Greeks at times interpreted plague as punishment for human sins. In the *Iliad*, for example, Apollo sent a plague upon the Greeks as punishment for the insult to his priest Chryses at the hands of Agamemnon[11]—who had captured Chryses' daughter and expelled Chryses[12]—raining down arrows of plague upon the Greeks for a period of nine days.[13] At other times, classical thinkers identified other causes of plague. Lucretius Carus (*c.* 99–*c.* 55 BCE), whose *On the Nature of Things* (*De Rerum Natura*) was rediscovered in the later Middle Ages, offered a powerful explanatory model that emphasized the role of environmental conditions, regional variations, and associated social conditions. According to Lucretius, whose explanatory model drew from other thinking of classical Antiquity and would have great appeal into the early modern period:

there are many seeds of things which support our life, and on the other hand there must be many flying about which make for disease and death. When these by chance or accident have gathered together, and thrown the heavens into turmoil, the air becomes diseased. And all these diseases in their power and pestilence either come from without down through the sky like clouds and mists, or often they gather together and rise from the earth itself, when through damp it has become putrescent, being smitten out of that novelty of climate and water affects any who travel far from home and country, just because there is a great difference in these things . . . Hence different places are dangerous to different parts and members; the variety of air brings that about.[14]

Combined with the biblical and rabbinic explanations, the classical sources provided a powerful explanatory model for understanding plagues.[15]

Plagues and Jews in Historical Context

The various intellectual understandings of the plague informed the ways premodern people approached plague. Their personal experiences and the stories they heard about the experiences of others also impacted how they responded when the plague broke out and the precautions they took when news of the spreading plague reached them.

The plague—in a wide range of forms and outbreaks—recurred regularly in Europe and the Ottoman Empire from the fourteenth into the early eighteenth century, with particularly virulent effects at certain times and in specific locations. It often combined with other diseases and other natural disasters and social or political upheavals to create particularly difficult conditions.

Two schools of explanation accounted for the spread of plague. Borrowing from Greek medicine as well as biblical writings, the spread of plague was attributed to contagion between people or to transmission through the water and air (miasma). The prophylaxis for and treatment of plague could be different depending on which of these theories was adopted. According to the former, for example, quarantine and fumigation were preferred methods;[16] this was the more common response to plague. Concern over miasma, on the other hand, could lead to a variety of civic responses, from shooting canons, constructing fires, draining swamps, or applying vinegar and aromatic oils to diseased houses.[17] The emphasis on bad air, which might be attributed to various meteorological or cosmic conditions, was frequently embraced by more learned people—though they also held, even simultaneously, the contagionist position—which often served as the justification for fleeing from plague in hopes of finding better, healthier air. Given the range of understandings and responses to plague, one of the most frequently debated issues in the early modern world was whether, in fact, one was permitted to flee from one place to another during the outbreak of plague, when even movement within a city or town could be highly regulated.[18]

Jews, like Christians, often fled the plague, as the Jewish memoirist Asher Levy of Reichshofen noted in describing the flight of people from the plague during the second decade of the seventeenth century.[19] One Yiddish writer similarly noted the situation in Prague:

> In the community, as soon as anyone caught it, a terrible fear gripped us. Everyone wanted to flee, to escape. Many people went to the authorities, who took them under their protection in the countryside. And here they were seen everywhere packing and departing, from every street and every corner [of the city]. All day long they were seen carrying cases, and what are they to do, the poor who remember seeing all the rich people leaving to save their own skin? We, we are compelled to stay behind in misfortune.[20]

Clearly not all the Jewish communal leaders fled Prague, for the same author recorded the piety of some scholars and communal leaders, who served the poor and worked to strengthen the resolve of the survivors.[21] Christian—Catholic, Lutheran, and Protestant—authors had also regularly addressed the question of flight from the plague.[22]

While the development, spread, and impact of plagues were often related to weather conditions and food shortages, and so could be rationalized or approached somewhat practically, particularly severe plagues invoked images of the end of days. This was certainly the case with the outbreak of the Black Death in the middle of the fourteenth century, which claimed more than 60 percent of the population in some places.[23] Later outbreaks of the plague could also be quite devastating. The plague of 1576–77 led to the death of 28 percent of the 180,000 residents of Venice. The great plague of 1630–31, which swept across central Europe, claimed 61 percent of the population in Verona, 59 percent in Padua, and 46 percent in Cremona and Milan, for example.

Plagues were at times part of everyday life experience, and there were significant periods of normalcy. Under these conditions, many communities evinced the ability to manage plagues. Despite the severity of the Black Death, a scholarly consensus has begun to emerge that the Black Death was not necessarily a watershed in European history, certainly not in the majority of places.[24] The conditions for and impact of plagues could vary a great deal by time and location, however.[25] In 1611, in Constance, for example, 300 people died between September 17 and October 12. Of the 700 houses within the city, 355 were quarantined at some time. But the disease had a particularly dire effect on the have-nots, who had a mortality rate of 39 percent; the very rich, by contrast, had a mortality rate of only 4 percent. Not surprisingly, the southern part of the city, with many poor areas, was particularly hard hit. Of the 1,462 recorded deaths, 552 were children and 221 were young people. Mortality was also high among workers in particular professions—bakers, health care providers, clergy, and, not surprisingly, corpse bearers. Although the number of taxpayers initially fell from 1,282 to 1,101, by 1620 it had again reached 1,244, due to both increased births and the migration of refugees.[26]

The plague could dramatically affect the poor and minority groups—the former who were often less resistant to the plague and had fewer means to treat it if they did contract it, and the latter who could be scapegoated as a result of or in advance of the plague.[27] As historian Brian Pullan notes, "Suspicion tended to spread from casual or seasonal migrants to refugee populations: in Venice it clung to Slavs and Albanians in the mid-fifteenth century, and a century later to Marranos or Portuguese New Christians from the Low Countries." "Relieving the poor," Pullan continues, "could at once be an act of placation addressed to God and a practical measure for containing an epidemic."[28] At the same time, the plague could intensify both the feeling that the poor were to be pitied for their suffering or needed for their labor,[29] on one hand, and that they were to be feared because of their role in spreading disease or in imaginary, nefarious plots against society, on the other.[30] Attacks against the Jews during periods of plague are well known—especially during the Black Death of the mid-fourteenth century—even if some recent scholarship has questioned whether the attacks were as deadly or widespread as once perceived.

Some Jewish accounts of plague can be found in early modern memoirs and songs, in both Hebrew and Yiddish.[31] The Hebrew translator of Glückel of Hameln's famous memoirs, Chava Turniansky, has identified three Yiddish songs, written shortly after a devastating plague in Prague in 1713. Perhaps even more deadly than the dreadful plague of 1680, the plague of 1713 claimed about a third of the 11,500 Jews in the city, who lived in cramped and unsanitary conditions in the ghetto.[32] The songs, though quite different in some regards, collectively offer a graphic picture of the plague, including its outbreak, with details about the victims, and suggested charms to protect against it and cures for when it was contracted.[33] The accounts are almost exclusively concerned with the plague within the Jewish quarter, dating the start and end to coincide with the effects on the Jewish community and rarely referencing life outside the *Judenstadt*.[34] Moses ben Hayim Eisenstadt, for example, supplicated in the introduction to his account that

> Almighty God, in the Heavenly realm, You always come to our aid when we are in peril: You brought us out of exile in Egypt and out of exile in Babylon, You have preserved us from all Evils. Merciful God, in the third exile, again You defend us, and in the fourth exile You will also protect us. Our hopes turn toward You, and we hope in these times that You will not try us so harshly.[35]

Formulaically, he attributed the devastation of the plague to "our sins." Not surprisingly, he called for prayer to God and penance: "Holy community of Prague, you must do penance! And remember this punishment for many years to come; and let us pray to God whom we love and in whom we hope, that He may never again send us such punishment."[36] Although most Jews perceived the plague as punishment for sin, Turniansky's reading of the texts leads her to conclude that there clearly were some who "questioned the link between sin and affliction," even if they were a small minority.[37]

The plague affected all segments of the Jewish community, frequently taking the lives of entire families. In addition to some embedded criticism of Jewish leaders who fled the plague[38]—before the Jewish quarter was sealed and residents were no longer allowed by the civic authorities to leave—and the appointment of several Jewish policemen to guarantee that no criminal activity was taking place within the ghetto,[39] there is some inter-communal dissonance presented in the accounts. According to Eisenstadt, "In this state of cruelty, people rose up against each other . . . no one could perform the *gemilut hesed* [giving of loving-kindness], for fear of being infected himself . . . I cannot be silent about what happened, how people began [to tear] each other to pieces."[40] In addition to tales about the dead, who could not be buried quickly and whose corpses often rotted in the sun, the report of the death of babies and children was particularly chilling.[41] Many people also became sick and impoverished. Eisenstadt described the length that some community members went to in order to set up temporary housing and provide food for the daily increasing number of poor. "There were eight hundred sick, and sometimes this number rose to a thousand at once," he rued.[42]

The Prague accounts reveal both concerns with bad air as well as personal contagion, with individuals attempting to protect or cure themselves in various ways, all the while engaging in the traditional acts of repentance, prayer, and charity.[43] Indeed, although we have few available sources, some previous early modern communal edicts (Yiddish edicts, e.g., from Prague, in the Hebrew month of Tishrei, 5373 (September/October, 1612), at the time of the well-known Rabbi Solomon Ephraim Lunshitz and posted in the synagogues) reveal the concern with Torah study and general communal morals, including the distancing of immodest behavior, with prostitution especially identified as in need of banishment. The decrees were prefaced by an introductory paragraph in Hebrew indicating that the regulations were established in response to the large number of deaths in a short period of time.[44] The regulations, incumbent on everyone in all their details, were intended as penance to placate God at such a difficult time. People were encouraged to learn Torah every day and to maintain their oaths.[45] Other regulations, akin to earlier communal ordinances and sumptuary laws, stipulated that women who engaged in business should not go alone to the houses of non-Jews, and in general, they should not be alone in rooms with men.[46] Likewise, unmarried women were not to stroll alone in the streets during the day or night, though exceptions were allowed for housemaids who might be traveling to or from work.[47] In distancing immorality from the community, prostitutes were no longer to be tolerated in the community—for the obvious reasons of their trade, as well as for the associated opportunities for evil deeds that their presence afforded—for example, the desecration of the name of God and the consumption of non-kosher wine.[48]

Eisenstadt's account ends with a variety of responses and practical treatments. In addition to "solemn services and supplications to Heaven," beseeching God to end his wrath,[49] Eisenstadt, who criticized communal leaders for leaving, ironically recommended fleeing when possible but remaining in one's house if flight was not possible. "When going out is unavoidable, it would be useful to wash your face and hands in vinegar, and also hold a sponge soaked in vinegar to your nose and mouth until you have returned home."[50] Like others, he suggested a plaster comprised of eggs and other ingredients to treat the plague.[51] As Eisenstadt's text reveals, however, Jews, like Christians, mixed religious and medical responses to the plague. Recent research has stressed the extent to which responses to sickness were similar among Jews and Christians, even to the extent that Jews participated in the broader culture that assumed the existence of demons, consulted astrological signs, and relied on amulets as well as the more intellectual world of books and formal medical training.[52] As historian Nimrod Zinger notes,

People who lived in the seventeenth and eighteenth centuries perceived their bodies completely differently from how we do today. In pre-modern times the body was viewed as a hermetically sealed entity which could not be observed 'beneath the skin.' People had a holistic view of health and sickness, in which the individual was a micro-cosmos of the universe and one's bodily condition was influenced by its position in society and geographic space.[53]

Plagues could also have significant communal and social implications. They could alter the trajectory of normal communal customs and celebrations, particularly in urban environments in which Jewish actions would be scrutinized and in which significant numbers of Jews and Christians might be impacted. It also revealed the complex social structures of early modern Jewish society. For the year 5426 (1665/66), Juspa, the Shammash of Worms, recorded an epidemic as follows: "I also saw … an occurrence that prevented men from assembling in the *Braut Haus*, for the *Braut Haus* was also impure because of all the sick people who had fallen victim to the epidemic." Although prayer and celebrations for the holiday of Simhat Torah were relocated to the inner courtyard of the synagogue, individuals were not required to attend or participate. "However, the gathering was not as large as it had been in previous years. Whoever wished to attend did so, but whoever did not wish to attend was not compelled to come. Happiness did not prevail, for the plague was still rampant."[54] For July 1666, Juspa recounted that the head of the rabbinical court had been selected to perform a circumcision. However, the household of the newborn was struck by the plague and "the rabbi withdrew his agreement to perform the circumcision." Other *mohelim* (circumcisers) subsequently also refused to perform the circumcision until Juspa himself agreed, rationalizing that "did not our rabbis, of blessed memory, teach that 'no harm will befall the one who performs a commandment?'"[55] This was particularly the case, asserted Juspa, for a commandment that even superseded the observance of the Sabbath. Juspa performed the circumcision and ended with the following supplication: "May God prolong this day, Amen. May He banish the Angel of Death and the plague from all the Children of Israel, Amen."[56]

The Case of Plague in Padua

In bringing various religious and medical thoughts and practical experiences together, premodern people crafted complex, and at times fairly effective, responses to plague. And still, absent modern medical advances, plague was recurring and often quite deadly. In order to understand plague more deeply, let's examine one significant case in more detail.

A major plague epidemic between 1629 and 1631 killed as many as 280,000 people throughout northern Italy. The plague had dramatic effect on Christian and Jewish residents of the region alike, with perhaps between one half to two-thirds of the residents of the region perishing.[57] In Padua, a staggering 19,000 out of 32,000 people—or 59 percent of the population—perished.

The plague erupted in Padua in the spring of 1630. While it did not initially affect the Jews of the city, it soon wreaked havoc on the inhabitants of Padua's ghetto during the ten days of repentance between Rosh Hashanah and Yom Kippur.[58] By Rosh Hodesh (the start of the new month of) Adar (5391), 170 Jews had died. Although the number of plague deaths decreased for a time, by the month of Sivan (June 1631) the plague began anew across the city.[59] The city's Jewish community, which had numbered 280 in 1585, and 439 by 1603, had grown to 721 in 1630–31.[60] Of that number, 634 were afflicted by plague and 421 subsequently died.[61] In response to the crisis, Jews in Padua received financial, food, and medical support from other Jewish communities, especially from the communities in Venice and Ferrara.[62] Although not without tensions, relations between Jews and Christians in the region were generally good during the crisis. Jews who fled from the city were able to find lodgings among non-Jews outside the city.[63]

By the time he wrote his account of the great plague epidemic in Padua (likely shortly after the events described), Abraham Catalano (d. 1642) had studied both Torah and medicine, and he had earned a medical degree from the University of Padua.[64] Although he was not registered as the rabbi of the community, he taught Torah and sat on the rabbinic court (*bet din*). In addition to his account of the plague, Catalano also authored a small book on good behavior (*midot*). The plague impacted him very directly, as his wife of twenty-one years was taken in the epidemic as was his first daughter.[65]

Catalano's plague account offers a good deal of historical information about the reach of the epidemic in Padua and the ways that it affected the Jewish community in particular. It details both the timing and spread of the outbreak of the plague and meticulously documents the deaths of many individuals caused by it.[66] Catalano records various rules and regulations issued by the Jewish community and non-Jewish local and Venetian territorial authorities upon the plague's arrival, such as travel restrictions, quarantine, and the disinfection of material possessions. He also presents a variety of theories about how the plague penetrated into the ghetto—via the family of the non-Jewish gatekeeper or the goods of a Jewish merchant from abroad, for example. Highlighting the important role that community structures and community-wide efforts played in mitigating the plague's impact on Padua's Jewish residents, Catalano referred frequently to community leaders' allocation of money, food, medical, and burial services to their fellow Jews during the epidemic. As the plague progressed, Catalano noted that prayers were sometimes held outside the synagogue. At other times, there were not enough men to be found to constitute a prayer quorum (minyan). Many stopped observing the particular customs that had structured their observance in the past. Yet, other prayers—including, for example, the prayer *Pitum Ha-ketoret* (Babylonian Talmud, Tractate Kerithot, 6a), related to the preparation of the temple incense—were added to the liturgy, as were various lamentations and supplications.

Catalano also had theological reflections—and admonitions—to offer his readers. Indeed, he began his account by writing, "I will speak and moan I will complain from the bitterness of my spirit (I am Abraham Catalano), to inform the generations to come and the children who should be born of things as they happened. And I will faithfully make known to the generations three useful lessons from this story."[67] These lessons included his conclusion that God's wrath had been kindled against the people of his generation and that it behooved them to end their transgressions—lest they die for their sins. Catalano's notion that God punished people by means of the plague was, as noted above, a common trope among both Christian and Jewish observers in the premodern era.[68]

As notable as his historical and theological sections were the many practical recommendations that Catalano's account included. In the manuscript, he discussed at great length the practical means to avoid and treat the plague and the measures people could take to try and save their families and community. In his conclusion, Catalano offered specific guidance related to quarantining, medicines, food preparation and supplies (including securing many days' supplies of wheat, wine, and oil), and properly cleaning a house and clothing (including sealing and stamping valuable clothing with a health seal) once plague appeared in one's home. Throughout, Catalano devoted much space to political concerns and negotiations with various non-Jewish authorities. He stressed the need for coordinated efforts regarding such things as the disinfection of Jews' belongings, as well as travel restrictions and the efforts of opening the ghetto. Understanding the complexity of the political conditions of his day, including relations with officials in Venice as well as local civic authorities in Padua, Catalano admonished his coreligionists:

> And you, people of my community, remember and do not forget, before a plague reaches you, send a trusted delegate from among the people of our holy community to Venice [the non-Jewish authorities] and pay his salary, so that he can help you when you are in trouble and if a matter comes up against you before the ministers, which is not religious [in nature], whether [for example] to hand over the ghetto or a single person, this one [the delegate] can stand there in the breach.[69]

Catalano wrote his wide-ranging account with the hope that recording his experiences and those of his community and city would benefit future generations who might experience similar disasters or, as he put it, so as to allow "the generations to come . . . [to] know how to behave and properly prepare for a devastating plague in the world in their days."[70] Many of Catalano's descriptions and warnings are reminiscent of the discussions—and enduring skepticism—about mitigation attempts and vaccines that we encounter even today.[71] Consider, for example, his counsel that not everything on offer as a cure for the plague was useful, or even safe:

> If the doctor tells you to take these drugs—Elettuario, Conservi, Preservativi—[saying] you will be protected from the plague, do not believe him, as this is not going to help you . . . [or] save you. I saw many who followed this course and died bitterly and many others who did not take any of them and were not infected, or were sick and recovered, and the plague did not distinguish between them. Many important doctors contracted plague and many were unaffected. I saw at that time that there were many who always placed a citron under the nose to filter the vapors leaving or temper impurities, which I thought was nonsense. Who knows if the smell from breathing the air resulting from those vapors stimulates good health. Although I was adorned with the crown of medicine and I know what the doctors say about Preservativi, I did not look to record anything from the writings in their

books. I only wrote what I remembered and thought would be useful for future generations.[72]

As both a chronicler of disasters and a trained medical professional, Catalano hoped that his account would be useful for those who might confront the next outbreak of bubonic plague, teaching them both what to do and what to avoid. Does it hold any lessons for us today as we confront and attempt to understand and respond to contemporary disease, notably the recent Covid-19 pandemic?

Certain lessons do seem to emerge. As Catalano himself emphasized, efforts to respond to disease and natural disaster are more effective when coordinated on a large scale. The work of local princes and cities during the second pandemic of the bubonic plague was not always systematic, but we know that when it was, the results were a great deal more successful and long-lasting.[73] The same was true for Jewish communities of the time, which instituted restrictions on religious gatherings and celebrations, developed systems to take care of the most vulnerable populations, worked (with varying degrees of success) with non-Jewish authorities, and set up communal structures to address the most pressing needs of their day.

Those who lived through bubonic plague pandemics learned improved measures to prevent and mitigate the spread of disease, some of which are still in use today, such as quarantines, social distancing, deep cleaning, and travel restrictions.[74] The account of the physician and Talmudic scholar Jacob ben Isaac Zahalon, which describes an outbreak of plague in the Jewish ghetto of Rome in 1656, to take another example, details the organization and management of isolation units as well as stay-at-home orders imposed on everyone except those who would today qualify as "essential workers," such as physicians.[75] Like their non-Jewish neighbors, Jews also introduced fast days and special prayers for the liturgy in order to appeal to God for salvation from the plague and to mark the event in communal history well after it had passed.[76] Just as some have used the safely distanced spaces of their verandas and terraces to deliver uplifting words, pray, and celebrate festive occasions in the time of Covid-19, early modern rabbis were known to deliver sermons from their windows or elevated porches to edify their congregants who could not assemble in the synagogue.[77] We may be in uncharted territory today, but there are still good reasons to look to the past for guidance—at both the individual and communal levels—as we look to the future with uncertainty.

Conclusions

Like other natural disasters, plague was seen by early modern Jews and Christians in both scientific and religious contexts. Utilizing a mix of ancient and contemporary medical knowledge, they concocted a range of preventative measures against and treatments for the plague. Often competing (or contradictory) responses of quarantine and flight appear to have been advocated and practiced. Many early modern writers recounted the ravaging effects of plague in often gruesome detail. Of course, the devastation could depend a great deal on localized conditions—including the concurrence of other disasters (such as food shortages or particularly harsh weather) and the effectiveness of local policies, as well as the specific virulence of the disease. Much civic and territorial legislation attempted to address epidemics and numerous modern civic and state policies and interventions were birthed in the context of early modern plagues. In the end, plagues affected daily life for many people, and they had an enduring impact on the human psyche of early moderns, regardless of religious observance or background. Still, we find evidence of long periods of normalcy and, especially for survivors, some sense of an ability to cope with the challenges brought by plague. We can learn a great deal from the ways that premodern people responded to plagues. As we found in our own recent Covid-19 experiences, response to disease can be most effective with the coordination of medical, public policy, and social actions. Absent modern medicine, premodern people identified important ways to limit the spread of disease, and they developed some (at times, limited) ways to address the physical and psychological impact of plague.

Unlike some other environmental conditions and natural disasters, such as floods, which were often easier to predict (even if with relatively short notice) and might be more expected in some places, the cycle of plague could be unpredictable. As a result, outbreaks of plague were, not surprisingly, seen as both natural occurrences and supernatural events. At times associated with various signs and wonders, such as comets, they were cast typologically as divine punishment for human sin and, as in the case of other natural disasters, diverse religious responses were forwarded to respond to these occurrences. The traditional resort to prayer and repentance, and in many Christian cases religious processions as well, was inflamed by often charismatic preachers who took the opportunity, frequently in an apocalyptic vein, to encourage moral reform. At times, such passionate preaching could lead to scapegoating or the further marginalization of outsider groups, including minorities such as Jews and foreigners—even when the plague refused itself to differentiate among its victims. Under some conditions, the plague could foment anti-Jewish preaching and lead to anti-Jewish activities, particularly in the form of looting and vandalism, as some of our authors note. Plague narratives—both Jewish and Christian—provide details about daily life and about the conditions of Jewish life, including the overcrowding and unsanitary conditions facing some Jews in larger ghettos. They also reveal multifaceted interactions between and perceptions of Jews and Christians that make it rather difficult to draw hard and fast conclusions about Jewish and Christian or other religious or social groups. The lessons we can draw about dealing with uncertainty are significant. Responding to the unknown can be terrifying; we often resort to faith traditions and other experiences to navigate these circumstances. While we may express our anxiety in compassion for others, we may also demonize and marginalize others, whom we might even blame for the spread of the disease. How do we maintain compassion at these times and also protect ourselves? Premodern people succeeded in some ways, although they often built upon and extended hatred and animosity in other ways. The impact of plague could fundamentally alter intellectual and social foundations and force new ways of thinking and relationships. It could also reinforce traditional ways of thinking and behaving. How might we assess the opportunities and challenges when we are not faced with a specific crisis so that we can be better prepared during a crisis?

Plagues had significant social and political dimensions, and those writing about them could utilize a range of polemics that could also inform and be used in support of political initiatives. Plagues could have impact beyond communal boundaries, and they often affected broad regions, with little respect for civic or territorial boundaries, in such things as economic conditions and travel. Nonetheless, they often had severe local consequences, and they revealed and incited local social tensions and communal conflicts. Responses to the plague were telling of such conditions and of the possibilities for significant and sustained change in many early modern societies. Combined with responses to other natural disasters and in the context of other significant issues, they allow a remarkable opportunity to uncover local conditions as well as broad social and cultural trends and changes. As we learned in the Covid-19 pandemic, political and geographic borders cannot protect individuals fully from the spread of disease and what happens in one place can have a significant impact on people in other places. In an ever-increasingly globalized world, how do we navigate local conditions and their potentially global connections and implications? This is one of the themes that will emerge more fully in the next chapter in the context of the religious ideas and practical experiences related to flooding.

3

Floods

From Theology to Technology—
Understanding, Mitigation, and Prevention

Introduction

Natural disasters can be localized; they can also cross borders and have implications far beyond the places where they may occur. As such, they have political and social implications. Natural disasters can cause a great deal of uncertainty, especially in the short term. They may also lead to longer-term concerns and needs for reconstruction and new ways of preparing for crises. Aside from the actual structural and physical damage that they may cause, natural disasters can challenge our inherited knowledge and, in some cases, even our faith. They may reinforce the way we see the world or call for a reconsideration of how we imagine the world and our own communities and behaviors. The same is true for how we relate to others, whether within our social and communal orbit or beyond.

Since many major rivers and seas traverse significant distances and often cross political boundaries, floods provide us with a valuable opportunity to examine these and other issues. Given the vast discussion of water and flooding in the Bible and rabbinic writings, this chapter follows a parallel structure to previous chapters in examining some of the religious texts and thoughts that informed how people framed their lived experiences and made sense of the challenges that flooding brought. After this brief overview, we turn more fully to an examination of the flooding of the Rhine in the late eighteenth century to consider these and other issues.

Floods are a frequent natural disaster, which can have significant impact on people, animals, and the broader environment, often altering natural ecological systems. This has been true throughout human history, but increasingly so, in some ways, in the Anthropocene and the significant human-induced climate changes that have defined it. Floods have often been described from both local experiences and in larger epochal dramas, eliciting a range of metaphors and ways of thinking and planning. In what follows, we consider some examples of biblical and rabbinic discussions about floods—including the biblical flood of the Noah story and its comparative Ancient Near Eastern renderings—followed by more specific flood histories drawn from a few select early modern Jewish examples. This overview, paralleling the structure of the other chapters in Part I, provides a foundation for an analysis of the central case study (the flooding of the Rhine in the last quarter of the eighteenth century) and it teases out some of the historical understandings of and responses to the environment and natural disaster.

Floods in Biblical and Rabbinic Texts and Thought

Flooding is a major event in the Hebrew Bible, and it is surrounded by a range of significant issues (in the text and in commentaries for millennia after) beyond the narrative sensation of the account. In Gen. 6, God is reported to have seen the wickedness of people on earth and that all the plans devised by humans entailed nothing but evil. God regretted creating man and was saddened. God determined to blot out humans, but Noah, who was a righteous man in his generation, found favor with God. God instructed Noah to make an ark, and the text provides details about the dimensions and characteristics of the ark. God announced to Noah that God will "bring the Flood—waters upon the earth—to destroy all flesh under the sky in which there is breath of life; everything on earth shall perish. But I will establish My covenant with you, and you shall enter the ark, with your sons, your wife, and your sons' wives." Noah did as he was commanded. Chapter 7 of Genesis provides a thorough overview of the animals that Noah took aboard the ark and the onset of the flood, and then it continues:

> And on the seventh day the waters of the Flood came upon the earth. In the six hundredth year of Noah's life, in the second month, on the seventeenth day of the month, on that day All the fountains of the great deep burst apart, And the floodgates of the sky broke open. (The rain fell on the earth forty days and forty nights.)

The familiar story, which has intriguing parallels with other Ancient Near Eastern accounts of a great flood—though from a different, polytheistic perspective—continues with the rise and receding of the floodwaters (in chapter 8 of Genesis).[1] Noah eventually departs from the ark and makes a sacrifice, resulting in God articulating a commitment to humans to never again destroy every living being and concluding that "So long as the earth endures, seedtime and harvest, cold and heat, summer and winter, day and night shall not cease."

The story continues in Chapter 9, when God establishes a covenant (with the rainbow as a reminder) with Noah and his future offspring, through which God promises to never again bring a flood to destroy the earth. The Biblical flood account sets a precedent for connecting flooding with human sin—a theme that gets further amplified in the book of Exodus, when the Egyptians pursuing the Israelites are drowned in the sea (Exod. 14:26-31), when Moses, at God's behest, holds his arm over the sea, turning the waters back on them. The Israelites witnessed the wondrous power of God, the passage concludes, such that they both feared God and had faith in God and Moses. The flood narrative also places nature into a broader natural and supernatural context, in which humans engage with God. The account, which shared some aspects of broader flood stories in the region (and intriguingly beyond), became fodder for later historical and scientific accounts as well as speculation and discussion among the rabbis on a range of theological and societal issues and concerns.

Biblical texts related to floods could also be leveraged in a range of more metaphorical ways. Flooding could be associated with destruction and the loss of hope, for example, as in Job 14:19: "Water wears away stone;/Torrents wash away earth;/So you destroy man's hope," or later, in Job 22:10-11: "Therefore snares are all around you,/And sudden terrors frighten you,/Or darkness, so you cannot see;/A flood of waters covers you."

If the flood was, in biblical mindsets, seen as punishment for sin by an angered divinity, the discussion of floods could open a range of more subtle theological discussions and reflections on human nature, beyond the simple "economy of sin."[2] The rabbis reiterated some of the reasons that God brought the flood. Some of these are articulated in a midrash, Vayikra Rabbah 17, around issues of miserliness, lack of neighborliness, and lying.[3]

The generation of the flood is discussed in a lengthy section in the Babylonian Talmud (Sanhedrin 107b–108a). The discussion is related to the notion of various groups labeled "wicked," which also includes the people of Sodom, the Biblical spies, the generation of the wilderness, and the assembly of Korach. Of what did their wickedness—especially that of the generation of the flood—consist? The generation became haughty (due to prosperity and pleasure), developed a sense of self and questions about the need for God, covetousness, corruption of the flesh (including mating with animals), and engaged in robbery. That generation also provided fodder for some analysis of the backstory of the biblical saga. In the Babylonian Talmudic tractate of Sanhedrin,[4] for example, the people of Noah's generation rebuked Noah for his warning and even for the actions he was taking to construct the ark. When he responded to them that God was bringing a flood upon them, they inquired what kind of flood it would be. If it would be a flood of fire, they claimed to have a fireproof tool to protect them; if it would be a flood of water, they claimed to possess iron plates with which they could cover the earth to prevent the water from rising. And if God sent the waters from the heavens, they possessed a substance that could absorb the water. What is intriguing in this response is that the people of the generation did not deny their evil ways and expressed no interest or need to repent of them; rather, they sought ways to mitigate the coming deluge and were planning the best strategy for a major event that they assumed they could somehow control or mitigate. Like their twenty-first-century cousins, the people of the flood generation possessed a certain hubris and comfort in their technology and abilities—rather than considering a change of the behavior that had led to the pending destruction, they sought to maintain their behavior and placed their future with confidence in their own abilities.

Noah, however, in this account, alerts his critics that God can send the flood in ways that they cannot imagine or prepare for. Their technology cannot save them. In this passage, he also circles back to reiterate some of the sins for which the generation was being punished, including wayward sexuality. Indeed, the rabbis also record Noah as having reminded the people of the generation that God had already given them a great deal of time to reconsider their behavior and repent.

Part of the biblical and rabbinic lesson is that righteousness—which we can assume has many meanings and manifestations—is a defense against disaster, in a way that self-aggrandizement and a sense of self are not. What is more, the passage points out that the flood did not come overnight and for insignificant reasons; rather, the people of the generation had a long time to change their ways (habits and behaviors). For indeed, God knew that changing behavior takes time for people; but still, there are limits. Noah, in his righteousness, convinced God not to bring such a disastrous flood again, and the rabbinic authors concluded that it is in part loving-kindness that helps stave off this kind of disaster:

> And we find that because of the sacrifices offered up by Noah, He swore that He would never again bring a flood over the world—whence we see that the world endures because of the sacrifices, and on lovingkindness, [as it is written (Psalms 89:3): "The world is built on lovingkindness." Lovingkindness consists of: rejoicing the groom, consoling mourners, visiting the sick, attending upon the dead, and the like.] (Pirkei Avot, 1:2)

Flood Histories

The biblical and rabbinic discussions of flooding offer significant insights into the moral considerations that people have often layered upon their experiences of floods and other disasters. They highlight the opportunity to improve behavior but also reveal the limitations on the knowledge that we think we have, especially with ever-expanding technology. How have we learned from floods, and how have we thought about such experiences within broader social and intellectual contexts?

The impact of floods on humans throughout history has varied based on many factors, from their intensity to their proximity to human settlements and the combination of other natural and social conditions. Floods, which regularly recurred in certain regions, could be understood through recourse to local history, particular experiences, and scientific explanations. At the same time, they were also taken as indicators of God's power and ability for punishment and salvation—depending, of course, on the sins or penances of human beings. The response to floods might have religious dimensions, at both the personal and communal levels. Indeed, religion continued to play a central role in discussions of floods well into modernity.

Narratives of floods, therefore, could take many shapes and be utilized in a range of writing and thinking. Historical flood narratives, whether reported in the context of other events or broader histories or as the primary narrative focus, often provided details about specific damages incurred. Clearly, the nature and scope of the accounts were different when authors presented personal experiences—at times they could be more immediate and related to specific themes, though they were not always as a result more objective or more "detailed," since many writers enhanced their accounts from later reports after the disasters. In any case, many accounts noted the practical responses to and results of flooding, including effects on crops, food prices, and travel. Flood narratives could reveal issues that were most pressing for particular communities (before, during, or after the floods), but they could also be more universal, drawing from specific experiences but then framing events in typological ways, often employing past history or biblical texts.

Floods often evoked prayers, calls for repentance, and the formation of civic processions, as well as broader calls for moral improvement. At times, more dramatic apocalyptic sensibilities could intensify such religious sensibilities. Flood narratives could also be co-opted, both consciously and subconsciously, for a range of polemical purposes. Sometimes this polemic served ends that were religious—to inform a return to tradition or instigate religious or communal reform, or as a way of marginalizing outsiders—or political—explaining past or contemporary political events, which were the result of or portended by unusual events in nature. Such narratives, therefore, could be important mechanisms for creating and defining community—at the level of neighborhoods, towns, and cities, or broader territories (later at the national level as well). Flood narratives revealed social tensions and resilience, dictated social behaviors, and all the while helped to define more clearly community and polity. Communal and generational memory was frequently referenced by chroniclers, creating boundaries and ownership of the events. Flood narratives could, therefore, have broader implications for particular communities or societies, beyond the mere statistics of damage and death.

Several floods (and periods of severe weather) are recorded in the book of customs by Juspa, the Shammash of the German city Worms, in the middle of the seventeenth century, and they offer a foundation for the analysis of the case study at the heart of this chapter. Juspa's flood entries detailed floods in the winter of 1651, the winter of 1658, and several summers during the 1660s and 1670s.[5] Many early modern German Jewish accounts of floods (and other natural disasters) balanced internal and external foci. The position of the Jews and their possessions and their legal standing appeared rather tenuous in some cases. Still, most accounts made no mention of negative consequences for the Jews and, as with Juspa's account, they revealed knowledge of the city beyond the Jewish streets or quarter. While Jewish authors generally focused on the impact of such events on the Jewish community, they also described the effects on the broader population, and they frequently extended their comments beyond the borders of their own city or town. As Juspa demonstrated, Jews were familiar with the Jewish section of the city as well as the city at large—"our place" or "our neighborhood," as opposed to "our city" Worms—and the broader countryside. Jewish accounts would continue this balancing well into the modern period.[6]

Within their own residential space, Jewish narrators had a clear sense of geography and hierarchy—noting the most extensive damage by location (heavily in the west of the Jewish quarter in Worms, it would appear) or by social status (noting the losses of particularly wealthy men or communal leaders).[7] Juspa revealed only a few names of individuals and their houses affected by the floodwaters. Unlike the accounts from the later eighteenth century, however, in which we can glean some details about internal Jewish social tensions and settlement patterns in various German cities, towns, and villages, Juspa presented little specific information.

Case Study: The Floods of 1784

Juspa's account provides us with valuable insights into the practical and day-to-day experiences and implications of flooding. Indeed, flooding was a constant threat in medieval and early modern cities, towns, and villages situated along coasts or close to riverbanks. Just a decade and a half before the great flood of 1784, in November 1770, significant flood waters inundated parts of the Rhineland.[8] But the Rhine River rose to particularly impressive levels in the 1784 flood. Based on high water marks on buildings, the waters of the Rhine rose to 12.55 meters on January 28, 1784.[9] The exceptional rise of the Rhine River in February 1784 led to massive destruction of goods and the loss of some lives. A week-long frost gave way to thawing that led to devastation in Cologne, Deutz, Mülheim, and Bonn, where houses and bridges were destroyed. According to one account, the villages surrounding Bonn were flooded to the point that only the tops of the houses were visible.[10]

The flooding of 1784 was one of the most calamitous environmental disasters in central European history. It evoked many diverse responses. We possess a range of Jewish and Christian accounts that offer a unique opportunity to explore how Jews and Christians experienced, understood, and remembered the events of 1784. The diversity of genres of these accounts allows us to understand nuances in Jewish and Christian perceptions and also to consider daily life and Jewish and Christian relations at the edge of modernity.[11]

The winter of 1783/84 was particularly harsh in Europe (and other places). It followed on the heels of major volcanic eruptions in Iceland and Japan and accompanying clouds of ashes and smoke—interpreted by some apocalyptically—intense heat across parts of Europe, and high levels of seismic activity in Italy.[12] The atmospheric cover caused by the volcanic ash resulted in a decrease in sunshine and average temperatures for at least five years after the eruptions, leading to severe cold especially from December 1783 through January 1784. Frigid temperatures cut across Germany and parts of northern Italy; in Heidelberg, the temperature fell as low as −30°C, for example.[13] Record-setting snowfalls accompanied the deep cold. The *Leipziger Zeitung* reported extraordinarily heavy snows across Germany, France, Italy, England, and Holland, with snow levels of fourteen feet settling in some areas.[14] In Mannheim, to take one example, twenty-nine snowfalls were recorded between December 24, 1783, and February 21, 1784, some lasting an entire day. In the Rhine-Neckar region, 45 cm of snow fell on December 27–28, 1783, alone.[15] Thousands of people and animals died because of the cold and snowy conditions.

Sudden warming at the end of February caused extensive flooding across Europe, with huge ice floes forming in the subsequent cold that again followed the brief increase in temperatures. These gruesome towers of ice flowed down rivers and destroyed many bridges and buildings.[16] Authorities in some places fired cannons both to break up the resulting ice and, later, to warn people of impending floods. Many contemporaries commented on the material destruction caused by the ice and flooding.[17] In Bamberg on Friday, February 26, the *Bayreuther Zeitung* reported that the water rose evidently to such a height that the entire city—even the areas where in human memory no water had come previously—with the exception of every part that lay on the mountain, was inundated, and indeed the water in many streets was 12 to 15 feet high. There was no other communication than by ships, where the inhabitants had to be passed essential foodstuffs through second storeys.[18]

The destruction caused by the flooding could be quite extensive. In Bamberg, the Seesbrücke, constructed in 1732 at great cost, was broken. Bridges and mills around Germany were smashed, houses were destroyed, and thousands of trees were uprooted in various locations.[19] In the small town of Mülheim near Cologne, hundreds of houses were destroyed or damaged.[20]

The flooding swept up people and animals almost instantaneously, and many eyewitnesses described horrifying scenes. Reporting on the situation in Pilsen, the author of an article in the *Regensburger Zeitung* wrote that dozens of people stood upon the wooden bridge at the Prague Gate to see the ice float. In an instant, the gate was demolished and the people were cast under the ice. Some people were saved—a fortunate man who was pulled up by the baton of an officer, a boy pulled out by a burgher and his horse, and "four other people, including an old woman," who "had so much presence of mind that they held on to a broken piece of the bridge and attempted to propel themselves until they could be saved by reaching the Schiesshaus." "Everyone else," the report continued, "13 or 14, drowned and presumably were crushed to pieces by the ice . . . One of the most sorrowful sights were the approximately 27 people who climbed one wall to another to escape the rushing water."[21]

Christians frequently referenced Biblical passages in sermons, poems, and other writings of the period that described the flooding and ice floats. Many passages from Psalms (such as Psa. 42, 69, 95, 124, 144)[22] were cited along with other passages from the Hebrew Bible (e.g., Job 47: 6, 9, 10) and the New Testament. Preachers often stressed the power of God, the opportunity that natural disasters provided for repentance, and the need for human brotherhood.[23] Sermons called for love and charity,[24] as well as the need to turn to God, who controlled nature and could provide protection.[25] Many writers responded to the event by thanking God for salvation from the flooding.[26] Not all responses were theological, of course. The activity of local and regional, even imperial, governments could be quite quick and extensive. People had a tremendous need for rebuilding in some places.[27] The threat of ensuing epidemics and food shortages was also significant in numerous regions and called for organized responses.[28]

Some of the oldest and most prestigious Jewish settlements in Germany developed along the Rhine River, a major highway for business, politics, and daily life through the medieval and early modern periods. As such, the flooding of the Rhine affected Jews, like their Christian neighbors, in many ways and evoked a similarly rich range of responses. The flood of 1784 left an indelible mark on individual and communal Jewish consciousness and writing of the period.[29] Jewish synagogues were damaged, and communities lost many ritual objects and books to the flood waters.[30] In the memory book for Bonn, the communal scribe recorded the damage to various prayer books and records by the rising waters.[31]

Aside from the accounts in local memory books, there are several other Jewish sources, including from *Sippur bekhi neharot* (Tale of the Weeping of the Rivers), written by Simon ben Jacob Abraham Kopenhagen, who was then living in Bonn. The booklet was published in Amsterdam in March 1784. We also have a Yiddish text written by Mendel Nathan. Although this brief report of the Mülheim events of 1784 contains a page that quickly described the flood of 1788, the events of 1784 appear to have been recorded approximately six months after the flood, in mid-August 1784.[32]

Although Jews had been expelled from Cologne in the early fifteenth century and would not be formally tolerated as residents until the end of the eighteenth, the thriving Jewish populations outside the city and throughout the broader region played an important role in early modern Jewish social and communal life as well as in the broader economy. In the region surrounding Cologne, where the flooding was particularly devastating, there were approximately 1,000 Jews in the middle of the eighteenth century, with several dozen very small settlements of a few Jews each throughout the region.[33] Jews in this area also maintained a trans-regional connection with the Landjudenschaft and Duchy of Berg, where small Jewish communities were likewise scattered across the countryside.[34] There were some larger Jewish communities in the region as well. Approximately, 300 Jews lived in Bonn (home to many court Jews in the eighteenth century[35]) and fifty-six in Deutz—making those the central communities of the region and the seats of rabbinic authority.[36]

Abraham, the son of R. Joseph Halevi, Kosman, authored the entry in the Deutz memory book about the great flood of 1784. He wrote "in order to narrate for the next generation the miracle that occurred."[37] Abraham was the son of the famous rabbinic scholar Joseph Juspa Kosman (d. 1758), who was the son-in-law of the famous regional rabbi Judah ben Joseph Mehler (d. 1750). Abraham described the flooding in detail. In the year 1784 "there was a great cold that trustworthy men could not remember the likes of."[38] In the month of Tevet (late December 1783 and January 1784), the ice and water grew strong and touched upon the walls. The ensuing cold led to ice that was seventeen feet thick, "a great novelty since the creation of the world"[39] Wagons and carriages traveled and conducted business upon the ice. Many people came from near and far to see this spectacle.

In early Adar (late February 1784), the waters became mighty, Abraham noted, and "poured down from the mountains, descended and broke through every opening and gate."[40] Only houses with roofs and high towers remained above the waters. The Jews broke through fortified walls of the synagogue to save the Torah scrolls. Thirteen scrolls were salvaged, though the rest had to be abandoned. As in the account from Bonn below, Abraham noted that the Jews cried out to God to hear their lament, to stop the harsh decree, and to save them from the water. The Jews, like others, were forced to flee to the local cloister, where they were given protection and joined in prayer to God with the non-Jews sheltering there:

> Very heavy is the hand of God; we are forced to walk to the houses of exile. We go to the cloister and to the towers. There they provided us, within the monastery, space for the sake of children and people of the world; and there we prayed to the

God of the world—all the nations around us prayed in the name of God, because they are despondent.[41]

The Jews called out, "God, see our doorways and give us providence immediately, take pity on us, don't forget bread and butter . . . send help and abundance of joy."[42] The unusual sight of Jews and Christians praying together was noted by another eyewitness. He reported that at the sight of the receding waters, the Jews sang out in such an intricate and noisy Hebrew tune that the Christians, who were unfamiliar with it, were silenced.[43]

Throughout the entry, Abraham narrated the terror and tense conditions during the flood. Due to the adverse conditions, Jews could not cook for the Sabbath, and children cried out in hunger. But devastation ran wild through the region, with herds of cattle and sheep drowned and other animals swept away.[44] As in other affected areas, local authorities sent ships from house to house and roof to roof to save people. More than 300 people were saved in this way. The synagogue was destroyed.[45] The water began to decrease already on the Sabbath. When each head of house returned to their dwelling, they found all the rooms covered in mud, however. People were forced to borrow bedding and vessels from neighbors and relatives as they went into exile. In this misery, Abraham noted, Jews were not distinguished from non-Jews, as they roamed about in streets that were filled with decay and terrible smells.[46]

In Deutz, Jews lived on a specially designated street. In these smaller enclaves, Jews would almost by default have been forced to live among the general population. Although such Jewish communities have generally been portrayed as marginalized and isolated from the larger society, awaiting later political integration,[47] Jews in some smaller settlements appear at times to have been physically, and even socially, integrated with the general population. During times of distress, as we saw above, the lines demarcating religion and social standing might be particularly blurred. Of course, the very fact that both Jewish and Christian authors went out of their way to note such episodes of positive interaction indicates how rare they may in fact have been in day-to-day life. And yet, it must also be noted that Jews and Christians could see themselves in civic roles that occasionally transcended solely religious boundaries. Participation in rescue efforts and common prayer services (probably more the result of geographical proximity in confined quarters than a harbinger of theological reconciliation) reveal that at times, daily social and religious interactions between Jews and Christians were not only possible but potentially important—a situation that has been increasingly documented for the early modern period.[48]

Abraham recorded that the Jews sang out their thanks to God. He offered special thanks at the end of the entry for the Jewish community of Bonn, from which some families sent wine and blessings at the holiday of Purim, shortly after the flood. Abraham ended the entry somewhat more positively, noting that the Jewish community "will say praises of God . . . Who saved our souls."[49]

The situation was equally bleak in Mülheim, an open small town of 420 houses that lay an hour from Cologne, on the right bank of the Rhine River in a plain. Mülheim was comprised of two main streets along the river, with a short middle quarter with gardens. These were intersected by two diagonal quarters, thereby dividing Mülheim into three distinct districts.[50]

A brief Yiddish account of the flood in Mülheim was written in the month of Elul of the Hebrew year 5544 (August 17, 1784) by the businessman Mendel Nathan, who also wrote to remind future generations of the events and of God's salvation of the Jews. Mendel had been in Mülheim for a while already by that time, perhaps since the early 1760s. His account is useful because it provides several details of the flooding and because it can be compared with non-Jewish accounts.[51] Mendel began by describing the severe freezing of the Rhine in late December 1783 and early January 1784. The Rhine remained frozen even as its waters rose higher and currents plowed through parts of the town, such "that no one could walk or drive through the water and men had to climb over the ridges on the roofs, in order to get from one to the other."[52] The author recounted the efforts exerted to deliver provisions to people and to rescue them using small boats.

As elsewhere, the temperatures in Mülheim dropped again, and the water receded so that people could travel about on foot. The Rhine itself remained almost completely frozen, so that men, horses, and wagons could travel upon it between Mülheim and Deutz. Ice drilled from the river was measured to be sixteen–eighteen feet thick or more in some places. Cold and heavy snowfalls blanketed the area throughout the Hebrew month of Shevat (late January and February, 1784), but by the second of Adar (the twenty-fourth of February) warm weather arrived and within days, by the fourth of Adar (the twenty-sixth of February), "the Rhine began to rise and in that night it rose so much that it already stood in the quarter by the Reform Church by three o'clock in the morning." The raging waters pulled down some walls of the Reform Church, even as canons could be heard from Cologne and drums were sounded locally to warn people.

As the Sabbath arrived, women lit candles with difficulty, and there was no food. As water entered the houses, the inhabitants dwelled in darkness and with the fear that the houses would soon collapse. They managed through the night, and

> on the day of the holy Sabbath, the weekly portion [of] Teruma, the 28th of February, around seven o'clock in the morning, foreigners came into my house through the roof-peaks and entered my attic. And with the help of the Eternal One we crawled with wife and children . . . from house to house and we came through the window into the house of Meir Katz and we were unscathed, with the help of the Eternal One. There we prayed and made Kiddush, since all we Jews who lived here, men and women and children, met in the house of Meir, with the help of the Eternal One. And with the help of the Eternal One no one suffered any bodily injury.[53]

Reports circulated that 162 houses were destroyed, including the house of Mordechai Katz, in which the synagogue was located. Traditionally, Mendel attributed the destruction to "our many sins." He also recorded specific damage, including the loss of six Torah scrolls, ritual objects, prayer shawls, and prayer books.[54] The houses of the author's son Izek, his sister-in-law Ms. Zerle, and Mr. Jüdel Horn were thoroughly destroyed. From government documents,[55] from June of 1784, we know that ten Jewish families had been living in Mülheim,[56] and that seven of them were directly affected by the flood.[57] The three families living at the highest elevations escaped damage to their property, but they had severe strains placed on their businesses and they sheltered, fed, and looked after the other Jews for a long time. While most of the Jews lost their possessions, they were, the author reiterated, saved from bodily harm by God's help. Mendel concluded that "only foreigners drowned and fell from the houses."

Without a synagogue, a minyan (prayer quorum) met in Mendel's house on Purim. But the community lacked a Torah scroll, "for we could not receive one, not one from the holy city of Deutz, which is a half hour from here but did not want to lend us any." But, he continued, "and then on the seventh day of Passover, we received a Torah scroll sent from the community in Amsterdam, may the Eternal One protect and guard her, sent with the post wagon." The father-in-law of his son Izek was an influential governor in Amsterdam, by the name of Berman Kohen, and he "sent us from Amsterdam haggadot, mahzorim, Prayer shawls, prayerbooks, and books of the Pentateuch."

Non-Jewish accounts of the events in Mülheim provide similar information in many regards. An account by the French language teacher J. W. Berger reviewed the general conditions, including the icing of the Rhine in early to mid-January 1784. In noting the rescue of people and their removal to dry ground, Berger frequently presented a rather universalistic picture that looked beyond social or religious boundaries. In one passage, he declared:

Here sit together Christians and Jews, Roman Catholics and Protestants, oppressed by the same dread, filled by a purpose and they pray in brotherhood to one God to save and spare them—There the father kneels with his children, and next to them the mother with the small infant on the arm or sleeping alongside in the cradle, and they send to heaven the innermost pleas with repeated wringing of their hands and loudly-resounding sighs . . . The one sighs to God, the other grumbles against Him. Some feel for the first time in their lives that they are sinners and they tremble before the approaching moment when they should pass over into eternal rest. Others seek God by reconciling themselves through vows that their unrepentant hearts will again forget with the passing of the emergency. Only a few give a lasting impression of a true improvement of life. Only a few pay the Lord their vows by discarding what displeases Him.[58]

Berger expressed a remarkably unified corporate sensibility in several other places as well: "All food stuffs, blankets, canvas, and pieces of clothing sent were distributed without regard to religion."[59] Or, consider: "dearest charitableness encouraged our eyes—dulled from anxiety, grief, and weeping—through a marvelous spectacle and a picture of the bliss that would rule the world was imagined if people lived together as brothers, as members of a family (which they really are), and each person felt the needs of another as his own."[60]

He portrayed a similar notion in describing the charity doled out to the citizens of the town:

they found from the citizens who escaped open doors and open hearts. They were taken lovingly into the houses and refreshed with food and drink by 10, 20, 30, even by a hundred, without differentiation of standing and religion. The best rooms were handed over for beds by the most distinguished citizens. From the lowest storeys up until the roof, the houses were filled with people of all class and age, who, even though they were pressed together so densely, nevertheless it was not nearly as narrow as in their abandoned huts. Happy that they now no longer had to fear every moment for the collapse of their dwellings upon their heads, they took delight in a small room in which they could only sit or lay.[61]

Charity was likewise sent from Protestant merchants in Cologne as well as the Catholic General Vicarius, "all of which was distributed according to the will of the donor without regard to the religion of the needy." Food was also delivered from other towns and communities close by, such as Solingen and Elberfeld.[62]

Non-sectarian cooperation led to Reform Christians allowing Lutherans to use their church.[63] The author declared: "God wanted that this might be a prelude that all prejudice and sectarianism would be eradicated at the root and not only tolerance, but actual love would be grounded in and blossom through the spirit of Christ. But as with all apparent toleration and everywhere increasing impartiality, this point appears to be still distant."[64] While such passages probably referred to Christian denominations primarily, if not exclusively, both Christian and Jewish writers recorded a close interaction of Christians and Jews, particularly during the most intense periods of the crisis. As in Deutz, it is not entirely clear what the emphasis on this crisis-invoked cooperation meant for daily interactions in more normal times. In fact, Berger suggests that many people did not take advantage of the conditions to improve themselves or their relations with others. Still, that Jews and Christians of varying denominations were thrown together without incident and in what appear to have been constructive, if temporary, results, forces us to consider the extent and nature of Jewish marginalization at the end of the early modern period.

Conclusions

Our limited sources[65] do allow us to make some general observations. Not surprisingly, as for much of early modern Jewish history in Germany, Jews frequently lived in small and dispersed settlements with regional associations. The individuals living in these settlements were connected to other Jews and Jewish communities for a variety of familial, economic, social, political, and religious reasons. The network of interactions that was regnant in smaller settlements was as clear in the personal relations that facilitated the loan of a Sefer Torah from Amsterdam to the Jews living in Mülheim as it was in the generous gifts and aid sent from Bonn to Deutz.

But the possible tensions between Jews within individual communities and between those living in different places were noticeable as well. In Bonn, for example, internal discord had divided the community for decades in the eighteenth century,[66] even as Jews appear to have supported one another for a long time during the recovery from the devastations of the floodwaters. While the authors writing about the flood stressed the unified response and mutual assistance of Jews in response to the crisis, they also hinted at long-held social differentiation, with some wealthier Jews leading the community and even housing the synagogue. Jews did not necessarily live together in every town, and the geographical dispersion raises questions about the importance of social standing and the extent of general communal integration. As we have experienced today, communal boundaries are real, even when they can at times be permeable. The specific needs of individuals and communities could be nested within larger social needs and conditions. At times of crisis, these needs could diverge and lead to conflict (even within specific faith traditions), or they could open opportunities for collaboration, which could be temporary or alter longer-term trajectories of interaction.

Jewish writers tended to emphasize the importance of recording the flood for posterity so that people would recognize the power of God and the fact that the Jews were deserving of being saved. Like many Christian writers, the Jewish authors frequently referred to the Providence of God and the need for and enactment of charity and prayer. The Jewish texts also addressed the theme of penance and the idea of God's punishment for sin, though the latter was generally less of a focus of attention. Rather, throughout the texts, the authors affirmed positive Jewish actions—exertions to save sacred objects, efforts to carry out religious obligations and services in the face of extreme adversity, and general internal cohesion in the face of the disaster. The Jewish communities quickly looked to restore or rebuild damaged or destroyed synagogues, and they paid premium prices to rewrite communal memory books so that the souls of the deserving deceased would be properly recognized.

Naturally, the genre of writing and the background of the authors must be taken into account as we consider what their writings can tell us. The memory book entries were in a sense sacred literature that formed an important communal and ritual function, as they were read aloud in the synagogue at certain times of the year. Simon clearly had extensive familiarity with Jewish law and was a scribe who functioned regionally. In a sense, then, the Jewish accounts were themselves crafted from a religious perspective, but one that was focused on broad theological issues as well as practical matters. In all cases, however, the texts served as important communal documents that would record the history and success of the Jewish communities in overcoming challenges and that would demonstrate that God was still protecting the Jews from external threats. Record keeping was important for a variety of tangible concerns, from property rights (and later insurance claims) to disputes over damage and liability. Records of disasters like floods also helped to create memory and forge identity; such events could become anchors for the individuals who experienced them, but also for those who would live in the community or the locale and may never have experienced the event or even, in some cases, the impact of those events.

The integration of Jews into the broader societies in which they lived could vary depending on a wide range of factors, including the size of the Jewish community and the occupations of its residents.[67] While the Jewish writers at times recognized the assistance non-Jewish neighbors and civic authorities provided, they nonetheless typically focused their accounts on internal issues confronting the Jewish community.

Jewish authors were generally less exuberant about national or regional sentiments, even as they espoused a certain, general civic consciousness. Jewish prayers could be universalistic while Jews used language and imagery that spoke specifically to Jewish exile and deliverance. In Mülheim, Mendel noted that the Jews were miraculously saved, even as some non-Jews lost their lives. In the very narrative structures of their accounts, Jewish writers referred to more general developments and, in some cases, apparently even borrowed from Christian accounts of the flood. Inevitably, however, they turned their attention to internal Jewish communal concerns, revealing engagement but not integration with the broader society in which they lived.

While environmental distress did not create civic harmony, it did allow opportunities for both Jews and Christians to look from their respective communities into a broader society in which real-world concerns encouraged a greater degree of integration and in which the struggles and interactions of daily life we can no longer see have left faint traces of their complicated and interwoven nature. Jewish life could vary a great deal depending upon specific circumstances. Often, the daily life and inner workings of the Jewish communities and settlements remain hazy due to limited sources. Environmental history may, in the end, allow us one more angle or view into the multifaceted, if opaque, early modern German Jewish experience that must consider a wide range of aspects of Jewish life and interactions both within and beyond the Jewish community.

In this chapter, we examined floods in eighteenth-century Germany and observed the ways in which people worked together within and across communities and differences (religious, social, geographic), as well as the limitations to such cooperation in the short and long term. We noticed that some changes, especially around prevention and response protocols, could take root and become part of the broader culture. Some changes were enshrined in legislation and rituals, and the memory of floods could connect people in important ways. Learning from the past in this case could provide opportunities to better manage disasters in the future and to engage the environment in more proactive and systematic ways to mitigate the possibilities for and impact of natural disasters. At the same time, we also noticed the challenges to change, especially with disasters that are beyond human control, and we saw that the marginalization of others remains a powerful and negative tendency during and after crises. Many of these issues emerged during other natural disasters, as we saw in Chapters 1 and 2 and as we will observe in the discussion of fire in the next chapter. As we will see in Part II, learning from disasters is significant, even when there are limiting factors and attitudes. Premodern experiences provide examples of significant learning and ways that practical experiences could dictate thinking and behavior, even as religious narratives provided different lessons and opportunities. As was the case in our discussion of earthquakes, religious and practical responses did not have to be separate or in competition. In fact, they could be mutually supportive, and the call for penance did not mean that people needed to forsake more practical measures at the same time. Preparing for future disasters with practical measures did not have to mean that humans should not improve their morals, and an emphasis on divine punishment did not mean that people had to live a passive existence, simply awaiting whatever cards God might deal.

$$4$$

Learning with Fire

Introduction

Chapter 3 revealed that at times of crisis community boundaries can be quite permeable; crisis, however, can also lead to a retrenching of boundaries and the exclusion of marginal or outsider groups. Disasters—whether natural or human-induced, unexpected, or recurring—can open windows onto otherwise unseen cultural structures, latent social tensions, and a full range of intergroup relations in different historical contexts. Such events may both reinforce and challenge existing norms and behaviors. How disasters are perceived and remembered can have a great deal to do with the perspectives and concerns of the individuals and communities that experience them, whether in person or even at a temporal or geographical distance. Recently that has been the case with wildfires in California (in the north in the 1990s) and the devastating infernos burning in and around Los Angeles as I prepare this book for publication.

Natural disasters can lead to conflict and collaboration (sometimes even at the same time!). They also serve as significant markers that help us create memories and set identities that can live on for a very long time. In this chapter, I examine one specific kind of disaster (that could be natural or human induced), namely fire, and then consider a case study focused on the fire that destroyed the Jewish ghetto in Frankfurt am Main in 1711. The chapter raises a number of questions, including: how we understand nature and the environment; causality; the relationship of theory and practice in responding to disasters; the types of considerations that must be taken into account in responding and rebuilding after a disaster; the means that can be employed for the prevention of future disasters; the role of politics and polemic in representing disasters; the impact on extant policies and the development of new policies for responding to and mitigating disaster; and the impact of changing demographics and settlement patterns on the outbreak and impact of fires and other natural disasters.

Biblical and Rabbinic Discussions of Fire

Harnessed for important domestic and industrial purposes, fire has been essential for human social development. Not surprisingly, fire was seen by the philosopher-scientists of

Antiquity as a primal element (along with earth, air, and water) and a self-generating key force of change.[1] Even when downgraded from "elemental status," fire remained a central process and key theme for reflection, investigation, and application.[2] Uncontrolled and wild fires, by contrast, while serving many natural functions, have at times devastated human communities. The ubiquity of fire in early modern society naturally fueled the chances for the spread of fire and nearly every urban area was scorched at some point in its history.

Biblical and rabbinic writings provided important orientation and insights for Jews when it came to a wide range of theological and practical issues, including natural disasters and various crises. Fire in the Hebrew Bible was a powerful force. God was present in the pillar of fire that guided the Israelites through the desert (Exod. 13:21), God came down upon Mount Sinai in fire (causing the mountain to tremble) (Exod. 19:18, 24:17), and God's messenger appeared in "blazing fire out of a bush" (Exod. 3:2). Not only God's presence, but God's wrath could also be revealed in fire. God was incensed by the Israelites' complaining, and God's fire broke out against them, ravaging the outskirts of their camp (Num. 11:1; or consider Num. 16:35). Fire is used in the Bible metaphorically to describe God's passion (Deut. 4:24) and fury (Ps. 89:47, Lam. 2:4). God's law is also described as fiery—whether because it was given amid fire on the mountain or, as the medieval Jewish exegete Rashi would note, referencing a midrash, because the Law was written by God in black fire upon white fire (Deut. 33:2). Indeed, God's word is described as like fire (and a hammer) (Jer. 23:29). Fire was also associated with the altar (Lev. 6:6) and "alien" or unauthorized fire—as that brought by Aaron's sons Nadab and Abihu—could lead to punishment by death (Lev. 10:1, 16:1; see also 2 Kgs 1:10-14).

The rabbis discussed these and other passages related to fire. The midrash Genesis Rabbah, expanding on the biblical text, for example, details the famous episode of Abraham and the fiery furnace:

He [Teraḥ] took him and handed him over to Nimrod. He [Nimrod] said to him [Abraham]: "Let us bow down to fire." Abraham said to him: "Let us better bow down to water, that extinguishes fire." Nimrod said to him: "[All right,] let us bow down to water." He said to him: "If so, let us bow down to the clouds, that bear the water." He said to him: "[All right,] let us bow down to the clouds." He said to him: "If so, let us bow down to the wind, that scatters the clouds." He said to him: "[All right,] let us bow down to the wind." He said to him: "Better let us bow down to a person, who can withstand the wind." He said to him: "You are saying mere words. I bow down only to fire. I will cast you into it, and let that God to whom you bow down come and rescue you from it." Haran was there and he was conflicted. He said: "Either way [I will know what to do]; If Abraham is victorious, I will say: I am with Abraham, and if Nimrod is victorious, I will say: I am with Nimrod." When Abraham descended into the fiery furnace and was rescued, they said to him [Haran]: "With whom are you?" He said to them: "I am with Abraham." They took him and cast him into the fire and his innards were scorched. He emerged and died in the presence of Teraḥ his father. That is what is written: "Haran died in the presence of Teraḥ." (38:13)

In this text, fire is a primal force that Nimrod, often understood as a descendant of Noah and a king rebellious against God, venerated. Abraham convinces him that there are other elements (water and wind) that deserve greater reverence. Nimrod returns to bowing down to fire and casts Abraham into the fiery furnace. Abraham survives. His brother Haran, who had made up his mind to follow Abraham if Abraham was saved and Nimrod if Abraham died, is himself thrown into the furnace and burned. The story elevates the power of fire and the religious devotion that could be given to it, while also noting that God is more powerful and can protect meritorious people like Abraham from it.

Rabbinic discussions about fire frequently involved discussions of damages caused by fire and associated liability.[3] Fire could also be associated with sin, as the rabbis discuss in the Babylonian Talmud (Sotah 17a): "Rabbi Akiva taught: If a man [ish] and woman [isha] merit, the Divine Presence rests between them. But if due to their behavior they do not merit reward, fire consumes them." Fire is likewise associated with sin and the evil inclination: "One who was born under the influence of Venus will be a rich and promiscuous person. What is the reason for this? Because fire was born during the hour of Venus, he will be subject the fire of the evil inclination, which burns perpetually" (Babylonian Talmud Shabbat 156a:11, Sefaria translation). Fire could be seen specifically as a punishment for the desecration of the Sabbath:

Rav Yehuda, son of Rav Shmuel, said in the name of Rav: Fire is only found in a place where there is desecration of Shabbat, as it is stated: "And if you do not heed Me to sanctify the day of Shabbat, and to refrain from carrying burdens and come to the gates of Jerusalem on the day of Shabbat, and I will light a fire in its gates and it will consume the palaces of Jerusalem and it will not be extinguished" (Jeremiah 17:27). The Gemara asks: What is the meaning of: And it will not be extinguished? Rav Naḥman bar Yitzḥak said: Fire will break out at a time when people are not found to extinguish it. Abaye said: Jerusalem was destroyed only because people desecrated the Shabbat in it, as it is stated: "And from My *Shabbatot* they averted their eyes, and I was profaned among them" (Ezekiel 22:26). Several punishments were decreed to befall Jerusalem as punishment for this transgression. (Shabbat 119b, Sefaria)

In fact, fire was one of the central punishments Jews would strive to avoid, as explicated in the high holiday liturgy:

On Rosh Hashanah it is inscribed, and on Yom Kippur it is sealed—how many shall pass away and how many shall be born, who shall live and who shall die, who in good time, and who by an untimely death, who by water and who by fire, who by sword and who by wild beast, who by famine and who by thirst, who by earthquake and who by plague, who by strangulation and who by lapidation, who shall have rest and who wander, who shall be at peace and who pursued, who shall be serene and who tormented, who shall become impoverished and who wealthy, who shall be debased, and who exalted. But repentance, prayer and righteousness avert the severity of the decree. (*Unetnaeh Tokef*)

The positive, Godly aspects of fire could find expression in rabbinic texts as well: "Rabbi Yehuda said to him: My son, open your mouth and let your words illuminate, as matters of Torah do not become ritually impure, as it is stated: 'Is not my word like fire, says the Lord' (Jeremiah 23:29). Just as fire does not become ritually impure, so too matters of Torah do not become ritually impure" (Babylonian Talmud Berakhot 22a).

The rabbis could also associate fire with more cosmic issues, as in the Babylonian Talmudic tractate of Pesachim, where the fire of hell (Gehenna) is discussed; in that passage, the time when fire was created is considered, and it is noted that Gehenna is one of seven phenomena that were created before the world was created—Torah, repentance, the Garden of Eden, Gehenna, the Throne of Glory, the Temple, and the name of Messiah (Pesachim 54a). Fire would be associated with God in a mystical sense too.

> Immediately, Rabban Yoḥanan ben Zakkai alighted from the donkey, and wrapped his head in his cloak in a manner of reverence, and sat on a stone under an olive tree. Rabbi Elazar said to him: My teacher, for what reason did you alight from the donkey? He said: Is it possible that while you are expounding the Design of the Divine Chariot, and the Divine Presence is with us, and the ministering angels are accompanying us, that I should ride on a donkey? Immediately, Rabbi Elazar ben Arakh began to discuss the Design of the Divine Chariot and expounded, and fire descended from heaven and encircled all the trees in the field, and all the trees began reciting song. (Chagigah 14b, Sefaria)

Other classical and medieval Jewish sources discussed the power of fire, aligning it with God's law as well as God's fury and as a tool for punishment for sin. As such, fire was a remarkable vehicle that could have different meanings in different contexts. Depending on whether it was used appropriately or inappropriately, it could have constructive or destructive results. From a biblical and rabbinic perspective, then, fire could be multivalent, representing religious practice and connection to God and simultaneously cast as divine punishment for human sin.[4] Regardless, fire was a very real element, which belonged to the world of creation and even pre-creation. It was also a malleable metaphor that accompanied a good deal of theological discussion and real-world action.

Fires in Early Modern History

Fire in biblical and rabbinic writing and thought surfaced many different theological ideas, and it also elevated important discussions about a host of related and mundane concerns, including damages and liability. Even day-to-day issues might have deep religious implications and serve as the springboard for discussions of moral and ethical questions as well. What were some of the practical considerations raised by fire in the premodern (and modern) world?

Fire has been presented in historical accounts as one of the greatest, if not the greatest, threats to early modern cities.[5] Whether the result of lightning strikes, dry weather conditions, or human actions (accidentally according to early modern writers or as a part of crime or warfare), fire could have devastating effects on cities and towns comprised of houses and buildings that were constructed largely from wood and that often lacked conscious planning and development or fire prevention. Although the deaths that resulted from fires might be fewer than those from other disasters, the broader damage and economic and social impact could be much greater.[6] Fires destroyed houses and other buildings; this destruction as well as the process of rebuilding could escalate latent economic and social tensions or confirm traditional social rules and privileges. They could reveal societal vulnerabilities and latent tensions. They could challenge, recalibrate, or reinforce social, economic, and political hierarchies.[7]

In describing fires, early modern people drew from a well of biblical, theological, scientific, and historical sources. Early modern chroniclers often did not specify who or what caused fires—at times they simply did not know. The lack of agency, however, also allowed writers to associate anonymity with divine punishment.

For many medieval and early modern people, fires were often part of a panoply of wonder signs and punishments from heaven, frequently seen in an apocalyptic vein,[8] along with other signs—including solar and lunar eclipses; rains of fire, brimstone, and blood; bloody snow; terrible winds and storms; earthquakes; and even locust infestations—all of which portended misfortune and divine punishment for an unrepentant and Godless world. Such accounts could be polemical, attacking adherents of other denominations or faiths,[9] or more general moral upbraiding or criticism of particular social groups, confessions, or behaviors.[10] The occasion of a fire could encourage self-reflection and calls for repentance,[11] especially for vices such as haughtiness, blasphemy, desecration of the Sabbath, and unchasteness.[12] Only repentance could stave off other disasters.

In seeking assistance from other cities or communities or to maintain order, civic governments might issue a range of edicts and ordinances regarding the measures necessary to prevent fire. These included construction regulations, the relocation of businesses or industries utilizing fire to less densely populated parts of town or even outside the city walls, precautions to be taken against wind and severe weather as well as the dangers of unattended candles at night, techniques to protect key structures such as bridges, and the development of surveillance and warning systems. Many ordinances stipulated the specific measures to be taken in the event of an actual conflagration: the types of machinery to be employed to battle the flames; the use of lights at night; fire watches, horn blasts, and other means to notify people of fires; measures to safeguard the food supply; and protocols for rescue efforts. Social and communal responses were at times standardized, as with other communal regulations such as those governing the collection of alms, for example.[13] The early modern response to fires also included the development of fire guilds and fire insurance.[14]

Fires, therefore, often led to increased regulation of daily life and industry, and by the seventeenth century, they broadly influenced architecture and urban planning, including even the selection of (stone) building materials.[15] The prophylactic attempt to prevent fires from beginning or spreading once they did could itself be expensive, with the investment in equipment and supplies, the creation of watch towers, digging of wells, and the staffing of various communal positions.[16] A great deal of money could also be required to respond to damages caused by fires, and as a result, special taxes might be collected to fund the reconstruction projects in cities.[17]

The particular response to a fire could vary by location and specific conditions, but often entailed a mix of theological and practical responses.[18] However, the question of where to lay blame for the outbreak of a fire was important and could be highly charged. Some premodern writers blamed the city magistrates for poor policies and insufficient or sluggish responses.[19] Accusations of arson were more complicated, but they were frequently directed at marginalized groups such as Jews, gypsies, and vagabonds. Even when early moderns maintained that fires were divine punishment,[20] those accused of arson could be seen as agents of divine wrath, though to many minds no less guilty of crimes against the city and their neighbors.[21]

Responses to fires could be complex and they revealed financial challenges in addition to latent social and political tensions.[22] Even when damage was localized within a city or urban district, the disaster could have significant resonance throughout the city and region.[23] Reconstruction had huge financial implications; likewise, any decision not to rebuild carried other, equally significant implications, as diverse populations were forced to compete for housing and interact more directly. Even in localized fires, weakened communal infrastructure and compromised food supplies could lead to epidemics, rebellions, or armed conflicts.

Fires, of course, have long affected urban life, and since the Middle Ages numerous fires have had a direct impact on German Jewish communities. As for other urban residents, fires affected Jews in a variety of ways. Already with the famous medieval charter for the Jews in Speyer we read that

> At the outset, when we came to establish our residence in Speyer—may its foundations never falter!—it was the result of the fire that broke out in the city of Mainz. The city of Mainz was the city of our origin and the residence of our ancestors, the ancient and revered community, praised above all communities in the empire. All the Jews' quarter and their street was burned, and we stood in great fear of the burghers. . . . The bishop of Speyer greeted us warmly, sending his ministers and soldiers after us. He gave us a place in the city and expressed his intention to build about us a strong wall to protect us from our enemies, to afford us fortification.[24]

Accounts of significant fires could reveal extreme danger to the Jewish communities because of loss of property or anti-Jewish animus that could manifest itself in accusations of Jewish conspiracy against or general malevolence toward Christians. For the year 1541, for example, the Jewish chronicler David Gans wrote, "There were many and great fires in the entire territory of Bohemia in the year 301, according to the shorter calculation, and it was not known who started them. And it was a libel against the shepherds and against the Jews, saying that they did this evil thing . . . and many were burned in martyrdom." Gans went on to note that "Ferdinand, King of Bohemia, because of the complaints of the people, expelled all the Jews of his Kingdom; only in the city of Prague there remained ten [Jewish] men for a short time" (Gans recorded that the Jews were recalled a short time later).[25]

Other Jewish chroniclers registered occurrences of fires as well. An anonymous chronicle from Prague discussed a fire in 1559. In a traditional approach to theodicy, the author ascribed specific suffering within the community, such as expulsions and fires in the Jewish street, to the sins of the community. "Due to our iniquities," he wrote,

> there was a fire in the Judenstrasse here in Prague, in which seventy-two houses were consumed by the flames, as well as the Hochschul. This occurred on the 17th of Tammuz [a fast day instituted to recall numerous tragedies in Jewish history, especially related to the destruction of the Second Temple]. A woman named Friedel Niches perished in the fire as well, due to our iniquities.[26]

Of course, fires affecting the Jewish communities were not limited to the lands of the Holy Roman Empire (see also Chapter 5). To take one further Eastern European, example, we have accounts of other fires that affected early modern Jewish communities. Consider, for example, the memoirs of Ber of Bolochow,[27] in which he detailed a conflagration in 1729 (5489).[28] That fire consumed five large buildings on the town's main street, and Ber noted the reconstruction and reallocation of housing, as well as the death of one woman.[29] The fire began in the church when a candle fell onto a covered table and spread to the main street before eventually dying out due to the gap created between the houses.[30] Ber mentioned other fires that were the result of military encounters.[31] In other cases, Ber noted the amount of damage and the need for Jews (including himself and his brother) to find other, temporary lodging with extended family.[32] Like their Christian neighbors, Jews understood and responded to fires in ways that were simultaneously theological and practical. As we will see below, early modern fires could also reveal complex, and at times, positive relations among Jews and between Jews and Christians—neighbors, clergy, and secular authorities.

Case Study: The Great Fire of 1711 in the Frankfurt Jewish Ghetto

Given the range of theological ideas associated with fire and the range of tangible regulations instituted to prevent and fight fires when they occurred, how can a review of the devastation of fire in history contribute to our work in this book? To answer that question, I turn now to a major conflagration that hit the Jewish ghetto in the German city of Frankfurt am Main in the early eighteenth century. The fire raised many theological debates even as it had significant civic and political implications during and after the reconstruction of the Jewish ghetto.

The relatively large Jewish population of Frankfurt am Main was sequestered into a special quarter in 1462, which initially enclosed some 10 houses and 100 residents. By the second decade of the seventeenth century, there were roughly 2,700 Jews from 453 Jewish households (occupying 195 houses) in Frankfurt,[33] with the population expanding to 3,000 by the end of the seventeenth century, constituting ten percent of the total city population, and then contracting a bit to over 2,400 in the early eighteenth century.

Some medieval and early modern German Jewish quarters were devastated by fire at various times. The Frankfurt ghetto suffered major fires in 1711, 1721, and again in 1774. The great fire of 1711, which was confined to the Jewish quarter, was seen by some contemporary Christians as the result of Jewish machinations against Christianity or, alternately, by later historians (regardless of religious background) as a result of the unhygienic and polluted nature of the ghetto (related to traditional anti-Jewish sensibilities that accused Jews of being dirty).[34] Most contemporary observers would have seen the fire as, to some extent, divine punishment for some transgression. Christians could argue that God was angry about Jewish stubbornness in rejecting Christianity, while Jewish writers could assert that the fire demonstrated the need for some form of communal or religious improvement. The fire would remain for decades a major event in Jewish communal identity and history, with real-life property implications.[35]

The fire broke out on Wednesday, January 14, around eight in the evening, apparently in the house of Rabbi Naphtali Cohen.[36] Accused by some Christian writers of kabbalistic intrigues, the rabbi was detained in prison and investigated before being released some four or five months later[37] and moving to Istanbul. The fire spread quickly and soon threatened walls and gates as well as some adjacent Christian houses.[38] However, on several occasions, strong winds turned the flames back on the Jewish quarter—a development that would be seen by some, Jews as well as Christians, as some sort of divine punishment.[39]

Christians arrived to douse the flames.[40] Fearing looting, however, the Jewish residents kept the doors locked. Finally, carpenters with axes smashed the door to the small bridge leading to the ghetto.[41] Realizing the futility of battling the flames, many Christians assisted Jews in moving their possessions with carts and wagons. The Jews' fears were partially realized, however, by looters who plundered some of the burning houses. Early on January 15, while the fire continued unabated, the City Council met, sounded fire signals, and formed a committee that was sent to the Jewish quarter to assess the situation. The Jews were accommodated in other parts of the city—the poor in the sick house—and supplied with provisions. By the evening of January 15, much of the ghetto and the Jews' possessions had been consumed.[42] Many Jews fled to the cemetery. Miraculously, only four people succumbed to the flames.[43]

Various Jewish and Christian writers attributed a range of causes to the fire. Some within the Jewish community criticized life in the ghetto as too worldly. As a result, the Jewish community council banned all comedies and plays for a period of fourteen years and issued stringent sumptuary laws.[44] The day of the fire was marked by the community as one of penance and lamentation, which continued to be observed annually for decades.[45] Others, including religious leaders, found other explanations. Some lamentations, like that written by David ben Simon Sougers of Prague and published in Frankfurt, drew parallels to the destruction of the temple and noted the complete devastation of and panic within the Jewish ghetto.[46] Inveighing standardized language, the author attributed the fire to "our great sins."[47] Still, the author recognized the protection and assistance provided by the authorities and concluded somewhat formulaically that "Day and night we pray for our lords and authorities that God should protect them from all misfortune."[48]

The Holy Roman Emperor responded to the catastrophe with a decree that was widely circulated.[49] In it, he noted the unforeseen and sudden conflagration that devastated the entire Jewish quarter, referring to it as a great misfortune for the Jews. The document mentioned several evil and licentious (Christian) residents of the city who took possessions from the burning houses. It also pointed out that there were certain citizens who threatened the Jews that if another fire were to break out, they would slay the Jews and cast them in the flames, causing great fear and angst among the Jews. The decree absolved the Jews of any guilt in the kindling of the fire. Any actions against, mishandling of, or threats to the Jews, the Emperor asserted, would be severely punished, since the Jews were under imperial protection. Finally, the Emperor dictated that arrangements had to be made as soon as possible for the reconstruction of the Jewish quarter, so as not to hinder or overburden the Jews.

Local Christian accounts of the fire revolved around some central themes. An illustrated broadsheet circulating in 1711, for example, summarized the events but also quickly turned to place the fire in the context of divine punishment against the Jews. The Christian author wrote that "[through] God's anger the fire suddenly came into the Jewish quarter."[50] He concluded more broadly, however, that "How this fire actually arose and began—regarding this much has been spoken: It is as He wills, so we must hereby learn of God's fire-burning anger, to distance [ourselves] from all vices, and pray to God that such fires will not destroy the city of Frankfurt."[51]

Negotiations between representatives of the Jewish community and the Frankfurt City Council related to the reconstruction of the Jewish quarter began immediately.[52] The Jews pressed the City Council for permission to rebuild already a month later (on February 12). The Council was not certain how the ghetto should be reconstructed and gave initial permission only for the synagogue to be rebuilt—its foundations were laid on March 23 and it was completed by September.[53] Negotiations for the reconstruction of the remainder of the ghetto proved to be a more protracted affair.[54] Although a construction ordinance was issued by the council on April 7, it would be challenged and debated over the course of the next two years.[55] What is more, many Jews lacked the funds for reconstruction, and the community was forced to seek financial assistance from other Jewish communities.[56] Still, the Jewish Construction Ordinance of April 1711, which was seen as too favorable to the Jews by some, provided important details for how the Jewish quarter should be reconstructed.[57] The Jews were to pay to have the quarter paved in such a way that water could flow unimpeded to fight future fires. The ordinance stipulated that all the Jews' houses should be the same height, and no more than three storeys—an ordinance from January 24, 1594, had long before, in part over concern about fire, dictated that no Jewish houses could be higher than three storeys.[58] The ordinance stipulated the height and construction of each storey, and it provided details about the scope and construction of firewalls, as well as the proximity of houses to the walls.

The ordinance further stipulated that "all the walls that surround the Jewish quarter should be visible [and demarcated] with eagles and a [letter] 'F' [for Frankfurt] . . . , as a sign that the city alone has jurisdiction," undercutting imperial authority over and protection of the Jews. According to the ordinance, houses were to remain elevated, and no sub-cellars were permitted, addressing a particularly volatile issue that would be discussed repeatedly over the next several years. The Jewish stables that had previously stood by the moat were to be relocated within the Jewish quarter, though no more houses were permitted to be added in compensation for the loss of living space. The Jews were to be allowed, at their own expense, to locate and build their own hospital, behind the synagogue and against the innermost quarter where the brewhouse and communal bake oven had stood previously.

Similar ordinances were enacted after other fires in the city. Consider, for example, the construction ordinance for houses that later burned down in the Bock-Gasse in 1719.[59] Aside from the labeling of the Jewish quarter as under Frankfurt jurisdiction, the legislation about the sub-basements, and the requirement for Jews to assume the costs of some construction and improvements, there is little that differentiates this ordinance. The initial response of the authorities to the fire in the Jewish quarter, therefore, was typical of responses to other fires in the city.

The reconstruction of the Jewish quarter, however, induced opposition from other parties. The Archbishop of Mainz registered a complaint in 1712 that a western row of houses opposite the monastery, and particularly the windows, were being constructed higher than before and that such construction was offensive to the Christian religion. The windows, the Council later decided, should be bricked over.[60] Even more quarrelsome, however, were the objections to the construction of sub-basements and the height of the buildings, which the burghers' deputies articulated.[61] They also raised concerns about the expansion of the Jews' spaces (cemetery, bake ovens, etc.) outside the ghetto, initiating a significant debate over the expansion of Jewish space into the public Bleichgarten (bleach-field).[62] The Council rejected any initial agreements to expand the height of buildings or the footprint of the ghetto. Imperial authorities stepped in, however, in 1714, and overturned the more limited and revised construction ordinance in favor of the original one, more favorable to the Jewish community, allowing construction to continue.[63]

Turning their attack now on the City Council, the irate deputies representing the burghers thundered that the burned-down quarter should not be improved and expanded, for that would favor the Jews, who, it was argued, are the ruin of the Christian citizens and only strengthen them in their obduracy and enmity against the name of Jesus and his adherents.[64] Similarly, in 1714—precisely as the Jews were displaced by the fire from their ghetto—local merchants submitted a petition to an imperial commission. Complaints were also raised about the number of Jews who had settled in Frankfurt—who were required to possess a certain amount of money—and their business practices.[65] Initial patience with and support for the Jewish community by local Christians appears to have given way to opposition in the months after the fire.[66]

In its objection to the expansion of Jewish trade into new commodities, the petitioners asserted that both the number of Jews involved in trade and the range of products with which they dealt had expanded. Jews were accused of being unfair by nature and of using improper trade techniques. Finally, the petition argued that Jews should be kept inferior to Christians; otherwise, their hatred of Christians would grow, and they would be further discouraged from conversion.[67] The merchants implied that the Jews were forming a "state within a state," and they called for a significant reduction in their numbers, a ban on additional Jewish settlement, and the removal of Jewish commerce to outlying rural areas.[68]

Nonetheless, the bulk of the Jewish quarter had been reconstructed by the middle of 1716.[69] By 1718, the construction outside the Jewish ghetto on the previous public Bleichgarten—with five community bake ovens and a hospital—was also completed.[70] While it made sense to relocate these Jewish spaces outside the ghetto because of space limitations and efforts to prevent fire, it is likely that this facilitated Jewish interaction with non-Jewish neighbors outside the ghetto. Already by January of 1716, the Council had ordered Jews to return to the ghetto and Christians no longer to house them.[71] During the period outside the ghetto, the Jews, in a notice to the Council, pointed out that "the entire time that we dwelled in the city there were no complaints raised against us."[72] Some Christian writers chided polemically that there were indeed some benefits to the temporary housing arrangements for the Jews, namely that, as the Christian Hebraist and Jew-hater Johann Jacob Schudt (1664–1722) asserted, "through their contact with the Christians [they] learned how to maintain their households better and cleaner."[73] Schudt, a native of Frankfurt, had studied theology at the university in Wittenberg and Orientalia in Hamburg with Esdras Edzard, the Protestant theologian noted for his missionary activity among the Jews and his contention that the full-scale conversion of the Jews to Christianity was a necessary precursor to the Second Coming of Christ.

The Frankfurt ghetto continued to be the topic of many legal, ethnographic, historical, and literary works.[74] Schudt himself authored a massive work on the Jews in Frankfurt, which, despite its polemical twists, remains a valuable source on Jewish history and society in the eighteenth century. His enormous *Jewish Curiosities* (*Jüdische Merckwürdigkeiten*) included four volumes—the first three published in 1714 and the fourth in 1718. Schudt had devoted earlier work to Jewish history. Given its tone and scope, *Jewish Curiosities* was not a book that would have secured Jewish conversions to Christianity. The work appears to have been inspired, at least in part, by the fire of 1711, which it referenced frequently. Schudt noted that within twenty-four hours the entire Jewish quarter was destroyed, and he recounted the vast suffering and crying of the Jews as well as the kindness of the authorities and burghers, who helped save and protect Jewish possessions and provided housing.[75] Individual Christian citizens took in Jewish families during the cold night and maintained them for several days until they could find food and supplies—for which many Jews expressed their gratitude.[76] Schudt did praise the Jews during this time for expressing no harsh words against God and patiently and quietly suffering, while proclaiming their own sins.[77] Overall, however, Schudt elevated many anti-Jewish themes, including that Jews were hostile to Christians in their rituals and social practices. He described Jews as blasphemers against Christianity and he urged Christians not to house Jews.

The fire left a lasting imprint on the Jewish community. The title page of the new Frankfurt memory book itself opened with a lengthy discussion of the Great Fire of 1711, pointing to the fire as a process of purification that wrought extensive damage:

> Suddenly, in the evening of Wednesday, at the eve of Thursday, the 10th of the month of Tevet, in the complete year 1711, God judged with fire. The fire causes purging and smelting of silver and gold (Malachi 3:3: He shall act like a smelter and purger of silver; and he shall purify the descendants of Levi and refine them like gold and silver, so that they shall present offerings in righteousness to eliminate filth) . . . for days we experienced trouble and were pained like a woman in childbed, and our faces were flaming, as many stood against us. . . . It is the Satan, it is the evil inclination, who ascended and accused us and then descended and then burned and destroyed the fences and vineyards. [Song of Songs 2:15] The fire crossed both sides of the public space . . . Above and below the fire caused great damage, such that one could not save even the commentaries to the Torah, books of the Bible, Midrashim, Tosefta, Aramaic translations of biblical writings, books in press, communal ordinances of the wise, "for gold and silver are in the crucible and furnace." [Prov. 17:2]

The memory book went on, in a more typical style for its genre, to recall the valiant efforts of a leading philanthropist to rebuild the synagogue—"And even when we were amid the children of the world: God gave us favor in the eyes of Egypt and sent a king who freed and released our people. We built synagogues as in previous days. We established the house so that God would open His eyes toward it day and night" [1 Kgs. 8:29]. The memory book then recounted in greater detail the deeds of Eliezer Oppenheim, who supported the new memory book and the reconstruction of the synagogue:

> And behold the Lord has aroused the spirit [Jer. 51:11] of the leader, very learned like one of the sages, the head and the judge and the philanthropist, R. Eliezer Lezer Oppenheim, May the Lord avenge his blood, father of the poor and the orphans. He returned the former glory, he built the fence and "leveled (prepared) the highway for the house of our God, to pray [there] days and nights." The intention of this holy work was to glorify God and His house and to make it possible to pray there three times a day in every generation. May God remember him well that he performed so many good deeds in his youth and old age. He published the ledger [*pinkas*] of the burial society [*chevra kadisha*] of the upright and pure men, in which all the names of the deceased were registered for more than 100 years. He commanded that the names of the holy pious men and women in the land be recorded and thereby remembered for all time.

In addition to the prayer penned by Rabbi Samuel Schotten, presented by Schudt and mentioned above, several other theological writings—lamentations and prayers—were also authored in response to the destruction of the fire, and they focused on some central themes of loss, punishment, and exile. One lamentation, referenced above, was written by David ben Simon Sougers of Prague. The author reviewed the outline of events—timing; location of the fire; destruction of vessels and other material goods such as clothes; loss of books and Torah scrolls; locking of the quarter; plundering of Jewish possessions when the gates were opened; as well as the burning of houses, study halls and synagogues. He noted that people were running around in a great panic. While he formulaically attributed the great fire to "our great sins," he also noted that such a punishment was unprecedented. In the lament, he mentioned that many Jews were scattered and their whereabouts could not be confirmed.[78] David wrote to console his readers, though he nevertheless questioned, "Why should we desire anything better in exile?"[79] Still, even in this catastrophe, he noted that God continued to be merciful to the Jews, as the authorities ordered that the Jews should be taken in and protected in all the areas where they were located.[80] Further, homes were opened up and the poor house was allocated for the common people and their children to spend the winter.[81] David petitioned God to measure justice with mercy.[82]

The fire of 1711 was not the last trial to face the Frankfurt Jewish community in the eighteenth century. Ten years after the first conflagration that destroyed the Jewish quarter, another struck (1721), destroying more than a hundred houses. Fears of plundering were indeed realized in 1721, as the Jews complained to the Council: "even in the houses that were preserved, the household effects, including oven, windows, and roofs, were stolen; not even victuals, wine, and precious flour were spared." Personal effects and furnishings that could not be secured were also wantonly carried off.[83] Jews remained outside the ghetto for another extended period, and they would be ordered back to the ghetto again only in May of 1727.[84]

Conclusions

Fire was a devastating and pervasive natural disaster in the early modern world, as it can still be today. Early modern people possessed a well of knowledge derived from religious, scientific, and historical texts. Theological sensibilities and worldviews structured much of the writing about and response to fires. This could lead to a sense that God was punishing human sin through fire and that humans needed to atone for their poor behavior. Such thinking could lead to both internal self-reflection as well as castigating and marginalizing others, who could be seen in a negative light and held responsible for disaster. We find the same tendencies even today, especially as our inherited worldviews can sometimes come into conflict with new experiences or the views and experiences of others.

At the same time, early moderns also had personal (and second-hand) experiences with fires that prepared them for their outbreak in some ways, but still left them highly vulnerable in others. Fires, of course, could be natural disasters or they could be human induced. As recent scholarship has shown, the boundary between these was porous, and the impact could vary depending upon human settlement and the specific context of various conflagrations and their impact on the plants and animals of the nonhuman world, many of which in turn affected humans near and far.

A review of the fire of 1711 and subsequent responses reveals that there was a range of interactions between Jews and Christians. In some cases, negative religious representations and economic accusations prevailed. Yet, there were many levels of response. The imperial authorities were quick, at least initially, to write in support of the Jews, and the early discussions about reconstruction fit largely into more general civic legal and practical responses to fires. Despite a long and protracted debate over various aspects of reconstruction, which surfaced a variety of tensions and anti-Jewish motifs, Jews did succeed in finding housing in the city and in surrounding areas for an extended period.

While many responses to fires drew from traditional religious texts and arguments about divine punishment for sin—thus casting the disaster as divine vengeance against the Jews and reinforcing many traditional anti-Jewish accusations and motifs—other responses provide evidence of more pragmatic and positive interactions between Jews and Christians that may force us to reevaluate the normative historical narratives that emphasize Jewish and Christian otherness and opposition. Some of the textual responses—in the form of historical accounts and liturgy—and some pointed political and economic debates strengthened perceived confessional differences. However, a wide range of other documents noted a degree of integration of Jews into broader early modern German society. Such integration was probably never thorough, but it did allow Jews to find housing after the destruction of the ghetto and it did result in the reconstruction of the Jewish space—still separated by walls—within the city. It suggests, however, that Jewish and Christian relations, at times of crisis and normalcy, were much more complex than generally explained in historical accounts that focus primarily on religious differences and theological debate, economic competition, or uneven and meandering toleration that largely served other political purposes.

Natural disasters such as fires could, and often did, surface latent social tensions as well as possibilities for collaboration, even if still uneven or short-lived. The response to fires revealed elasticity and a certain resilience and adaptiveness of society and highlighted the ability of individuals and communities to learn from experience and develop technology in order to mitigate the impact of natural disasters and, in some cases, even reduce the possibility of them in the first place. While fires could be quite devastating, responses to disasters provided opportunities for new thinking about policies and responses and new ways of constructing the built environment. Though generally local, fires could affect many people across broader regions and have significant political and cultural impacts, especially when coterminous with other societal stresses and natural disasters.

As we saw in the first three chapters, religious discourse could compete with but also be taken together with the knowledge and lessons of science, medicine, and technology. The boundaries between these various fields could be quite fluid at times, just as the borders between communities could be permeable. In each case, premodern people had to find ways to navigate the wisdom they inherited and the actual experiences they had. Natural disasters could challenge their sense of self—especially when cast as punishment for sin—and offer opportunities to think in new ways and in a larger social context. Natural disasters could reinforce ways of thinking and structures of power; they could also undermine and topple them. Somewhere in between, the crises spawned by natural disasters required premoderns to bring both sets of knowledge into conversation with one another. Premodern natural disasters highlighted the fact that many disasters were local or experienced locally and that they could have implications far beyond local contexts. Finally, the disasters that we have examined played an important role in the creation of identities and traditions that helped to create continuity and learning, even as they could construct barriers that excluded some people. In the next and final chapter of Part I, I turn to consider whether the same kinds of issues emerged for Jews living in a different religious context, namely under Islam in the medieval and early modern periods. Shifting cultural, religious, and spatial lenses will help us identify how different contexts could lead to different ideas and responses and how they might underscore more general transformations across difference and on the edge of modernity.

5

Comparative Perspectives

Natural Disasters, Jews, and Islam

Introduction: Jews under Islam

In Chapters 1–4, I explored natural disasters in Jewish history in the context of Jewish life in Christian Europe. We saw ways in which Jews drew from internal biblical and rabbinic thought and culture. We also noted the ways in which Jews shared in larger social and cultural developments, incorporating non-Jewish thought and experiences and engaging with non-Jews in multiple ways. Although the majority of Jews before modernity lived in areas under Muslim control, a good deal of Jewish history has focused (and continues to focus) on the experiences of Jews in the Christian West. In this chapter, I turn to consider, in a comparative vein, some of the same types of natural disasters to see how Jews (as well as Muslims) responded—in ways that were different and similar to Jews under Christianity and Christians. Such a comparative approach allows us to see more general trends in the premodern period as well as broader lessons that may be useful (and limiting) for the modern and contemporary periods as well as for the future.

Jewish life under Islam could be complex in the medieval and early modern periods. In terms of sheer population (see below), but also in terms of opportunities for broader advancement and engagement in society, Jews could fare comparatively well in the often cosmopolitan and diverse Islamic lands, especially in the far reaches of the Ottoman Empire. At the same time, Jews, like Christians, remained second-class citizens—in theory and frequently in practice as well—and they were squeezed for extensive taxes and, at times, they experienced significant social precarity.

As with their coreligionists under Christian rule, Jews in Islamic lands shared many social, cultural, political, and religious views and orientations with the members of the dominant, in this case, Muslim group—though, of course, Muslims themselves were never a cohesive and unified group. The result was that Jewish responses to natural disasters drew both from internal Jewish traditions and Islamic beliefs as well as local, regional, and imperial policies and practices. This chapter reviews the responses of Jews in a few select cases related to fires, earthquakes, and plagues to add to the range of Jewish understanding of and responses to natural disasters that we have explored in the first four chapters. As we will see, in many ways, the responses of these Jews were quite similar to those provided by their coreligionists farther west. And yet, some of the differences are also helpful as we offer a fuller picture of historical accounts and approaches.

Jewish Demographics

The experience of Jews under Islam could be different from that under Christianity. At the very least, the Jewish demography of the premodern period had important implications for Jewish communal structures, integration, and intellectual development. The Jewish population and settlement of the Ottoman Empire were extensive, due in part to the widespread settlement patterns and relations that had existed before the Ottoman state formed and the forced migration of Jews from Iberia at the end of the fifteenth century. The Ottomans absorbed Greek-speaking Jewish populations in Anatolia and the Balkans as well as large Jewish centers that had existed under Mameluke rule in Egypt. Combined with the complexity of Ottoman settlement policies, Ottoman Jewry was quite diverse in terms of customs and histories.

Some Ottoman Jewish communities were quite large by early modern (and even modern) standards, when a very large city might have no more than 10,000 inhabitants. Ottoman expansion in the Middle East during the second decade of the sixteenth century had far-reaching consequences for the Jewish populations in those areas. Some scholars have suggested that a third of the 300,000 residents of the land of Israel were Jewish in the sixteenth century.[1] By the 1560s, half of Safed's 10,000 inhabitants were Jewish.[2] In the Ottoman Empire, Constantinople and Salonika each held an excess of 20,000 Jews in the middle of the sixteenth century. In other areas absorbed by the Ottoman Empire, large and long-standing Jewish populations could also be found. In Algiers, in North Africa, there were 8,000 to 9,000 Jews in 1600, a number that had at least doubled from a century before and that would increase by at least another quarter in the century to follow.[3] And while not of the same magnitude, other Jewish communities were also significant in their size and/or influence.

North Africa had a long and rich, if at times complicated, history of Jewish settlement. Many Jews emigrated to North Africa during the terrible persecutions of 1391 in Spain. Fez in Morocco was also a bustling Jewish center, where in the early seventeenth century, one chronicler writes that 10,000 Jews, mostly expelled from Spain, occupied the *mellah* (Jewish quarter).[4] The emigrations of Jews and conversos had a significant impact on local Jewish culture. Indeed, many of the scholars in Fez were émigrés. It was newly transplanted Jews who also established the first Hebrew printing press there in 1516. The combination of various ethnic and regional backgrounds and religious traditions could lead to complex communal structures and internal communal conflict. A much smaller Jewish population resided in the Persia of the Shiite Safavid Empire, where the position of the Jews was at times very difficult, and Jews were not granted the same degree of freedoms and opportunities as in the Ottoman lands,[5] and where there were religious restrictions on Jews and pressures to convert to Islam.

Fire

Concerns about fires were omnipresent in the premodern world (and continue to be significant today). As in Europe and other parts of the globe, fires devastated many places in the Ottoman Empire. In Istanbul alone, there were seventeen fires recorded by one chronicler between 1563 and 1600. The fires of the fifteenth and sixteenth centuries often resulted in significant destruction of houses, shops, and religious institutions. They could be quite deadly as well. A fire in 1539 burned some 700 prisoners to death when it reached the prison. The largest fire of the sixteenth century began on September 28, 1569, coming on the heels of a drought, and is thought to have begun in a bakery in the Jewish neighborhood, the busiest district in the city. Another fire destroyed the Jewish neighborhood in 1589, with some properties being looted amid the chaos, and yet another fire in 1606 also led to widespread damage. In response to these and other fires, government authorities moved from wood to stone as the primary construction material already in the seventeenth century, though this did not seem to yield significant results until the nineteenth century.[6]

We have Jewish accounts about some of these fires. Hakham Meir ben Shemtov Melamed,[7] for example, reports that a certain Mr. Yohanan ben Samuel came before the rabbinic court of Salonika to recount events and misfortunes that had befallen him in 1620.[8] Flames, he said, grew up in the heavens and took strong hold of an inn in which they were staying. At that moment, he told his son that they would be fortunate to save themselves, but that they could not attend to their material possessions. In the "economy of sin" vein, he asserted that the fire was an evil that was the result of "our multitude of sins."[9] He reported that he and his son wrapped themselves in a cloak and, along with four other Jews, were able to run through the flames, the cloak burning but protecting them.[10] The son could not see the father through the smoke, and he apparently thought that the father had been burned. Apparently, he returned into the flames to look for him. The next morning, which was the holiday of Tisha b'Av (commemorating the destruction of the Temple as well as many misfortunes in Jewish history), the father went about town looking for his son, asking various Turks whom he met if they had seen him. The father eventually discovered that his son had, in fact, been burned to death in the flames—he had been able to recognize his remains by his shoes, which had remained unburned. This tragic story elevates certain themes related to perceptions of the connection between (or at least literary motifs associating) sin and punishment, and specifically the tradition of bad things happening on Tisha b'Av when the Temple was burned and many other disasters occurred throughout history. It also reveals the causal relations between Jews and others, and it points to the daily challenges that fires could create.

The great fire of Istanbul in 1660, to take another example of fires that impacted Jews and Jewish communities, revealed latent political and religious tensions and allowed for significant reorganization of the urban landscape and polemic against the Jewish minority, as parts of the city were reconstructed.[11] In a growing process of Islamization, the deteriorating position of the Jews, especially in comparison to that of Greek Orthodox Christians, allowed for the appropriation of Jewish property and the expulsion of Jews from several areas and their relocation to other districts. The endowment deed for the great mosque that was built—expanded from the foundations that had lain incomplete for many years—gathering many Jewish properties that had surrounded it, made a significant statement about Jewish marginality and precarity and it cast a highly visible and prominent image for people entering the city. The deed included the following language:

> By the decree of God the exalted the fire of divine wrath turned all the neighborhoods of the Jews upside down. The effect of the flames of the wrath of God made the homes and abodes belonging to the straying community resemble ashes. Every one of the Jewish households was turned into a fire temple full of sparks. Since the residences and dwellings of Jews, who are the enemy of Islam, resembled the deepest part of Hell, the secret of the verse which is incontrovertible, "those that do evil shall be cast into the fire" (Q 32:20), became clear, and in order to promise and threaten those who deny Islam with frightening things, the verse, "woe to the unbelievers because of a violent punishment" (Q 14:2), also became manifest.[12]

Jews and other minority groups could be blamed for starting fires directly or for causing them by their alleged poor behavior. The great fire in Galata in 1696 was similarly portrayed by Muslim authorities as punishment for the "blasphemy, impiety, superstition, idolatry, and adultery" of the Jews and Christians who had recently settled in the affected quarter, and it served as an excuse for the confiscation of burned-down Jewish and Christian houses as part of a larger project of Islamization.[13]

In assessing Ottoman responses to natural disasters, historian Yaron Ayalon concludes that "Overall, state authorities on the local and imperial levels responded to plagues and famines in ways that reflected deliberate interests, well-calculated priorities, and sincere concern for the well-being of their subjects,"[14] regardless of religious differences.[15] However, there were times when such responses were colored by religious sensibilities, including during the fire of 1660, which witnessed discrimination against Christians and Jews in the context of the "Islamization of the urban landscape."[16] Ayalon concedes that "While the state underwrote the restoration of buildings that bore a clear Islamic function (mosques and madrasas) and many that did not (citadel and port structures), I could not locate even one structure that specifically served only non-Muslims, such as a church or a synagogue, that was to be restored by the government."[17] As we have seen in other natural disasters, described in previous chapters, such events could surface latent tensions in some cases but also lead to, often temporary, collaboration across differences. Ayalon highlights the complications of cross-confessional relations, and he concludes that interconfessional boundaries could be porous but that in crises, internal religious community affiliation was quite significant.[18]

Earthquakes

Jews under Islam circulated in a culture that had similar ways of thinking about earthquakes as did Jews living in the Christian world. Take, for example, a geniza fragment (Letter (T-S 18J3.9)), part of a letter dated 1033, in which Solomon b. Semah described the effects of an earthquake in Ramla on 12 Tevet (December). The letter is written in a Hebrew style intended for public recitation (probably in Egypt). The author references numerous biblical passages that are relevant to the theme, including Isa. 24:1, Jer. 10:10, Ps. 104:32, Job 9:6, Amos 9:5, Hos. 4:3, Nah. 1:6, Joel 2:13, Hos. 6:1, and Jon. 3:9. In the midst of the disaster, the author of the document calls for penance, including fasting and mourning. While describing the scope of the destruction caused by the earthquake, Solomon also notes that God was simultaneously merciful: "God was merciful and did not carry out full destruction." "He even showed great generosity by, before the quake, summoning up dark clouds that rained heavy raindrops. Two great rainbows were seen, one of which appeared divided, and fire was seen from the south-west, at the very moment of the quake, such as had not been experienced since ancient times." The author seems to indicate, as one recent reinterpretation concludes, that "local Muslim authorities provided disaster relief to the Jewish population of Ramla": he writes that "Also the governor of the city, with the men in the caliph's employ, put up tents for them outside the town, and they are still there even now."[19]

At the beginning of the letter, the author notes that residents came out into the streets because the walls of their houses were "buckling back and forth" and fortified structures were collapsing. Many people died as a result, while others fled:

> Everyone came out of their houses, each one leaving behind all that they had, and fled for their lives. Wherever they turned, they could see the evidence of God's mighty deeds. Walls had been thrown one on top of another and cast down, and all those that remained were damaged and broken open. No one is living within them because their owners are afraid that they might even now fall on them.

The author locates the events to a specific time—before sunset on Thursday, 12 Tevet:

> Were it not for the mercy of our God, who showed us mercy because of his great kindness, and caused it to happen before the end of the day, so that everyone could see each other and warn each other, then it might have happened in the night, when everyone would have been asleep in their beds unable to escape, bar a very few.

He also notes that the tremors continued Friday and Saturday and then another eight days. He provides additional information on the affected region:

> in Ramla, and in all of the land of Palestine, in the fortified towns and the rural villages alike, even in all the coastal fortresses up to the fortress of [. . .] and in all the towns of the Negev and in the hill country as far as Jerusalem, and in all the towns up to Shechem (modern Nablus) and the villages as far as Tiberias, and in all the [. . .] of the hills of Galilee and all of the Land of Israel.

As was true for other premoderns, Solomon thought that the earthquake was the result of God's anger, and he concludes by requesting God's ongoing kindness and compassion.

Between this event in 1033 and the middle of the eighteenth century (1759), there were sixteen earthquakes recorded in the region—nine strong and five major (7 or above on the Richter scale).[20] The account of an earthquake in Izmir in 1688 by Rabbi Elijah HaCohen (ca 1659–1729), who lived through it, offers details regarding Jews. Some 400 Jews perished in the earthquake and two synagogues were damaged.[21]

HaCohen begins his account by enumerating miracles experienced by the Jews during the earthquake. These include that the earthquake happened during Shabbat and at midday, when Jews were at home and not in the streets and markets. Indeed, most of the devastation occurred in non-Jewish quarters. What is more, the specifics of the event and the associated escape of the Jews provided ample evidence of the protection of the Jews by God, as "all the nations attested to this miracle."[22] Other miracles listed included that the earthquake happened in summer not winter, all the dead were retrieved and buried, the associated fire did not reach the Jewish neighborhood, and no Jews were harmed in collapsed houses. The author concludes his brief account with a story of personal salvation:

> the place where I found myself during the earthquake was a narrow place surrounded by four high walls that fell on top of me, and it became dark from the dust caused by the collapse. I did not know what to do. There was no spirit left in me and I was trembling and confused. I rose to my feet and said "God is the King, God has ruled, God will rule forever . . . " about ten times, as was customary on such occasions, and yet the tremors did not cease, so I recited "Hear, O Israel" . . . and other verses. And when [the earthquake] did not subside I almost died and was silent. As soon as the moment of anger ceased and the darkness cleared I found myself in a pit of stones consisting of the four walls [that had collapsed] . . . and I was not hurt at all. Blessed be He that does good to those who are undeserving![23]

These earthquake accounts highlight the fact that natural disasters could often take place across communities and regions and that they might appear together with other natural disasters and societal disruptions—in this case, the outbreak of plague that killed many Jews and non-Jews alike.[24] The experiences of and responses to earthquakes could create cross-communal and interreligious cooperation, even when they could highlight and even stoke differences as well. Natural disasters played out in individual and daily life and could impact areas for years to come, especially given the destruction of buildings and infrastructure. While many premodern people could see earthquakes, like other disasters, as punishment for sin, they also understood and responded to them in practical ways as well.

Plague

Diseases have at times played havoc on individuals and communities throughout history—sometimes inflecting historical events and even the direction of history itself. Bubonic plague, especially in the late medieval and early modern periods, had a devastating effect on human society, especially in some places that suffered through recurring waves of plague, becoming something like a regular part of life. Jews, Christians, and Muslims often understood plague as both a punishment for sin and as a disaster that could be mitigated or resolved through various policies and behaviors.

In Arabic, writers utilized several different words to connote communicable disease more generally: *'adwā* (contagion); *wabā* (plague); *al-mard al-wāfid* (epidemic); and *tā'ūn* (pestilence). As with both Latin and Hebrew words, the range of Arabic terms is related to "hitting" or "striking."[25]

Plagues impacted many cities and regions. Numerous plagues in the last half of the fifteenth century significantly depopulated the city of Istanbul, and Ottoman authorities responded with forced resettlement, forming part of a larger political plan often mentioned in historical accounts.[26] As with other disasters, the plagues that hit Istanbul almost invariably swept into nearby areas, such as Edirne, as well.[27] Plague next struck Istanbul in the early 1490s, reaching numerous other Ottoman lands, including Syria and Egypt.[28] Epidemics in and around Istanbul were recorded almost constantly between 1497 and 1533 (including seventeen years of major outbreaks).[29] Additional plague outbreaks would haunt the city in the 1520s, between 1533 and 1549, and again between 1552 and 1567, culminating in a major epidemic in the 1570s, which continued in various forms into the seventeenth and eighteenth centuries.[30] In the eighteenth century alone, plague occurred in sixty-eight individual years in Istanbul.

Plague recurred throughout the lands of the Ottoman Empire more generally— throughout the Balkans in the early 1580s,[31] and across Anatolia and the Arabian Peninsula in the 1590s.[32] In the seventeenth century, we find references to ten plagues in various parts of the Ottoman Empire.[33] Many places within the Ottoman Empire faced ongoing cycles of plague during the eighteenth century as well: Aegean Anatolia, for example, for 57 percent of the century.[34] The duration of epidemics might vary considerably. In the period between 1700 and 1850, for example, the largest number of plague outbreaks in the Ottoman Empire lasted one year (45 percent); 26 percent lasted two years; and around 4.5 percent seven years or more (the approximately 25 percent remaining plagues lasted less than one year).[35] Between 1713 and 1792 there were only twenty years entirely plague-free in the large city of Smyrna and during the collective period of epidemic, death tolls reached up to 35 percent of total population.[36] In Smyrna, in the course of the eighteenth century, there were fifty-four years of plague. As in Europe, these events were connected to other calamities, such as famine and major conflagrations, which either preceded or came on the heels of the epidemic.[37]

The sixteenth-century Ottoman chronicler Selâniki Mustafa Efendi, who lived during a period of severe and repeated plague outbreaks, frequently referenced the plague as well as other disasters.[38] In most cases, he did not employ the standard term *tā'ūn*, with Arabic origins, but rather referred to the plague as "blessed" or "manifest," perhaps euphemistically, though perhaps also suggesting divine origins of the plague or simply its appearance without making a causal connection to the plague as punishment for sin.[39] In his use of particular expressions, one recent scholar suggests that Selâniki emphasized that it was the will of God, not the actual plague, which killed people.[40]

In Islam, the approach to plague was dictated by religious texts and traditions as well as scientific knowledge. Muslims frequently attributed disease to the *jinn*, hidden and supernatural creatures.[41] In response, a variety of plague prayers were written that invoked God's divine names.[42] Some plague responses, however, suggested ongoing religious or even magical conceptions of disease. In Muslim lands, a variety of religious responses to plague and disease more generally were possible. In Cairo, the response to the plague of 1430—which at its height may have claimed 10,000 people daily—resulted in religious services at mosques, pious activities, and communal processions.[43] Early modern Muslims could draw from a range of texts and tales in which religious figures encountered and combatted manifestations of plague. The prophet-saint Hizir (a mystical figure described in the Quran), for example, was thought to help those in need and fight against the horseman of pestilence and plague and healing wounds.[44] The thirteenth-century Anatolian mystic Haci Bektaş utilized apples collected in the dead of winter from a bare tree to treat illness, and the fourteenth-century Anatolian mystic Abdal Musa was known to be able to predict and combat plagues.[45] Other mystical or saintly figures with the power to heal were also known in Ottoman society. Through magical signs, incantations, and talismans, individuals pleaded for God's curative interventions, referencing Quranic verses and the knowledge of letters and numerological values of letters.[46] Muslim scholars similarly drew from classical sources, their own traditions, and specific experiences.[47]

Various Hadith examined the question of flight from the plague. According to one text, for example, "Narrated Saud, The Prophet said, If you hear of an outbreak of plague in a land, do not enter it; but if the plague breaks out in a place while you are in it, do not leave that place" (*Sahih Al-Bukhari*, Hadith—7.624). Islam has generally been presented as being resistant to flight from plague—polemically cast by its opponents as infused with a certain degree of "fatalism" and a more "passive" response to the outbreak of disease.[48] The increasing Islamization of the Ottoman Empire in the sixteenth century, especially with the acquisition of lands in the Islamic heartland, it has been argued, naturally led to a more fatalistic and less pragmatic response to plague, at least when it came to the decision whether to flee or not.[49] Traditional interpretations have noted that in Islamic thought three basic principles or assumptions based on teachings of the Prophet shaped response to the plague: plague should be interpreted as a form of mercy and a means of martyrdom for the faithful, but a punishment for the infidel; Muslims should not enter into an area with plague, but also should not flee an area if already there; and the plague was not transmitted by contagion but rather through God directly.[50]

Recent scholarship, however, has complicated that assumption significantly. The concept of "contagion" was not universally rejected by Islamic scholars[51] and the most prominent Ottoman jurist of the sixteenth century, Ebussund Efendi (1491–1574), approved flight as a preventative option against the plague.[52] In support of his position, Efendi could cite earlier Islamic scholars as well as some sayings of Muhammad and historical examples of Caliph Umar to support his position. Flight from the plague was certainly practiced at various times, and it was recommended in some Ottoman medical circles as well.

The Jewish physician in the Ottoman Empire, Ilyas bin Ibrahim al-Yahudi (d after 1512), who had traveled to Istanbul and converted at the end of the fifteenth century, wrote a treatise on "The Refuge from Plague and Pestilence" for Sultan Bayezid II. He indicated flight as the first recommendation against the plague. Absent the opportunity to flee, however, he identified particular places that were best suited for refuge—namely, places in high altitudes and facing north. He also indicated that other related precautions were beneficial, such as disinfecting the air with vinegar, sandalwood, and rosewater, in addition to fumigation.[53] In treating the plague, he also mentioned a variety of remedies that were frequently discussed in other works.[54] Contagionist theories certainly existed across cultures and religions. Bin Ibrahim had arrived in the Ottoman Empire at the end of the fifteenth century. He referred to Hippocrates as well as other classical scientific sources and noted that disease can be transmitted through direct contact between people or through eye contact. True to the somewhat fluid connection between contagion and miasma, he simultaneously asserted that putrefied air could transmit disease.[55]

Islamic writers during the second pandemic of the bubonic plague drew from a variety of scientific sources, including the classical medical and scientific thought of Hippocrates and Galen, as well as the great Avenzoar (Ibn Zuhr), a highly regarded twelfth-century Muslim physician and surgeon and contemporary of Averroes. Ibn Khātima in the fourteenth century offered advice on how to protect oneself from plague. This included (like the Jewish physician noted above and his European counterparts) making certain to have fresh air—"by living in houses facing north, by filling them with cold fragrances and aroma of flowers, such as myrtle and oriental poplars, by sprinkling the houses with rose water mixed with vinegar, and also use the same on oneself." In advice that would be followed well into the early modern period, he suggested that people anoint their face and hands with cool fragrances and frequently smell these fragrances as well as sour lemons and limes and cooling flowers, including roses and violets. He recommended food and air that could produce heat. Beyond this, he suggested that one should seek agreeable company; read books on history, humor, and romance; and avoid disparaging others. Bleeding was also of great value. Primarily, however, "Rely on God; He is the best and most compassionate protector."

In late medieval and early modern Islamic plague treatises, a variety of causes of plague were identified, including natural causes such as the alignment of stars, disasters such as earthquakes, natural conditions related to the sanitation of air and water, human-induced causes such as warfare, in addition to divine will.[56] Therefore, beyond religious responses, among some Islamic plague writers, fumigation, diet, folk remedies, and even changes in location were suggested to protect against or ward off the plague.[57] In the early modern period, new emphases on medical over religious or magical approaches to the plague—including the use of quarantine—may be explained by scientific advances, political agendas, as well as greater foreign influences in some places, such as the expanding Ottoman state.[58] Early modern Ottoman authors, in fact, increasingly suggested other means beyond religious practice for combating the plague, such as medical treatments and fumigation of the air.[59]

As Yaron Ayalon notes, "Natural disasters were hardly ever entirely *natural*. A human factor played at least a nominal, and sometimes significant, part in the outcome of almost every disaster."[60] As in other parts of the globe, other disasters such as famine could intersect with plagues.[61] As in Christian Europe, in the Ottoman Empire, governmental legislation combined with a range of scholarly treatises when it came to the response to natural disaster, especially plague. What is more, theory and practice could diverge, making it hard to know to what extent the writings of Muslim scholars on response to plague reflected popular perception and practice.[62] Medieval Muslim thinkers believed that disasters such as plague were caused by God,[63] and they seem generally to have opposed fleeing from plague, though some authors under certain conditions might allow or even encourage it, especially later into the early modern period,[64] and in general, there was little in the way of systematic thought on how to respond to plague.[65] Ayalon writes that "Muslim scholars managed to reconcile the two approaches by suggesting that, even though contagion existed, it was God's decision whether or not a person would become ill."[66] Plague treatises provided general medical advice, such as avoiding moist places, avoiding excessive movement and maintaining a low body temperature.[67] Pervasive ignorance about plagues conditioned people's responses in many ways.[68]

Ottoman authorities introduced policies that improved cleanliness in cities,[69] though they did not always draw a clear connection between hygiene and disease.[70] Ottoman authorities could provide substantive assistance when plague broke out—including tax breaks in affected areas[71] and quarantine,[72] allowing local agents some flexibility in developing their own policies,[73] and redistribution of grain and foodstuffs.[74] The government also took steps to mitigate other disasters, including measures to reduce the risk of fires[75] and new approaches to urban planning[76] and building construction. At the same time, supplication to God might still be seen by many as the best form of preventative self-protection.[77]

Conclusions

Jews, Christians, and Muslims shared many of the same understandings of and approaches to plague and other natural disasters, despite the traditions in historiography that have often cast Muslim responses as more primitive and "religious." In the heterogeneous cities of the Ottoman Empire, a wide range of ideas and practices circulated, and Jewish experiences were inflected both by the broad surroundings and personal experiences as well as Jewish law and tradition. As with Jewish communities in the West, Jewish communities and their Jewish inhabitants engaged with the world around them and learned from their experiences in important ways as they sought to navigate the challenges of early modern natural (and other) disasters.

Like Europe and other parts of the globe, the Ottoman Empire suffered from many natural disasters. These included fires, plagues, earthquakes, as well as droughts and famines. The response to disaster operated at personal, communal, and government levels. Such responses might include, for example, the prohibition of the use of hay as construction material for rooftops (prompting rebuilding with wood) in the case of fires;[78] street cleaning to rid the city of foul smells associated with the outbreak and spread of plague[79] or quarantine (as in the 1760–62 pandemic);[80] price regulation during plague and famine—as in Aleppo in 1696;[81] or the transfer of wheat (as in the famine in Aleppo in 1728).[82]

Jews and Jewish communities in Islamic lands likewise responded in various ways to disasters. Jewish communities might try to secure funds to assist with the burial of members who died[83] or rebuild communal spaces such as the synagogue after destruction during earthquakes (as in Aleppo 1822).[84] At the same time, plague, as in the example of Aleppo, could lead to the desertion of synagogues and perhaps even the collapse of communal infrastructure and authority.[85] Jews, like others, might flee infected cities (see Damascus in 1576 or Aleppo in 1760–1762)[86] and damaged neighborhoods after earthquakes, as in Aleppo in the large and famous trembler of 1822, when the Jewish quarter was destroyed. Jews left the city—many setting up tents outside the city for over a year and returning to houses that had been ransacked in their absence.[87] Just like the case of Jewish experiences in the Christian West, the history of Jews and natural disasters under Islam provides valuable information about how the environment and natural disasters were understood before the modern period and what successes and limitations Jewish and more general societal responses have informed modern and contemporary perceptions and actions.

Modernity is often blamed for climate change and environmental degradation. Though we have come to recognize that humans have always had an impact on the environment, the growth of the human population and the acceleration of change wrought by humans through their settlement patterns and technology over the past century or two have been greater than previous changes ushered in by humans. Many of the issues that we have come to associate with modernity have been seen as responsible for the worldviews and behaviors that encouraged and made possible the conditions for dramatic changes to the environment. These have included a focus on the self (to the exclusion or minimization of the common good), progress and the belief in the limitless possibilities of both growth and consumption, the increasing global connections and footprint of humans, the innovations of science and the expanded application of technology, the increasing complexity of world systems and networks, and the acceleration of time (in which changes happen much faster and with greater impact and when that impact affects people in the future in much deeper and more profound ways). Premodern people may have had a smaller footprint in the world, but they struggled with notions of individual and collectivity, emerging technology and productivity, expanding geographic horizons, and what for them felt like an incredible acceleration of life. In some ways, the experiences they had and the lessons that we can intuit from those experiences are valuable. However, in other ways, premodern people felt similar limitations and perhaps even more in understanding the world around them and in living through uncertainty.

Modernity has been held accountable for the (artificial) separation of nature and culture and the displacement of people from inhabiting, and constructive engagement with, the environment. Of course, modernity does not have a monopoly on this purported separation. Some have ascribed the disconnect to the emergence of Judaism, Hellenism, and Christianity some two thousand years ago and more, creating the intellectual foundations for the later domination and exploitation of nature. The study of environmental history has reckoned with the modern and contemporary challenges of environmental degradation while also looking at the complicated relationship between humans and nature throughout a long history.

Premodern people grappled with disasters and changes around them. They put on record their experiences and looked for possible solutions. At times, they made incredible progress, and we have continued on their path in certain areas, including most recently social distancing and quarantine during pandemics. In this regard, history itself provides us with valuable insights into how people lived and responded to changing conditions. At other times, the limitations or shortcomings of premodern people and their responses to natural disasters are also helpful as we learn from our own experiences and those of the past. Indeed, the nature of the history that we have been writing has also changed, inflected by contemporary situations and needs.

Early modern history has often seemed to me to be at the cutting edge of theories—things we can apply in particular contexts—and the start of a significant expansion of source materials for the study of the past. My medieval colleagues are always a bit jealous of the variety and number of source materials that I seem to be able to summon for any given number of historical themes! While history once seemed to be very much aligned with specific historical periods, increasingly historians cut across traditional periods and explore a broad range of topics, all the while considering a multiplicity of experiences, that is, differing pasts. These skills and orientations will be helpful, as we will see in Part II, as we extract learning from the past as part—not as the full sum—of the ways to engage with the changes of today and as we see more clearly the connections between pasts, presents, and futures.

Whatever culpability we might ascribe to it, religion (and Judaism in particular) in its more traditional forms, including premodern, has also offered some significant perspectives to understand, and remedies to respond to, natural disasters and environmental crises, which we have seen throughout the first part of this book (and which we will unpack more fully and systematically in Chapter 8). These include the call to take responsibility (and being held responsible) for our actions and repenting of our behavior, reflected in moralizing and discussion of ethics and social justice, as well as reflection on the covenant with God. Other tools and views that religion has provided include practices that recognize the need to value and steward nature and to contract and look beyond ourselves.

Premodern Judaism has often been seen as traditional and static. Recent scholarship has revealed it to be far more open to a certain halakhic flexibility and tolerated dissent than was once recognized. Modernity, with its secularization and the bifurcation of Judaism into various denominations, has often also been seen as the demise of "tradition." Tradition was recreated and re-entrenched in the modern world and could lead to the creation of strongly polarized views of the world, religion, and politics. The binary thinking that has emerged at the end of the modern period is perhaps related to the uncertainty of a quickly and ever-changing world, on one hand, and the search for comfort and truths to hold onto during such uncertainty, on the other. While premodern Jewish flexibility did not mean that there were no conflicts within Jewish communities or that there was no competition for authority and power, the notion that there are different ways to believe and behave (whether accepted or not) may be taken constructively with the challenges wrought by modernity to help us find grounding and ways to adapt as needed. Such flexibility is necessary given the complex and multilayered changes to and within the environmental system that have been caused and accelerated by human actions as well as changes within nature itself.

There is much to learn from premodern understandings of and approaches to religion. There are also opportunities to rethink our assumptions as we confront radically changed circumstances. The responses to premodern natural disasters that we have reviewed supply examples of ways that religion has been helpful in creating frameworks for understanding, making experiences personal, and developing common purpose and action. They have also highlighted that religion can coexist with other forms of knowledge and practice. At the same time, our premodern cases have offered examples of polemics, stereotyping, othering, and closed thinking that can make it difficult to learn and adapt from our experiences. Part II will examine ways to build on the positive aspects of religion (especially Judaism) and open new ways of engaging with religion (including Judaism) to overcome the challenging parts of religion when it comes to understanding and responding to natural disasters and environmental crises.

The observations that we have made from the examination of Jewish environmental history in Part I, including the opportunities and limits of both history and religion, will be discussed in greater and more theoretical ways in Part II. Since learning and adaptation are key to understanding, responding to, and mitigating environmental and climate crises, the more nuanced ways of thinking about both history and religion that emerge in Part II will be applied in Part III to help us think through key issues that have animated and stifled progress on the climate and environment today. These include: increased complexity and the interrelation of human and environmental systems; binary thinking that makes it difficult to find a middle ground (overcoming polarization) and that balances multiple needs and approaches to responding to crises; the apparent inability to make the radical changes needed to stem the tide (to the extent possible) of climate and environmental change; developing deeper and more meaningful relationships, especially across differences in order to cooperate in more significant and longer-term ways; finding ways to understand and take seriously the challenges that others are experiencing even when we ourselves do not always have an immediate or direct parallel experience; and developing ways to find more resilient ways to respond to the significant changes that are occurring all around us. Let's turn now to this work.

PART II

Disaster, History, and Religion

Tradition and Innovation

Beyond History

Disasters and Crises in the Anthropocene

Introduction

The earthquakes, plagues, floods, and fires that we examined in Part I of this book offer a range of ways to understand the nature of and response to natural disasters in Jewish and more general history and thought. They highlight experiences and worldviews that layered scientific, philosophical, and theological ideas onto diverse political, economic, social, and cultural sensibilities. As we examined the context and impact of those select historical examples, we had a chance to see traditional ways of thinking and acting, many of which still play a role in disaster prevention, mitigation, and response today. We also viewed innovations that would change the very lived experience of people (especially in Europe, but by extension around the globe and in many different settings as well).

Especially as modernity has been cast as the main culprit in human-induced climate change and increasing environmental degradation, many scholars have seen the benefit of returning to a premodern, and in some cases indigenous, approach to the environment. At the same time, however, historical responses to natural disasters and changing environmental conditions—many of which are the result of the growth and expansion of human society and human actions (throughout human history and especially in modernity)—have their limits. The "acceleration" of many aspects of human life and changes to the earth system more broadly temper some of the thinking and practical responses that animated the premodern world. While some aspects of the historical record and experience continue to be useful as we consider how we understand and respond to changes in and to the world, many of which we and our ancestors have initiated, there are many ways in which the lessons of the past are insufficient for the challenges that the present and possible future realities hold in store. What, then, can history teach us, and how might we need to think differently about history as well as the present and future if we are to address the impact of the increasing reach and influence of humanity?

History might assume that natural disasters had a single cause and that there were direct connections between disasters and subsequent developments and behaviors. That could often be the case; however, recent natural disasters alert us to the fact that we may not always understand the combination of causes that result in a disaster and that disasters can have ripple effects far beyond the area in which they occurred in ways that many of the premodern people we studied may not have imagined. While premoderns learned from prior experiences, they were sometimes locked into particular ways of thinking that did not allow them to consider other possibilities. The spread of disease, to take one example, might be seen to be associated with the behavior of criminals, deviants, witches, and foreigners as opposed to other sources they could not see or along with other explanations they might have at hand (of course we have not progressed much farther than our ancestors in many ways in this regard!). If the emphasis on divine punishment for sin was taken to its logical conclusion, people might be encouraged to repent of poor behavior even when that behavior might be irrelevant to the disaster at hand or when such penance absolved them from other direct and intentional practices. Religion in the premodern world, as now, could be used to emphasize narratives and practices of domination and marginalization. Yet there are wonderful ideas and practices in religion that have been identified and cultivated for both personal growth—notions of grief and care, for example—as well as for communal benefit—taking the idea of contraction and expanding it to societal practice.

In transitioning to Part II of this book, I will revisit many of the same themes that emerged in the case studies in Part I. However, in each case—be it human society, history, or religion—I will suggest both limits and opportunities in traditional narratives, thinking, and practices that are indebted to and also go beyond what traditional "history" and "religion" can offer. In that sense, Part II is an effort to craft a new approach to history and religion (beyond what has become a typical approach to environmental history and ecological theology) that will give us tools and perspectives that might usefully direct the way we think and behave now and in the future. Throughout, my main focus is on Jewish history and Judaism, though these are placed into conversation with other religions and scholarship from other fields.

The final chapters (Chapters 10 and 11), which comprise Part III, serve as a conclusion to this book. They consider change in broad strokes. While change is part of what historians typically study, the final chapter suggests that a much more complex approach to change will be required for the future: history has constraints but also significant insights, especially when placed into conversation with religion, and, in this case, Judaism in particular. These chapters focus on the complexity and uncertainty that characterize environmental systems and the rapid growth and changes in technology and society today. They ask history and religion to provide tools for understanding agency and causality in new ways, for seeing relationships and impact in less direct and more multilayered ways, for helping us get past binary thinking that fails to see different perspectives and new ways of thinking, for allowing us to cultivate new ways of learning and adapting, for encouraging ways to imagine multiple and different futures, and for conceiving new ways of understanding community and common goals and needs.

I begin Part II, and this chapter in particular, with a discussion of natural disasters in history as a reference. I will consider the nature of disaster—characteristics and definitions, the relationship between "natural" and "human-made" disasters, dangers and opportunities, and the continuities and transformations in the scale and impact of disasters in the contemporary world. I expand the discussion of the contemporary impact in the second and larger section of the chapter that considers the "Anthropocene," a term that designates a new period in Earth's history defined by the significant impact of humans on the Earth. In that review, I will examine the term, its origins, and what it represents. I also place it in conversation with other monikers to describe the dramatic changes in the environment and society, as well as criticisms of the term itself. Much of the section engages with the "modern" context of the Anthropocene, with special attention to the debate over the universal and the particular, the idea of the self, notions of progress, globalization, science and technology, the acceleration of time, and complexity. I conclude this chapter with some thoughts on the conflict and possibilities embedded in the Anthropocene and signal new ways of thinking that will be developed in the remainder of the book.

Disaster(s)

As we saw in Part I, there are many kinds of natural disasters, and they have a diverse range of impacts, which seem increasingly interconnected. In the twentieth century, famine and drought accounted for 87 percent of overall deaths from disasters.[1] Floods are estimated to have been 9.2 percent, earthquakes and tsunamis 2.2 percent, storms 1.5 percent, and volcanic eruptions and landslides each 0.1 percent.[2] Often, these disasters were localized.[3]

There can be a difference between natural and "man-made" disasters—though they can also be closely connected; in either case, the reaction to disasters can tell us a great deal about the societies and people who experience them.[4] Disasters and their impact can be measured in many ways—from casualties (often higher for the most vulnerable populations) to destruction of property and changes to social, cultural, and other systems.[5] Some scholars have maintained that disaster itself is a "social construction." As historian Jerry Toner writes:

> The distinction between natural and man-made disasters is misleading in this respect because it suggests that there is no human influence on the outcome of a physical event. In fact, the effect that a natural agent such as an earthquake has on a society is purely a reflection of the particular ways in which that society has chosen to inhabit its environment.[6]

More recent research on disasters extends this analysis even farther, focusing on time frames beyond the immediate impact, especially as expressed in social order, human relations with the environment, and "historical structural processes."[7]

Disasters have been defined in many different ways,[8] including based on their physical impact, level of social disruption, type of social construction (of reality), effect on politics and political structures, as well as a more general imbalance of ratios related to demand and capability.[9] According to one definition, "Disasters in general are portrayed as nonroutine, destabilizing, causing uncertainty, disorder, and sociocultural collapse."[10] Disasters can disturb habits and typical ways of doing things, creating social dysfunction and elevating tensions that may have existed under the surface.[11] They can lead to political upheaval and scapegoating, with some groups blamed for the events and their consequences.[12] At the same time, as the case of historical disasters in the Roman Empire shows, the suspension of some societal norms in the short term does not necessarily lead to chaos. What is more, many societies throughout history proved to be anything but passive in the face of disasters, taking many measures to respond to them and mitigate the impact of future ones.[13] The return to more "normative" conditions and behaviors might be relatively quick in some cases.[14] The response to disasters might also afford the opportunity for regnant authorities, which might be conservative and seek to restore the previously disturbed order,[15] "to reassert dominance and supposed benefit dominance could bring to society."[16] At the same time, disasters hold out the possibility of challenging existing authority and they could help to create crises of and for leadership.[17]

As evident in the Chinese symbol for disaster, disasters could be said to be a combination of two different characters—one symbolizing danger and one opportunity.[18] In the same vein, crises—which are often seen as the challenges we face when change occurs at a rate faster than we or our systems can handle[19]—are often presented as turning points or moments of decision or resolution. The ways people respond to disasters are informed by the infrastructure they have built and the learning they have accumulated. They are also informed by context and the range and nature of other (often related) disruptions. Here history, with its emphasis on context, can be quite helpful in understanding the dynamics of a situation as well as strategies that may have been helpful in previous situations.

Disasters, like "crises" more generally, can offer an opportunity for the activation of social networks and religious communal engagement.[20] In ancient Roman culture, for example, disasters highlighted the relationship between the human and upper worlds, and most explanations of disasters involved religious ideas of some kind, with disasters often seen as a manifestation of divine will and a breach of the covenant with the divine or punishment for human sin.[21] Christians in the Roman Empire could see disasters as a chance to show the resoluteness of their strength; interpretations of disasters could also serve polemical roles in interreligious debates.[22] Associated apocalyptic visions served at times to enforce or reinforce codes of behavior or signal divine retribution against oppressors.[23] Some groups were more impacted by disasters, but a significant amount of infrastructure allowed the Roman authorities to provide food and other supplies during difficult times,[24] even as the disasters could surface weaknesses in systems and lead to criticism of imperial power and authority.[25] As such, disasters were both unusual events with great significance and simultaneously part of daily life.[26]

Disasters could pose a significant test of the status quo. The French Jewish philosopher Emmanuel Levinas (1906–1995) cited the French philosopher Maurice Blanchot (1907–2003), who noted that a disaster "signifies neither death nor an accident, but as a piece of being which would be detached from its fixity of being, from its reference to a star, from all cosmological existence a *dis-aster*."[27] Similarly, some scholars maintain that disasters disrupt the status quo and they can force different behavior and thought–innovation[28]—as we try to understand and respond to them. Disasters can literally create alternative spaces in history when "other rules of change apply."[29] At the same time, there are many possible ways for a crisis or disaster to unfold.[30] As John Robb notes, crisis is relational and not absolute. As a result, he notes, "The effects of a catastrophe depend not only on how severe it is and how long it lasts but also on how people are organized and relate to the world around them."[31]

Given the massive changes in human society and the environment, especially over the past half century, are disasters different from those in the past? Do we need different ways to think about, mitigate, and respond to them in contemporary society? To begin to answer these questions, we must first understand the new period of human and ecological history that we are now living in—what some call the Anthropocene.

The Anthropocene: The Human and the Nature of Humanity[32]

By many accounts, we are in a new geological period, the center of which is humanity. Evidence has been assembled for years now to craft a formal proposal to create an official new geological time for the period in which we currently live.[33] Although not fully accepted in the scientific community, the term Anthropocene has gained a significant foothold. The Anthropocene, or the period in which humans are exerting a significant influence on and even domination of the global environment—the earth system[34]—which has been described as bigger than an "age" but less than a "period,"[35] is quite literally the intrusion of humans into the geological footprint and time frames of the Earth. It has been characterized by rapid and deeply accelerated change, as well as some of the accompanying challenges associated with industrialization and human growth—including climate change[36] and degradation of the environment.[37] It is often characterized by dramatic increases in population growth and energy use,[38] since the eighteenth century, and in a particularly accelerated manner since the middle of the twentieth century, with the expanded use of fossil fuel and then later nuclear energy.[39]

Naming the period may help us understand the challenges we face, though it will not necessarily give us the foresight or tools to address the associated challenges. As one recent assessment notes:

> Humans will not find it as easy to live in the Anthropocene as they did in the Holocene. It now seems clear that life as we have experienced it for the last ten millennia is going to be changing very rapidly and largely for the worse: the air carries a third more carbon dioxide and so the climate will, almost certainly, soon be hotter than it has ever been in the history of *Homo sapiens*. The seas are rising. Global biodiversity is shrinking. Fresh water is becoming more scarce. Topsoil is being lost [at] the rate of at least 36 billion tons every year, endangering food supplies. The pressure on the systems that nurture, shelter, and fuel us will become ever more intense in the years to come. These intensifying pressures will impact our societies unevenly and unfairly, but no part of the globe will be unchanged.[40]

Given the diverse challenges associated with the Anthropocene, we will need a wide range of changes in how we think and how we act to live through it. This will include multi-scalar and multidisciplinary interventions that are more systemic—understanding the interconnection between human and earth systems[41]—and less hierarchical and increasingly flexible and adaptable.[42]

The changes associated with the Anthropocene affect humans, but also broader biodiversity and the scope and quality of habitations.[43] According to one recent assessment, "The environmental crises of the present and the future include not only climate change but also nested issues and wicked problems such as ocean acidification, black carbon, environmental justice, species die-off, human overpopulation, loss of topsoil, plastic gyres in our oceans, air pollution, and overconsumption, to name only a few."[44] Pollution, to take one example, is a significant aspect of environmental degradation. However, as is the case with most ecological crises in the age of the Anthropocene, the brunt of the impact is felt by the poor and individuals in particular geographical locations. In examining the situation in the city of Detroit, for example, one recent study observes that "when you layer the environmental and social data that is publicly available, the top 5 percent most polluted areas are composed of 81.5 percent people of color, compared with 25.1 percent of the general population."[45]

The carbon added to the atmosphere in the process of burning fossil fuels and through deforestation has numerous planetary effects, including changes to the chemical makeup of the oceans and warmer temperatures that lead to an increased capacity of the air to hold water vapor, resulting in stronger tropical storms.[46] Although humans have no control over phenomena such as hurricanes, these natural events are influenced by human activity and resultant weather patterns.[47] And while natural disasters—as we have seen—are often negative for humans, they can at times have "positive" outcomes, at least for some people in some places.[48] Of course, the impact of natural disasters on human society, as in the case of earthquakes, depends in part on preexisting social vulnerabilities that can impact recovery and rebuilding responses.[49] That is to say that the effects of the Anthropocene are hardly simple or linear.

The Anthropocene has been characterized as a period when infinite growth has been seen as both possible and desirable by some.[50] With this in mind, some scholars have referred to the period not as the Anthropocene but instead as the Capitalocene, to signal this sensibility, which, with that moniker, serves as a fairly easy target for criticism at the same time. In this reframing, nature can be understood as an external condition that does not need to be considered when examining (and maximizing) economic productivity.[51] One challenge of seeing the "products of nature" as interchangeable with those of human manufacture is that it leads to an unrealistic evaluation of nature's products, for which there is no substitute.[52] What is more, we may need to find ways to estimate not simply the products of nature, but the very services and processes that nature provides—including, for example, "pollination, nutrient cycling, genetic resources, and soil formation."[53] While the appeal of economic growth is not always negative or simply the purview of a greedy minority of wealthy people and states,[54] the earth system's resources are finite.[55] In addition, as the environmental historian J. R. McNeill and strategist Peter Engelke note, sustainable development work has highlighted that the global economy since the middle of the twentieth century has been socially unjust to the detriment of the poor and it threatens to "outstrip ecological limits, mainly due to the patterns of consumption in the rich world."[56] On the other hand, others propose that there is evidence that when we understand that humans are a planetary force that can disrupt the earth system[57] and we focus on "well-being" as opposed to productivity, we might foster societies with greater social and ecological sustainability and equality.[58] To do this, some scholars argue that we may need at times to adopt what appear to be "antisocial postures" that rupture traditional ways of thinking and, some assert, give up modern notions of liberty for what might appear to be "eco-authoritarianism."[59]

Other scholars have preferred still other terms rather than Anthropocene. Archaeologist Monica L. Smith, for example, writes of the "anthroscape," "as a description of the ways humans have physically altered the physical environment through selective consumption of plants and animals and the modification of terrestrial slope, gradient, hardscapes, watercourses, and vegetation regimes."[60] She refers to relations between humans and nature that are iterative and innovative (and sometimes incremental),[61] and that allow for large and small scale perspectives.[62] In a similar vein, she also chooses to refer to "mass events" as opposed to "catastrophes," in order to avoid value judgments "assessed within the frame of reference of the people who experience the event and its aftermath and who move forward from that experience through subsequent actions."[63] That also means that she eschews "the consideration of intentionality and human efforts as prime movers of physical change, focusing instead on the physically measurable effects of action rather than considering animacy, intentionality, or personhood."[64] As we will see, this raises intriguing questions of agency—indeed, the very notion of what an agent is and what an action is.

Modernity as/and the Anthropocene

The Anthropocene is frequently associated with modernity. As theologian Michael S. Hogue beautifully articulates:

> Sustainability and climate ethics are concerned with the challenges provoked by the mutually amplifying systemic trajectories of modern life: the exponential growth of the human population, the magnitude of our technological and industrial impacts on natural systems, the global expansion of a fossil-fueled economic system that generates inequality and concentrates economic and political power, the increasingly radical forms of energy extraction needed to maintain the economic system and the growing population, and the fact that marginalized and disempowered individuals and communities tend to suffer the most immediate and negative consequences of this juggernaut of dynamics.[65]

The exact starting dates of both modernity and the Anthropocene are somewhat open to debate. Whether sometime in the eighteenth century or the twentieth,[66] what is clear is that some of the key issues raised (and in some ways created) by modernity play a significant role in how we think about the environment and how we respond to environmental issues today and into the future. These include the distinction between universal and particular, notions of the self, ideas of progress, expanding globalization, advances in science and technology, and ever-increasing experiences of time and complexity.

Universal and Particular

One prevalent issue often associated with modernity is universalism, which became a hallmark of modern thinking, eschewing particularisms, especially those that sometimes emerged in religious spaces. Universalism is under fire in a postmodern culture, especially when, as Susan Neiman writes, "on the left because it's conflated with fake universalism: the attempt to impose certain cultures on others in the name of an abstract humanity that turns out to reflect just a dominant culture's time, place, and interests."[67] But universalism never fully won the day in modernity. Indeed, even among Jewish and other religious reformers of the nineteenth century, a certain degree of particularism merged with a quest for universal morals and ethics. The positive aspects associated with the ideals of universalism, especially around rights and equality, were always in conversation with particularistic tendencies, contexts, and challenges. As we saw in the case of flooding (in Part I), responses to disasters could be complex and pivot between "universal" and "particular" concerns.

The Self

Modernity, and especially notions of the modern self and individualism, have often been discussed in the context of contemporary social and political issues, including environmental degradation and climate change. Alexander J. B. Hampton, for example, argues that "This buffered self, the paradigm of modern social imaginary, has given us profound powers to reshape nature, while simultaneously disconnecting from it, with devastating consequences."[68] Using the Covid-19 pandemic as a prompt for this discussion, Hampton notes that modern notions of the self engage a number of important issues that are central for understanding how we think about and respond to disaster. These include identity, agency, and authority.[69] While the modern construction of autonomous identity leaves out both eternal and natural worlds, shearing them of "inherent meaning and value," Hampton offers that premodern conceptions provide a different opportunity:

> The modern self therefore is established in the context of a subject-object dynamic, where individual subjects and their internal concepts are set over and against external objects, creating the framework for the modern sense of autonomy.[70] Alternatively, for the premodern self, identity is manifested through a relational framework, where meaning and value are intelligible ontic realities, adhering both in the external corporal realities that instantiate them, and in the internal mental thoughts of the minds that think them.[71]

While modern identity seeks invulnerability, premodern identity is far more relational and vulnerable to extrinsic ideas and others (including nonhuman agents).[72] In this case, the premodern is elevated as a more organic and relational way of being than the modern—and, as I have sometimes mused with my students, seems far closer to the postmodern, which has also rejected the metanarratives and truths of modernity that have appeared to many to be the source of the environmental challenges we face today.

Progress

Some scholars have further argued that modernity, with its notion of progress and separation of "Nature" and "Culture," agitates and deepens the environmental crisis.[73] Indian writer Amitav Ghosh, for example, writes,

> To want to be ahead, and to celebrate and mythify this endeavor, is indeed one of the most powerful impulses of modernity itself. If Bruno Latour is right, then to be modern is to envision time as irreversible, to think of it as a progression that is forever propelled forward by revolutionary ruptures; these in turn are conceived of on the analogy of scientific innovations, each of which is thought to render its predecessor obsolete.[74]

While progress often suggests a specific, and true or best direction, recent discussions of progress offer a more nuanced conception that may be helpful in discussions about the environment. Neiman writes that "Here Philip Kotcher's pragmatic conception of progress is helpful. It's a matter of changing direction: rather than thinking of progress as directed *to* a particular goal it can be useful to think of progress *from* a problematic situation to one that is less constrained."[75] Regardless of how one sees it, progress is a key consideration in narratives about modernity and it has enormous significance in understanding and addressing environmental challenges.

Globalization

Globalization has been another concept associated with modernity, and it has been understood in both positive and negative ways.[76] On one hand, it has led to the integration of nation-states as well as cultures and economies.[77] On the other hand, some scholars contend that it actually erodes the nation-state and serves to redefine time and space.[78] It can harm nature and foster environmental degradation[79] and "critics note that globalization theorists tend to 'privilege economic and technological explanations and to downplay questions of agency, historicity, and social construction of meaning.'"[80] Some have noted a countervailing phenomenon termed "glocalization"—"in which an individual, group, community, or social network may be simultaneously global and local."[81] One result is that "'Local knowledge' and 'global knowledge' are ever more entangled, not only for indigenous people subject to the forces of modernity, but also for those responsible for its accelerating destruction."[82] It does seem increasingly difficult to separate activities and events where they occur and their impact in other, often geographically removed places; it is also the case that such global lenses can distract attention from local developments and concerns.

Science and Technology

If science in modernity seemed to promise an objective truth, we have come to learn that science can also in some ways be understood as a construct and far more subjective than we once believed. Like others, the philosopher Hans Jonas notes—returning to a premodern paradigm for comparison—that early modern science began a process by which quantity was seen to be the "at once essential and truly knowable aspect of reality: cognition accordingly consists to him in measurement and comparison of measurements. . . . motion instead of fixed spatial proportions became the main object of measurement . . . In the early stages of modern science, analysis of becoming supplants contemplation of being."[83] At the same time, "transcendental monotheism" eliminated "nature-gods and divine powers within the world," leading to an emphasis on the rational over the spiritual and an externalization of nature that led to its representation as mindless and lifeless.[84]

Technology has been a major force and driver in the Anthropocene.[85] Human technology has simultaneously been blamed for environmental ills by some and hailed by others as a means to rectify human-induced climate change and environmental degradation. This tension is reflected in the writing of Francis Van den Noortgaete, who argues that

> The Anthropocene does not so much reveal an emergent capability of humans to intervene on a truly global scale, which is sometimes suggested to render conceivable and to legitimize planetary interventions like climate engineering. Rather, it unveils the human inability to foresee what is in fact possible, despite our considering it impossible—or more frequently: despite the impossibility of our even considering it.[86]

Technology, therefore, holds the promise of being able to help in stemming climate change and environmental degradation. Yet even some efforts—technological and otherwise—that appear to be "green," can create their own environmental problems. They can also have significant social and economic downsides. Artificial Intelligence (AI) scholar Kate Crawford notes that "If we visit the primary sites of mineral extraction for computational systems, we find the repressed stories of acid-bleached rivers and deracinated landscapes and the extinction of plant and animal species that were once vital to the local ecology."[87]

Technological knowledge and its application have accelerated dramatically in modernity. Innovations that once took generations occur today in the span of days or months. But the speed of thinking can keep us from thinking deeply. In discussing technology, Jacob Ward writes that there are different ways of seeing an object. One way is consciously perceiving it and making decisions regarding it; a second is instantaneously guiding our action—akin to Kahneman's slow and fast thinking.[88] The latter—with instinctual recognition of patterns—is what AI developers seek.[89] Ward notes that for our brains, sacred values are nonnegotiable, and so we react more quickly than for things that we do not hold as sacred values.[90] Regarding the social psychologist Jonathan Haidt, Ward writes about the idea that "people develop their moral intuitions about the world almost automatically, and then essentially reverse engineer a system of reasoning that supports those moral intuitions."[91] Michael S. Hogue helpfully notes

> the challenge posed by technology's cultural *pattern* is its influence over moral consciousness, our conceptions of the human good and of moral responsibility. We are no longer merely the subject-agents driving technology, technology is not merely the extension of human efficacy, and so we need to think not only about what we are doing with technology but also about how technology is fundamentally transforming human moral life.[92]

Technology has fundamentally changed our world and our very system of human relations and morality, which can have significant (positive and negative) implications for human society and the future of humanity and the world.

What are the implications of this assertion for how we understand and respond to technological advances and acceleration? One implication surely is that we seek the easiest and quickest responses. And this can lead to attempts to simplify at the expense of engaging with nuance. It may also lead to increasing polarization as people refuse to look at divergent perspectives and attitudes, as we will see in the discussion of polarization.

Acceleration of Time and Complexity

Part of the complexity of the Anthropocene is related to the size (planetary) and multiplicity of scales of events and changes, and the varying time frames that merge into them (deep past, past, present, future, geological and social), along with different levels of impact (perceived and invisible, short and long term) and their interlocking aspects of causality, in addition to the vast networking of forms and contents of information and knowledge that have literally exploded, especially over the past generation or two.[93] The Anthropocene forces consideration of diverse experiences and the potential and actuality of enormous transformation, far beyond the simple or particular change that we once imagined. As a result, the Anthropocene is often taken as a metaphor for a reality that is unstable, quickly changing, and multi-valent. And yet, the impact of this instability—for now anyway—can be very unequally distributed, with some paying the current and steep price for the advancement of others. What is more, the Anthropocene may just force us to consider what we even mean by human and humanity, intersecting as it does with deep machine learning and artificial learning that some have associated with a kind of posthumanism.

Though the Anthropocene is short by geological standards, the depth and acceleration of change, as well as the time that may be needed to adapt to (or reverse) associated changes, is enormous.[94] Deep history has taught us that humans and their activities have always impacted the environment—regardless of whether we assess human history from prehistoric, Enlightenment, industrial, or contemporary lenses.[95] While the Holocene was a period of diverse conditions, it was characterized, in retrospect, by greater predictability than the emerging period of the Anthropocene, which is working to transform the earth system, rather than merely changing conditions in particular regions.[96]

Time has been a significant issue in contemporary discussions of complexity. In examining temporality, Hans Jonas argues that

> with respect to the organic sphere, the external linear time-pattern of antecedent and sequent, involving the causal dominance of the past, is inadequate: while mere externality is, at least can be presented as, wholly determined by what it was, life is essentially also what it is going to be and just becoming: in its case, the extensive order of past and future is intensively reversed.[97]

As we will see in Chapter 7, in an accelerated and quickly changing world, history must grapple with the connections between past, present, and future in new ways that are not segregated and that have significant impact on one another.

The Anthropocene highlights that human and earth systems operate differently—in terms of time, as well as "scales, methods, and questions"[98]—but nonetheless in ways that are still deeply intertwined. The nature of human and environmental impact is two-way.[99] There are many ways to begin to understand and measure the impact of humans on the environment—from the creation of new materials such as plastics that now occupy a significant space and impact within the Earth[100] to the immense increase in the numbers of certain animals used for food (such as chickens) or the decline of other species (such as flying insects) that have an impact on the functioning of natural environments.[101] At the same time, changes to the earth system, such as rising sea levels, are already impacting humans, especially given the built societies that humans have constructed along coastlines, an example of what some describe as "manufactured vulnerability."[102]

What exactly do we mean by "complexity?" According to one definition of complex systems:

> They are composed of multiple constituent elements interacting in both time and space that create a network structure that connects all or most of the constituent parts. The interactions among those elements develop processes and products that cascade across the network in linear and nonlinear feedback processes. This produces emergent properties and dynamics that initiate additional changes that ripple across the network. The dynamic nature of these interactions and the cascade of influence across both time and space means that these systems are inherently unpredictable. More precisely, it is difficult to untangle the convoluted interactions in a complex system that give rise to the patterns that emerge. At any given time and any given spatial scale, a complex system is defined by all interactions across the system and by external influences from other systems that is nested in.[103]

This kind of complexity means that we cannot think or behave in the same ways as in the past; that we cannot expect the same results from the same interventions.[104] German environmental historian Frank Uekötter writes that we can not understand global flows if we study them one by one. They have mixed and interacted in an eminently haphazard manner, and that has created plenty of crosscurrents and secondary and tertiary vortices. The vortex also features a lot of intended and accidental obstacles that shape the flow in one way or another There is a lot of movement inside a vortex, there are moments of calm, and it can be smooth sailing for a while, but there is ultimately no escape from the material heft of masses in motion.[105]

He uses the concept of a vortex to get at the "sense of dynamism and forces beyond control, particularly if we think of it on a planetary scale," as well as the associated turbulence and chaos. Humans may retain some agency in the vortex, but it is in constant flux and the power of the nonhuman world is central as well.[106] He concludes that "History cannot solve this puzzle [of global environmental crisis], but it can provide an idea of how we came to this point. More precisely, it can provide a multitude of ideas to that effect."[107]

The complexity of the Anthropocene (as we will discuss more in Chapter 10) is part of what makes the crises of the Anthropocene so challenging to understand and address. It is what appears to make it a challenging problem. But, as one recent assessment notes "The reason is that the Anthropocene presents not a *problem*, but a *predicament*. . . . A problem may be solved, sometimes using a single physical or conceptual tool produced by experts in the only appropriate field, but a predicament presents a challenging situation requiring resources of many kinds. We don't solve predicaments; instead, we persevere with grace and decency."[108] This also means that what we once took to be obvious causality is far from it. Instead of causality, some, like the Humanities scholar Ian Baucom, suggest we think in terms of forcing and forces— the former disturbances in a system, without will and neither good nor bad; the latter "happenstance, inevitability, and intention" that merge indistinguishably as historical forces.[109] In the age of the Anthropocene, causality is much more complicated than we once assumed and it involves many different factors and considerations. This can lead to conflict (see below) and to challenges to traditional ways of thinking and behaving (see the next chapters). Regardless of how we may want to respond, the Anthropocene and its associated challenges will force us to respond differently in many ways than we have in the past.

Conclusions

The Anthropocene has been characterized in part by conflict relating to the use and governance of the natural world and its resources.[110] Indeed, the issue of power has been central to many discussions about environmental degradation—including Lynn White Jr.'s argument about the theological understandings of the nature of human power (which we will discuss in Chapter 8) to contemporary debates about disinformation and hoarding of resources to neoliberal politics of invulnerability/resilience. The philosopher Giorgio Agamben identifies the connection—as did others such as Michel

Foucault—between institutions and power, in this case in the biopolitical body. He asserts that

> The present inquiry concerns precisely this hidden point of intersection between the juridico-institutional and the biopolitical models of power. What this work has had to record among its likely conclusions is precisely that the two analyses cannot be separated, and that the inclusion of bare life in the political realm constitutes the original—if concealed—nucleus of sovereign power. *It can even be said that the production of a biopolitical body is the original activity of sovereign power.*[111]

The connection between power and the environment takes on particular significance today, as we compete for natural resources and political predominance.

Collaboration can be difficult in the context of the Anthropocene, but it can be fostered through principled engagement, shared motivation, and joint capacity.[112] As research scientist Joshua Fisher argues, "by understanding that societies and systems are not trapped in linear timelines but instead follow cycles of stability, conflict, and reorganization, it becomes possible to design or redesign the institutional architecture that makes collaboration and constructive engagement more likely than polarization and deadlock."[113] In these various situations, power dynamics and legal structures play significant roles.[114]

Environmental concerns can lead to various forms of conflict, which can be the result of changes within and outside a system.[115] They can at times be complex and "wicked," that is "they prove to be incredibly protracted, constantly evolving, self-reinforcing, and unpredictable."[116] Indeed, environmental problems can include a variety of ecological, scientific, and societal relationships and processes.[117] Uncertainty can drive conflict.[118] However, conflict is not inherently bad or good, as Fisher notes—and there can be constructive conflicts,[119] through which "stakeholders" learn about the views of others as well as their own and develop social capital "that they can draw on when new precipitating events occur. This in itself creates a reinforcing process for cooperation and facilitates future constructive dynamics." "Conversely," however, "destructive dynamics reduce social capital and create inhibiting feedback processes that limit stakeholders' abilities to cooperate when new precipitating events occur."[120]

There may be a downside to the "metanarrative" of the Anthropocene. The French philosopher and anthropologist Bruno Latour argues that "The Anthropos of the *Anthropocene* is nothing but the dangerous fiction of a universalized agent capable of acting like a single humanity."[121] That is, the broader concept of the Anthropocene, in its full sweep, might allow individuals to not take individual responsibility. On the other hand, the collectivization reflected in the notion of the Anthropocene might also foster a kind of apocalyptic sensibility[122]—or a series of mini apocalypses as one colleague once suggested to me. And yet, if the Anthropocene reveals humans as having godlike technical powers that have planetary implications, humans also have a corresponding moral responsibility to address contemporary and future, intergenerational, concerns.[123]

Not all of the challenges and changes ascribed to the Anthropocene are new. We found many of the same issues already in the premodern world as well. The scale, speed, and interconnected nature of these changes and challenges, however, are different from those in the past. The Anthropocene calls our attention to the need for broader systems thinking and greater proactive rather than reactive, and at times passive, action. It also forces us to revisit our relationship with the environment—re-placing ourselves within it rather than in opposition to it. It increasingly makes the traditional distinctions of modernity between subject and object less clear and less relevant as we find that these concepts are inextricably linked and themselves shift in many different ways, complexifying when we act and when we are acted upon, and how we understand ourselves, others, and the environment as they interact with each other. With these observations in mind, let's take a closer look at history (Chapter 7) and religion (Chapters 8 and 9), before considering change (Chapters 10 and 11) and ways to address environmental degradation, climate change, and natural disasters.

History, Narratives, and Temporality

Introduction

Even beyond the current period of the Anthropocene, and as we saw in Part I, environmental change, including climate change, along with various natural disasters and the spread of infectious diseases, had significant impacts on societies in the past. Historians have noted the devastation that these events caused, as well as the opportunities that they sometimes created.

A number of recent studies have examined these issues in the historical context of the Roman Empire. Kyle Harper, for example, observes that "the influence of the climate on Roman history was by turns subtle and overwhelmingly alternatingly constructive and destructive." It affected demography and agriculture as well as social and political structures. "With good reason," he writes, "the ancients revered the fearsome goddess *Fortuna*, out of a sense that the sovereign powers of this world were ultimately capricious."[1] The successes and failures of responses to disaster can teach us a great deal about historical periods, and they also hold more general lessons. Harper notes that "The resilience paradigm allows us to see why the response of the system to an impulse was nonlinear; feedback mechanisms, critical thresholds, and changes operative on different timescales meant that one drought might have invisible effects, while another of just the same magnitude might seem to tip society irreversibly toward catastrophe."[2]

In fact, history often provides us with valuable examples of the impact of and response to natural disasters and changing environmental conditions. Where once we assumed that we could only effectively respond to and mitigate disasters with modern technology, we now know that people in the past learned from disasters and created systems and ways to respond to current and mitigate future episodes that could be quite effective. In writing about flooding in early modern Europe, for example, Lydia Barnett notes that "The long-standing misperception that premodern people could only see themselves as the passive victims of forces beyond their comprehension or control likely drew some of its force from an implicit assumption that belief in an active, interventionist, and punishing God was incompatible with an account of humanity's power to make or mitigate significant changes in the natural world."[3] This could be true even as theology (especially in the often discussed "economy of sin") and religious polemics were used as part of the explanation for natural disasters.[4] In the early modern world, the characterization of floods as biblical deluges served to merge temporal spheres and pointed to a severity of experience that was seen to have a providential meaning when linked to the biblical flood narrative.[5] This was a key example of ways in which global disasters could be displaced onto the past (including the very distant and even mythic past) but also cast upon the future (especially in apocalyptic veins).[6]

Even when climate and natural disasters cannot be linked directly to historical events, they could affect collective and individual mindsets. "Climate convulsions," writes Philip Jenkins, "have been understood in religious terms, through the language of apocalypse, millennium, and Judgment—with premodern peoples often association divine favor or displeasure with human actions in the form of climate and environmental conditions."[7] Such apocalyptic thinking could continue to exist into modernity and the Enlightenment as well.[8] These upheavals could cross political and geographic regions and, importantly, they were often connected with a range of other crises, both political (e.g., warfare) and environmental (e.g., drought, storms, flooding, famine, pestilence). Due to the ephemeral interest of mass media, lack of memorials, and what can appear as their random and singular character,[9] natural disasters today can (and in the past could) often receive attention that is minimal or fleeting. How humans respond to natural disasters depends on collective learning[10] but also their particular "social and cultural patterns, values, religious belief systems, political institutions, and economic structures."[11] There is, in fact, a social and political context for and component of natural disasters, even in shorter-term periods.

There is benefit, then, in examining natural disasters and crises in history more broadly. As we saw in Part I, such history allows us to see the relationship between nature and culture (see below), to understand human interactions with the environment, and to understand the intellectual and physical responses of people in the past, which may be useful today, on one hand, and simultaneously highlight insufficiencies that must be addressed in decidedly accelerated times today and into the future.

Some of the recent developments in the study of history, along with innovations in the interdisciplinary approach of environmental history, provide new and deeper ways to leverage the study of the past to spark new understanding and encourage new ways of thinking today and in the future.

One significant emphasis in recent work in history is related to the learning process. The environmental historian Franz Mauelshagen argues that "The 'circle of impact' between society and the environment has always politicized the discourse on natural hazards, which helps to explain the need for communication as a means of coping with contingency."[12] Regarding learning in this context, Christian Pfister distinguishes between "what" knowledge (observation, classification, measurement of natural phenomena, and the establishment of governing principles and regularities) and "how" knowledge (techniques, practices, instructions).[13] Performance, Mauelshagen notes, improves with repetition, and innovation occurs when learning leads to the modification of existing processes or the development of new strategies to reduce future vulnerability.[14] History can be helpful in thinking about and responding to natural disasters today and not simply, with hindsight, in the past. Rene Favier and Anne-Marie Garnet-Abisset write that the historiography of disaster has largely focused on three main issues: agrarian and demographic concerns; the development of individual and communal coping strategies; and the environmental causes and consequences of disasters.[15] They call on historians as archival experts to analyze accumulated data on past disasters that can be used to place development and models into a broad chronological perspective.[16] In this way, we may actually learn from history; however, that means we must engage and think about history beyond mere examples of responses in particular contexts.

Historical records can provide evidence of cultural adaptation to environmental threats as well as examples of coping mechanisms during those difficult times.[17] As Christian Pfister notes, historical narratives in this context emphasize the importance of empirical evidence and provide flexibility in analyzing specific events—"They present the only means that allows us to project into the future while we are restricted to drawing exclusively on the past and what is known."[18] In addition to understanding specific contexts, then, a broad historical engagement with the environment allows us to observe larger trajectories and changes that may be helpful in new settings and conditions, especially the dramatic acceleration of the Anthropocene.

Another significant development in the study of history relates to the work of "deep ecology" and "deep history," which have attuned us to the need for and benefit of writing longer-term and more interconnected histories. There are, of course, opportunities and challenges in this work, which requires us to look beyond traditional methods and national and geographical boundaries.[19] But the benefits are substantial. Such depth and fluidity in engaging history afford us opportunities to contextualize ecosystems as well as the effects of long-term climate (and other) changes and the ecological trajectories that may result.[20] They can also allow for a certain "rewilding" and "restoration," even when we cannot fully know the original conditions of an environment or ecological system.[21] With this additional context, it is important to turn to the development and focus of environmental history—which often bridges such geographical, political, social, and temporal boundaries, and which challenges distinctions between nature and culture. This chapter will conclude by reexamining narrative and temporality, which are central to the work of history and can profitably be thought of in new and deeper ways, before considering the limitations and opportunities of history as a framework and discipline for engaging with climate change and the environment.

Environmental History

Learning and deep history represent two relatively recent emphases in the study of history. Another is interdisciplinary history, which engages across a wide range of scholarly fields, including Humanities, Social Sciences, and even Sciences. Environmental history is a relatively recent interdisciplinary field, with roots in the last half of the twentieth century, though by some accounts it can be traced back well into the nineteenth century.[22] While the study of climate (the average weather over time) might include physical and measurable forms of climate (e.g., temperature and precipitation), it is now commonly recognized that climate is more than these physical manifestations; it is in many important ways also a cultural construct.[23] As we will see, the boundaries between nature and culture are far from precise. Natural events have social impact and are interpreted through particular societal and cultural lenses.[24] As such, historians can bring important perspectives in studying nature and climate, including in the ways that technology intersects with and affects human-environment relations (and vice versa).[25]

Historians studying the environment bring some valuable and more general perspectives into the broader field of environmental humanities, as Andrew Isenberg details, including attention to change, causation, contingency, and context.[26] In fact, environmental historians bridge diverse academic disciplines, collecting and analyzing a range of data and materials from the natural sciences (natural archives) as well as the human and social sciences (human archives).[27]

The complexity of contemporary climate change challenges traditional notions of time and space,[28] as climate can be local, regional, hemispheric, or even global. Furthermore, environments are not linear, and they can change unpredictably.[29] Similarly, landscapes themselves are never pristine, but always hybrid[30] and the boundaries between nature and culture are porous.[31] Environmental history, therefore, reminds us that there are a variety of factors at play in historical change.[32] Discussions about the environment have often hinged on notions of experience. While experience has been typically considered as something related to and existing in the past, experience is also valuable for "memory" and for "judgement," and so it has present and future value as well.[33] As the intellectual historian Martin Jay observes, "Experience thus grows out of experimentation, which moves us into the future rather than tying us down to the past."[34]

Climate change has, in some ways, also blurred the distinctions between objects and subjects. Modernity tended to privilege the "'objective' instruments whose registering of stimuli from the external world were purportedly more accurate and disinterested" over the bodily learning derived from the senses.[35] Science, which was often seen as "objectively true," however, has itself increasingly been seen as a construct and regularly in need of revision.[36] And, as we now recognize society, science, and environment as in constant flux, we need more dynamic ways of thinking about each individually and together.[37]

New Historical Assumptions and Approaches: Nature and Culture

Given the emphases of environmental history, as well as some of the new, less binary ways of thinking about the past and human experiences, there are new opportunities to reconsider and reevaluate the relationship between humans and nature. Historians have for a long time segregated human and natural experiences and histories, but that way of thinking is being reconsidered. In explicating an American immanental theological framework, for example, Michael S. Hogue notes that "there is no outside of nature, nature is infinite and inexhaustible and it is without center or periphery."[38] In the context of the climate crisis, he writes that "Two interrelated assumptions about nature drive the human-centered patterns of thinking and behavior and meaning and value that have led us into the Anthropocene and the climate crisis: the idea that humans and nature are ontologically distinct from each other and the idea that nature is a fixed and stable backdrop to the dynamism of human culture and history."[39] Challenging these assumptions is key to making progress in addressing climate change and environmental crises.

The difficulty of seeing nature and culture as opposing, Bruno Latour points out, has been that such opposition leads to a simplistic and largely polemical notion of nature that serves other (human) ends. Superimposing human historical notions onto nature is also problematic. Latour notes that discourse about natural history is being framed by concepts of human history.[40] That is challenging since no discourse is neutral. Latour writes that "This claim of descriptive neutrality made it possible to forget that one never plunges into description except in order to act, and that, before looking into what must be done, we must be impelled to action by a particular type of utterance that touches our hearts in order to set us in motion—yes, to move us."[41] And, he argues, acting brings "one's existence, one's subsistence, *from the future toward the present.*"[42] The connection between narration and action here is intriguing, for the challenges it can create but also, as we will see in Part III, for potential solutions it offers as well. Latour's postmodern sensibilities also signal a move that connects future to present through action in ways that remind us of our ties and responsibilities beyond current temporalities.

Latour, among others, has reexamined the (modern) bifurcation of nature and culture, and he has suggested that they are not two separate domains, but rather two parts of one concept.[43] He cautions that "The concept of 'nature' now appears as a truncated, simplified, exaggeratedly moralistic, excessively polemical, and prematurely political version of otherness of the world to which we must open ourselves if we are not to become collectively mad—*alienated*, let us say."[44] For Latour, modernity allowed many people, especially the wealthy, to cross to another side, in which historicity ended. That is, an apocalypse has already occurred so that these people cannot comprehend that their world has ended and that they need to change their way of life[45]—"To rediscover meaning in the question of emancipation, *we have to free ourselves from the infinite*"[46] and "*To live in the time of the end* is first of all to accept the finitude of the time that passes and to put an end to negligence."[47]

Yosef Hayim Yerushalmi noted the ruptures of modernity and the separation of an organic sense of memory in which Jews were directly connected with their pasts, and an objectifying modern identity in which Jews wrote history as a way of connecting to a past to which they no longer had direct access. Yerushalmi famously referred to Jewish history as the faith of fallen Jews.[48] I have argued elsewhere that Yerushalmi's distinction is perhaps a bit too stark and that we need to examine more closely the nature of memory and historical thinking, the concepts of subjectivity and objectivity, and the characteristics of the rupture that he associates with aspects of modernity. Still, given the central role of modernity in the assessment of climate change and environmental degradation, there is an opportunity—indeed, a need—to consider these issues afresh.

In his work, Latour also problematizes the notion of intentionality. In discussing chemist James Lovelock and the concept of Gaia (a self-regulating and complex planet), he notes, for example, that the greater the intentionality of the individual actors, the less intentionality will be found in the whole of the organism.[49] However, Latour argues that "it is only when you feel the repercussions of your own action that you understand to what extent you are *responsible* for it."[50] The rebuff of the bifurcation of humanity and nature, and of the modern notion of history, is sometimes presented in what we might call a return to "indigenous" experiences that bridge the divide and pull us out of modernity and modernizing tendencies.

This move is well represented in the work of the French anthropologist Philippe Descola, who argues that in modern thought nature attains meaning only when "set in opposition to human works."[51] In modernity, he argues, humans move from being part of nature to being external and superior to it,[52] especially since the scientific advances of the seventeenth century that separated mechanistic and organicist worlds[53] and when the notion of "nature as an autonomous ontological domain, a field of inquiry and scientific experimentation, and object to be exploited and improved" gained supremacy.[54] However, Descola blurs the lines between the human and animal—and perhaps the rational and sympathetic—by noting that in some First Nation narratives and worldviews humans can become animals but also that animals can become humans as well as other animal species.[55] This means that "Their taxonomic grasp of reality is thus always contextual and relative, for the permanent swapping of appearances makes it impossible to attribute stable identities to the environment's living components"[56] As a result, humans relate to nonhumans just as they do to other humans[57] and that nonhumans in this perspective possess "a reflexive awareness and intentionality that enable them to experience emotions and exchange messages with both their peers and also members of other species, including humans."[58] As such, humanity is merely a "condition" and humans do not obtain a privileged position vis-à-vis other living beings.[59]

Furthermore, such a line of thinking serves to elevate the relationships between (and networks of) different individuals over what Descola calls a "construction of stable and mutually exclusive macrocategories."[60] The environment in this approach is what links everything together.[61] Rather than differentiate between human and nonhuman, some indigenous peoples, like the Chewong, differentiate based on geographic proximity. Descola observes that "rather than distinguish, deep down, between humans and nonhumans, they draw a line of demarcation between what is near and what is distant, between, on one hand, communities of persons of heterogenous aspects who nevertheless share the same mores and habitat and, on the other, the mysterious periphery where other languages and other laws hold sway."[62] Such an approach allows us to break free from the assumption that there is a deep divide between domestic and wild, for the wild is itself "highly socialized."[63]

The connection between humans and nature is much more complex than we often recognize or admit. Many writers have sought to address and deepen our understanding of this relationship. The environmental writer Wendell Berry, to take one prominent example, asserts that "People cannot live apart from nature; that is the first principle of the conservationists."[64] What is more, the notions of wildness and domesticity are not in opposition, but they are deeply interdependent.[65] Berry continues, "And yet, people cannot live in nature without changing it. But this is true of all creatures, they depend upon nature, and they change it. What we call nature is, in a sense, the sum of the changes made by all the various creatures and natural forces in their intricate actions and influences upon each other and upon their places."[66] The human and nature relationship is complex, interdependent, and changeable, which makes it hard to understand and negotiate, and perhaps even more important than a simple binary would suggest.

In this assessment, Berry posits significant differences between what he terms "two minds,"[67] which reflect two mindsets or worldviews. The Rational Mind, on one hand, believes in objective science and truth.[68] He concedes that "My own belief is that the Rational Mind has been performing impressively within the narrowly drawn boundaries of what it probably knows." However, "it has been doing badly in dealing with the things of which it is ignorant: the future, the mysterious wholeness and multiplicity of the natural world, the needs of human souls, and even the real bases of the human economy in nature, skill, kindness, and trust."[69] By contrast, the

> Sympathetic Mind would not forget that so-called environmental problems have causes that are in part political and therefore have remedies that are in part political. But it would not try to solve these problems merely by large-scale political protection of "the environment." It knows that they must be solved ultimately by correcting the way people use their home places and local landscapes.[70]

Berry recognizes that our knowledge can be limited and limiting when we get to the unknown or to systems that are too complex for our typical ways of understanding and analyzing.

Narrative(s)

The reconsideration of a starkly dichotomous way of thinking about humans and nature has led to and also been advanced by reflections of a more personal nature in the form of nature writing (essays, poetry, memoirs) and in the intersection of history and literature (including historical fiction), which have suggested alternate ways to think about the past and, importantly, possible future(s) as well. Such work opens us to different perspectives and areas of emphasis. It encourages different questions and topics. It has the potential to make historical experiences more relatable and poignant.

Wendell Berry's work highlights the importance of narratives in understanding and engaging with the environment. Narratives have been useful in a range of Humanities disciplines, but increasingly in the Sciences as well—consider the power of narrative medicine.[71] A central concern of history is storytelling, which holds out the promise of helping people to navigate complexity with stories that offer opportunities to make meaning and to connect more directly with the subject matter. Stories can also help to decenter the emphasis on separating subject and object, creating instead a more integrated and holistic perspective and worldview.

Rabbi Natan Margalit writes that "Our reductionist, atomistic perspective—seeing ourselves as isolated, free-floating individuals instead of as parts of a greater whole—has led to terrible harm to the living systems of the world, both biological and social."[72] The emphasis on systems thinking and complexity has been important for understanding and even reframing human relationships with nature.[73] Margalit points to such concepts as emergence, nestedness, bifurcation events, and tipping points.[74] These can be helpful as we complexify the modern notion and culture of control.[75] But in considering these issues, Margalit, like others, also points to the meaning that emerges from telling stories.[76]

A significant challenge in raising awareness about and addressing environmental crises is the distance between some people and the actual impact of environmental degradation, which makes it difficult to motivate people, to connect them with the suffering of others, and even to verify information and claims.[77] Information in and of itself does not, in any event, necessarily incentivize people to respond to climate and other environmental changes.[78] On one hand, information can be dubious—a situation exacerbated by the prevalence of post-truth and fake news—and the general reticence of people to change and the anxiety that many feel about the state of the world.[79] However, narratives such as storytelling and the use of specific imagery[80] have been identified as possible ways to more effectively engage people and change their behaviors. Maxwell Boykoff writes that "telling human stories about humans (e.g., about people affected by climate change and how they're responding to it), not necessarily scientific ones, can engage with new audiences and enhance possibilities for collective action."[81] But that is not true of just any stories. Dramatic and scary images can distance and disengage people, even if they can capture their attention.[82] More dialogical and conversation-based narratives can be more effective.[83] Even when we might disagree, broad framing and open discussion can be quite helpful.[84] Similarly, bridge building is more useful, in this case, than shaming others.[85]

Literature, like history (and historical narratives), can be a useful tool for engaging environmental issues. Aside from the narrative power that it brings, literature also provides evidence[86] and opportunities to test assumptions and engage with critical thinking. This is particularly true in futurological fiction, which also confronts people with and, to some extent, opportunities to experience a range of futures that result from contemporary actions.[87]

Temporality

One additional development in the study of history has been the willingness to examine multiple time periods (including the deep history I noted earlier in this chapter) and the interconnection between them. Some history, especially in an environmental context, has been willing to engage with the future in ways that traditional history would have avoided. Consider, for example, the recent work on "anticipatory environmental histories."[88] In addition to a future focus, some environmental history has taken a very long view of human development and the relationship between humans and the environment. This is a particularly helpful approach because environmental degradation and climate change have varying temporal contexts and impacts. Until recently (and still for some), climate change has seemed to be a far-off concern. We are learning that it requires a potentially long time span to address it in any significant ways.[89] But understanding the complex temporal interactions may be helpful to encourage collective commitment and action, especially as it becomes clearer how climate change plays out locally, in our daily lives and livelihoods, and the impact it may have beyond the local and on the futures that we can imagine even if we may not experience them ourselves.[90] Given these considerations, temporality is a significant consideration in historical, and also in ecological discussions. As Stephen Gardner notes,

> Temporal dispersion creates a number of problems. First, . . . the resilience of climate change implies that sustained action across many decades is required, and that this needs to anticipate (and so avoid or moderate) negative impacts that are some way off . . . Backloading makes it hard to grasp the connection between causes and effects, and this may undermine the motivation to act; it also implies that by the time we realize that things are bad, we will already be committed to much more change, undermining the ability to respond . . . Third, the deferral effect calls into question the ability of standard institutions to deal with the problem.[91]

The future is imbricated in the present in many deep ways. Gardner notes that future generations are vulnerable to present and past ones in what he terms a kind of "tyranny of the contemporary."[92] What is more, we seem to lack "the resources with which to deal with large-scale problems involving the long-term future."[93]

The issue of time, relative to environmental issues, has at times been seen as a result of modernization. However, the relation of time and modernity could move in somewhat different directions. According to one interpretative framework, on one hand, much like the alleged transition from subjectivity to objectivity, experience moved from an active exploration before modernity to a more passive perception with modernity. The German historian Reinhart Koselleck argues that the prior experience of time was "denaturalized" in modernity (1750–1850).[94] The verb "to experience," which previously denoted "exploration," "inquiry," and "trial" became more passive over time, he argues, the mere perception of objects absent a sense of movement and inquiry.[95] At the same time, modernity ushered in the sense of historical rupture as we noted above. Until the early modern period, Koselleck asserts, experience taught that the "future could bring nothing fundamentally new," and things remained fundamentally the same, at least until the end of the world.[96] Modern time, by contrast, "was identified with progress, since it was progress that conceptualized the difference between the past so far and the coming future."[97] Modernity, as we saw in Chapter 6, was associated with progress, among other things, and it crafted a more dynamic sense of the connection and possible relationship between different time periods even as part of the modern mindset led to the separation or rupture between periods.

In general, history seemed to be of limited value in addressing the future (and in some cases even the present).[98] The past as past seems "empirically verifiable," something that cannot be said about the future.[99] Still, Koselleck signals that "in every case, prognostics draws its evidence from previous experience that is treated scientifically. To this extent, forecasting the future is an art of combining data from diverse experiences."[100] Prognoses are possible to the extent that they are because there are formal structures in history that repeat, even if concrete expressions and experiences are unique.[101] Koselleck argues provocatively, that "the transformation of experience can also take place over the long term, gradually or in phases, beyond all spontaneous effects and unexpected turns, and thus modify all generation-conditioned, continuous, and ritualized experience: then, in a relatively short time, the previous framework of experience is entirely transformed in practice."[102] This kind of generational experience that history sometimes fosters can help create connections across longer periods of time. It is perhaps what Roy Scranton means when he quotes philosopher Hannah Arendt regarding the need to keep experiences a part of active conversation over time in order to activate thought:

> If it is true that all thought begins with remembrance, it is also true that no remembrance remains secure unless it is condensed and distilled into a framework of conceptual notions within which it can further exercise itself. Experiences and even the stories which grow out of what men do and endure, of happenings and events, sink back into the futility inherent in the living world and the living deed unless they are talked about over and over again. What saves the affairs of mortal men from their inherent futility is nothing but this incessant talk about them, which in its turn remains futile unless certain concepts, certain guideposts for future remembrance, and even for sheer reference, arise out of it. (On Revolution)[103]

So, history can engage with various temporal modalities beyond the past. Not that history predicts the present or future; however, history allows us to understand contexts and connections and construct meaning. Of course, the acceleration of change that we are witnessing in the Anthropocene complicates things a great deal. Koselleck admits that prognoses are becoming more difficult, even in short time spans, given the greatly increased complexity of the world.[104]

Despite the acceleration of modernity, history can take a lesson from literature, which at times helps us to imagine multiple (possible) futures. In his novel *Einstein's Dreams*, Alan Lightman engages playfully with notions of time as Einstein might have dreamt them. He writes that

> These three chains of events all indeed happen, simultaneously. For in this world, time has three dimensions, like space. Just as an object may move in three perpendicular directions, corresponding to horizontal, vertical and longitudinal, so an object may participate in three perpendicular futures. Each future moves in a different direction of time. Each future is real. At every point of decision . . . the world splits into three worlds, each with the same people but with different fates for those people. In time, there are an infinity of worlds.[105]

Historians often unearth multiple pasts, so a historical frame of thinking should not be troubled by multiple futures. This observation can also lead to intriguing questions about agency and causality—in both the past and future—and Lightman also addresses issues of causality. He writes, "Consider a world in which cause and effect are erratic. Sometimes the first precedes the second, sometimes the second the first. Or perhaps cause lies forever in the past while effect in the future, but future and past are entwined."[106] If history is not about monocausal pasts and comprehensive understanding of individual events, but rather a way of understanding and probing, the same sets of skills remain helpful for the future—not in the sense of learning what has worked or not, but perhaps in the sense of learning about the range of how people responded and what they learned, and importantly, how they reasoned. In that sense, history is a powerful tool that can complement other ways of thinking as we imagine environmental concerns as pressing case studies that may have no specific or even best answer but which require a diversity of considerations and strategies.

Given the significant changes associated with human-induced climate change, history may increasingly veer into areas that were once more properly in the realm of philosophy—including ethics—and even within its own traditional purview, history may have to reassess questions of intentionality, authority, and impact. Willis Jenkins argues that "Received ideas of justice do not anticipate moral agency exercised cumulatively across generational time, aggregately through ecological systems, and nonintentionally over evolutionary futures. Climate change involves dimensions of human action without precedent in our traditions and institutions of justice."[107] Jenkins finds, as a result, that ethics is challenged not by human power that can be evil and destructive but "by the difficulties of interpreting and taking responsibility for the complex and ambiguous story of humanity's social intelligence growing into a geophysical force."[108] Like others, he sees a challenge in differentiating social and environmental problems in the context of ethics,[109] and he notes the significance of economic and political considerations as much as the technical.[110] Climate change is a difficult problem; perhaps even a wicked problem as we explored in Chapter 6.[111] Climate change, Jenkins concludes, is less a problem that can be solved than "new and enduring relations of human power and thus new and enduring questions of responsibility."[112]

Conclusions: The Role and Limits of History

In a study that quickly became a classic—first as an article and then as an extended book-length analysis—the historian Dipesh Chakrabarty noted that the planetary climate crisis has led to a range of responses at various levels "ranging from denial, disconnect, and indifference to a spirit of engagement and activism of varying kinds and degrees."[113] Reflective of our observations above, for Chakrabarty, the crisis has disconnected the present and future and made both the past and the future feel incomprehensible from a historical perspective.[114]

In assessing this situation, Chakrabarty advanced four theses. According to the first, "Anthropogenic explanations of climate change spell the collapse of the age-old humanist distinction between natural history and human history."[115] As we have seen, the divide that was imposed between nature and humanity in past historical epochs is now effectively crossed. The climate crisis has upended the notion that the environment changes so slowly that it does not impact humans or human history. As is clear in the discussion of the Anthropocene, humans are now a geological force and not simply a biological agent.[116] In the fuller study, Chakrabarty observes that "humans have acquired the capacity to interfere with planetary processes but not necessarily—at least not as yet—the capacity to fix them."[117]

Chakrabarty's second thesis is that "The idea of the Anthropocene, the new geological epoch when humans exist as a geological force, severely qualifies humanist histories of modernity/globalization."[118] Many of the issues we have raised in this chapter and the previous one have been centered around notions of modernity and the changes associated with modernity. From Chakrabarty's perspective, we must deploy reason in a global sense, and we must develop new political imperatives. At the same time, "the crisis of climate change should produce anxieties precisely around futures that we cannot visualize"[119]—the very concern we have seen around futuring and proscription.

The third thesis builds on the second: "The geological hypothesis regarding the Anthropocene requires us to put global histories in conversation with the species history of humans."[120] This is the conversation, in a sense, between deep ecology and deep history—something far deeper than the *longe duree* structural history of the Annales school in the twentieth century. Chakrabarty admits that the climate crisis is related to "capitalist Management,"[121] as in the various metaphors associated with the Anthropocene, but it is also related to a deeper history: "The crisis of climate change calls for thinking simultaneously on both registers, to mix together the immiscible chronologies of capital and species history. This combination, however, stretches, in quite fundamental ways, the very idea of historical understanding."[122] Or, as he adds, "We need to connect deep and recorded histories and put geological time and the biological time of evolution in conversation with the time of human history and experience."[123]

In the final thesis, Chakrabarty argues that "The cross-hatching of species history and the history of capital is a process of probing the limits of historical understanding."[124] Chakrabarty notes that we experience parts of the crisis but not all of it.[125] As a result, we must recognize that there is a need for a global political approach without assuming a global identity.[126]

In unpacking the political implications of the climate crisis, Chakrabarty cites Hannah Arendt to argue that "*any* action undertaken with the aim of addressing climate change over a time span covering the lives of multiple generations is political."[127] That is, political action extends beyond the time of individual lives and, in addition, in relations between rich and poor, it also extends to the nonhuman world.[128]

The collapsing of multiple chronologies—including the history of the earth system, the history of life including human evolution, and the history of industrial civilization[129]—that Chakrabarty and others have identified has significant implications.[130] For Chakrabarty, it leads to a change in the human condition.[131] He asserts that "The climate crisis thus produces problems that we ponder on very different and often incompatible scales of time. Policy specialists think in terms of years, decades, at most centuries, while politicians in democracies think in terms of their electoral cycles."[132] This change can also lead to significant gaps between thought and action[133]—certainly a need to reconsider the gaps and connections. For example, Chakrabarty argues that

> Those who connect climate change causally to historical origins/formations of economic inequalities in the modern world raise valid questions about historical inequalities, but seeing it as the only cause not only reduces the problem of climate change to that of capitalism . . . it also blinds us to the action—or agency, if you will—of Earth system processes and their unhuman temporalities.[134]

History, and environmental history in particular, can provide us with valuable examples and models of human relationships with the environment and the variety of ways that humans have thought about and responded to environmental issues. They also signal some ways that historical thinking can be valuable in the future as we face new challenges. At the same time, history can force us to think in static ways that often assume certain things about agency, causality, time, and context that make it hard to understand and reconceptualize the world at times of dramatic and accelerated change. As we will see in the final chapter of this book, there are opportunities for learning from past experiences and leveraging new thinking about core historical concerns to help us today and in the future. But before we get there, we must examine religion, and especially for this project, Judaism—for religion provides a similar series of opportunities and challenges in addressing environmental degradation and climate change in a contemporary context.

Religion and the Environment

Some Traditional Assessments and Applications

Introduction: Religion as the Cause of Environmental Degradation: The Lynn White, Jr. Thesis and Beyond

Religion, especially in its more conservative expressions, has often been cast as opposed to environmentalism. In part, this is due to the notions of human exceptionalism and domination that many see in religious writings, particularly in the Judeo-Christian tradition and the story of creation. At the same time, religion (and even the same creation story) offers important ideas of stewardship and environmental justice, as well as a range of concepts and behaviors that can be important in addressing environmental challenges. These include repentance, which, as we saw in Part I often appeared in the guise of the "economy of sin," in which God punished people for their poor behavior; through repentance, people could potentially reverse the punishment. Other religiously relevant concepts include the idea of the covenant—which could be read as an agreement with the divine that entails both responsibility and obligation and real consequences for behavior (positive or negative)—as well as exile from the land, and Sabbath or rest (of God, humans, and the land), which could be valuable in crafting responses to the abuse of the environment. Some religious ideas, such as the apocalypse, could lead to either a sense that we should exploit the current world since it will end, or it could dredge up deep-seated fears for our souls in the next world, urging us to take care of others and the environment in this world.

In a famous article that has had a very long shelf life, the medieval historian Lynn White, Jr. associated environmental challenges with the thinking linked to a notion of domination that he argued was inherent in the Judeo-Christian biblical and religious traditions. In a seminal essay, "The Historical Roots of Our Ecological Crisis," published in 1967, he argued that,

In sharp contrast, Christianity inherited from Judaism not only a concept of time as nonrepetitive and linear but also a striking story of creation. By gradual stages a loving and all-powerful God had also created light and darkness, the heavenly bodies, the earth and all its plants, animals, birds, and fishes. Finally, God had created Adam and, as an afterthought, Eve to keep man from being lonely. Man named all the animals, thus establishing his dominance over them. God planned all of this explicitly for man's benefit and rule: no item in the physical creation had any purpose save to serve man's purposes. And, although man's body is made of clay, he is not simply part of nature: he is made in God's image. . . . By destroying pagan animism, Christianity made it possible to exploit nature on a mood of indifference to the feelings of natural objects. . . . Both our present science and our present technology are so tinctured with orthodox Christian arrogance toward nature that no solution for our ecologic crisis can be expected from them alone. Since the roots of the trouble are so largely religious, the remedy must also be essentially religious, whether we call it that or not.[1]

White argued that Christianity (more specifically, the Judeo-Christian tradition) inherited a creation story that sees humans as made in God's image and outside of nature in some regards, leading to an arrogant sense of domination over nature and indifference to nature (and its objects).

Many scholars have pointed out that White's thesis is too simplistic and not completely accurate. But the controversy stoked by the argument led to a significant examination of themes related to the Bible, religion more generally, and the environment. As we saw in Part I, there is a strong tradition of associating divine punishment, in the form of various natural disasters, with human sin. Indeed, biblical literature, like much other writing, appears to see environmental problems as moral dilemmas.[2] Given this general orientation, it is not difficult to see why White's thesis struck a nerve.

It was not all bad news, though. If White argued that Western Christianity (and the Judeo-Christian tradition more broadly) was culpable in the environmental crisis, he also argued that it held solutions at the same time.[3] It has been pointed out that White's later writings actually provide a description of some ways Christianity can, in fact, positively address environmental concerns, including through progressive revelation, the embrace of minority interpretations, and the replacement of anthropocentrism.[4]

If White was focused on the theme of domination, it has been pointed out that there is another side of the human relationship with the divine as outlined in the biblical text related to stewardship and cultivation of nature. Some scholars have maintained that the concept of stewardship of nature is, in fact, as central as any notions of domination that exist in Western religion.[5] As the late chief rabbi of the United Hebrew Congregations of the Commonwealth, Rabbi Jonathan Sacks wrote, glossing Gen. 2:15:

"The Lord God took the man and put him in the Garden of Eden to work it (serve) and to guard it": The two Hebrew verbs used here are significant. The first— le'ovdah—literally means "to serve it." The human being is thus both master and servant of nature. The second—leshomrah–means "to guard it." This is the verb used in later biblical legislation to describe the responsibilities of a guardian of property that belongs to someone else. This guardian must exercise vigilance while protecting, and is personally liable for losses that occur through negligence. This is perhaps the best short definition of humanity's responsibility for nature as the Bible conceives it.[6]

It is precisely this strand of stewardship that many "green religious" movements have emphasized in their theology and activities. In Protestantism, for example, Michael S. Northcott argues, nature was gradually desacralized based on growing individualism and the belief in progress, and yet at the same time, Protestantism "proved fertile ground for a new 'turn to nature' as a subject of post-Reformation art and as a source of moral redemption and spiritual inspiration for the inhabitants of early industrial cities and towns in the New World and in Europe."[7]

Still, the limitations of such stewardship have been pointed out by others.[8] Despite "green" traditions in many religions, religion in a Western context is often still seen as supporting a doctrine of human domination of the natural world. Humans, after all, were given power to name the animals and were created in the image of God. As a result, right-leaning religious groups, especially in Christian traditions, are often characterized as adherents of climate change skepticism.[9] While recent research suggests greater diversity in attitudes about the environment, even in more fundamentalist circles,[10] there is still evidence that "a larger, more politically engaged contingent was convinced that the climate was not changing at all—or, if it was changing, that humans were not the cause and/or that the changes would not be catastrophic."[11] In addition to evangelical concerns with end times,[12] the battle with secular and liberal culture (and modernity)—and the sense of being attacked by it[13]—has affected much of the climate change discussion in these circles; and as climate change is associated with secular and liberal circles, ascribing to the same or similar ideas can lead to social isolation.[14]

Some evangelicals are nonetheless engaging in discussions about climate change, but in ways that may seem less familiar in traditional environmental parlance; they are instead leveraging religious terms and sensibilities and framing their own thoughts as part of their evangelical identity.[15] Religious Studies professor Robin Globus Veldman notes that many evangelicals advocate a "practical environmentalism," with a heavily inflected local concern: "they maintained that human treatment of the natural world should be governed by common sense, in keeping with local mores, apolitical, enacted at the individual level, locally scaled, and proudly anthropocentric."[16] Unfamiliar with some issues like habitat loss and threats to biodiversity, they often advocate a common sense approach to care for the environment,[17] based in large part on their own experiences in nature.[18] Aligned with this position is the tendency to believe that social, and also environmental, issues are more related to individual choices than broader systems or structures.[19] There are some groups within the evangelical umbrella, like Adventists, that do view environmentalism positively,[20] and, in any event, even some groups that have been seen as in the climate skepticism camp, such as Southern Baptists, are not a monolithic group of climate skeptics.[21]

While evangelicals, broadly speaking might agree that people need to take care of the environment, they often do articulate that notion within the context of human domination over the earth.[22] Drawing from the Bible, the environment and discussions about it continue to exist in a framework related to human sin.[23] At the same time, believing in climate change could, in these circles, be akin to a lack of faith in divine omnipotence.[24] What is more, for those firmly ensconced in biblical texts and ideas, there is a lack of clear scriptural guidance on climate issues.[25] Religious climate skeptics may be motivated by a number of concerns. One is related to justice; they worry that climate action might negatively impact economies and economic growth and hence, along the way, hurt the poor.[26] What is clear is that religion offers a range of, at times, even conflicting, ways to understand and respond to climate change and natural disasters. Attitudes about the environment can be complicated and layered and take on different meanings in different contexts.

Some Jewish Contributions to the Discussion

While some scholars have associated the desacralization of nature with the rise of monotheism,[27] others have offered a more nuanced range of options. Here, the discussion about and within Judaism is instructive. As some have noted, Judaism values preservation and protection of nature, but it also views nature as something that is to be used. As David Vogel cautions, "while Judaism may be consistent with many contemporary environmental values and doctrines, its teachings are not identical to them."[28] In commenting on the rabbinic text "Rabbi Ya'akov says: One, who while walking along the way, reviewing his studies, breaks off from his study and says, 'How beautiful is that tree! How beautiful is that plowed field!' Scripture regards him as if he has forfeited his soul," environmental anthropologist Jeremy Benstein identifies three broad approaches of rabbinic Judaism to nature: subordination, in which nature is denigrated and revelation and study of Torah are elevated; a more moderate and prevalent approach that recognizes creation as subordinate to revelation but still recognizes and values the acts of creation; and, finally, the position that all nature reflects divine action and can teach us about God.[29]

Rabbinic writings at times elevated the natural world in discussing God's creation. According to a midrash (Kohelet Rabbah), when God created Adam, God led him around the Garden of Eden and said: "Look at My works! How beautiful and praiseworthy they are. Everything that I have created, I created for you. Take care not to damage and destroy My world, for if you destroy it, there is no one to repair it after you."[30] Rabbinic culture also clearly articulates a notion of thanksgiving that individuals must express when utilizing nature. In the Babylonian Talmud Tractate Berakhot (35a), for example, it is related that "The Sages taught in a Tosefta: One is forbidden to derive benefit from this world, which is the property of God, without reciting a blessing beforehand. And anyone who derives benefit from this world without a blessing, it is as if he is guilty of misuse of a consecrated object."[31]

Indeed, despite the critique of Judeo-Christian traditions, when it comes to the environment many biblical stories and passages attest to a more complex relationship with nature and the earth. Biblical scholar Mari Joerstad writes, "Torah does not ease responsibility, it increases it. Israel is expected to act with circumspection in every part of its life; dietary laws, agricultural precepts and cultic regulations suggest that carelessness is not only unfortunate, but dangerous and destructive."[32] What is more, the concept of environment can have many meanings[33] and the place of humanity in ecology is complex.[34] In the context of the Bible, Jewish Studies scholar Hava Tirosh-Samuelson argues that the biblical text can be read in numerous and conflicting ways,[35] but that "The most distinctive feature of biblical environmental legislation is the causal connection between the moral quality of human life and the vitality of God's creation."[36] She concludes that Jewish environmental ethics is characterized by several core features: it focuses on human obligations toward nature, action in specific contexts, long-term perspective taking and sustainability of human practice, and the common good (aligning social justice and environmental well-being).[37] The diversity of Jewish theological approaches to nature throughout time is, according to Tirosh-Samuelson, the result of the various contexts in which Jews have lived as well as the theological agendas of the rabbis themselves.[38]

The rabbis noted the significant dependence that people had on the world and the elements. In the Midrash Bereshit Rabbah (13:3–8), to take one example, it is noted that

> "Because the Lord God did not cause it to rain upon the earth"—it mentions a complete name in association with a completed world. Rabbi Ḥilfai said: Just as it mentions a complete name for a complete world [in that verse], so it mentions a complete name [here,] regarding rainfall.
>
> Rabbi Shimon bar Yoḥai said: Three matters are of equal importance to one another, and they are: Earth [eretz], man [adam], and rain [matar]. Rabbi Levi bar Ḥiyya said: The three of them are each of three letters, to teach you that if there is no earth there is no rain, and if there is no rain there is no earth, and without the two of them, there is no man.[39]

Nevertheless, Tirosh-Samuelson has suggested that Jewish Studies and Jewish environmentalism have not always been closely aligned or in step:

> The preponderance of activism and advocacy in Jewish environmentalism explains why the academic discipline of Jewish studies has been rather slow to respond to the growing Jewish interest in environmentalism for the following reasons: First, the academic study of Judaism is decidedly textual, whereas environmentalism cares about material and social reality outside the texts. Second, the academic study of Judaism is committed to disinterested and objective analysis of the past, whereas Jewish environmentalism is about the present; and third, whereas academic study of Judaism is interested in theory for its own sake, Jewish environmentalism is primarily interested in praxis for the sake of addressing acute and compelling social problems.[40]

As we have seen, in engaging with White's thesis, numerous Jewish and Christian scholars turned first to the texts cited by White as well as the long interpretative traditions of these texts. The result has been both rebuttal and reframing. The Jewish medievalist Jeremy Cohen, for example, offered a deep and trenchant review of the relevant biblical passages identified by White, as well as subsequent commentary on these passages. He concluded that "Rarely, if ever, did premodern Jews or Christians construe this verse [Gen 1:28] as a license for the selfish exploitation of the environment."[41] Examining the response to White's thesis, Cohen points out that the various words often isolated in the passage to refer to domination actually do not denote consumption or exploitation of other creatures and instead might refer to peaceful dominion.[42] Donning a biblical critical hat, Cohen notes that the biblical author/redactor P wrote in the context of the destruction of the temple, which led to a theology of despair, but one that also led to stress on God's covenant with Israel and God's control of history.[43] Citing Jewish theologian Michael Fishbane, Cohen suggests that divine dominion over humans leads to boundaries and subservience as well as autonomous agency of humans.[44] Indeed, it has been noted that some traditional Jewish sources emphasized the responsibility that humans were given as much as any domination.[45] In this world, human beings straddle relations with the natural world and God;[46] Cohen writes that "The idea that human beings straddled the colloquial fence dividing heavenly (spiritual) and earthly (material) worlds, blending characteristics of both somehow marking the point of transition between them, enjoyed considerable popularity in ancient and medieval thought."[47]

Some Key Aspects of Religion and the Environment

Through the balance reflected in the domination vs. stewardship narratives, as well as new ways of thinking about religion as an active and changing concept (see Chapter 9), there are several ways that religion—and I would argue Judaism in particular—can help us to adjust our attitudes and behaviors toward the environment. Some of these were evident already in the historical cases that we examined in Part I. Others rely on interpretations of core religious texts and theological ideas. Still others have emerged as we have begun to think about religion in new, more contemporary—perhaps postmodern—ways.

In addition to the sometimes varied—and contested—notion of stewardship, it has been argued that religion can foster social connection and collective action.[48] Before we turn to some of the exciting discussions of religion over the past generation, it is worth noting that religion—even in its older or more traditional manifestations—has a good deal to offer when it comes to thinking about the environment in the past, present, and even future. Religious and theological ideas often intersect with a range of ethical and philosophical discussions. In what follows, we will consider some of these considerations, especially as they play out in questions of repentance, responsibility, covenant, contraction, fighting idolatry (broadly defined and especially as reflected in a critique of modernity), and social justice.

Repentance and Grief

While the Hebrew Bible records many instances of punishment for sin—especially the sin of disloyalty to God—that involve curses, some in the form of natural disasters, these same texts also discuss and offer the opportunity for repentance.[49] Such repentance is often seen to include confession of guilt, humbling the self and returning to proper observance of divine precepts, restitution, and accepting the punishments for sin.[50] In many biblical texts, God seems to assume that humans will voluntarily repent[51] and that repentance can lead to a new beginning.[52] Related to repentance are a range of concepts that involve reflection and change of attitude and behavior.

Grief is one concept that has been discussed more frequently in recent years in relation to climate change and human responsibility for climate change. Leslie Davenport introduces grief as containing a "powerful transformative component" that can prepare us for change[53] (as we find in repentance as well). She identifies five stages of climate grief: denial, anger, bargaining, depression, and acceptance.[54] She similarly articulates seven perspectives that guide the work of self-care for therapists that can be helpful in addressing climate grief: connection, deep listening, creativity, presence, commitment, resolute compassion, and resiliency.[55] Davenport notes that people are not very likely to change their behavior based only on data.[56] In fact, we know that once set in their ways, data that conflicts with people's views often serves to make people entrench further and hold their ideas more firmly (see the discussion on polarization).

Some emotions can keep us from acting. In a religious setting, some theologians have noted that the apocalyptic sensibilities that religion can produce and promote can feel overwhelming. Davenport refers to these as "apocalypse fatigue,"[57] leading to inaction or overwhelm. Humans, after all, are more likely to prioritize, and rationalize, immediate concerns over longer-term considerations.[58] What is more, we can sometimes be convinced that products or actions are more environmentally friendly (more green) than they are—what Davenport refers to as "greenwashing."[59]

One can experience "empathy burnout," especially when witnessing the greater impact on certain groups and the inequity of climate change. While individuals can experience trauma in their own ways, communal recollections of experiences, in which "the past becomes a collective story of grief, and compassionate bonds help build emotional buoyancy among members helping to facilitate the healing process"[60] that also leads to "redemptive moments."[61] Arguing that only crisis produces real change, Davenport asserts that although trauma can narrow the window of tolerance,[62] love of place can spur people to action.[63]

Responsibility[64]

Relatedly, a good deal of more recent discussions about climate change has focused on human responsibility—to other humans today and especially in the future, as well as to animals and other life forms. Responsibility is a complicated concept, and there are open questions about whether all people have the same responsibilities when it comes to the environment, given the unequal harm and benefits that humans in modernity have inflicted on the environment and on different groups (often at the expense of other groups).[65] Responsibility is, in some important ways, related to notions of stewardship that have religious as well as social and political hues.[66] Of course, these discussions are closely intertwined with how people understand and think about the past and future.[67] For the philosopher Emmanuel Levinas, therefore, responsibility was "responsibility for the Other, thus as responsibility for what is not my deed, or for what does not even matter to me, or which precisely does matter to me, is met by me as face."[68]

Traditional Jewish texts offer opportunities to reflect on notions of responsibility. In the Babylonian Talmud, tractate Shabbat 54b, we read, for example:

> Whoever is able to protest against the transgressions of his own family and does
> not do so is held responsible for the transgression of his family. Whoever is able
> to protest against the transgressions of the people of his community and does not
> do so is held responsible for the transgressions of his community. Whoever is able
> to protest against the transgressions of the entire world and does not do so is held
> responsible for the transgressions of the entire world.[69]

The text raises important considerations around protesting (moral, ethical, religious,
and other) transgressions in a variety of settings. In an environmental context, this
is a powerful text, for it also signals that when we do not protest, we share in the
responsibility of the transgressors themselves.

Sustainability

While many of the challenges associated with environmental degradation, and
specifically climate change, are new, some have been discussed for a long time and relate
to fundamental concerns about human values and ethics. In that sense, both history
and religion may help us think through a range of behavioral and moral considerations
in these challenging times.[70] As Jeremy Benstein has suggested, we need technological
and textual skills as we navigate these changes.[71] As he points out, religious texts may
need to be interpreted to help us address contemporary issues, especially since, as we
have seen, many aspects of Judaism (and other religions) are not inherently positively or
negatively inclined toward the environment.[72] Still, Judaism, like other faith traditions,
offers valuable insights about notions of sustainability: "a sustainable society is one that
integrates social, environmental, and economic concerns of health and justice, and
can both *sustain itself* over time, living up to responsibilities to future generations, as
well as *sustain* and *nourish* its members, materially and spiritually, in the present and
in the future."[73] Benstein concludes that the environmental crisis is less a crisis of the
environment than it is of ourselves and our thought and behavior:[74]

> it is not our conception of the human as sovereign that is the constitutive feature
> of environmental degradation. Rather, it is our view of nature as mere stuff, as
> so much raw material and replaceable parts, coupled with belief in unlimited
> technological potential to invent or replace the "spare parts," that has led to the
> absence of moral responsibility and the enabling of ecological destruction. . . .
> The converse is also true: the frequent *inability* to experience those deeply human,
> and deeply religious, emotions stem from the complete transformation of nature
> into commodities, and therefore the diminution of the self to a one-dimensional
> consumer, someone who uses nature but doesn't live in it.[75]

In threading the diverging creation stories of Genesis, Benstein writes that because
humans are created able to transcend nature, they are simultaneously directed to
protect it as well.[76] For Benstein, dichotomizing the spiritual and physical "means
that spirituality is de-physicalized, with no bodily expression, and physicality is
de-spiritualized, lifeless and inert."[77] However, in reality, we are both separate from

and interdependent upon the world.[78] Similarly, we must look at the impact of our actions on future generations while remaining grounded in the here and now, paying attention to the impact of our actions in the present.[79] Benstein advocates for a model that is related to a "rooted identity" and a "portable sanctity," "in varying combinations, relations, and dosages in different places and periods,"[80] a combination of the dynamic between wandering and return.[81]

In his well-known *The Lonely Man of Faith*, the orthodox Jewish thinker Joseph B. Soloveitchik offered an examination of the two biblical accounts of the creation of humans. The results of his reflections add further depth to the conceptions and considerations above. In addressing the duality of the creation accounts, Soloveitchik turns the duality into an opportunity to explore various conditions and natures of humans as well. He writes that

> the answer lies not in an alleged dual tradition but in dual man, not in an imaginary contradiction between two versions but in a real contradiction in the nature of man . . . Adam the first received the mandate from the Almighty to fill the earth and subdue it. Adam the second was charged with the duty to cultivate the garden and to keep it . . . God, in imparting the blessing to Adam the first and giving him the mandate to subdue nature, directed Adam's attention to the functional and practical aspects of his intellect through which man is able to gain control of nature . . . Hence Adam the first is aggressive, bold, and victory-minded. His motto is success, triumph over the cosmic forces. He engages in creative work, trying to imitate his Maker (*imitation Dei*) . . . In order to answer this triple question [Why is it? What is it? Who is it?], Adam the second does not apply the functional method invented by Adam the first. He does not create a world of his own. Instead, he wants to understand the living, "given" world into which he has been cast. Therefore, he does not mathematize phenomena or conceptualize things. He encounters the universe in all its colorfulness, splendor, and grandeur, and studies it with the naivete, awe, and admiration of the child who seeks the unusual and wonderful in every ordinary thing and event.[82]

This and other approaches we have noted challenge the notion of the monolithic domination of nature that many have read into Biblical narratives and religious history. They also help us to understand core values and approaches to the world that are embedded in religious thought and behavior.

Covenant

In the biblical text, God enters into a covenant with the Israelites. Covenant has been seen as one way to approach the issue of the human relationship to nature and the divine. Covenant also raises important questions about the particular and universal— what are the specific conditions of the covenant, to whom do they apply, and under what circumstances? Discussing the prolific Jewish theologian Yitz Greenberg's notion of multiple covenantal communities,[83] interfaith scholar Alon Goshen-Gottstein quotes Greenberg at length:

The fundamental and universal biblical statement is that God wants creation (the world as it is now) to be redeemed. Out of love for humanity, God imposes self limits and calls humans to be partners in the process of *tikkun olam*. God commits to uphold the laws of nature that allow humans to live constructive, dignified lives within the framework of a stable, dependable, natural order. Humans pledge to live in harmony with the rhythms of the universe—that is, God's plan—to increase life and improve nature and society to fully sustain the value of life, especially human life with its fundamental dignities. This is the universal covenant with all humanity, biblically called the covenant of Noah. This covenant is never superseded. Every religion that accepts these values and goals derives its legitimacy directly, its direct access to God and its partnership with the Deity from this covenant open to all people, all the time.[84]

Goshen-Gottstein also explores the particular aspects of covenants that are relational and create moral communities—and so are also pluralistic.[85] As such, there are two biblical covenants—one with humanity (Adam and Noah) and one with the people of Israel (from Abraham to Moses).[86]

The Jewish notion of covenant signals, for some thinkers, that a relationship between the earth and its owner does not mean that the "owner" prevails in that relationship.[87] Jewish discussions of the very nature of humans—as created in the image of God—can lead to multiple interpretations (and not just the sense that humans can dominate nature).

The relationship between humans and God and the associated moral and ethical considerations is developed by many different thinkers. Lawrence Troster, for example, argued that

These three interpretations of *tzelem* present a composite portrait of humanity as a nexus between God and the natural world. As the *tzalmu* of God, humanity is the physical extension of God's power and presence on earth. Having characteristics of both "higher" and "lower" creatures, and of our earthly origin and limitations as well. Finally, our consciousness provides us with the self-awareness to realize our responsibilities to God and to the earth which we tend.[88]

Covenant has been a powerful theological concept and it has great significance in framing and deepening the relationship between humans and God as well as humans and nature.

Fighting Idolatry

In exploring the theme of idolatry, Goshen-Gottstein offers another important theological contribution that can help to enhance the discussion of environmental concerns. He notes that idolatry can be seen as worship of the part at the expense of the whole.[89] In his discussion of the Sabbath, he points out that "The Sabbath teaches us where our control over nature ends and where God's dominion is affirmed," leading to a contrast "between lording over nature and being a part of a greater totality."[90] This resonates with discussions of responsibility as well as the interaction of particular and universal sensibilities, which are often central to religious discussions, especially when chosenness is involved. Indeed, Shaul Magid, in discussing the theology of Arthur Green, argues that "Judaism is idolatry the extent to which it focuses on its exclusivity, and exceptionalism, certainly chauvinism, in relation to God."[91] On one hand, divine truth is expressed in the "oneness and unity of all creation";[92] at the same time, God is infinitely fragmented into all things.[93]

The concept of idolatry has particular valence in the context of the critique of modernity (the "idolatries of modernity"), which has been associated with ecological devastation. Eilon Shamir sharpens this critique of modernity, with a particular emphasis on unrestrained capitalism:

> the connection with capitalist culture is clear: consumption culture is based on the belief that money and objects whose value can be expressed with money are the answer to our wishes, our needs, our wills. And the will is not static. It can be shaped and manipulated so we want more than we have. We will always want more, because we believe these objects will fulfill our inner needs. Thus, the more we buy the more we add fuel to the engine of late capitalist economy. . . . Yet, we remain dissatisfied, because we don't find answers to our anxieties, to the void in our heart. The will, the center of the self, becomes disintegrated. We become confused. We don't know what we really want anymore. We chase shadows in order to escape our confusion, our inner doubts, and our fears, but we don't find answers, so we continue compensating by chasing, more and more.[94]

The anti-modern and anti-capitalist sentiment that is sometimes linked to the climate crisis has been connected with the concept of idolatry by other scholars as well. Haviva Pedaya points to a four-fold expression of idolatry that underscores the challenges associated with modernity. Pedaya notes the issue of selfishness (a worship of self rather than God), the trampling of social morality in the pursuit of power and money, and the confluence of religion and state or nationalism, as well as a fourth idolatry—"the destruction of the environment to the point of threatening our very survival on Earth in the name of insatiable corporate greed."[95] Jonathan Wittenberg also elevates the preoccupation with self in modernity as a significant challenge.[96] One antidote to this self-centeredness, he argues, is to restore the sense of awe and wonder and reverence for and before all living things[97]—and God's presence in nature.[98]

Morality and Social Justice

David Aberbach notes that environmental disaster follows moral collapse in the Hebrew Bible and that human misbehavior literally scars the landscape, as morality and the environment are often merged, and nature in the Hebrew Prayerbook can itself be seen as Torah.[99] The Bible, he argues, is less concerned with theology than the earth and human behavior, especially given the Bible's agricultural contexts.[100] Aberbach asserts further that "The Bible weeps for the alienation from Nature, for the loss of innocence, the twisted dark of the human heart. The natural world demands reverence, being divinely created, a gift to humankind. Human dominance is temporary and conditional."[101] On the other hand, the natural world represents justice and truth.[102] As such, the landscape represents connection with the divine.[103] And yet, humans retain free will to choose their behavior, unlike nature, which is created holy, as the voice of God.[104] As a reflection of this, Torah is a tree of life and trees provide guidance and advice (therefore, deforestation often follows the disasters of things such as drought and war throughout the Bible).[105] In this sense, humans may have dominion at various times, but such dominion is actually temporary and contingent on their moral behavior.[106] Property ownership in the Bible, according to this reading, is not permanent, and restraint and regularity are core to moral virtue.[107]

Indeed, the scholars of the rabbinic period often connected human and natural behavior, particularly through their interpretation of biblical passages. The famous Rabbi Akiba, for example, leveraged biblical passages to associate the lack of rain with punishment for neglecting pilgrimage and certain religious rituals.[108] Other rabbinic figures made explicit connections between rain and the performance of various ritual aspects of the holiday of Sukkot. According to Jeffrey Rubinstein,

> Even if the liturgical "mention" of rain developed after the destruction, this connection to Sukkot rituals represents a desire for continuity with temple practices. Just as the festival temple ceremonies were directed towards rain, so the liturgical "mention" oriented the rabbinic celebration of the festival towards rain. With the destruction of the temple prayer became the main vehicle for petition and was no longer ancillary to cultic ritual.[109]

Aspects of nature and the environment are, in these ways, core to religious belief and practice, and they have particular significance for morality and ethical behavior.

Tzimtzum—Contraction

The theological notion of divine contraction—tzimtzum—received a good deal of attention in kabbalistic thought and it has been usefully employed in commenting on human behavior and addressing ecological issues in contemporary thought. In his extensive treatment of the history of the concept, Christoph Schulte writes that

> Zimzum, human self-restraint in response to the use and abuse of natural resources, is an ecological imperative today, theological overtones aside. Hans Jonas's "ecological imperative" that stipulates that we should "act so that the effects of [our] action are compatible with the permanence of genuine human life" is not possible without humans exercising reasonable self-restraint with the earth's natural elements and resources . . . Ecologically responsible self-restraint as one of the options is not the renunciation of action, but rather the responsible, active, productive choice of a different course of action, one that allows new things to continue to emerge and makes it possible for the people on this planet to live in health, freedom, and dignity. Even God, as kabbalists, artists, theologians, and

philosophers imagine him, does not always use all his power and possibilities. He remains creative and free for this very reason.[110]

Here, the notion of divine contraction is seen as parallel to human self-restraint, especially in the context of the environment. Contemporary Jewish theologian Shai Held similarly notes that "These twin notions of *tzimtzum* suggest that God is radically present while still making space for us. . . . we must be present while making space; we must make space while remaining present."[111] The notions of contraction and presence (and when we need each) draw from long-established religious traditions and thinking and can still be valuable as we think about human responsibilities and actions generally and specifically as related to environmental issues. While there is value in shrinking our footprint, so to speak, we must also do so with intentionality and consciousness if we are to have a more significant impact.

Practice

Like other religions, Judaism has a few principles and practices (including around kashrut) that have been much discussed in the context of environmentalism (in the form of eco-kashrut, for example). Perhaps the most prominent is *bal tashchit*, the prohibition against wasteful destruction.[112] This practice is based on a relatively small number of textual sources, especially interpretations of a passage from Deuteronomy, which describes what constitutes proper behavior during a time of war, along with a number of rabbinic prohibitions.[113]

In explicating the concept of wasteful destruction, there is an extensive discussion in the Talmud (Babylonian Talmud tractate Bava Kamma 91b-92a):

> In connection with the prohibition against cutting down trees the Gemara notes: Rav said with regard to a palm tree that still produces fruit in the amount of a *kav*, that it is prohibited to cut it down due to the prohibition of: "When you shall besiege a city . . . you shall not destroy the trees." (Deuteronomy 20:19, Sefaria)

In a typical analytical approach, the rabbis of the Talmud ask how much fruit must be on an olive tree that would prohibit it from being cut down. The response is a quarter of the same measure (quarter-kav), because olive trees are different, and more significant, than palm trees. As the passage unfolds, Rabbi Hanina reports that his son died because he cut down a fig tree before its time. With a practical bent, however, Ravina adds that a tree might be cut down despite the prohibition if the monetary value of its lumber is greater than that of its fruit. The discussion continues about what types of trees might be cut down, which includes trees that are not for food; though some trees that bear fruit may also be cut down in certain circumstances. Still, precedence is given to cut down barren trees before trees whose fruit is used for food.

The value of trees in this discussion is related to what they produce, lending a set of economic considerations to the issue.[114] However, as Eilon Schwartz notes, "Death as divine punishment for cutting down the tree, even though it is permitted by the halachah, certainly demands that we relate to *bal tashchit* as something far more substantial than simply respecting the economic value of fruit-producing trees for human society."[115] Along the way, some rabbinic discussions emphasize other issues—such as prohibitions to injure oneself.[116]

Added to these are many medieval and modern commentaries around the destruction associated with cutting down trees.[117] In discussing the medieval commentaries, Schwartz writes that

> Human responsibility for the tree is based on human dependence upon the tree. Trees are a source of food and thus cutting them down reduces the food supply available after the siege. [The medieval scholar] Ramban [Moses ben Nachman] goes on to suggest that such an act is a sign of loss of faith, for the trees are being cut down to help in the siege. The soldiers, not believing that God will lead them to victory, destroy their own future food supply, fearful that the day of victory will never come.[118]

The medieval Jewish philosopher and legal scholar Maimonides [Moses ben Maimon] argued that the prohibition of destruction extends to the destruction of household goods, buildings, springs, and food.[119] *Bal tashchit* was also seen in the context of excessive consumption, in which consumption beyond necessity is akin to destruction.[120] However, mitigating this sentiment is the notion that human comfort and enjoyment should also not be forsaken.[121] There are other things that override *bal tashchit* as well, including honoring royalty, observing mitzvot (commandments), and some educational considerations.[122] Schwartz concludes that there are multiple approaches to *bal tashchit* in Jewish tradition. A minimalist position that "has human needs and wants taking precedence over the rest of creation," is the more dominant position. However, it is counterbalanced by a maximalist position that "has human wants counterbalanced with the legitimate claims of the natural world."[123]

In Jewish ethics, Schwartz sees morality as transcendent of the natural world.[124] The Bible, he claims is less concerned with nature as "a pristine state of the world" than "a temporal reality that needs to be redeemed."[125] Within Judaism, legal considerations are often more prominent than ethical ones, and so there is more of a focus on practical duties rather than rights.[126] Schwartz notes that "Judaism's relationship with the natural world is far more ambivalent than that with which many Jewishly committed environmentalists would feel comfortable."[127] He contends that "Judaism has traditionally offered a plurality of approaches, each moving dangerously close to extremes, but with safeguards to insure remaining within acceptable boundaries."[128]

Are there other Jewish experiences, concepts, or texts that have been, or could be, leveraged in the throes of the challenges of the Anthropocene? Laurie Zoloth argues that "the traditions, histories, and texts of Jewish thought address precisely the sort of existential crisis that we face now, and thus deepen and enrich our public discourse about what to do, how to live, and who to be in our fraught time."[129] Zoloth encourages a Jewish mode of argumentation, commentary, debate and discussion.[130] She identifies exile as a useful conceptual tool, writing that "The move of theological ethics toward a consideration of exile is an approach that is promising. It allows us to think about our duties as exiles, as opposed to our rights as landowners, and to fear their curtailing.

Now we can begin to envision a world that is a cultivation with limits, between physical necessity and ethical task."[131] She also discusses the theology of interruption and the ethics of hospitality as valuable ways of addressing climate change.[132] Zoloth concludes that religions, generally, have at least four powerful capacities: they confront the enormous terror of each of us as we face death; they allow ordinary people to believe in their own power to change unjust situations, despite all odds and everything arrayed against them; they allow for prophecy (imagining a future that can be changed and redeemed); and they exist without borders.[133]

Conclusions

Willemien Otten writes,

> In the Western religious tradition nature has, on the one hand, been too narrowly identified with Christian "creation," which is placed opposite God, and, on the other, too often regarded as a foreign force or immoral entity rivaling God and hence something to be shunned or kept at bay. As a result, two streams of nature discourse run through the Western religious tradition: the discourse of exegesis and ongoing theologizing of the theme of biblical *creation*, on one hand, and a more elusive sense of *nature*, which is seen as wily and wild, transgressive and unbridled, and at times, considered tinged with pagan (not to mention feminine) overtones, on the other.[134]

Thinking about nature allows us to grapple with our own thoughts and perhaps allows us to see that "whatever we think must always be provisional and is always only one perspective."[135]

Religion has a great deal to offer in the discussion of the environment. Beyond the notions of domination and stewardship, we have seen that religion, in its range of prior and contemporary thinking and usage, surfaces many significant beliefs and practices that can be important in the Anthropocene. Referencing the complex notion of religion, Willis Jenkins argues that "religious ethics holds promise for confronting unprecedented problems not because it possesses a special kind of moral resource (values, beliefs, worldviews) but because it works within traditions that are constantly being renegotiated and redeployed in order to meet new contextual demands."[136] Religious people engaged in environmental concerns have drawn from their traditions and (as we will see in the next chapter more fully) also evolved. They have identified and encouraged a range of practical measures. As Michael S. Hogue notes,

> In response to these questions, some religious leaders, thinkers, and practitioners have discovered wisdom in their traditions they had previously overlooked. Others have sought to imagine and theorize new moral and religious concepts, values, traditions, and practices. Responses include formal statements made by official bodies of all major religions of the world; scholarly works written and debated

by theologians and religious ethicists; and educational, legislative, and grassroots initiatives across the traditions at local, regional, and international levels.[137]

Religion, as Hogue argues, has a great deal to offer as it enriches our thought and helps to shape our actions.

In some ways, traditional ways of thinking about the world in various religious contexts can lead, especially in modern settings, to environmental challenges. At the same time, embedded in religious texts, interpretation, and discourse are strands of thought, belief, and practice that see the complexity in nature and offer ways to engage constructively with the world. While religion opens a range of ways of thinking about and engaging with the environment, in the next chapter we will turn to other ways of conceptualizing and engaging with religion that have emerged recently and consider in what ways they may potentially help us even more to navigate the concerns of the Anthropocene.

9

Religion

New Conceptions and Opportunities

Introduction: Religion and Ecology

As we have seen throughout this book, and especially in Chapter 7, history can be useful in addressing environmental concerns.[1] Theology also has some valuable assets in this regard, as we saw in the last chapter, especially with repentance, responsibility, covenant, social justice, contraction, Sabbath, and eschatology (which can be relevant in the area of conservation activism).[2] Religion, as we will see in this chapter, offers a form of grounding (a binding if you will) as well as adaptability in the face of change (perennial revelation, reconsideration). Religious tradition, to take one specific aspect of religion, can be connective (across time and geographies) and it can also be adaptable, when applied to new conditions and concerns. As such, religion and the traditions often associated with it are part of a learning process that engages "theory" and "practice" through reflection and interpretation. Judaism especially reflects this stance, which offers opportunities to think about the environment in new ways amid change and to develop new practices to address changed circumstances. In seeking religious insights to stem environmental degradation and climate change, some scholars have harvested the insights of Eastern and indigenous religions and faith traditions. Often the focus of these traditions on practice and connection with nature is highlighted. As we will see, Judaism offers a range of ways of thinking and behaving, some of which can be quite valuable in confronting and reversing contemporary environmental challenges.

The connection between religion and ecology is long-standing and can be deep. Willis Jenkins writes, "Religion is ecological, at least in the sense that it is a significant part of humanity's evolutionary history."[3] This is particularly true, as a broad understanding of ecology refers to "(a) the scientific study of organisms in relation to their environment, (b) an ethical worldview about appropriate human relations to their environment, (c) a political movement for adaptive social change, (d) a metaphor of interconnectedness, or (e) a materialist research frame for interpreting religious phenomena."[4] Given these interconnections, there is potential benefit, then, when religious leaders can engage with scientists, environmentalists, and politicians on themes related to the environment.[5] Religions often provide responses to suffering and violence and the predicament of the poor and marginalized,[6] and they can offer the framework for social connection and collective action.[7] If some scholars have pinned environmental degradation, even in part, on religion, many have also argued that religion both preserves traditions but also can provoke social change.[8]

Even when religion does not provide a specific perspective, answer, or response, it can surface significant issues and stir new ways of thinking. As Michael S. Hogue puts it, as moral and cultural creatures, humans live in multiple registers of time and space, and so the climate crisis that humans precipitated "may require that we think beyond the resources of existing moral and religious traditions, perhaps even against their grain."[9] Building on the ways in which religion can assist in thinking about and addressing environmental crises, this chapter probes a bit deeper into some of the key issues raised in the last chapter, while reading religion against the grain, as Hogue suggests, especially in regard to the notion of tradition. In this way, we explore the rich and, at times, novel ways that religion can help us navigate the challenges of the present and future.

Beyond some of the more discussed aspects of religion—such as repentance, responsibility, covenant, combating idolatry, and so on—that we reviewed in the previous chapter, there are some other, and often newer, ways of thinking about and leveraging religion and insights drawn from various faith traditions that can be helpful in engaging with the environment and redressing environmental degradation. Some scholars have, for example, focused on the restorative and renewing power of religion and of religious interpretation and rituals.[10] Similarly, considerations of Jewish law at times intersect in important ways with discussions about relationships and systems that we find in ecology. Rabbinic sources and thinking can themselves be seen as a kind of system. Avi Sagi describes halakhah (Jewish law) as a process that does not lead to "closedness or rigidity." He writes that "It may even help to justify epistemic openness, as long as it assumes that truth is attained through discourse rather than intuitively or through some similar process."[11] Leveraging medieval Jewish thinkers, he emphasizes the tension between innovation and original revelation. Discussing the medieval theologian Joseph Albo, for example, Sagi concludes that "The law of God cannot be perfect so as to be adequate for all times, because the ever new details of human relations, their customs and their acts, are too numerous to be embraced in a book."[12] This leads to a discussion of the notion of perennial revelation:[13] "Instead, disputes occur because perennial revelation unfolds through each sage's autonomous reasoning. As individuals differ in their reasoning, the articulation of revelation changes accordingly."[14] The concept of perennial revelation and religious law as a process offer valuable ways to apply religion—which in this reading is neither static nor dichotomous—in ever-changing environmental conditions and associated moral and ethical considerations.

Reconceptualizing Religion

Like Sagi's discussion of perennial revelation, a significant amount of work in religious studies has described the adaptability of religion—including some of the most "traditional" religious expressions—mirroring the discussions in broader Humanities and Social Sciences research (as well as the hard sciences). Religion scholar Mark Taylor notes that the term religion derives from two Latin terms: *religare* with an implication of binding and obligation and *relegere* with the implication of being thought through again.[15] Religion can encourage regularity and lead to predictable patterns of thinking and behaving; it can also adapt,[16] helping us to reset boundaries and encourage new thought.

With its rootedness and adaptability, religion provides a potentially valuable tool to address the complexity we face today, especially regarding the climate and environment. Complexity forces us to take a larger systems perspective, and it can help us go beyond polarities and single-mindedness—as we will see regarding approaches to complexity and polarization (Chapter 10). Grappling with complexity means that we must address messy and at times seemingly contradictory information and competing values—orientations that are essential (and ever more visible) in the accelerated and uncertain conditions of the Anthropocene. As the political scientist Peter Coleman and others argue, simplistic concepts and, in Taylor's argument, unbending faith, can lead to violence and destruction.[17] Recognizing complexity and the interconnection of beings—as well as nature, society, and culture more broadly—allows us to see how they "codetermine" each other through a network or system that is not linear or always clear.[18]

Taylor notes that "Biological organisms are not isolated systems but are imbricated in constitutive and transformative networks that both encompass and surpass them"[19] and that "Far from a simple biological force, life is impossible apart from the ceaseless interaction of mutually conditioning networks of social, cultural, and technological factors."[20] Drawing from these and other observations, Taylor offers several conclusions relevant to this project. He argues that life needs creativity, which requires novelty, which needs surprise.[21] Given the increased connectivity in the world, there is greater uncertainty and instability, with people feeling that things are out of control; in response, they seek "simplicity, certainty, and stability."[22] Instead of leaning into this uncertainty, Taylor finds that people turn to the past for guidance in order to address present unsettling and future uncertainty. But he asserts, "Old maps cannot provide adequate guidance for new territories."[23] What is more, he believes that "There is, in fact, a crisis of values, but it is caused by the militant moralists who are leading the crusade to return to a past that never existed."[24]

Taylor concludes that we need a new vision of the world that "not only helps to understand our place in it but also provides guiding principles for negotiating conflicts that often seem nonnegotiable."[25] This vision must combine theory and practice. He cautions that "theory without practice is empty; practice without theory is blind. Theory and practice, in other words, are inextricably interrelated and, therefore, mutually conditioning. Theories or interpretative schema always have practical consequences, and human activities transform the frameworks that inform them."[26] The result is that religion has been called upon to provide tools and perspectives in an ever-changing world, while still rooting people in certain behaviors and worldviews.

This connection between theory and practice through reflection and interpretation can be quite powerful. In discussing drought and disaster in rabbinic writing (especially in the Babylonian Talmud tractate of Ta'anit), Julia Watts Belser argues that the interpretation of events can have a powerful influence on the actual experiences that people have.[27] She writes that

> Through a series of biblical interpretations that contest the meaning of God's curses against Israel, Bavli Ta'anit argues that what appears to be curse is actually blessing, that what seems a sign of degradation actually expresses God's beneficent protection and care. By cultivating a discourse of ambiguous appearance and by emphasizing that hidden meaning often lurks beneath the surface of things, Bavli Ta'anit develops a theological sensibility that destabilizes the apparent meaning of misfortune—and blunts the moral condemnation inherent in disaster. The signs of divine disfavor are no longer entirely clear.[28]

Reframing disasters in this way points to the importance of context and perspective, as well as the meaning behind misfortune, which can also be nuanced. In this way, religion can cultivate an ambiguous stance toward disaster that allows for interpretative value and innovation. Devorah Steinmetz similarly notes that religious texts allow for engagement with big ideas and issues.[29] In the context of discussions about rain, Steinmetz observes that rain was depicted in Tanakh as an instrument of judgment, but it could be an instrument of social justice later in rabbinic midrash, pointing to changed perspectives and realities in the transition from biblical to rabbinic experiences and worldviews.[30]

Rethinking Tradition

While we often view religion as "traditional," which is generally taken to mean consistent or unchanging, religion (not only during periods of reform) has always been adaptive. The history of Judaism demonstrates this as much as any religious or faith tradition. Let's consider the very notion of "tradition" itself within Judaism. For some, tradition evokes images of deep connection and community. A guiding light to help us navigate the world, transmitted to us from sages and leaders from the past. For others, however, perhaps drawing from Enlightenment dualism that pitted tradition and its authority against rationality and free will, or postmodern notions of subjectivity, multiple truths, and anti-essentialism,[31] tradition dredges up a more sinister view. We are a bit in the "Fiddler on the Roof" conundrum—literally singing the praises of and need for tradition on one hand, even as we grapple with the reality that for many, tradition is insufficient to chart the turbulent waters and difficult questions of contemporary and future life: moving in one scene from extolling the virtues of inherited beliefs and activities and then grappling with changes to that very culture—how we arrange marriages, who we marry, and how we transgress long-standing communal norms, for example. Indeed, our relationship with tradition is both deep and complex.

But what exactly is tradition? In Roman law, tradition was a method of transferring ownership of property. The sociologist Edward Shils observed that "Tradition is whatever is persistent or recurrent through transmission, regardless of the substance and institutional setting . . . It includes beliefs thought to have been divinely revealed as well as interpretations of those beliefs. It includes beliefs formed through experience and beliefs formed by logical deduction."[32] Another typical definition can be found in the *Encyclopedia Judaica*, which notes that tradition in English is derived from the Latin "trader," to transmit or to give over. In Judaism, tradition (Hebrew mesorah) "Generally . . . refers to beliefs, doctrines, customs, ethical and moral standards, and cultural values and attitudes which are transmitted orally or by personal example. Under this designation, the process of transmission itself is also included. Theologically, in Judaism, tradition is the name applied to the unwritten code of law given by God to Moses on Mount Sinai."[33] The Hebrew root letters *mem samech resh* have a range of meanings in Hebrew: to give, deliver, hand, transmit, hand down, inform against, risk one's life, suffer martyrdom, complain against someone before heaven, give one's regards to someone, make a public statement, announce publicly, devote oneself to—as well as "to saw." The themes of transmitting (for good and evil, making the word something of an amoral concept), devotion, and public engagement help to define some of the contours of tradition as we typically think about it.

There are rich biblical and rabbinic discussions about tradition. In Ezek. 20:37, for example, tradition means a bond (of the covenant). In *Pirkei Avot* (Ethics of the Fathers), 1:1, we learn that mesorah is an act of transmission: "Moses received the Torah at Sinai and transmitted it to Joshua, Joshua to the elders, and the elders to the prophets, and the prophets to the Men of the Great Assembly. They said three things: Be patient in [the administration of] justice, raise many disciples and make a fence round the Torah." In the Talmud, tradition has a sense of handed-down interpretations that provide information about both the biblical text and its lessons. In the Babylonian Talmud, Tractate Sotah (10b), for example, the rabbis discuss the idea that the biblical figure Tamar covered her face in the home of her father-in-law Judah (explaining why Judah did not recognize her when he comes across her without her face covered). The biblical text does not reveal this information, which we know instead from "a tradition that we received from our ancestors."[34]

Other kinds of more practical information, with halakhic implications, are similarly derived from tradition. According to the Talmudic Tractate of Chullin (63b:11):

> Rabbi Yitzḥak says: A kosher bird may be eaten on the strength of a tradition that it is kosher, without inspecting for the signs listed in the Mishna. And the hunter is deemed credible to say: My teacher conveyed to me that this bird is kosher. Rabbi Yoḥanan said: And this is the halakha only when the teacher is familiar with the non-kosher birds and with their names.

Here, experience in particular fields (with halakhic implications), along with its associated teaching, composes the "tradition."

Other, later discussions explain more fully the notion of tradition, especially as related to the correct text of the Bible and, as such, a halakhic fence that protects against illegitimate novel interpretations. Rabbeinu Yonah (d. 1264), for example, in his commentary on *Pirkei Avot* noted that

> Tradition is a safeguarding fence around Torah: Traditions are the full spellings
> and incomplete spellings [of the words in the Torah] and the cantillation notes that
> the sages passed on to their students. And they are a safeguarding fence around
> the written Torah, such that you do not find differences among the books [of the
> Torah], except in a few places.[35]

But tradition has taken on a much more fluid sense in contemporary Christian
discussions. In engaging tradition to make it relevant to contemporary situations,
some theologians have noted the more fluid and evolving aspects of tradition. Colleen
Mary Mallon, in *Traditioning Disciplines: The Contribution of Cultural Anthropology to
Ecclesial Identity*, for example, argues that even in the ancient church, tradition could
take on different expressions and meanings due to changing historical and cultural
contexts.[36] In more contemporary settings, tradition is at times presented as a dynamic
and changing locus theologicus . . . "the unfolding of tradition as a 'natural process of
causation' emanating from the Holy Spirit"[37] that "grounds the believer in the life of
faith."[38] That is, "Living tradition is inherently continuous with the original apostolic
teaching because 'the word of the divine spirit moving through all centuries' cannot
produce an outward expression that is inconsistent with its ultimate source and
identity."[39]

The idea of textual canons often emerges in the discussion of traditions, given
the importance of selection, text, and interpretation in tradition. But the act of
engaging with canons reveals traditions to be both set and open. As Mallon argues,
"Individuals within a tradition both receive tradition as a gift and engage in the task
of questioning, refuting, and contesting aspects of the tradition that are seemingly
irrelevant. The experience of inhabiting a tradition is never a matter of pure receptivity
or pure challenge."[40] What is more, she finds that "As the community moves through
history, new situations pull new meanings from traditional symbols. Moreover, growth
in social awareness can offer critical assessment of previous formulations exposing
past and present complicity in systems of oppression."[41] Mallon concludes that "The
conserving character of tradition does not eliminate progress and growth, but novelty
must be avoided by maintaining an organic continuity with the past. . . . Understanding,
knowledge, and wisdom grow, but always within the limits that conserve their essential
character as Christian faith."[42] Tradition, then, in a Western, Christian tradition can be
seen as multivalent and multilayered. It can operate in social, ideological, and cultural
arenas, and it may manifest power as well as reveal the complexity of relationships and
interactions.[43]

Tradition[44] may be more nuanced and complicated than we imagine, even in more
"traditional" denominational circles. This is true in recent Jewish assessments as well.
At times, tradition is linked with historical or theological continuity. In *Changing the
Immutable: How Orthodox Judaism Rewrites Its History*, however, Marc B. Shapiro
examines cases of the conscious crafting of messages and even false ascriptions that he
finds at times in haredi communities, asserting that "There is often a tension between
the quest for historical truth and the desire of communities of faith to pass on their
religious message. This is because lifestyles and outlooks often change drastically over
the generations, while the traditional religious mindset views itself as carrying on the

values of the past, the latest links in a lengthy chain."[45] Shapiro argues that altering the past can be the result of concern over what may happen if the mass of common people are exposed to certain ideas or practices. But the alteration serves another purpose, namely to control the past in order to control the present and future.[46] In this regard, Shapiro quotes Yoel Finkelman, who writes that: "Haredi writers of history claim to know better than the great rabbis of the past how the latter should have behaved. Those great rabbis do not serve as models for the present. Instead, the present and its ideology serve as models for the great rabbis."[47]

Of course, the manipulation of traditions and histories is not a novelty in modern or contemporary Jewish communities of any flavor. Shapiro notes that in the twelfth century, Maimonides had already differentiated "true beliefs" and "necessary beliefs."

"True beliefs" are those which teach, in a literal fashion, some truth about God, such as His existence, unity, eternity, and omnipotence. Their purpose is to enable one to attain intellectual perfection. "Necessary beliefs," the basis of which is tradition and not philosophy, are expressed in a figurative manner and fulfill a political function in that, by instilling obedience to the Torah, they regulate the social relations of human beings. In addition, they[48] enable people to acquire noble qualities.[49]

We can even identify several examples from the Talmud that supported, or at least reported, knowingly false attributions to strengthen an argument or convince someone else to accept a contested point.[50] In Jewish debates, tradition could be leveraged to maintain certain practices or attitudes, even in the face of halakhic or scientific evidence to the contrary.[51] As the scholar of Jewish mysticism, Gershom Scholem, once wrote: "Tradition is not simply the totality of that which the community possesses as its cultural patrimony and which it bequeaths to its posterity; it is a specific selection from this patrimony which is elevated and garbed with religious authority. It proclaims certain things, sentences, or insights to be Torah, and this connects them with the revelation."[52] But this also means, as one recent scholar has argued, that "Upon closer inspection, however, mesorah, in all its usages, is not static but fluid. Even the textual mesorah, despite its aspirations for precise recall, consciously includes selective innovations by certain salient rabbinic greats to eliminate inauthentic variants that have become manifest."[53]

As we have seen, tradition can be (and often has been) a complex concept that is understood and utilized in many ways. The nature of tradition has received a good deal of attention in the past several decades. Among the most influential thinkers on the topic was the German philosopher Hans-Georg Gadamer (1900–2002), known for his pioneering work on hermeneutics. There are several important arguments that underpin Gadamer's discussion of tradition in his seminal work from 1960, *Truth and Method*.[54] First, in the footsteps of other philosophers (Edmund Husserl in particular), Gadamer challenges the traditionally accepted opposition of subjectivity and objectivity.[55] This move allows Gadamer to assert that even when we are open to analyzing a text or experience, we always bring context, or "fore-meaning," to everything we experience. He writes that "All that is asked is that we remain open to the meaning of the other person or text. But this openness always includes our situating the other meaning in relation to the whole of our own meanings or ourselves in relation to it."[56]

The second argument that is core to Gadamer's notion of tradition is a similar dismissal of an opposition—in this case, the Enlightenment distinction between faith in authority and the use of one's own reason.[57] While such a distinction might, in fact be legitimate, Gadamer fears that it can easily preclude the reality that authority can be a source of truth (we do not need to denigrate all authority). While the Romantics defended tradition in opposition to the Enlightenment worldview, Gadamer criticizes them too for suggesting an unconditional antithesis between tradition and reason.[58] He writes that "However problematical the conscious restoration of old or the creation of new traditions may be, the romantic faith in the 'growth of tradition,' before which all reason must remain silent, is fundamentally like the Enlightenment, and just as prejudiced."[59]

A final argument in which Gadamer rejects a generally accepted opposition regards the antithesis between tradition (history) and historical research (the knowledge of history).[60] In part, this frees him to efface the difference between the past as an experience disconnected from us and our contemporary life. Instead, Gadamer asserts that "But understanding it will always involve more than merely historically reconstructing the past 'world' to which the work belongs. Our understanding will always retain the consciousness that we too belong to that world, and correlatively that the work too belongs to our world."[61] What is more, "the process of construal is itself already governed by an expectation of meaning that follows from the context of what has gone before."[62] In our efforts to understand a text, we therefore are not "transposing" ourselves into the author's mind but rather into the larger perspective in which his or her views were formed, what he terms "a sharing of common meaning."[63]

Drawing on Martin Heidegger, Gadamer concludes that the process of understanding a text is neither subjective nor objective, but the interplay between the movement of tradition and the movement of the interpreter.[64] He concludes that

> Every age has to understand a transmitted text in its own way, for the text belongs to the whole tradition whose content interests the age and in which it seeks to understand itself. The real meaning of a text, as it speaks to the interpreter, does not depend on the contingencies of the author and his original audience. It certainly is not identical with them, for it is always co-determined also by the historical situation of the interpreter and hence by the totality of the objective course of history.[65]

Gadamer also introduces the notion of horizons of understanding. He offers that understanding tradition requires a "historical horizon,"[66] and yet the "horizon of the present" is continually in formation through a process of testing our prejudices by engaging with our traditions.[67] And while the self-understanding of the present is impacted, so is the tradition itself.[68] That is, "Every encounter with tradition that takes place within historical consciousness involves the experience of a tension between the text and the present," and understanding is affected by and has an effect upon tradition.[69] To clarify, for Gadamer, a written tradition—a text—is not a fragment that represents a past world, at least not simply. Instead, it "has already raised itself beyond this into the sphere of the meaning that it expresses."[70] As a result, according to one Gadamer scholar, tradition is, therefore, inexhaustibly open to new interpretations and additional dimensions of meaning.[71]

Despite the complexity and changeable nature of parts of tradition in Gadamer's model, some have criticized his notion of tradition as overly conservative. Jürgen Habermas, notably, found Gadamer's idea of tradition too optimistic and worried that it could serve as a tool for manipulation and oppression.[72] Others have noted that Gadamer and others in this philosophical camp are forced to make assumptions that there is in fact one "mainstream" tradition and particular "valid" works within it. Some have raised questions about what appears to be an unbroken continuum for Gadamer, in which tradition has been, and will continue to be engaged.[73]

And yet, for Gadamer, engagement with tradition (and what he calls traditionary texts) provides a powerful opportunity to see and test our prejudices. Gadamer writes that

> It is impossible to make ourselves aware of a prejudice while it is constantly operating unnoticed, but only when it is, so to speak, provoked. The encounter with a traditionary text can provide the provocation. For what leads to understanding must be something that has already asserted itself in its own separate validity. Understanding begins, as we have already said above, when something addresses us.[74]

In explicating his notion of hermeneutics, Gadamer points out that hermeneutics is divided into three parts: understanding, interpretation, and application.[75] Yet while these are three separate parts, they are inextricably connected: for him, understanding is always application at the same time, for example:[76] "If the heart of the hermeneutical problem is that one and the same tradition must time and again be understood in a different way, the problem, logically speaking, concerns the relationship between the universal and the particular. Understanding, then, is a special case of applying something universal to a particular situation."[77]

Similarly, Gadamer asserts that all interpretation of a past text entails a dialogue between past and present.[78] As literary theorist Terry Eagleton nicely captures it, "Gadamer can equably surrender himself and literature to the winds of history because these scattered leaves will always in the end come home—and they will do so because underneath all history, silently spanning past, present and future, runs a unifying essence known as 'tradition.'"[79]

With an educational focus, Gadamer argues that knowledge is gained through experience[80] and that experience is a process.[81] Regarding the hermeneutical experience, he maintains that, "I must allow tradition's claim to validity, not in the sense of simply acknowledging the past in its otherness, but in such a way that it has something to say to me."[82] The engagement with tradition helps to surface meanings that would likely never have been anticipated by the original author or a contemporary audience.[83]

Gadamer also engages with another key concept—questioning; which he believes opens up the possibilities of meaning.[84] Indeed, rather than reflecting an unquestioning form of conservatism, Gadamer's approach does not imply that questioning or even challenging existing traditions is impossible.[85] As one recent scholar notes, "On the contrary, Gadamer perceives tradition as an inherently reflective ontological structure that is in a continuous state of revision and self-transgression through processes of understanding where historically inherited presuppositions are relentlessly questioned and challenged."[86] Educational experiences, for Gadamer, therefore, at the same time appropriate and transform the tradition.[87] Anniina Leiviskä concludes that

> What follows from this is that tradition inevitably has a different meaning and relevance for each historical time period, and therefore every generation must reconsider this meaning from the viewpoint of its unique place in history. Educators as representatives of a previous generation are therefore unable to give students a ready-made answer to the question of how they should understand and appropriate the tradition they inherit.[88]

Sociology has reinforced this notion. Edward Shils argues, for example, that "every tradition, however broad or narrow, offers a possibility of a variety of responses. Every tradition, given though it is, opens potentialities for a diversity of responses."[89]

Gadamer's approach requires us to engage with others and otherness to some extent—in the form of previous texts (of tradition)—forcing us to understand the claims of others and evaluate and potentially revise our own preconceptions.[90] Learning, in this way, involves "transforming the unquestioned appropriation of tradition to its reflective reappropriation in a way that creates new value."[91] Along the way, we may transform tradition, but we also identify and evaluate our own prejudices, problems, and deficiencies, and evaluate what is worth preserving or restoring from the past.[92]

Are there implications of this reassessment of tradition—in the broad sense and as it relates to learning—as we consider Jewish notions of tradition, Jewish education, and Jewish approaches to the environment? In *Textual Knowledge: Teaching the Bible in Theory and Practice*, Barry Holtz advances the discussion of some of these key issues.[93] Holtz asserts that we have a model for rewriting tradition in Judaism, in the form of midrashic reading.[94] Grappling with aspects of postmodernism and literary deconstruction, Holtz himself examines the pull in two directions—tradition as encompassing "ideas, competencies, attitudes, virtues, and proscribed behaviors" on one hand and the encouragement "to enter that conversation actively, to create new tales, new readings of the law, new interpretations, new ways of understanding the old," on the other.[95]

Instead of focusing on teaching a body of knowledge and rulings, the process of questioning and reasoning with Jewish tradition is essential in Judaism. Instead of telling our students what our tradition says for today, we should allow our students to encounter tradition through their own lenses and experiences so that they can make meaning (or not) from and, more importantly, in conversation with texts and traditions. Rather than emphasizing the notion of tradition as handed-down wisdom that determines how we must behave and believe, it may be more constructive to conceptualize tradition as a system—with expressions and boundaries, to be sure, but with a dynamism and fluidity that encourages questioning and exploration rather than adherence. What we can say is that most students today and for the future (and for some time) will not be compelled or coerced by commandments. They may embrace aspects of tradition—and we can decide in some ways which are most essential and how we present them to speak most deeply and clearly to our learners. However, seeing tradition as a system, with each of us part of that system that is forever cycling through development, growth, decline, and reconfiguration, we have the chance to do what Gadamer in fact suggests—learn from tradition (and hopefully make tradition the fore-knowledge that all our students possess) while testing it and helping to transform it and improve ourselves at the same time. In this way, people can also find themselves in parts of tradition that resonate with them. While this may feel overly selective to some among us, in reality, that has been the cycle of tradition in history, in which tradition has been fluid and adaptable. We may want to establish red lines or essentialisms, and yet an openness to engaging (and deciding) may open people, perhaps ironically or counterintuitively, to accepting more rather than less of tradition. If tradition is more about interrogating texts, evaluating evidence, assessing arguments, and posing questions with contemporary relevance, we are likely to witness an excited turning to tradition to learn—and by learn, I mean emulate, critique, and reshape. For, an openness at one point in the system will draw our students into further exploration and a graciousness in considering what else our texts and traditions might in fact have for them.

Such a systems approach draws from work in ecology and environmental sciences (see, for example, the notion of panarchy) and is particularly well adapted to navigating crises and change of all sorts. If we see Judaism as a complex network (with tradition itself as a system), we may be able to accommodate social and technological acceleration, increasing interconnection, and expanding complexity in society and life.[96] Such an approach is evolutionary, continuous, and organic, and it allows us (and the system) to be more resilient in volatile and unstable conditions, while open to and offering adaptiveness to more creative and innovative opportunities, which have been central to much of the historical and intellectual developments of Judaism over millennia.

Rethinking Religious Responses to Environmental Crises: Return to Indigenous Approaches?

Scholars of other religious traditions (beyond the Jewish and Christian ones I have primarily discussed in this book) have also grappled with issues related to religion and ecology. In addition to considering other faith traditions and making religion and tradition more active verbs, other trajectories in religious studies have opened new opportunities for thinking differently, especially around environmental issues. Perhaps more than any other subject, the engagement with indigenous societies and religions has provided many opportunities to think differently than we have in Western and, in some cases, even Eastern traditions. A fruitful approach to religion and the environment has been displayed in the work of David Abram, in his well-known

The Spell of the Sensuous: Perception and Language in a More-Than-Human World.[97] Drawing from the philosophical work of Maurice Merleau-Ponty, Abram notes that all knowledge, including scientific knowledge, is derived from a particular point of view or some experience.[98] Perception for Merleau-Ponty involves a reciprocity between the body and the surrounding entities,[99] with the implication that neither the perceiver nor the perceived are wholly passive in "perception."

Leveraging the work of the philosopher Edmund Husserl (like Gadamer), Abram reframes the traditional differentiation of subjective and objective.[100] He writes that

> The "real world" in which we find ourselves, then—the very world our sciences strive to fathom—is not a sheer "object," not a fixed and finished "datum" from which all subjects and subjective qualities could be pared away, but rather an intertwined matrix of sensations and perceptions, a collective field of experience lived through from many different angles. The mutual inscription of others in my experience, and (as I must assume) of myself in their experiences, effects the interweaving of our individual phenomenal fields into a single ever-shifting fabric, a single phenomenal world or "reality."[101]

We have, however, he argues, become estranged from our direct experience, so that "conventional scientific discourse privileges the sensible field in abstraction from sensory experience, and commonly maintains that subjective experience is 'caused' by an objectifiable set of processes in the mechanically determined field of the sensible."[102] This leads to setting ourselves apart from "the rest of animate nature."[103] Human speech inscribes humans in the animate landscape; however, the diminishment of the biotic diversity on earth through the expansion of technological civilization also diminishes language (provided by the sensuous world).[104]

Abram notes that many people have accused the ancient Hebrews and Greeks of offering a mental context to foster civilization's mistreatment of nonhuman nature.[105] This is due in part to the central role of writing in these cultures, which distances them from the actual experiences that are reflected in oral culture. The Hebrew written character no longer refers us to any sensible phenomenon out in the world, but "solely to a gesture to be made by the human mouth . . . A direct association is established between the pictorial sign and the vocal gesture, for the first time completely bypassing the thing pictured."[106] Greek, according to Abram, leads to an even greater abstraction as the letters and words become meaningful on their own, shorn from the very things they represent.[107] The Greek philosopher Socrates saw genuine knowledge as eternal and unchanging in contrast to the material world that was variable and fleeting:[108]

> The fact that one's scripted words can be returned to and pondered at any time that one chooses, regardless of when, or in what situation, they were first recorded, grants a timeless quality to this new reflective self, a sense of the relative independence of one's verbal, speaking self from the breathing body with its shifting needs. The literate self cannot help but feel its own transcendence and timelessness relative to the fleeting world of corporeal experience.[109]

Writing, Abram therefore argues, leads to forgetfulness and an inability to remember except through marks external to the thing in question.[110] "By contrast, for indigenous people, the landscape is still alive, aware, and expressive."[111] Abram argues that "In this uniquely oral form of community censure, a topographic place becomes the guarantor of corrected behavior, the visible presence that reminds one of past foibles and that ensures one's subsequent attentiveness."[112] The erosion of oral culture leads, Abram suggests, to loss of the "felt power and personality of particular places."[113]

At the same time, alphabetic writing was important to the emergence of "abstract, homogeneous space" as well as "abstract, linear time."[114] "Recording mythic events in writing establishes, as well, a new experience of the permanence, fixity, and unrepeatable quality of those events"[115] Time, however, is curved (and cyclical) in oral culture; it becomes linear in the printed line.[116] The cyclical or circular is spatial and temporal—for some indigenous people, such as the Navajo, existence is a continuous manifestation, series of events rather than states or situational persistence through time and the future is experienced as a "stock of possibilities if incompletely realized events and circumstances."[117] For them, there is no distinction between space and time, "The vitality of each place, moreover, is rejuvenated by the human enactment, the en-*chant*-ment, of the storied events that crouch within it."[118] Additionally, for the Navajo, "that which we call the 'mind' *is not ours*, is not a human possession. Rather, mind as Wind is a property of the encompassing world, in which humans—like all other beings—participate."[119]

Citing the renowned scholar of religion Mircea Eliade, Abram asserts that the Hebrews were the first to discover linear, nonrepeating time:[120] Eliade noted that

> For the first time, the prophets placed a value on history, succeeded in transcending the traditional vision of the cycle (the conception that ensures all things will be repeated forever), and discovered a one-way time. This discovery was not to be immediately and fully accepted by the consciousness of the entire Jewish people, and the ancient conceptions were still long to survive.[121]

Such an approach allowed the Hebrews to preserve their cultural stories even when cut off from the lands where those stories took place—"the written text became a kind of portable homeland for the Hebrew people."[122] Still, the Hebrews were never entirely linear.[123] Hebraic religiosity was far more corporeal and responsive to the sensuous earth than we might commonly assume.[124] Hebrew renounced animistic engagement with the visible forms of the natural world but retained a participatory relationship with the invisible medium of that world, the wind and breath.[125] Indeed, the Hebrew vowels were expressed as unsounded breath, and in order to read Hebrew texts, the reader's breath had to be added (in the form of the vowels), potentially changing the very meaning of the words.[126] That is, the Hebrew text required the reader's conscious participation.[127] This led to an experience of the world around us as "a continual, ongoing utterance."[128] And, the holy name, the Tetragrammaton, was the most breath-like consonants in the Hebrew alphabet (aleph-beth).[129] The medieval kabbalists, Abram argues, went even farther in their meditation on individual letters.[130]

Abram writes that "It remained for the ancient Greeks, possessed of their own version of the alphabet, to derive an entirely placeless notion of eternity—a strictly intelligible, nonmaterial realm of pure Ideas resting entirely outside the sensible world."[131] For the Greeks, then, now became a dividing point separating past from future.[132] Unlike the Hebrews, the Greek scribes introduced written vowels into a previously consonantal system of letters.[133] "For by using visible characters to represent the sounded breath, the Greek scribes effectively *desacralized* the breath of the air."[134] This trend was expanded by the spread of Christianity, which relied on the spread of the alphabet,[135] and reached its apex with the scientific advances of the early modern period, especially in the work of Isaac Newton and, later, Immanuel Kant.[136]

Religious Methods to Combat Environmental Degradation

While some have seen religion as a source of environmental degradation, others have noted the power of religion as a moral force that can be useful in combating it.[137] Professor of Environmental Humanities Evan Berry writes that

> religion is an important means by which to articulate the status of other-than-human beings in the moral economy of climate disruption; (b) climate change infrastructures are spaces that encourage, constrain, or refract religious engagement; (c) religion is a domain in which alternative conceptual frameworks are the basis of knowledge about environmental change and (d) transdisciplinary theorization about religion is a useful means of comparing the social and cultural impacts of climate change.[138]

Practical responses to climate change at times relate to social and cultural (as well as economic and political) considerations. Indeed, sustainability can be framed as a social learning process.[139] Willis Jenkins outlines four ways that the concept of "environmental pragmatism" has been used: "By supposing that (1) civic engagement with practical issues determines norms for meaningful theory, environmental pragmatists (2) use a problem-oriented approach to critique theories that stymie ongoing investigative debate by claiming an objective finality. Pragmatists thus want (3) theories that cleave closely with social experience, in order to satisfy (4) the activist concern for factual consequences."[140] There are, indeed, specific religious practices that are helpful in this regard. These include recording the memory of suffering, contemplative kenosis, and solidarity with vulnerable others.[141] Such approaches often take quite practical form, in Judaism in contemporary liturgy and the adoption of the kabbalistic ritual of conducting a seder for the New Year of trees on Tu b'Shevat.

For Jenkins, environmental ethics must describe "nonhuman entities in such ways as to warrant their moral standing,"[142] "link nature's standing with practical obligations and motivations for human agents,"[143] and engage with human practices.[144] Religion can allow us to recuperate creation and also reinhabit (see below) the environment, opening opportunities for "desire and wonder."[145] Indeed, ecology and religion can be thought of as profitably intertwined.

Climate change has destabilized our notions of nature.[146] For Jenkins, it functions in broader social thinking and practice as well: "Climate change becomes dangerous when the magnitude and pace of the changes exceeds the capacity of social and ecological systems to adapt, thus degrading sustaining goods."[147] As climate change can harm collectively and in different ways for different people,[148] the goals of responding to it (and associated actions and responsibilities) can be diverse.[149]

Jenkins notes, "Past generations are not present to be held accountable for their actions, while future generations have no political voice, so the present generation must decide justice while facing a strong incentive to defer the questions to the next generation."[150] Unfortunately, the futurist thinking that responding to climate change requires is not well aligned with the human mind's ability to handle complex causation, uncertainty, and multiple temporal and geographic scales.[151] While denial of climate change in some religious circles may be a form of avoidance or lack of taking responsibility, apocalyptic sensibilities (as discussed in Chapter 8) can also be counter-productive in the same kinds of ways.[152] Jenkins, therefore, discusses a variety of advocacy, missional, and survival strategies in addressing climate change.[153] Important in this regard are pragmatic strategies that can tap into the power of religious traditions and community.[154] What is more, religion has some capacity to be useful in this regard, as it can take a global ethical position and sense of responsibility.[155] Of course, there can be tensions between such "universalism" and local conditions and needs.[156]

If sustainability is about meeting both present and future needs, it can, in a sense, be seen as a "secular salvation idea."[157] But it must not weaken commitments to today's vulnerable in this quest, even as it identifies sacrifices we must make today, and it must also not discount the interests of the future.[158] Utilizing a complex notion of religion, which we also suggested in the discussion of tradition above, Jenkins asserts that "religious ideas, cosmologies, and alternative worldviews do not imply foundationalism. They may also function as important tools for solving problems."[159] And perhaps one of the benefits of apocalyptic thinking, Jenkins notes, may be that it encourages us to use new metaphors and engage in new thinking and behavior.[160]

As in discussions of tradition, the notion of practice has also been enriched through recent scholarship about geography and space. Religion, Thomas Tweed argues, involves geo-spatial practices—dwelling and crossing[161] "are most useful for analyzing what religion is and what it does: spatial metaphors (*dwelling* and *crossing*) signal that religion is about finding a place and moving across space, and aquatic metaphors (*confluences* and *flows*) signal that religions are not reified substances but complex processes."[162] Underlying these observations are a series of assumptions, including that religions are not static; they are simultaneously individualistic and collective; and they can interpret and ease suffering.[163] In a provocative move, Tweed suggests the use of the term religioning instead of religion,[164] as "Religions are partial, tentative, and continually redrawn sketches of where we are, where we've been, and where we're going."[165]

Religion, as Lynn White, Jr. had himself already suggested, has the potential to solve problems as well as create them. Dave Aftandilian[166] cites the work of Roger Gottlieb, which identified four paths that religious environmentalists have taken to respond to the environmental crisis: recovery of neglected pro-environmental parts of their spiritual traditions; reinterpretation and/or critique of existing traditions; evolution of new models within existing traditions; and radical innovation, creating entirely new liturgies, rituals, stories, traditions, and so on.[167] These paths are reflected in much of what we have seen in this chapter: notions of grounding (including dwelling and re-inhabiting) and change (and the realization that everything is in constant flux and that there exist large environmental systems with great complexity), the process of questioning and interpreting (as part of learning), the reduction or elimination of the binary opposition of object and subject (and the realignment of relationships as a result), and that space and time can be collapsed in some important ways.

Given the range of religious ideas, sensibilities, and behaviors that can be helpful in understanding and responding to the environment (as we saw in Chapter 8), combined with some of the new and more complex ways of thinking about and leveraging religion (throughout this chapter) and history (as in earlier chapters), where might we go from here? In the final chapters, we now turn to the question of change and how we use history and religion, especially Judaism, in all of their complexity and opportunity to address not just the past and present but the future as well.

PART III

New Approaches in the Anthropocene

10

Complexity, Polarization, and Resilience

Introduction

The chapters in Part I and Part II have highlighted a range of historical experiences for Jews and others related to natural disasters and the depth and multivalent nature of history and religion in their more "traditional" manifestations and in more recent scholarship. We learned how premodern people understood, experienced, and responded to a range of natural disasters (including earthquakes, plagues, floods, and fires) in various historical settings. We saw that their worldviews were shaped by their religious and intellectual traditions as well as their practical experiences. In many ways, they developed significant and at times sophisticated and successful ways to cope with and mitigate disasters. Premodern religion, while sometimes blamed for encouraging domination of the environment, objectifying nature, and encouraging exploitation of the world's resources, also provided ways of thinking about stewardship and tools—intellectual, spiritual, and practical—from repentance to environmental and social justice to mitigate the damage that humans could cause to the environment.

Their approaches were helpful in some, though not all, ways. What is more, the approach that we found among premodern people is helpful but not sufficient given the range of disasters and the acceleration of environment and climate change, especially since the middle of the twentieth century. In Part II, therefore, we considered some of the ways that history (including Jewish history) and religion (especially Judaism) have been useful in thinking about and responding to environmental change, but we also explored new ways of thinking about both that may be even more helpful in the rapidly changing age of the Anthropocene.

In history, we examined new ways of thinking about causality and agency, the importance of connecting across time periods, the opportunity for history to help us chart multiple futures (and not just multiple pasts), and the relevance of narratives and metaphors that can call people's attention to the need for environmental action and behavioral change. In religion, we considered how engaging with other faith traditions (especially indigenous ones) can help us reconsider binaries that are stifling, understand the complex systems of nature and human society, and the ways that traditions can be connective and grounding but also adaptive and dynamic. This can lead to deep and relevant learning that can help people adjust their behaviors in ways that are positive for the environment and relations with others.

In these final chapters (Part III), some of the core themes that have been raised will be placed into a more synthetic review of some promising approaches to grappling with the complexity and polarization that have emerged in Parts I and II, as well as ways to develop resilience and stir behavior change.

Complexity

As we have seen throughout this book, the relationship between humans and nature has always been complex. In the first section of this chapter, we will consider the very notion of complexity itself, as it offers the chance to examine the challenges associated with environmental crises and, given our discussions of history and religion, provides some ways to consider how we might think about and respond to natural disaster and climate change today and into the future. As part of this discussion, we will engage with concepts of emergence, non-binary organization, change, relationships, and space and time.

Emergence

Scientists think of nature as a series of complex systems. What exactly do we mean by a complex system? According to one basic definition, a complex system is "a system that exhibits nontrivial emergent and self-organizing behaviors."[1] A key component of this definition is "emergence," which is "the idea that new structural properties and patterns can appear spontaneously in complex adaptive systems that are not present in its individual parts."[2] Self-organization refers to an intelligent collective behavior that goes beyond that of individual behaviors.[3] As one recent study of plants notes, "In humans, the brain is thought to be a kind of control center for the entire body, but in plants and other creatures without nervous systems, intelligence is distributed across the entire system."[4]

Other discussions identify some core characteristics of complex systems: they involve a large quantity of elements that interact with each other; the interactions in such systems are nonlinear and even minor changes can have significant consequences; and they are unpredictable. Importantly, complex systems are dynamic, reversible, and emergent.[5]

Increasingly, we have begun to see history and religion as systems as well, with the result that we find in them complexity, autonomy, and change. Some recent approaches to religion have in fact applied the notion of emergence to the divine. That is to say, the emergence and development of the world were not fashioned by an entity "God," but are instead a process that we have termed God.[6] The behavior of such systems (whether divine or not, or whatever we term them) can be impossible to predict, and yet even apparently chaotic systems possess some order.[7] While a systems approach is essential for understanding the environment and environmental change, it is also useful for crafting more robust concepts of history and religion and developing more agile responses to the changes of the Anthropocene. Though science has not been able to study consciousness objectively[8]—"Consciousness was not some substance in the brain but rather emerged from the complex relationships between the subject and the world"[9]—an increasing range of studies, which have recalibrated how we think about and identify consciousness in animals and plants, provide a valuable opportunity to understand emergence as well as non-binary thinking.

Beyond Binaries

Several academic theories have helped to complexify thinking in ways that offer new insights, especially when applied to environmental crises. Queer theory, to take one example, helps us to consider the range of complexity that exists between binary poles, and it has constructively challenged traditional categories and dualisms. As Whitney A. Bauman and Heather Eaton write, "Queering understanding of what it means to be male, female, human, plant, mineral, animal, organic, and machine means recognizing that such designations are abstractions from the ever-shifting and evolving relationships that constitute our daily planetary lives."[10] Queering blurs the boundaries between natural and unnatural, and it questions broader notions of human exceptionalism[11] and the notion of the "stability" of nature itself.[12] This leads Bauman and Eaton, like others such as French philosopher and anthropologist Bruno Latour, to question the very notion of the concepts of nature and culture.[13]

Racial theorists offer a similar deconstructive approach, as they challenge dichotomies, especially as they lead to exploitation and marginalization.[14] The racial lens also highlights the uneven impact of environmental degradation and disasters on some groups. Carol Wayne White notes that "the proximity of certain groups to environmental disasters is not incidental. Rather, decision makers, regulatory agencies, and local planning and zoning boards have too often made it easier to place such facilities in low-income African-American or Latino communities than in primarily white, middle-to-upper income communities."[15] Understanding systems more fully, and the fluid relationships that constitute them, allows us to see different perspectives, assess impact in more nuanced ways, and design solutions to problems that often seem intractable.

Change

Another significant conceptual challenge in complexity relates to change. Here, history provides a useful tool for identifying and contextualizing change. However, as we have seen, new approaches to history are necessary as we engage with the most significant and rapid changes of today and the future. A challenge that we have faced in the past in addressing environmental concerns is that we have often viewed the environment as a static and cohesive concept. But we know now that the environment, as a complex system, is in constant flux, is multi-scalar and multi-dimensional, and that it is constantly reshaping and reorganizing in response to a variety of internal conditions and external stimuli.[16]

In addressing environmental concerns, social action must take into account the fluidity of nature, as well as of society.[17] As David Harvey suggests, citing the philosopher Alfred North Whitehead, "nature . . . is always about the perpetual exploration of novelty."[18] We need to explore possible worlds and, as such, it may be useful to replace the "fixed idea of values" with a "process of valuation."[19] Harvey accordingly diagnoses six distinctive "moments" of the social process: language/discourse, power, thought, fantasy, desire, institution building, material practices, and social relations.[20] Different ecological movements have engaged these processes in different ways, he notes. Radical ecological critique, for example, has roots in anarchism, emphasizing community, locality, place, proximity to "nature," peculiarity, and decentralization.[21] As Harvey writes, "The radical ecological literature that focuses on place construction, bioregionalism, and the like has something creative to offer, partly as an excellent ground for critique of capitalism's production of waste. . . . as well as its production of serial conformity in urban design and the like."[22] Such an approach represents a change in how we think about nature and space, even as it itself grapples with the accelerating changes around us.

Relationships

Complex systems also highlight the centrality of relationships—within and between systems. The discussion about relationships is relevant in many ways, including in educational settings. At times, relational approaches in education have been associated with the self and contrasted with complexifying approaches (focused on the collectivity).[23] As Stephen Kosslyn and Ben Nelson note in writing about new approaches to higher education, "although it can be useful to study complex social systems in isolation, ultimately they must be understood in relation to other systems."[24] Or, as recent work on plant intelligence has taught us, plants' "attention and awareness is localized in each of their parts, but each of their parts communicates and strategizes across the whole, producing consciousness all the same."[25] Plants, like people, it turns out, are not simply individuals with clearly demarcated boundaries.[26]

Of course, relationships are not always harmonious; rather, they describe encounters and engagement in a variety of ways. William R. Jordan, III argues that "environmental thinkers have typically sought communion in exactly the wrong places—in parable and models of harmony rather than in those troubling aspects of life and relationships in which the shame and tensions inherent in them are revealed and made accessible."[27] With regards to the last conception, therefore, he argues that we should not lose sight of the fact that community is not necessarily harmonious, homogeneous, nor solidary.[28]

What, then, are the possible implications for humans and their collective action as we navigate relationships between people and between people and the earth system, especially as we head ever more fully into the complexity and uncertainty of the Anthropocene? One rabbinic text offers some guidance as we navigate individual and collective sensibilities. Consider Leviticus Rabbah 4:6:

> Hezekiya taught (Jeremiah 50:17): "Israel are scattered sheep"—why are Israel likened to a sheep? Just as a sheep, when hurt on its head or some other body part, all of its body parts feel it. So it is with Israel when one of them sins and everyone feels it. (Numbers 16:22): "When one man sins [will You be wrathful with the whole community]." Rabbi Shimon bar Yochai taught a parable: Men were on a ship. One of

them took a drill and started drilling underneath him. The others said to him: What are you sitting and doing?! He replied: What do you care. Is this not underneath my area that I am drilling?! They said to him: But the water will rise and flood us all on this ship. This is as Iyob said (Job 19:4): "If indeed I have erred, my error remains with me." But his friends said to him (Job 34:37): "He adds transgression to his sin; he extends it among us." [The men on the ship said]: You extend your sins among us. Rabbi Elasa said: a gentile asked Rabbi Yehoshua ben Karha: In your Torah, it is written (Exodus 23:2): "After the multitude will you side." We are more numerous than you, so why don't you become like us in practicing idolatry?[29]

The text compellingly points out that the actions of individuals can affect others—literally in this case by sinking a ship. What is more, individual errors may also affect others when an individual shares them. And yet, the end of the passage signals that there are times when individuals must choose to follow their own path and not succumb to the bad acts of others (idolatry) even if that is practiced by a majority of people. That is, the passage teaches that individuals are never fully separate from their environments, but that they must choose different paths and behaviors in some circumstances.

Spatial and Temporal Considerations

In understanding the complexity of environmental systems, some ecological work has focused on notions of space and place,[30] as well as time, all of which can themselves be affected by social practices and power relations[31]—especially as space, place, and time (which also impact deep ecology) can themselves be seen as social constructs in some ways.[32] In the context of environmentalism, Jordan argues that environmentalist social movements have elevated three ideas about the relationship of humans with nature,[33] which all have some spatial components. These include a colonial conception, in which nature is seen as a resource and is valued as a source of goods and services;[34] a sacred space conception, in which nature transcends economic or merely human interests;[35] and a community conception, in which humans are seen to be in community with the rest of nature—a notion introduced by the conservationist Aldo Leopold.[36]

Some scholars have noted differences between space (as undifferentiated and abstract) and place (as particular, familiar, and laden with meaning).[37] Place is a particularly significant, if layered, concept for environmental considerations. As Brian Campbell writes, "The essence of a place is not only a matter of features we passively perceive. We actively encounter place, with intentionality and with particular behaviors and practices. . . . Self-consciously or not people make places significant."[38] What is more, "modern people lack intimate knowledge of any one place. Their interior landscape is disordered, and they see the world in instrumental terms—as resources to be exploited."[39] These observations help explain, in some ways, how geographical distance can reduce our sense of concern about developments in other parts of the world.

Places cannot be assumed to be natural, but are constituted and constructed through complex social, economic, and political processes.[40] In a certain sense, nothing is exactly "natural." Places are permeable, comprised of relations that extend beyond temporal and spatial boundaries. They may have multiple identities that coexist and include diverse groups that contest meaning.[41]

Place plays out particularly poignantly in considerations of the local and global. As we have seen elsewhere in this book, the tensions between local and global can be significant (they can occur naturally and be constructed). Localization is related to notions of the sacred (the unique) on one hand and mundane practices that include things like growing and eating food, on the other.[42] Globalization engages local places but reshapes them within networks and systems (of information, people, and economies).[43] The local and the global (as well as the particular and universal)—and both together—need to be addressed for the future, even as they were at times (if briefly) raised in more theological terms in some of the historical examples we explored in Part I. The relationships between them are important as we attempt to stir action by increasing a sense of connection and immediacy.

Given the importance of place in discussing the environment, one approach to environmental crises is to "reinhabit" place.[44] As many scholars have noted, there is also a strong connection between place, memory, and identity,[45] and so discussions of space and place may be fruitful in understanding the environment and our relationship to it in new ways. David Harvey writes that "The preservation or construction of sense of place is then an active moment in the passage from memory to hope, from past to future."[46] Harvey quotes the Norwegian architectural theorist Christian Norberg-Schulz, who utilizes the philosopher Martin Heidegger's conception of "dwelling":

> "When man dwells, he is simultaneously located in space and exposed to a certain environmental character. The two psychological functions involved, may be called 'orientation' and 'identification.' To gain an existential foothold man has to be able to *orient* himself; he has to know *where* he is. But he also has to *identify* himself with the environment, that is, he has to know *how* he is in a certain place." . . . Dwelling consequently entails above all "identification with the environment; and from this it follows that the 'existential purpose' of building, architecture, and urban design is 'to uncover the meanings potentially present in the given environment.' To think this way is not to concede anything to environmental determinism, nor is it to insist upon a static conception of place."[47]

Dwelling here requires a presence within the environment, in both physical and spiritual ways, and it opens opportunities for connecting individual and communal social and environmental experiences.[48] Given this connection, some have focused on the need to "resacralize" place.[49] Places can be sites of collective memory and social identity[50] and so they have political value and power (they can also be the sites of the contestation of power). If place is particularistic, however, it can run into tension with a more universalizing sensibility in social justice, which looks to universalizing conceptions and values.[51] Finding ways to balance universal considerations within grounded, localized realities and experiences that we noted above is a challenge but one that we need to engage, if we are to address environmental issues with any success.[52]

Harvey intriguingly argues that universality can never be avoided, but that it needs to be constructed in dialectical relation with particularity:[53]

> All propositions for social action (or conceptions of social justice) must be critically evaluated in terms of the situatedness or positionality of the argument and the arguer. But it is equally important to recognize that the individuals developing such situated knowledge are not themselves homogeneous entities but bundles of heterogeneous impulse, any of which derive from an internalization of "multiple othernesses" within the self.[54]

At the same time, Harvey and others note the need for balance between some level of permanence and multiple and shifting identities.[55] That is, to some degree, we must consider how we can be "situated" within a world of difference[56]—or, as my colleague Keren Fraiman and I have explored—how we can create a sense of communal belonging (peoplehood) through diversity and not uniformity,[57] issues that are core to systems thinking and new approaches to both history and religion.

In considering ecological systems and environmental concerns, another exploration of the distinction between space and place is important. Timothy Morton argues that space is an objective phenomenon and place a subjective one.[58] Morton continues to play provocatively with the distinction between object and subject. In another work, he writes that

> because a thing just is a rift between what is and how it appears, for any entity whatsoever, not simply for that special entity called the (human) subject. What ecological thought must do, then, is unground the human by forcing it back onto the ground, which is to say, standing on a gigantic object called *Earth* inside a gigantic entity called *biosphere*.[59]

For Morton, global warming is itself an object and, more than that, what he terms a hyperobject,[60] meaning that it is something that does not come and go, but rather "looms around us constantly."[61] Hyperobjects, Morton contends, have a temporal dimension, and they are future facing.[62] He writes that "hyperobjects last so long that utilitarian concepts such as the social discount rate, a sliding scale for determining the value of future people for present actions, cannot be ethically or even meaningfully applied to them. Hyperobjects compel us to adopt attitudes for which humans are not well prepared in an age of advanced consumer capitalism."[63] According to Morton, global warming is also a wicked problem, for which there is no rational solution. More than that, he argues that global warming may even be a "super wicked problem," in which there is no central authority to address it and even efforts to mitigate it can contribute to it.[64]

Polarization

One response to complexity and uncertainty has been increased social and political polarization. As the Columbia University political scientist Peter Coleman argues, we have become so polarized ("simplistic, dichotomized, and tribal") that we have lost any middle ground and anything we hear becomes fodder to reinforce our beliefs or, when it does not align with those beliefs, is easily marginalized and dismissed.[65] Coleman writes that

> This suggests that [most] of us are putting much less time and energy into seeking accurate information about the people on the other side of the divide or on the many different challenges facing our world, choosing instead to think and feel in ways that are consistent and conforming with our tribes. We are devoting much more energy to obtaining a sense of *belonging* and comfort from our groups than to seeking accurate information about our increasingly complicated world.[66]

Part of the reason that polarized thinking has become more widespread is that people often cannot tolerate complexity,[67] and the collapse of complexity itself leads to more "intractable conflict."[68] The opposite is also true: in the midst of complexity and uncertainty, we often seek simplicity.[69]

Coleman's discussion of polarization, therefore, has a few lessons for engaging with environmental concerns. Coleman asserts that most of the issues over which we are divided have more than two sides.[70] So, it is not generally a question of truths or right and wrong, but of nuance. There may be some hope, however. Coleman argues that complex systems can be significantly affected by even simple changes.[71]

At the same time, the effects of changes on complex systems can sometimes be obvious and immediate but also delayed, and importantly, they can lead to unintended consequences.[72] Coleman notes that there are "unarticulated assumptions and beliefs that we hold about aspects of ourselves, others, and the world around us that shape how we engage with the world."[73] Nonetheless, Coleman identifies some important theories of change that have resonance in other fields as well. Here, Coleman introduces a concept with ecological overtones, namely radical relandscaping—to further expand the discourse on space we noted above. He describes it in the following terms: "Rather than fight, flee, or fix the conflict, it recommends working with the flow of the (self-organizing) situation to realize sustained change."[74] This radical relandscaping stresses situations and collective action over individual agency:

> it offers a less direct, multicausal nonlinear view of some types of change. This perspective recognizes that direct action in cloudy, unpredictable situations often misfires. Rather than proposing a mastery approach to directly intervening with such divisions, this theory recommends a harmony orientation, working with existing trends, movements, programs, and other inherent sources of energy and political will in the environment.[75]

It also requires a more comprehensive and holistic view of the "constellation of factors perpetuating the conflict."[76] Coleman articulates five modes for the practice of radical relandscaping, namely reset, bolster and break, complicate, move, adapt.[77] Such relandscaping requires that we break our fixity, reconsider our current ideas and actions, and seek more nuance and complication.

Another theory of change that Coleman references relates to the work of behavioral psychologists Amos Tversky and Daniel Kahneman about the powerful effects of positive (vs. negative) semantic framing on decision-making.[78] In the context of environmental decision-making, could the celebration of nature, for example, as opposed to punishment for poor environmental decisions, be more successful in making real and lasting change in behavior? Indeed, as we learned about Jewish approaches to interpretation, the very way we frame a situation or ask questions (and what questions we actually ask) can have a significant impact—"the questions we ask when seeking change not only shape our understanding of the challenges (and opportunities) we face but also determine our expectations and sense of hope and possibility for the future,"[79] revealing resonance around communal sensibilities and shared interests or needs.[80]

Coleman suggests some strategies for complicating our thinking and views that can help us to overcome polarization. First, we must identify and own our own internal contradictions.[81] This work opens us to be vulnerable to our own assumptions as well as those of others. This leads to a tolerance for ambiguity, which Coleman argues helps make "people who are more able to accept and not become destabilized by uncertain, inconsistent, or otherwise ambiguous situations and information," leading to greater happiness, health, and ability to deal with complexity.[82] Relatedly, Coleman advocates for dialogue over debate.[83] Dialogue allows us to hear others and also be heard,[84] amplifying contradictions, widening lenses, and complicating narratives.[85] Coleman suggests emphasizing movement (from tensions), with a literal change in physical space allowing a shakeup of how we traditionally see, feel, and understand.[86] He also recommends "synchronization," the operation of two or more things simultaneously, which he claims science shows can lead to enhanced cooperation, ability to achieve joint goals, increased compassion, and greater concern for a partner's outcomes.[87]

Complex problems and future considerations often lead to worse judgments.[88] Coleman asserts that we have trouble making decisions when we are stymied by the quest for efficiency, when we have to think about, plan for, and respond to situations that do not currently exist, when we are concerned about our esteem, and when a multitude of situational demands (such as "complexity, volatility, opacity, unfamiliarity etc.") impair our cognitive capacities.[89] The issues of temporal distance and cause and effect,[90] which we have noted in reexamining history, can lead to decision-making errors such as failing to anticipate the side effects or long-term repercussions of the actions we take and assuming that the absence of obviously negative consequences immediately means that whatever actions we have taken were successful.[91]

Others have also noted that polarization comes from the inability to see that we ourselves and our preferences are interdependent with those of others. One challenge is that in polarization, people can begin to define themselves by a particular point of view.[92] Brian Emerson and Kelly Lewis write that "When people who are attached to a perspective bump up against others who hold the 'opposite' perspective, they can get resistant and even recalcitrant as the things they value, and thereby their identity, are being threatened."[93] They note that when we focus on a pole, we appear to get short-term benefits, but ignoring the other pole can lead to negative outcomes. Instead, they assert that it is beneficial to pull the poles apart and understand benefits and overuses and identify the "Third Way" that occurs when harmonizing the tension:[94] "Standing in the Third Way is a commitment—to personal development, to growth, and to being with the truth of the interdependent relationship."[95] Navigating the polarities, therefore, requires a willingness to be vulnerable in some ways[96] and, importantly, it takes practice.[97] Thinking beyond polarities and embracing complexities can be aided by the lessons of history and the thinking and practices of religion, and especially by the new systemic approaches to both that we outlined throughout Part II of this book.

Resilience

In addressing complexity and uncertainty, along with the penchant for polarization that often comes along with it, some scholars have advanced the concept of resilience. In a postmodern world, ideas of climate are themselves constructed, unstable, and changeable.[98] In this context, resilience recognizes such change(ability) and reflects the ability of a disrupted system to return to a new configuration of stability (not a previous status quo)[99]—after all, change is the very nature of life.[100]

Resilience has been much discussed in the field of disaster preparedness and response and, because of its close connection with systems thinking and ecology, in the broader field of environmental studies. The theme of resilience has proven fertile ground for a range of studies and approaches in leadership, history, and religion as well. Not everyone has been persuaded of the value of resilience thinking, and some associate it with the very neoliberal regimes that are frequently held responsible for environmental degradation in modernity and contemporary life. Nonetheless, in the context of thinking about the Anthropocene, resilience seems to bring some potential value in identifying key issues and reorienting approaches to and possible solutions for addressing environmental and societal concerns.

Stephanie Wakefield, Kevin Grove, and David Chandler argue that "Resilience thinking engages problematic situations that exceed modernist practices of security, such as problems of non-linear ecosystem change and collapse."[101] Resilience, in this reading, offers new ways to understand and redistribute agency,[102] engage with feedback, and enable flexibility in responses because it is focused on processes, inter-relations, and interactive emergence—it is "less concerned with 'top-down' interventions—seeking to impose direction and ends—and more with 'facilitating,' 'enabling' or 'engendering' existing powers and capacities or seeking to redirect them to new possibilities."[103] That is, it offers significant antidotes to the challenges brought about by complexity.

This notion of resilience challenges fixity and so also linear causality,[104] opening opportunities to understand the multiple connections that intertwine to create current realities and challenges. Along the way, it can suggest different approaches to problem-solving as well.[105] It has often been the case that humans have applied fixed or static approaches to the problem of environmental degradation, though the problem itself is multivalent and fluid. Not surprisingly, such approaches have not been fully satisfactory or truly effective, as we discovered in the historical cases in Part I. The emphasis on systems and relationships affords the opportunity to recalibrate the interrelationship of humans and that of humans and nature in new and potentially fruitful ways. Indeed, de-centering humans may be a first, important step in reconceptualizing nature and our (mutually entangled and co-constitutive) connections with and to it.[106] It also reminds us of the many ways in which nature is beyond human knowledge and human control.[107]

The simple resilience of bouncing back to a status quo is not sufficient for the complexity of contemporary and future challenges.[108] Such simple resilience was informed by a simple binary that separated inside and outside and that relied on "top-down technologies or technocratic interventions."[109] As David Chandler notes

> As long as policy-makers and academic theorists presumed a modernist "world" external to us and amenable to governing and policy interventions, resilience-thinking could "reabsorb" or "metabolize" shocks and "bounce-back" through learning from disasters—even reimagining catastrophes as "emancipatory"—or as facilitating new forms of self-growth and improved systems of self-management.[110]

The process approach (rather than the solutions approach) is helpful, for as an expert on climate change, environmental security, and geopolitics, Simon Dalby reminds us, contemporary changes are taking place on a scale and speed that is unprecedented: "The complexity of the earth system and the scale of human activity make it clear that resilience understood in terms of systems recovery after a disruption isn't anything like enough to grapple with the overall crisis."[111] Contemporary climate change is occurring quickly, but that change is also rooted in very long ecological time—time for development and "recovery" or "restoration."[112] Our responses, therefore, require short- and longer-term responses. Quick temporal response is limited by the political reality that many politicians are loathe to make changes that would have political implications while they are in office (or seeking office).[113] Long-term responses require changes to current political and social structures. Resilience, with its systems approach and possibility for adaptation across time, may be helpful in reframing how we see ourselves and our relationships with others and the environment—especially since we have learned from cybernetics and other disciplines that it can be easier to adapt than to anticipate and control change.[114]

There has been criticism of the concept of resilience in some corners, especially in the field of climate justice, since notions of recovery to a status quo can "codify inequities."[115] As Kian Goh writes, "The movement for climate justice is born of historical global inequities and disparate vulnerabilities. It builds on notions such as 'ecological debt'—the assertion that historical and current exploitative and exchange relationships between richer countries of the Global North and poorer countries of the Global South perpetuate unequal environmental burdens—and calls for a 'just transition' to a postcarbon economy."[116] Resilience is positional, and so Goh argues that a just resilience "requires attention to the possibilities of radical imaginaries and practices of place-based, ground-up community voices as well as public institutions across levels of urban governance to remake places and social relationships across scales."[117] My colleague Mike Hogue and I have posited that a "complex" resilience, in which we learn and adapt through disruption, can be acquired through the combination of vulnerability (an openness to evaluating our own assumptions and understanding those of others), intentionality (in our thoughts and actions), trust (building strong and engaged relationships), and awareness (the ability to pay attention to what is happening with ourselves, around us, and in the broader environment). We term this approach VITA, which in Latin means life, making this approach to complex resilience a life stance and practice.[118] Resilience is, therefore, not the solution, but it can nonetheless be a significant tool as we try to respond to and mitigate climate change and environmental degradation.

Conclusions

Natural disasters and climate change are complex—they have been described as wicked and even super wicked problems. That means that there is not simply one answer to address them and that some of the actions we take may have an impact, sometimes an adverse one, which we may not even (yet) be aware of. Part of the complexity is also associated with the humans who created and are struggling with the manifestations of this complexity. Polarized views on these issues, the dangers and implications they bring, and what, if anything, to do about them, make it even more difficult to address them. The polarization that has developed and become regnant all around us does not position humanity well to address a complex problem, which requires a larger systems approach and an ability to navigate with and through gray and nuance. As we have seen in this chapter, understanding the nature of relationships (between humans and nature, as well as within human and environmental systems) is essential if we are to stem the tide of climate change and the natural disasters and human conflicts that are associated with, and often caused by, them. Many of the assumptions we have had about the environment and our impact on it have had to change as we see changes within the earth system that we ignited but cannot control, as we see multiple causes of disasters converge in new, powerful, and accelerated ways, and as we see the layered impact of these changes. The world is much more fluid and changeable than we may have once believed.

In this chapter, we identified some ways to understand this complexity and the polarization that has impeded our ability to navigate complexity and uncertainty. We have also considered how some aspects of resilience, which emerged in important ways from studies of ecology and disaster preparedness and management, may be useful. Some of the perspectives and considerations that have emerged in this chapter were anticipated in the chapters in Part II, where we saw the importance of thinking about society (through history and religion) with an eye toward systems: by cutting across geographies and temporalities; by eschewing simple binaries as explanations; through the introduction of new ways of learning that benefit from traditions (including the traditional understanding and responses we outlined in Part I) and interrogate and transform them as part of robust learning; and through the identification and development of practices that can help us shift behavior and mindsets in ways that can help us to be more agile in an age of hyper-accelerated change. In the next and final chapter (Chapter 11), we now turn to possible ways to bring all of these experiences and thoughts together to provide some practical guidance in what feel like ever more challenging and uncertain times and situations.

11

From Conceptual Challenges to Practical Applications

Introduction

Part I introduced us to ways that premodern people, especially Jews, understood, experienced, and responded to natural disasters. This gave us a chance to understand the worldviews and wisdom of people before (or at the very outset of) modernity, when the influence of humans on the environment took an ever sharper and more profound increase. We observed that premoderns could have similar notions and responses to their later, modern cousins. We learned that they could adapt in important ways and apply their learning to make progress in addressing the disasters that they experienced. Their approach drew on religious texts and ideas (especially Jewish ones), the work of philosophers and scientists from Antiquity and throughout history, as well as reflections on their own experiences. Indeed, history and religion could serve them well since they both provided examples of how to behave and respond and explanations for what they were experiencing.

Much of the hard-earned knowledge that premodern people acquired is still relevant and useful today. It still guides a good deal of our behavior. And yet, as we pointed out in Part II (Chapter 6), the scale, severity, frequency, and, importantly, impact of disasters today (and for the future) that have been caused in some significant ways by human activity will require humans to continue to apply what they have learned in the past and from their faith traditions. It will also require them to develop new ways of thinking and new behaviors to help stem the tide of climate change and the increase in natural disasters, as well as respond to them when they occur. New developments in history and religion—and in Jewish history and Judaism in particular—emerge from the challenges of contemporary life but may also be helpful in addressing those challenges. In addressing the complexity of climate change and natural disasters today, (Jewish) history and religion (Judaism and other religions and faith traditions) provide us with valuable tools related to critical thinking, adaptation, learning, communications, scenario planning, innovation, solidarity building, relationship building, and justice work.

Thinking, Writing, and Learning in the Anthropocene

While there has been a good deal of emphasis on the value of science (in both identifying environmental issues and offering ways to reverse or mitigate them, including some intriguing and some troubling geoengineering ideas), the Humanities have also been harnessed as we think about the environment and, especially, the ways we think about human behavior and change. The relatively new field of environmental humanities offers important opportunities for critical rethinking in many areas and diverse ways. As one recent scholar declares, "One contribution of the environmental humanities is to make clear normative arguments: to describe the world not merely as it is, but as it could be."[1] Environmental humanities have been used to help apply moral claims in the midst of ever-changing technology.[2] Many academic disciplines and subdisciplines have been brought into conversation with environmental issues. Feminist Studies and Queer Studies, for example, offer an opportunity to look at a plurality of factors and to test traditional assumptions and binaries, as noted earlier in this book.[3] Philosophy has also been quite helpful in understanding our current relationship with nature and the environment and in identifying ways to think about the ways we interact with and impact it, providing needed nuance in the very ways that we perceive the world.

In addition to the new perspectives that Humanities can offer, we have learned that Science, like all other disciplines, is subjective, changeable, and conditioned by context and a wide range of factors. At the very least, as scientist Niels Bohr (1885–1962) noted, we cannot understand what occurs in the world without accounting for ourselves and our own minds.[4] Or, as American writer and essayist Meghan O'Gieblyn writes, "There is no Archimedean point, no purely objective vista that allows us to transcend our human interests and see the world from above, as we once imagined it appeared to God. It is our distinctive vantage that binds us to the world and sets the necessary limitations that are required to make sense of it."[5]

Given the challenges to objectivity, the field of ethics is important in evaluating many significant conversations and considerations related to environmental matters. Land and water resources and usage discussions (as we will see below), for example, offer an opportunity for consideration of questions of social and political relations as well as the ethical questions related to how we see and use the environment. Aldo Leopold (1887–1948) formulated a land ethic that helps in this regard. For Leopold, the land is a living being and must be treated with love and respect—not as a thing to be exploited. The land, from this perspective, is a community of interdependent organisms including soil, water, plants, animals, and people; and a land ethic flows from a land aesthetic.[6]

Writing has been shown to be a powerful way to introduce people to, and help change behaviors when addressing, environmental (as well as other) concerns. Writing is a "strategy" that can have a personal and broader impact. Realities change what we write about and change us; but what we write about can also change us.[7] Narratives (discussed more fully in Chapter 7) are cultural practices that are related to some form of change. Not just a story, they are a communicative act of storytelling.[8] As consumerist educator and futurist scholar Vuokko Jarva writes, "Narratives are always comments, often on the deviations from the social convention, embedded in habitual scripts. Narratives are not only mirroring but performing, acting upon the world. They always have a mission, a message to deliver."[9] Storytelling, in particular, is an effective tool for individual and collective identity formation and for developing critical thinking skills. Matthew S. Henry argues that "Storytelling, through a range of media, can help link the individual to the collective, revealing shared experiences and empowering groups and communities to identify shared goals—all critical for overcoming doom-and-gloom environmental narratives centered around trauma, catastrophe, and inertia"[10] He stresses the importance of cultural representation, the incorporation of local knowledge, and collective interdependence that can be highlighted and that can emerge from storytelling as a powerful way to help address environmental conditions and problems.[11]

Not only the (meta)narratives we tell, but the very language that we employ in these narratives, can be powerful. Language matters in how we describe nature and natural disasters. Language, especially the metaphors we use, can quite literally shape how we process events and respond. Consider the use of certain terms when it comes to addressing social issues. AI expert and law professor Orly Lobel notes that

> The way we frame problems informs how we think of solutions. Lera Boroditsky, a psychology professor at the University of California, San Diego, ran an experiment that demonstrates how metaphors shape the way people are motivated to address social issues. In the study, one group of people was told that crime is a "beast" preying on a community. The other group read a description of the crime infecting a community as a "virus." With just a difference of one word, people supported different solutions to the same problem of high crime rates. Looking at it through the lens of the "beast" led them to want more policing and harsher punishment. Those who saw it through the lens of a "virus" supported social reforms and constructive solutions such as education, community support, poverty-alleviating measures, and the creation of more housing and jobs for the poor.[12]

The broader work in humanities and environmental humanities also involves significant thinking in the field of education and learning theory. In some of his work, Eilon Schwartz casts the discussion of the environment into a broader context that involves education, and especially Jewish education. "At its heart," he writes,

> the environmental crisis is a crisis of how we see and relate to the world around us. It is a crisis of culture, society and politics. Jewish education, framed as a cultural endeavor, should therefore be extremely relevant to the questions of the environmental crisis and the ways we are part of the problem, and the ways we can nevertheless become part of the solution.[13]

Schwartz calls for educational activities that instill a sense of wonder in nature, which create opportunities for dialogue between science and religion, facts and values, and allow students to see the interdependence humans have with each other and the responsibility we have for our actions.[14] This involves understanding that our actions—as well as climate change—represent a legacy that we are leaving for future generations; it also means that we need to foster a meaningful sense of place (as noted in Chapter 10) and that we need to understand that the habits we form become commonplace and impact our behavior and that of others.[15] "The first step," Schwartz argues, "in changing habits is exposing what is unsustainable about our present ones, and then creating alternatives."[16]

Schwartz suggests an environmental agenda that is focused on simplicity, community, and the centering of nature in human life.[17] He asserts that Jewish environmentalism offers an opportunity for dialogue between traditional texts and contemporary society[18] and he argues that real change will be more likely to be bottom up than top down,[19] leading him to advocate for a particular form of engagement:

> Engagement demands both belonging and criticism. We need to be part of the community, but we also need to change it. Being part of the community is a necessary condition for any engagement—criticism without a deep sense of belonging often strips criticism of sympathy, an important component in any effective criticism. But belonging without criticism does a profound disservice to the rich, dynamic tradition of which we are a part.[20]

Some have challenged the efficacy of "community." Michael S. Hogue argues that community privileges shared identity, which can divide people by differences and reinforce a politics of special interest. He writes that "while the lure of community makes sense in a splintering, fracturing, polarizing world, the privileging of shared identity within community can reinforce those splinters, fractures, and polarities. We may need community, but the complexity of the challenges we face demands more than communities."[21] Instead of community, Hogue calls for "solidarities," which "are a special kind of association an association that performatively answers the question of who they are as a 'we.' While communities tend to define themselves as a 'we' in terms of common identity, racial or cultural or otherwise, solidarities comprise diverse individuals or communities organized around common purposes."[22]

Various other responses to the ecological crisis have emphasized the need for protecting "diverse cultural and environmental commons," developing "strong Earth democracies," in addition to developing education "based learning to encourage students to identify the causes, and remediate effects, of social and ecological violence in the places they live."[23] In addition to a pedagogy that stresses responsibility and diversity,[24] other education areas of focus have been seen to have value. This includes outdoor and experiential education, place-based education, holistic education, environmental justice, and ecopedagogy.[25]

The ecological crisis we are experiencing today has cultural and educational dimensions. Rebecca Martusewicz, for example, argues that

> the ecological crisis is really a cultural crisis—that is, a crisis in the way people have learned to think and thus behave in relation to larger life systems and toward each other. It can be shifted if we learn to think differently about our relationships

to each other and to the natural world, and if we help students to identify and revalue those critical practices of mutual support and interdependence that still exist in communities all over the world.[26]

In particular, some scholars have pointed to ways that modern thinking and experience have undermined local and global systems (as we have discussed), entrenched patterns of unjust domination, and led to hyper-consumerism and commodification.[27] Education is an important tool in addressing these and other concerns.

Education about conflict, to take one particular area, may teach us valuable lessons about ecological issues. Keren Fraiman, in addressing how educators engage with the Israeli-Palestinian conflict in Jewish educational spaces, argues that there are four distinct barriers to such engagement. These have applications in other areas—including environment and environmental conflict—as well. They are: 1) knowledge—about the subject and context; 2) pedagogy—facilitating challenging conversations; 3) emotions—supporting students' emotions that emerge when learning about and discussing the conflict; 4) communal pressures and institutional support.[28] Addressing environmental issues will require us to leverage the knowledge that we have already, as in the historical cases in Part I, but also develop and maintain an openness to think differently as well. For some, there is a romantic notion that returning to a premodern sensibility,[29] which predates all the problems associated with modernity and its associated Anthropocene, will advance our work to mitigate climate change and environmental degradation. But, as we saw in Part II, this "return" is helpful but insufficient, especially given the significant and accelerated changes of the contemporary world. Fraiman reminds us that we need deep content expertise but also an ability to engage across differences and in uncertain and often emotional contexts if we are to bridge gaps and make real progress in conflicts and sensitive discussions and work.

As Fraiman signals, we know that learning is about far more than knowledge acquisition. Learning helps with critical thinking and analysis and in decision-making and problem-solving. Scenario planning has always been important, especially during periods of crisis. There is often a gap between scenarios and related actions, and it has been noted that good forecasts lead to action (not that they are necessarily accurate in their predictions).[30] There are many ways to think about decision-making, however, which reflect a range of social and ethical considerations. In many cases, these approaches have a good deal of relevance and have, at times, been applied to environmental issues. Famously, there is the tragedy of the commons, described by Russell and Norvig as "if nobody has to pay for using a common resource, then it may be exploited in a way that leads to a lower total utility for all agents." They note that "one approach for dealing with the tragedy of the commons is to change the mechanism to one that charges each agent for using the commons."[31] Carbon credits, to take an environmental example, have been one approach to addressing inequity among developed and developing nations.[32]

As a complex, perhaps wicked, problem that is highly relational, environmental degradation requires multiple and multilayered responses. As such, political and cultural knowledge is needed along with science.[33] Historical and cultural contexts are also required when identifying and applying technological fixes.[34] As Robert Emmett and David Nye argue, "The global environmental crisis demands new ways of thinking and new communities that produce environmental solutions as a form of civic knowledge. The crisis cannot be addressed solely by finding technological solutions to particular problems that are delivered 'downstream' to a population of passive consumers."[35] Responses to natural disasters have always required a range of skills and learning across multiple sectors of life and society. That is even more true in the Anthropocene. Framing environmental issues as complex and even wicked problems affords us the opportunity to bring different perspectives and approaches to bear on our responses. As we have seen, newer ways of thinking about (Jewish) history and religion (Judaism) align with these new approaches and allow us to bridge previous experiences into new, uncertain, and complex situations today and in the future. In addition to new ways of thinking, our behaviors will have to change as well—just as history and religion have shown us in different contexts.

In discussions about machine learning, which invariably circle back to how humans learn as well, the decisions that we all make are interrelated. The shaping of behavior through the use of simple rewards for the "successive approximations of that behavior" in the machine learning world may translate into human learning and behavior change as well.[36] In a certain sense, this approach is about rewarding specific states rather than individual actions.[37] Brian Christian notes that previous work of researchers "suggested that shaping rewards could enable an agent with limited ability to look ahead and forecast the effects of its actions to behave as if it was more farsighted than it really was."[38] A related discussion is about how to create intrinsic as opposed to extrinsic motivation to behave in certain ways.[39]

Behavior Change[40]

One of the impediments to behavioral change, especially when it comes to environmental issues, is the notion that the actions of any one individual are not important or extensive enough to make any real impact. Indeed, I have heard communal leaders say that it really does not matter what individuals do—the only thing that will move the proverbial needle are changes in the largest companies that are doing the most damage. But that is a challenging position to take. For, regardless of the weight of individual impact, the transformation of thinking in the individual, and by extension everyone with whom they interact, can be quite significant. The Hasidic master Rabbi Levi Yitzhak of Berdichev (1740–1809), in his *Kedushat Levi,* wrote that:

> The main thing that brings a person to the fear of God is when he recalls constantly that the entire world depends on his deeds, as the sages said—every person must say, for my sake the world was created. And a person should always see himself as if he is half righteous and half unrighteous and with one single deed he can tip the scales, for himself and for the entire world (Bavli Kiddushin 40b). So, when he reflects on how the entire world depends on him and on his actions, and for him the entire world was created, he will be heartbroken for his sins and will engage

with enthusiasm in God's commandments and his Torah, so as to bring bounty to all the worlds, all the angels, all souls and to the lower (physical) world.[41]

There is also a fine balance between theory and practice, as the rabbis already pointed out. In Avot 3:18, we find an intriguing passage that notes the important connections between Torah and correct conduct, understanding and knowledge, Torah and sustenance, and, particularly relevant for this discussion, wisdom and deeds. The passage runs:

> Rabbi Elazar ben Azariah said: Where there is no Torah, there is no right conduct; where there is no right conduct, there is no Torah. Where there is no wisdom, there is no fear of God; where there is no fear of God, there is no wisdom. Where there is no understanding, there is no knowledge; where there is no knowledge, there is no understanding. Where there is no bread, there is no Torah; where there is no Torah, there is no bread. He used to say: one whose wisdom exceeds his deeds, to what may he be compared? To a tree whose branches are numerous but whose roots are few, so that when the wind comes, it uproots it and overturns it, as it is said, "He shall be like a bush in the desert, which does not sense the coming of good. It is set in the scorched places of the wilderness, in a barren land without inhabitant" (Jeremiah 17:6). But one whose deeds exceed his wisdom, to what may he be compared? To a tree whose branches are few but roots are many, so that even if all the winds in the world come and blow upon it, they cannot move it out of its place, as it is said, "He shall be like a tree planted by waters, sending forth its roots by a stream. It does not sense the coming of heat, its leaves are ever fresh. It has no care in a year of drought; it does not cease to yield fruit" (ibid, 17:8).

In this passage, wisdom is important, but it does not create the deep and robust roots that deeds do. Literally, our work roots us and creates deep connections from the bottom up that can sustain us under difficult conditions. Here, the value of grounding, space, and dwelling that we discussed in the last chapter takes on even greater significance.

Wendell Berry similarly argues that action must proceed from the bottom up. He writes in his essay, "Think Little," "While the government is 'studying' and funding and organizing its Big Thought, nothing is being done. But the citizen who is willing to Think Little, and, accepting the discipline of that, to go ahead on his own, is already solving the problem."[42] In his work, Berry offers an analysis that distinguishes between what he terms "industrialism" and "agrarianism," which relates to different forms of land use as well as how we understand ourselves, other creatures, and the world.[43] "Industrialism," he asserts,

> begins with technological innovation. But agrarianism begins with givens: land, plants, animals, weather, hunger, and the birthright knowledge of agriculture. Industrialists are always ready to ignore, sell, or destroy the past in order to gain the entirely unprecedented wealth, comfort, and happiness supposedly to be found in the future. Agrarian farmers know that their very identity depends on their willingness to receive gratefully, use responsibly, and hand down intact

an inheritance, both natural and cultural, from the past. Agrarians understand themselves as the users and caretakers of some things they did not make, and of some things that they cannot make.[44]

A competing sense of nurturing and a propensity for exploitation exist within and between people—"We are all to some extent the products of an exploitive society, and it would be foolish and self-defeating to pretend that we do not bear its stamp."[45] So, we need to understand ourselves and our contexts, recognizing the complexities that we face, and simultaneously striving for reflection, understanding, and action.

Many scholars and activists have suggested a range of practical actions as we address environmental issues. Mike Berners-Lee, for example, identifies three strands of an environmental strategy: improving our own impact; enabling others to improve their impact; and pushing for global arrangements where needed.[46] These approaches focus on self and local and global collectives. Similarly, our own reflections can be a point of transformation, as one classic Jewish story recounts:

> When the Holy Seer of Lublin was a little boy, he was known to skip school for hours or even days. Once, his teacher followed the young boy to see what became of these free moments. The Seer walked to the edge of the town, into the deep woods, and there, in a small, green circle of trees, he began to pray. The next day the teacher asked the boy what drew him to those woods. The Seer of Lublin replied, "I can find God there." "But," said the teacher, "surely God is the same in the town as in the woods." "That is true," replied the Seer, "but I am not the same."[47]

For many writing amid environmental crisis, it is human behavior that is at the root cause of the negative changes. Wendell Berry rues the "doctrine of limitlessness" (which we saw in the critique of the "Capitalocene") or "the desire to be 'efficient' at any cost . . . "[48] He argues that "However it came about, this credo of limitlessness clearly implies a principled wish, not only for limitless possessions, but also for limitless knowledge, limitless science, limitless technology, and limitless progress. And necessarily, it must lead to limitless violence, waste, war, and destruction. That it should finally produce a crowning cult of political limitlessness is only a matter of mad logic."[49] Limits (like the contraction we introduced in Chapter 8), he contends, by contrast, are not confinements but "inducements to formal elaboration and elegance, to *fullness* of relationship and meaning."[50] Inverting the metaphor of domination that some have seen in the biblical text, Berry writes that "To recover from our disease of limitlessness we will have to give up the idea that we have a right to be godlike animals, that we are at least potentially omniscient and omnipotent, ready to discover 'the secret of the universe.'"[51] What is more, Berry asserts that through our own individual abuses of the world we contribute to the larger devastation and that we should not wait to do what is right in reversing this abuse until "everybody does it."[52]

Many, in fact, advocate for changing how we live. Berry, in "A Native Hill," writes that

> We have lived by the assumption that what was good for us would be good for the world. . . . We have been wrong. We must change our lives, so that it will be possible to live by the contrary assumption that what is good for the world will be good for us. And that requires that we make the effort to *know* the world and to learn from what is good for it.[53]

Beyond individual sensibilities and actions, several approaches focus on larger communal and societal concerns. While there are many notions of "nature,"[54] seeing nature in a more complex and fluid way allows for opening new ways of thinking and behaving. Michael S. Hogue, leveraging the thought of John Dewey, argues that thinking of nature as a process "demanded a dismantling of the supremacy of unchanging ideas, final causes, and theoretical problems over ideas of change, efficient causes, and practical challenges."[55] This can open important innovations and changes in perspective and behavior. At the same time, Dewey highlights that changing environments encourage people to seek security and certainty, which, according to Hogue, favor "thinking, knowing, and theory over acting, doing, and practice."[56] How do we leverage the notion of change for innovation as opposed to resistance?

Behavior change extends to social conditions. German sociologist Ulrich Beck argues that climate change "creates an entirely different way of conceptualizing the world and our chances of survival within it."[57] He refers to this transformation as metamorphosis, which is "not social change, not transformation, not evolution, not revolution and not crisis. It is a mode of changing the nature of human existence. It signifies the age of side effects."[58] While climate change ushers in physical change, it also alters social relations, part of power structures that redistribute social inequalities.[59] Beck concludes that "Metamorphosis then also means that the past is problematized through the imagination of a threatening future."[60] Urban ecologies, to take another example, suggest that there are some ways to contest inequities and vulnerabilities, especially through "design—urban, landscape, architectural, and infrastructural— which is often the platform through which contesting spatial agendas are visualized and prioritized."[61] In this regard, space can be a product of social relations and have multiple concepts and uses.[62]

Some scholars attribute some (or all) of the blame for the climate crisis to overconsumption (and consumerism)[63] by humans or a certain sense of "exceptionalism," by which humans feel entitled to whatever they may desire.[64] Sally Weintrobe suggests, instead, that "the starting point for building a more caring society is never forgetting that care and uncare are inherent parts of us all, and that each seeks expression and dominance over the other; also remembering that just because care wins a struggle with uncare one day, it does not mean its way will endure."[65] That is, she calls for new frameworks of care.[66] Such an approach involves nurturing feelings of containment (which also work against overwhelm).[67] Weintrobe notes that people often adopt psychological negation or denial when it comes to climate change.[68] She also identifies a condition she terms "eco-anxiety"[69] and she asserts that we need to develop not just awareness, but "formed awareness," in which we know that we bear some responsibility for climate change.[70] So, behavior change can take many forms and it is enhanced when combined with personal and psychological reflection and practice.

Other strategies suggested for addressing environmental issues, and especially climate change, require radical innovation, imagination, or cultural realignment. Some are simply about beginning with recognition, which is about attaining knowledge. As the novelist Amitav Ghosh writes,

> Recognition is famously a passage from ignorance to knowledge. To recognize, then, is not the same as an initial introduction. To recognize, then, is not the same as an introduction. Nor does recognition require an exchange of words: more often than not we recognize mutely. And to recognize is by no means to understand that which meets the eye; comprehension need play no part in a moment of recognition. . . . The most important element of the word *recognition* thus lies in its first syllable, which harks back to something prior, an already existing awareness that makes possible the passage from ignorance to knowledge: a moment of recognition occurs when a prior awareness flashes before us, effecting an instant change in our understanding of that which is beheld.[71]

There have been many discussions about what keeps people from understanding and addressing environmental issues, especially climate change. Some individuals and industries have worked hard to circulate misinformation or to cast doubts on the validity of scientific findings—or in some cases to produce counter scientific claims.[72]

Even more challenging, as we have seen, the temporal and at times geographic distance between the impact of environmental degradation and the experiences of some people makes it difficult for those people to understand fully the scope and nature of the crises. Natural systems are "highly structured, ordered and regulated steady-state natural systems"; however, they are a mix of geographical scales (local, national, global), as well as temporal scales (in which past actions affect the present and those of the past and present impact the future), and are highly changeable.[73] In the case of water, David Sedlak notes that the very cadence of political office can significantly affect how such issues are understood and approached: "Although public sentiment is important to decisions about emissions controls, many of the key decisions will be made by politicians and business leaders whose success depends upon near-term economic impacts of their actions."[74] Such distance between various geographical and temporal scales, and the changeable nature of systems, can create a disconnect between how we feel about environmental degradation and what we actually do about it.[75]

Or, as Jonathan Safran Foer has noted,

> We are aware of the existential stakes and the urgency, but even when we know that a war for our survival is raging, we don't feel immersed in it. That distance between awareness and feeling can make it very difficult for even thoughtful and politically engaged people—people who *want* to act—to act . . . Compounding the *over there* quality of the planetary crisis is a fatigue of the imagination. It is exhausting to contemplate the complexity and scale of the threats we face . . . And we find it hard to remember how much the world has already changed.[76]

As we have seen, humans seem to have a particularly difficult time processing future times and even understanding and describing their own future selves.[77] Indeed, there may be numerous impediments to engaging with the climate crisis. These include the fact that the victims of climate change are often far away, that we tend to focus more on suffering when it is socially proximate, and that the issues often feel "abstract, distant, and isolated."[78] And while most people are interested to do "what is right," they are often more loath to do it when it comes at personal expense.[79] What is more, as Safran Foer writes,

> Social change, much like climate change, is caused by multiple chain reactions that occur simultaneously. Both cause, and are caused by, feedback loops. . . . When a radical change is needed, many argue that it is impossible for individual actions to incite it, so it's futile for anyone to try. This is exactly the opposite of the truth: the impotence of individual action is a reason for everyone to try.[80]

Future narratives may not exist in real life, but they help construct and influence our lives. Jarva notes that "Future narrative then has multiple continuities, different options and open endings. . . . Thus they represent several scenarios included in one narrative whole. The receiver has an active role as a participant in the narrative process. The receiver participates in the 'performance of meaning' . . . The meaning is cocreated."[81] While historical examples of disaster and response can engage us and provide lessons, they can also lack the visceral connection that is necessary to adjust attitudes and behaviors. The benefit of cocreating meaning and imagining futures can place us front and center in problems that have often felt distant and disconnected.

Conclusions

Behavior can be difficult to change, not least because people are used to doing things the way they have done them before and because they may be accustomed to certain things. What is more, there can be competing interests between people. The conflict over water resources, for example, raises many significant issues in this regard. Scholars and researchers Christopher Ward and Sandra Ruckstuhl point to the conflict between people upstream and downstream, the fact that water has social and economic roles, and that it intersects with politics and power struggles and may be part of larger conflicts.[82] In this sense, community collaboration is essential to resolving or at least mitigating conflict.[83] They conclude that "Structural conditions fuel water conflict. And so, the objective of peacebuilding is *positive peace*: the removal of structural conditions—laws, institutions and social structures—that lead to physical harm, prevent parties from satisfying their basic needs and limit human potential."[84]

Consider one case discussed in the Babylonian Talmud, tractate Nedarim (80b):

> The Gemara raises a contradiction between this statement of Rabbi Yosei and another statement of Rabbi Yosei. It was taught in a *baraita*: In the case of a spring belonging to the residents of a city, if the water was needed for their own lives, i.e.,

the city's residents required the spring for drinking water, and it was also needed for the lives of others, their own lives take precedence over the lives of others. Likewise, if the water was needed for their own animals and also for the animals of others, their own animals take precedence over the animals of others. And if the water was needed for their own laundry and also for the laundry of others, their own laundry takes precedence over the laundry of others. However, if the spring water was needed for the lives of others and their own laundry, the lives of others take precedence over their own laundry.

There is a dissenting view, however: "Rabbi Yosei disagrees and says: Even their own laundry takes precedence over the lives of others, as the wearing of unlaundered clothes can eventually cause suffering and pose a danger." (Sefaria translation; A much longer and intricate case is presented in BT Gittin 60b)

The Talmud presents a range of positions. Here, the needs of local residents are prioritized over those from other locations (their lives, livestock, and laundry take precedence over those of others). However, the lives of others take precedence over one's own laundry. A dissenting view suggests that everything local takes precedence over everything foreign. Of course, the importance of water is highlighted here, but so are collective communal needs and, notably, the needs of animals as well as people.

Noah Toly reminds us that environmental challenges have significant social, and we might add political, dimensions.[85] "More specifically," Toly writes, "environmental governance challenges often involve choices that entail foregoing, giving up, undermining, or destroying one or more goods in order to secure one or more other goods."[86] Toly quotes anthropologist Joseph Masco: "We are now facing a three-fold crisis in the crisis of climate change: climate change and its material consequences; a crisis in our conceptual structures that struggle to work on novel scales and temporalities to address climate change; and the crisis of crisis saturation, especially in our media narratives."[87] Emphasizing the temporal span of climate change, Toly reminds us that "the cumulative warming effects of one generation's emissions cannot be borne entirely by that generation, but only distributed over future generations"[88] and that "Arresting climate change and pursuing climate stability would require us to forego, give up, undermine, or destroy other goods intrinsic to the modern energy regime"[89] We will need a plurality of responses.[90]

Given all these observations, it is clear that there is no single answer to environmental degradation and climate change. What is more, it is equally clear from our explorations of Jewish history (and history more generally) and Judaism (along with religion more generally), as well as contemporary thinking about environmental and climate (and associated) issues, that there are many vested interests that have helped to create the problems we are facing and different perspectives and needs in changing attitudes and behaviors.

History teaches us that humans do learn from experiences; it also teaches us that they often return to previous ways of doing things once crises have subsided. Religion teaches us that we can find ways to explain the world, but sometimes those explanations displace our immediacy or our responsibility. The environmental crises we have discussed are not going to subside, and the new approaches to history that connect futures with pasts and presents, and that take deeper temporal views while complexifying causality, can be helpful for the future.

Although some people have laid the climate crisis squarely at the feet of religion—and specifically the Judeo-Christian tradition—religious approaches to nature and the world are nuanced and far from simply exploitative. Many aspects of the practical and moral dimensions of religion provide valuable frameworks for addressing the environmental issues we are now facing on a massive, global scale. As with history, the trends that see religion as evolving and finding new ways to address a changing world—indeed contributing to positive changes in many ways—also build on a range of new thoughts around change, systems, practices, and communities (or solidarities!).

Taken together, we can say that history and religion in a premodern key provide many valuable lessons that have and will continue to impact how we respond to environmental changes and challenges. Moreover, we can add that new approaches to both of these fields—as displayed in developments in Jewish history and Judaism as well as other faith traditions—may be valuable as we face radically new and accelerating changes that have been human induced and will challenge traditional politics, social, and economic structures, and scientific mindsets. Especially when these changes seem to call for a different strategy of non-binary orientations, decentralization of power and response, and grappling with the unknown.[91]

I'd like to suggest a few opportunities for Jewish history and Judaism in light of all the ground we have covered. Jewish history has often been multi- and interdisciplinary. It will continue to benefit from that approach, as Jews belonged to their own communities and the broader societies in which they lived. There is value in comparing and contrasting the ways that Jews thought and behaved and the experiences that they had, especially given the limitations on historical source materials. At the same time, expanding the geographies and temporalities of the study of Jewish history allows us to ask new questions that have relevance in the past and today; they also allow the opportunity to consider future considerations as well. Not that Jews will become prognosticators, rather they will be able to contribute to identifying multiple futures and future scenarios that are important for Jewish (and by extension human) existence but that also enrich the ways that we understand Jewish history itself. Jewish history will continue to benefit from engagement with nature's archives as well as a diverse range of sources beyond written documents and visual materials. Discussions of agency, causality, and impact may provide new and significant ways to imagine the Jewish past. Jewish history can at times feel internal and one-dimensional. The move to discard a lachrymose view of the Jewish past as well as the embrace of multiple historical narratives and experiences (within and beyond the Jewish world) enriches our view of Jewish pasts and also provides important tools for engaging with environmental change.

Judaism—the study and practice of it—will also benefit from the innovations we explored in Part II. The idea that tradition is connective and evolving has been accepted more fully in some circles than others, but it is relevant in all aspects of Judaism, especially in an ever-accelerating world in which old problems and issues take on new dimensions and new issues arise with greater frequency. The study of Judaism has benefited from the "material turn" in the academy as well as the study of comparative religion. Placing Judaism into conversation with other religions and faith traditions will become ever more important, and the expansion of thinking about Judaism through the prism of material culture and practice—which is already embedded in the very fabric of Judaism—can be leveraged in valuable ways as we consider practical steps to address the environment and environmental change.

Judaism has a rich tradition of rejecting binaries and dichotomies and in seeking learning in the most mundane of experiences. These orientations will continue to inform how we think about and practice Judaism; they also have real value for other academic and religious approaches to climate change and the environment. Judaism, as we saw, is not always "green" or apparently prepared for change. However, Judaism has deeply woven into it a range of ways of thinking about and engaging with the world that can be surfaced and elevated around core issues and in ways that can contribute to larger discussions within and beyond the Jewish world. The Jewish penchant for asking questions and challenging (even God) can be an important tool in environmental work. The turn to learning from indigenous societies and religions has received a lot of attention, with the result that written faith traditions have been subject to a good deal of criticism—with the argument that they distance people from the objects that writing merely represents but does not experience. But Judaism sits in a very helpful place where oral traditions (even when canonized and recorded in writing) engage with the written word to offer a dynamic possibility for addressing change and changing needs.

Let me offer a few final observations related to the issues of environmental degradation and climate change by way of conclusion. These are some of the things that this book has identified that really matter as we address environmental concerns now and for the future—from natural disasters to climate change—as well as many other aspects of life:

History matters. It has important things to teach us about how humans have understood, experienced, and responded to the environment and natural disasters in the past. Many of these conceptions and strategies still have value today. History provides tools for contextualization, comparison, and critical thinking. It allows us to understand change over time—and recently, especially over vast periods of time and across diverse locations. History and the narratives and stories that animate it can help us to understand more deeply and facilitate changes in worldviews and behavior. History never exists only in the past; it teaches us that the past, present, and future all need to be accounted for.

Religion matters. Although there are some aspects of religion (especially, but not only Western religions) that have been faulted for helping to create the current environmental crisis, religion (and faith traditions more broadly) also has an amazing capacity to adapt and to mobilize people. It can provide moral and ethical frameworks and create a sense of community and shared destiny. In the more fluid notions of tradition and the ability to navigate change we discussed, religion offers a particularly valuable tool for reflection, repentance, responsibility, and improvement.

Education matters. Education, as Paulo Freire famously said,[92] is not primarily about the accumulation of knowledge (imparted to us by someone else), but about the development of critical thinking skills. That is not to say that we do not need deep and meaningful content; only that kind of knowledge is not sufficient. In this regard, we might more profitably see education (and learning) as verbs and not nouns. That is, education needs to be active and ever evolving. We cannot become complacent—we should regularly identify and assess our assumptions and perspectives, and those of others. Education is also profitably seen as a system, with significant connections across areas of life experience and thinking and opportunities for deeper insight with interdisciplinary exploration.

Complexity matters. The world is complex—human society, the nonhuman world, and the earth system are remarkably complicated and diverse. Complexity can be scary and overwhelming. But we must embrace complexity in order to see and honor the diversity of perspectives and experiences that are present in the world. We must equally eschew simple and dichotomous ways of viewing the world and others. Without the nuance within this complexity, we will continue to spiral into conflictual polarization and get stuck in an inability to move forward to address the most pressing issues of today and the future.

Responsibility matters. We have responsibility for ourselves, our families, and communities. We also have responsibility for others—human and nonhuman life and matter, as well as future generations. Despite the central role that humans have played in the world over the past centuries, leading to the coining of the term Anthropocene, we must recognize and remember that we are not the only creatures on the earth or the only ones who matter. If we take the Judeo-Christian creation stories seriously, we know that they can be interpreted to emphasize human power and ingenuity, indeed human dominance. But they also contain elements of stewardship and care, for which humans are just as responsible.

Change matters. Change can be hard for people. Sometimes it is truly impossible. But everything is always changing. We used to believe that there was something like a status quo and that we could find ways to hold onto it or return to it after challenges or disruptions. We have learned that there is no true status quo and that all things change constantly, including ourselves. This is a helpful reminder that we need to pay attention to the changes around us and to the fact that we need to constantly assess whether the ways we think and behave need to change as well as we confront ever new situations and conditions. If we take a more flexible change mindset, we have the opportunity to adjust in more meaningful and timely ways to environmental and other changes and concerns.

Notes

Introduction

1   See, for example, Dean Phillip Bell, "The Little Ice Age and the Jews: Environmental History and the Mercurial Nature of Jewish-Christian Encounters in Early Modern Germany," *AJS Review* 32, no. 1 (Spring, 2008): 1–27.
2   On the value of taking lessons, or at least new perspectives, from premodern history, see Annette Kehnel, *The Green Ages: Medieval Innovations in Sustainability*, trans. Gesche Ipsen (Waltham: Brandeis University Press, 2024).

Chapter 1

1   See David Sedlak, *Water for All: Global Solutions for a Changing Climate* (New Haven: Yale University Press, 2023), 71.
2   Laurie Zoloth, *Ethics for the Coming Storm: Climate Change and Jewish Thought* (Oxford: Oxford University Press, 2023), 76–7.
3   Aristotle, *Meterologica*, trans. H. D. P. Lee, Loeb Classical Library (Cambridge, MA: Harvard University Press, 1952), II Chapter VII, 199ff.
4   Ibid., 205.
5   Ibid., 207.
6   Ibid.
7   Ibid., 217.
8   Ibid., 219.
9   Ibid., 213–15, 217.
10   Consider also Seneca, *Naturales Quaestiones Volume II*, trans. Thomas H. Corcoran, Loeb Classical Library (Cambridge, MA: Harvard University Press, 1971), Book VI, "Earthquakes," 133ff.
11   Pliny, *Natural History, Volume I*, trans. H. Rackham, Loeb Classical Library (Cambridge, MA: Harvard University Press, 1938), Book II, Chapter LXXXI, 324–25.
12   Ibid., 327–31.
13   Arno Borst, "Das Erdbeben von 1348: Ein historischer Beitrag zur Katastrophenforschung," *Historische Zeitschrift* 233, no. 3 (1981): 529–69, here at 536.
14   Ibid., 540, 558.
15   Ibid., 539–40, 553.
16   Ibid., 541–43.
17   Ibid., 556ff.
18   For a general assessment of medieval and, more specifically, early modern, notions, see, for example: Peter Coates, *Nature: Western Attitudes since Ancient Times* (Berkeley: University of California Press, 1998), 67–81; Keith Thomas, *Religion and the Decline of Magic* (New York: Charles Scribner's Sons, 1971), 78–112.

19   Here and following, see David B. Ruderman, *Jewish Thought and Scientific Discovery in Early Modern Europe* (New Haven: Yale University Press, 1995), 14–53.
20   Ibid., 21–23.
21   Ibid., 17.
22   Ibid.
23   Carlos del Valle, ed., *Los terremotos de Girona de 1427 en la fuente hebrea* (Madrid: Aben Ezra, 1996), Hebrew text with Spanish translation.
24   The Hebrew text begins on page 39.
25   Consider, for example, section 9: "And already it was written in Tolomeo in the introduction of the book, that when stars are aligned what transpires, and *earth* ['*s foundation*] *tremble* (Isa 24:18) *it sweeps him from his place* (Job 27:21)."
26   Ibid., section 4.
27   See, for example, the beginning of section six: "[In] the city of Barcelona and Gerona each man turned to his God above."
28   See ibid., sections 7 and 20, for example.
29   Ibid., section one reads: "*The earth is tottering, tottering* (Isa 24:19) and *behold the Lord will strip the earth bare, and lay it waste, and twist its surface, and scatter its inhabitants* (Isa 24:1) because they transgressed Torah, changed law, *broke the ancient covenant* (Isa 24:5) . . . "
30   Earthquakes are one of the mysteries of God beyond our understanding (ibid., section 15) that demonstrate the power of God (sections 19 and 20, for example).
31   For a general discussion, see Lester A. Segal, *Historical Consciousness and Religious Tradition in Azariah de' Rossi's* Me'or 'Einayim (Philadelphia: Jewish Publication Society, 1989).
32   See Joanna Weinberg, "The Voice of God: Jewish and Christian Responses to the Ferrara Earthquake of November 1570," *Italian Studies* 46 (1990–91): 69–81. See also her introduction to Azariah de' Rossi, *The Light of the Eyes*, trans. Joanna Weinberg (New Haven: Yale University Press, 2001).
33   Weinberg, "The Voice of God," 70–1.
34   De Rossi, *The Light of the Eyes*, 15.
35   Ibid., 13.
36   Ibid.
37   Ibid., 12.
38   See, for example, ibid., 16–18, 14.
39   Ibid., 9.
40   Ibid., 10.
41   Ibid., 29–30.
42   Ibid., 29.
43   Ibid., 18.
44   Ibid., 24.
45   Ibid., 18, 21.
46   Ibid., 8.
47   See ibid., 20, 22, 23.
48   For biographical information and discussions of Gans' historiography, see Mordechai Breuer, "Modernism and Traditionalism in Sixteenth-Century Jewish Historiography: A Study of David Gans' Tzemah David," in *Jewish Thought in the Sixteenth Century*, ed. Bernard Dov Cooperman (Cambridge, MA: Harvard University Press, 1983), 49–88 and Dean Phillip Bell, *Jewish Identity in Early Modern Germany: Memory, Power and Community* (Aldershot: Ashgate, 2007), 122ff.

49 See Matthias Pohlig, *Zwischen Gelehrsamkeit und konfessioneller Identitätsstiftung: Lutherische Kirchen und Universalgeschichtsschreibung 1546–1617* (Tübingen: Mohr Siebeck, 2007).

50 See David Gans, *Zemah David*, ed. Mordechai Breuer (Jerusalem: Y.L. Magnes, Hebrew University of Jerusalem, 1983), introduction to book II. Parts of this passage are translated in Michael Meyer, *Ideas of Jewish History* (Detroit: Wayne State University Press, 1987), 128ff.

51 See Dean Phillip Bell, "The Little Ice Age and the Jews: Environmental History and the Mercurial Nature of Jewish-Christian Relations in Early Modern Germany," *AJS Review* 32, no. 1 (Spring 2008): 1–27, as well as Breuer, "Modernism and Traditionalism."

52 Gans, *Zemah David*, 225.

53 See Bell, "The Little Ice Age and the Jews."

54 Gans, *Zemah David*, 390.

55 Coates, *Nature*, 72.

56 Ibid., 78–9.

57 Jelle Zeilinga de Boer and Donald Theodore Sanders, *Earthquakes in Human History: The Far-Reaching Effects of Seismic Disruptions* (Princeton: Princeton University Press, 2005), 88.

58 Ibid., 92, 98.

59 See ibid., 102ff, for example.

60 Ibid., 99.

61 See Zoloth, *Ethics for the Coming Storm*, 72.

62 See, for example, Matthias Georgi, "The Lisbon Earthquake and Scientific Knowledge in the British Public Sphere," in *The Lisbon Earthquake of 1755: Representations and Reactions*, eds. Theodore E.D. Braun and John B. Radner (Oxford: Voltaire Foundation, 2005), 81–96. See also Robert G. Ingram, "'The Trembling Earth is God's Herald': Earthquakes, Religion and Public Life in Britain during the 1750s," in *The Lisbon Earthquake of 1755*, 97–115.

63 Ingram, "'The Trembling Earth is God's Herald'," 101.

64 See Georgi, "The Lisbon Earthquake and Scientific Knowledge," 93.

65 Ibid., 93ff; see also Robert Webster, "The Lisbon Earthquake: John and Charles Wesley Reconsidered," in *The Lisbon Earthquake of 1755*, 116–26.

66 For a full biography, see Jakob J. Petuchowski, *The Theology of Haham David Nieto: An Eighteenth-Century Defense of the Jewish Tradition* (New York: Ktav, 1970 (orig., 1954)). See also Cecil Roth, "Isaac Nieto," in *Encyclopedia Judaica*, eds. Michael Berenbaum and Fred Skolnik, second edn, vol. 15 (Detroit: Macmillan Reference, 2007), 261–2.

67 Roth, "Isaac Nieto," 262. See also Matthias Georgi, *Heuschrecken, Erdbeben und Kometen: Naturkatastrophen und Naturwissenschaft in der englischen Öffentlichkeit des 18. Jahrhunderts* (Munich: August-Dreesbach-Verlag, 2009) and "Christlicher Bedrohungsraum und protestantische Identität: Die englische Selbstwahrnehmung in der Debatte um das Erdbeben von Lissabon (1755)," in *Europäische Wahrnehmungen 1650–1850: Interkulturelle Kommunikation über Medienereignisse*, eds. Joachim Eibach et al. (Hannover: Wehrhahn, 2008), 185–205.

68 Isaac Netto (Nieto), *A Sermon Preached in the Jews Synagogue on Friday, February 6, 1756; Being the Days appointed by Authority for a General Fast* (London: Richard Reily, 1756), i. See also Reinhard Munk, ed. *Moses Mendelssohns Metaphysics and Aesthetics* (Dordrecht: Springer, 2011), 347, citing Mendelssohn regarding massive violence and disorder as in the aftermath of the earthquake in Lisbon.

69 Netto, *A Sermon Preached*, 1–2.
70 Ibid., 2–3.
71 Ibid., 4.
72 Ibid., 5.
73 Ibid., 9.
74 Ibid., 9–10.
75 Ibid., 15ff.
76 See, for example, Petuchowski, *The Theology of Haham David Nieto*, 24.
77 Ibid., 94ff.

Chapter 2

1 See Samuel Cohn, "Changing Pathology of Plague," in *Le interazioni fra economia e ambiente biologico nell'Euopa preindustriale, secc. XII-XVIII*, ed. Simonetta Cavaciocchi (Florence: Firenze University Press, 2010), 33–56.
2 John Aberth, *Plagues in World History* (Lanham: Rowman and Littlefield, 2011), 1–2.
3 Num. 14:37.
4 Num. 24, Num. 14:1–4, 11–12.
5 See Ezek. 5: 8–12; Num. 25; see also Deuteronomy 28: 20–1.
6 David's counting of the people in II Samuel 24.
7 Aberth, *Plagues in World History*, 4.
8 William D. Barrick, "The Eschatological Significance of Leviticus 26," paper (1999). https://biblicalelearning.org/wp-content/uploads/2022/01/Barrick-Lev26Eschat.pdf, 99.
9 Barrick, "The Eschatological Significance of Leviticus 26," 102.
10 18b-19a, 21a-22a Chapter III, in the *Mishnah*.
11 "And which of the gods was it that set them on to quarrel? It was the son of Jove and Leto; for he was angry with the king and sent a pestilence upon the host to plague the people, because the son of Atreus had dishonoured Chryses his priest. Now Chryses had come to the ships of the Achaeans to free his daughter, and had brought with him a great ransom: moreover he bore in his hand the sceptre of Apollo wreathed with a suppliant's wreath and he besought the Achaeans, but most of all the two sons of Atreus, who were their chiefs."
12 Aberth, *Plagues in World History*, 2.
13 "Thus did he pray, and Apollo heard his prayer. He came down furious from the summits of Olympus, with his bow and his quiver upon his shoulder, and the arrows rattled on his back with the rage that trembled within him. He sat himself down away from the ships with a face as dark as night, and his silver bow rang death as he shot his arrow in the midst of them. First he smote their mules and their hounds, but presently he aimed his shafts at the people themselves, and all day long the pyres of the dead were burning. For nine whole days he shot his arrows among the people, but upon the tenth day Achilles called them in assembly-moved thereto by Juno, who saw the Achaeans in their death-throes and had compassion upon them. Then, when they were got together, he rose and spoke among them."
14 Titus Lucretius Carus, *De Rerum Natura*, trans. W.H.D. Rouse (Cambridge, MA: Harvard University Press, 1937), 521ff.

15 See Gerrit Bos, "The Black Death in Hebrew Literature: Abraham Ben Solomon Hen's 'Tractatulus de pestilential,'" *Jewish Studies Quarterly* 18, no. 1 (March, 2011): 32–63.

16 See also Edward Eckert, *The Structures of Plagues and Pestilence in Early Modern Europe: Central Europe, 1560–1640* (Basel: Karger, 1996), 24.

17 Mary Lindemann, *Medicine and Society in Early Modern Europe*, second edn (Cambridge: Cambridge University Press, 2010), 51–3.

18 Eckert, *The Structures of Plagues and Pestilence in Early Modern Europe*, 26.

19 Ascher Levy, *Die Memoiren des Ascher Levy aus Reichshofen im Elsass (1598–1635)* (Berlin: L. Lamm, 1913), 12 (German), 5 (Hebrew).

20 Quoted and translated in full in Sylvie Anne Goldberg, *Crossing the Jabbok: Illness and Death in Ashkenazi Judaism in Sixteenth- through Nineteenth-Century Prague*, trans. Carol Cosman (Berkeley: University of California Press, 1996), 163.

21 Ibid., 167.

22 See Dean Phillip Bell, "Ministry and Sacred Obligation: A Late Medieval context for Luther's 'On Whether One May Flee from the Plague,'" in *The Medieval Luther*, ed. Christine Helmer (Tübingen: Mohr Siebeck, 2020), 197–212.

23 Lindemann, *Medicine and Society in Early Modern Europe*, 55–6.

24 Ibid., 58.

25 Clusters, according to Eckert.

26 Eckert, *The Structures of Plagues and Pestilence in Early Modern Europe*, 27–9. Despite plagues in Württemberg from the middle of the sixteenth through the first third of the seventeenth centuries, the population tended to recover quickly (Paul Warde, *Ecology, Economy and State Formation in Early Modern Germany* (Cambridge: Cambridge University Press, 2006), 28).

27 See Alfred Haverkamp, "Die Judenverfolgungen zur Zeit des Schwarzen Todes in Gesellschaftsgefüge deutscher Städte," in *Zur Geschichte der Juden im Deutschland des Späten Mittelalters und der Frühen Neuzeit*, ed. Alfred Haverkamp (Stuttgart: A. Hiersemann, 1981): 27–93.

28 Brian Pullan, "Plagues and Perceptions of the Poor in Early Modern Italy," in *Epidemics and Ideas: Essays on Historical Perceptions of Pestilence*, eds. Terence Ranger and Paul Slack (Cambridge: Cambridge University Press, 1992), 101–23, 105.

29 Ibid., 117.

30 Ibid., 106, 118.

31 Daniella Zaidman-Mauer, "'May God Shield us from the Plague.' Vernacular Remedies for the Plague from Moyshe Kalish's Yiddish Self-help Medical Book Seyfer Yerum Moyshe (Amsterdam 1679)," *Zutot* 19, no. 1 (2022): 144–62.

32 Chava Turniansky, "Yiddish Song as Historical Source Material: Plague in the Judenstadt of Prague in 1713," in *Jewish History: Essays in Honour of Chimen Abramsky*, eds. Ada Rapoport-Albert and Steven J. Zipperstein (London: P. Halban, 1989), 189–98.

33 Ibid., 191.

34 Ibid., 192.

35 Goldberg, *Crossing the Jabbok*, 163.

36 Ibid., 169.

37 Turniansky, "Yiddish Song as Historical Source Material," 196–7.

38 Ibid., 197.

39 Ibid., 195.

40 Goldberg, *Crossing the Jabbok*, 164–5; Turniansky, "Yiddish Song as Historical Source Material," 194.

41 Goldberg, *Crossing the Jabbok*, 164.
42 Ibid., 165.
43 Turniansky, "Yiddish Song as Historical Source Material," 196.
44 Isaac Rifkind, "Kuntres takkanot Prag," *Reshumot* 24 (1926): 345–52.
45 Ibid., 347–8.
46 Ibid., 348–9.
47 Ibid., 350.
48 Ibid., 350–1.
49 Goldberg, *Crossing the Jabbok*, 169.
50 Ibid., 170.
51 Ibid.
52 Nimrod Zinger, "'Our Hearts and Spirits were Broken': The Medical World from the Perspective of German-Jewish Patients in the Seventeenth and Eighteenth Centuries," *The Leo Baeck Institute Year Book* 54, no. 1 (2009): 59–91, here at 62, 69, 90, 66; for a discussion of Jewish uses of Christian saints in the Middle Ages, see Ephraim Shoham-Steiner, "Jews and Healing at Medieval Saints" Shrines: Participation, Polemics, and Shared Cultures," *Harvard Theological Review* 103, no. 1 (2010): 111–29.
53 Zinger, "'Our Hearts and Spirits were Broken,'" 67.
54 In Shlomo Eidelberg, *Medieval Ashkenazic History: Studies on German Jewry in the Middle Ages*. 2 vols (New York: Sepher-Hermon Press, 1999–2001), vol. 1, 130–1; Compare the comments of Bacharach to the customs book in the notes in *Wormser Minhagbuch des R. Jousep (Juspa) Schammes*, prepared by Erich Zimmer, 2 vols. (Jerusalem, 1988) [Hebrew], here at vol. 1, 232.
55 Eidelberg, *R. Juspa, Shammash of Warmaisa (Worms)*, 31.
56 Ibid., 32.
57 Abraham Catalano, *Olam hafukh ve-hu sipur ha-magefah asher neheytah be-yamav be-geto Padova be-shnat 5391*, seventeenth century, MS X893 Ab8, Rare Book and Manuscript Library, Columbia University Libraries, https://exhibitions.cul.columbia .edu/exhibits/show/hebrew_mss/communities/x893_ab8.
58 This particular outbreak of plague in 1630–31 also claimed 46,000 of 140,000 residents in Venice. Similarly, there was a 61 percent mortality rate in Verona, where 38,000 died. See Dean Phillip Bell, *Plague in the Early Modern World: A Documentary History* (London: Routledge, 2019), 26.
59 Abraham Catalano, "Olam Hafukh," ed. Cecil Roth, *Kovetz al Yad* 4, no. 14 (1946): 67–101, here at 67. Partial translations into English can be found in Alan D. Crown, "The World Overturned: The Plague Diary of Abraham Catalano," *Midstream* (January 1973): 65–76 and, more recently, Bell, *Plague in the Early Modern World*, 192–7. For more recent studies of Catalano, see Joshua Teplitsky, "Plague, Passover, and Perspectives on Social Distancing," Columbia University Libraries, April 21, 2020, https://blogs.cul.columbia.edu/rbml/2020/04/21/plague-passover-and-perspectives -on-social-distancing-dr-joshua-teplitsky/, and Susan L. Einbinder, "Poetry, Prose and Pestilence: Joseph Concio and Jewish Responses to the 1630 Italian Plague," in *Shirat Dvora: Essays in Honor of Professor Dvora Bregman*, ed. Haviva Ishay (Beersheba: Ben-Gurion University of the Negev Press, 2019), especially 76–80. See also Susan L. Einbinder, *Writing Plague: Jewish Responses to the Great Italian Plague* (Philadelphia: University of Pennsylvania Press, 2022).
60 Catalano, "Olam Hafukh," 68; see also Bell, *Plague in the Early Modern World*, 191.
61 The devastation was terrible across northern Italy. The mortality rate in Milan in 1630 was 46 percent, with 60,000 of 130,000 dying; 57 percent in Verona in 1630, with

30,000 of 53,000 dying; in Venice in 1631, 33 percent, with 46,000 of 141,000 dying. Bell, *Plague in the Early Modern World*, 26.

62 Catalano, "Olam Hafukh," 68.

63 Ibid., 69.

64 Ibid., 70.

65 See the introduction in ibid., 67–71.

66 Ibid., 70.

67 Ibid., 73.

68 For the association of God's punishment of human vices with natural disasters such as earthquakes—see, for example, Isaac Nieto's 1756 sermon, discussed in Dean Phillip Bell, "The Trembling of the Earth: Jewish Descriptions of Earthquakes in the Early Modern World," in *Studies in Jewish Civilization 20: 'The Mountains Shall Drip Wine': Jews and the Environment,"* eds. Leonard J. Greenspoon et al. (Omaha: Creighton University Press, 2009): 1–20. For a Christian view of how God employs plague as a "means to upbraid his sinful children," see Bell, *Plague in the Early Modern World,* 113–14.

69 Catalano, "Olam Hafukh," 67–9.

70 Bell, *Plague in the Early Modern World*, 192.

71 See, for example, Nancy A. Anoruo, "Doctors Rebuff Unproven and Potentially Dangerous Oleander Chemical Falsely Touted as COVID-19 'Cure,'" *ABC News,* August 19, 2020, https://abcnews.go.com/Health/doctors-rebuff-unproven-potentially -dangerous-oleander-chemical-falsely/story?id=72428650.

72 Bell, *Plague in the Early Modern World*, 196.

73 For one such case of successful outcomes in Castile, see Ruth MacKay, *Life in a Time of Pestilence: The Great Castilian Plague of 1596–1601* (Cambridge: Cambridge University Press, 2019).

74 As early as the fifteenth century, Marsilio Ficino famously advised his readers to "Avoid conversations, especially when on an empty stomach, and when you do converse, stay at least 2 *braccia* (6 feet) from your companion." Remi Chiu, *Plague and Music in the Renaissance* (Cambridge: Cambridge University Press, 2017), 74.

75 Joshua Leibovitz, "The Plague in the Roman Ghetto (1656) according to Zahalon and Cardinal Gastaldi," *Korot* 4, no. 3–4 (1967): 155–69; Jacob Zahalon, "The Treasure of Life," in Harry A. Savitz, "Jacob Zahalon, and His Book 'The Treasure of Life,'" *New England Journal of Medicine* 213, no. 4 (July 25, 1935): 167–76.

76 Examples of these ritual adaptations can be found across Europe and the Ottoman Empire; Bell, *Plague in the Early Modern World*, 86–7, 90–1, 104–5.

77 For some recent examples, see a sermon from a *mirpeset* (balcony): "Shi'ur Torah be-mirpeset be-beitar 'ilit," *Kikar ha-shabbat*, accessed August 21, 2020, https:// www.kikar.co.il/abroad/355827.html; for *minyanim* (traditionally a quorum of ten Jewish men over the age of thirteen required for Jewish public worship), see "Minyan mirpeset," *Ha-michlol*, accessed August 21, 2020, https://www.hamichlol.org.il/%D7 %9E%D7%A0%D7%99%D7%99D7%9F_%D7%9E%D7%A8%D7%A4%D7%A1%D7 %95D7%AA; regarding weddings, see, for example, "Hatunah be-tsal ha-koronah: Ha-misamahim hagagu 'al mirpeset ha-yeshivah," *Hidabrut*, accessed August 21, 2020, https://www.hidabroot.org/article/1135999. For the early modern context, Jacob ben Isaac Zahalon wrote of his experience living through an outbreak in Rome's Jewish ghetto in 1656: "Because none of the people were able to go to the synagogue, therefore on Sabbath of the Torah portion *Toledot Isaac*, I, Jacob Zahalon, preached a sermon on Catalana Street, at the corner of the street in the house of Rabbi David Gategni, may

God protect and preserve him, in the window of his house . . . and the people were standing in the street to hear the sermon." Bell, *Plague in the Early Modern World*, 207.

Chapter 3

1 See Otto Kaiser, *Die mythische Bedeutung des Meeres in Ägypten, Ugarit und Israel* (Berlin: A Töpelmann, 1962) which also addresses floods.

2 Drought could also be seen as a moral crisis. See Julia Watts Belser, *Power, Ethics, and Ecology in Jewish Late Antiquity: Rabbinic Responses to Drought and Disaster* (Cambridge: Cambridge University Press, 2015), 3.

3 This is what is written, "That one's household will be cast forth by a flood, Spilled out on the day of God's wrath" (Job 20:28). When will this happen? On the day that anger of the Holy One of Blessing will be stirred up against that person. How would it happen? When a person says to their neighbor, "could you lend me a kav [roughly 1.5 liters] of wheat?" And they reply, "I don't have any." "A kav of barely?" "I don't have any." "A kav of dates?" "I don't have any." Or a woman says to her neighbor, "could you lend me a strainer?" And she replies, "I don't have one." "Could you lend me a seive?" And she replies, "I don't have one." What does the Holy One of Blessing do? The plague erupts within that house, and while the person is bringing out their possessions, the people see, and say, "Didn't they say they didn't have anything at all?! Look at how much wheat there is, how much barely, how many dates there are! A cursed house with these curses!" Rabbi Yitzchak in the name of Rabbi Eliezer, "Better to derive this from the following verse (Vayikra 14:37): '[If, when the kohen examines the plague, the plague in the walls of the house is found to consist of greenish or reddish streaks that appear to] go deep [into the wall]' [the word for 'go deep,' sh'kah-arurot, being broken into two words, sh'kah arurot, the curses sink down.] The house sinks with these curses." Therefore, Moshe cautioned Israel (Vayikra 14:34), "When you enter the land of Canaan . . . "

4 BT Sanhedrin, 108b.

5 See Dean Phillip Bell, "Vulnerability in Judaism: Anthropological and Divine Dimensions," in *Exploring Vulnerability*, eds. Heike Springhart and Günter Thomas (Göttingen: Vandenhoeck and Ruprecht, 2017), 93–106.

6 See Dean Phillip Bell, "Navigating the Flood Waters: Perspectives on Jewish Life in Early Modern Germany." *Leo Baeck Institute Yearbook* 56 (2011): 29–52.

7 See Fritz Reuter, Warmaisa: *1000 Jahre Juden in Worms* (Worms: Verlag Stadtarchiv Worms, 1984), 92–3 and 132–3 for historical lists and maps of houses in the Jewish quarter.

8 Thomas P. Backer, "Alltag auf dem Lande," in *Eine Gesllschaft zwischen Tradition und Wandel: Alltag und Umwelt im Rheinland des 18. Jahrhunderts*, ed. Frank Günter Zehnder (Cologne: DuMont, 1999), 9–22, here at 18.

9 Clemens von Looz-Corswarem, "Zur Entwicklung der Rheinschiffahrt vom Mittelalter bis ins 19. Jahrhundert," in *Düsseldorf und seine Häfen: Zur Verkehrs- und Wirtschaftsgeschichte der Stadt as Anlaß des 100jährigen Hafenjubiläums 1896–1996*, eds. Horst Rademacher, Clemens von Looz-Corswarem, and Annette Fimpler-Philippen (Wuppertal: Müller + Busmann, 1996), 9–31.

10 See *Leipziger Zeitung*, no. 54, for Köln, den 27. February 1784 for details on the hourly flooding in Cologne, Deutz and Mühlheim, and Bonn (Bell, "Navigating the Flood Waters").

11 I have treated this more fully in "Navigating the Flood Waters." Here, I focus on one of the affected areas as a form of historical case study.

12 Rüdiger Glaser, *Klimageschichte Mitteleuropas: 1000 Jahre Wetter, Klima, Katastrophen* (Darmstadt: Primus, 2001), 203, 204f; www.bernd-nebel.de/bruecken (last visited November 2024); Guido N. Poliwoda, *Aus Katastrophen Lernen: Sachsen im Kampf gegen die Fluten der Elbe 1784 bis 1845* (Cologne: Böhlau Verlag, 2007), 56, 59ff. Curt Weikinn, *Quellentexte zur Witterungsgeschichte Europas von der Zeitwende bis zum Jahre 1850. Hydrographie. Teil 2: (1501–1600)* (Berlin: De Gruyter, 1960).

13 www.bernd-nebel.de/bruecken.

14 *Leipziger Zeitung*, no. 44, regarding Altona, February 24, 1784 (see Bell, "Navigating the Flood Waters"); last visited July 2010); for statistics on the flooding of the Elbe, see Poliwoda, *Aus Katastrophen Lernen*, 52ff.

15 Glaser, *Klimageschichte*, 205; see also www.bernd-nebel.de/bruecken; Poliwoda, *Aus Katastrophen Lernen*, 62–3.

16 Glaser, *Klimageschichte*, 205–6; for the Elbe, see Poliwoda, *Aus Katastrophen Lernen*, 65ff.

17 Glaser, *Klimageshichte*, 203.

18 *Bayreuther Zeitung*, no. 28, March 1, 1784 (see Bell, "Navigating the Flood Waters").

19 See *Bayreuther Zeitung*, no. 28, March 1, 1784, for Bamberg (see Bell, "Navigating the Flood Waters"). In other places, along the Elbe river, the flood of 1784 was frequently compared to other significant, but lesser, floods, such as those in 1595 and 1691. (See "Denkmal der Kälte und Wassefluth des 1784sten Jahres in einem Gedichte" (Dresden, 1784), v.)

20 Berghaus, *Allgemeine Länder- und Völkerkunde* (see Bell, "Navigating the Flood Waters"); 130–40, according to the *Regensburger Zeitung*, no. 30 (see Bell, "Navigating the Flood Waters"); 170 according to "Historische Nachrichten von den schrecklichen Wasser-Ergießungen von den entsetzlichen Eiß-Fahrten und von den dadurch . . . ," Lauban 1784, unpaginated.

21 *Regensburger Zeitung*, no. 30, Stück Pilsen vom 29. February 1784 (see Bell, "Navigating the Flood Waters").

22 See Johann Gottlob Hartmann, "Predigt nach überstandner großer Wassernoth am Sonntage Oculi 1784, in der Kirche zu Eutzsch gehalten" (Wittenberg, 1784), 6, 8, 12.

23 "Sachsens Ueberschwemmung im Jahr 1784: Ein Denkmal unserer Zeiten . . . " (Leipzig, 1784), 43.

24 Johann Christian Tiemann, "Predigt am grünen Donnerstage 1784. über den gewöhnlichen Text I. Car. XI. zum Besten der auf Landesherrlichen Befehl . . . ," (Leipzig, 1784), 3.

25 Johann Friedrich Ursinus, "Predigt nach der am 29sten Februar und folgende beyde Tage ausgestandenen schrecklichen Eisfahrt und Wassernoth am . . . ," (Desden, 1784), 5.

26 "Denkmal der Kälte und Wasserfluth . . . ," 5; or consider J.W. Berger, "Beschreibung der schrecklichen Ueberschwemmung und Eisfahrt wodurch den 27 und 28sten Februar 1784 ein großer Theil von Mülheim am Rhein verwüstet worden ist, verfasset von einem, der selbst vieles mit gesehen, gehöret und empfunden hat," (n.p., n.d.,) in *Die Stadt Mülheim am Rhein: Geschichte und Beschreibung, Sagen und Erzählungen*, ed. Johann Bendel (Mülheim am Rhein: Self-Published, 1913), 112–39, here at 121.

27 See Poliwoda, *Aus Katastrophen Lernen*, 75–80.

28 Ibid., 80–4.

29 Adolf Kober, *Cologne*, trans. Solomon Grayzel (Philadelphia: Jewish Publication
    Society of America, 1940), 344.
30 See the outstanding article by Aubrey Pomerance, "'Wasser wie nie seit
    Menschengedenken': Eine unbekannte jiddische Quelle zum Rheinhochwasser von
    1784," in *Memoria—Wege jüdischen Erinnerns: Festschrift für Michael Brocke zum 65.
    Geburtstag*, eds. Birgit E. Klein and Christiane E. Müller (Berlin: Metropol, 2005),
    177–92, here at 177.
31 Quoted in Pomerance, "'Wasser wie nie seit Menschengedenken,'" 178. There is also
    extant an account that Abraham bar Joseph Kosman composed in Hebrew regarding
    the flooding of the area, the destruction of the synagogue, and the rescue of the Jews
    in the Benedictine abbey, which is included in the Deutz memory book. (Pomerance,
    "'Wasser wie nie seit Menschengedenken,'" 178–9—see Adolf Jellinek, ed., *Märtyrer
    und Memorbuch: Verzeichniss der Märtyrergemeinden aus den Jahren 1096 und 1349,
    das alte Memorbuch der Deutzer Gemeinde von 1581 bis 1784 nebst Auszügen aus
    dem neuen vom 1786 bis 1816* (Vienna: Löwy, 1881), 63–6 and v for some general
    background.
32 Pomerance, "'Wasser wie nie seit Menschengedenken,'" 180.
33 Shulamit S. Magnus, *Jewish Emancipation in a German City: Cologne, 1798–1871*
    (Stanford: Stanford University Press, 1997).
34 Bastian Fleerman, *Marginalisierung und Emanzipation: Jüdische Alltagskultur im
    Herzogtum Berg, 1779–1847* (Neustadt an der Aisch: Verlagsdruckerei Schmidt, 2007).
    Monika Grübel and Georg Mölich, eds. *Jüdisches Leben im Rheinland: Vom Mittelalter
    bis zur Gegenwart* (Vienna: Böhlau, 2005).
35 Zvi Asaria, *Die Juden in Köln: Von den Ältesten Zeiten bis zur Gegenwart* (Cologne: J.P.
    Bachem, 1959), 60.
36 Ibid., 60; Birgit Klein and Rotraud Ries, "Zu Struktur und Funktion der jüdischen
    Oberschicht in Bonn," in *Eine Gesellschaft im Wandel: Alltag und Umwelt im
    Rheinland des 18. Jahrhunderts*, ed. Frank Gunter Zehnder (Cologne: DuMont, 1999),
    289–315, here at 300.
37 Jellinek, *Märtyrer und Memorbuch*, 63f.
38 Ibid., 63.
39 Ibid.
40 Ibid.
41 Ibid., 64.
42 Ibid.
43 Carl Brisch, *Geschichte der Juden in Cöln und Umgebung*, 2 vols. (Mühlheim am
    Rhein: C. Meyer, 1879–82), here at v. 2, 144.
44 Jellinek, *Märtyrer und Memorbuch*, 64.
45 Ibid.
46 Ibid., 65.
47 Fleerman, *Marginalisierung und Emanzipation*, 70; see also Asaria, *Die Juden in Köln*,
    59–61. The concessions of the late eighteenth-century replicated limitations on Jewish
    settlement and stipulated a range of Jewish behaviors, as was the case throughout
    Germany. See the ordinances reproduced in Fleerman, *Marginalisierung und
    Emanzipation*, 393ff.
48 See Dean Phillip Bell, *Jewish Identity in Early Modern Germany: Memory, Power
    and Community* (Aldershot: Ashgate, 2007) and Cili Kasper-Holtkotte, *Die jüdische
    Gemeinde von Frankfurt/Main un der Frühen Neuzeit: Familien, Netzwerke und
    Konflikte eines jüdischen Zentrums* (Berlin: DeGruyter, 2010), for examples.

49 Jellinek, *Märtyrer und Memorbuch*, 65.

50 Berger, "Beschreibung der schrecklichen Ueberschwemmung und Eisfahrt . . . ,"
    112–13.

51 I draw here from the German translation of the Yiddish original by Pomerance,
    "'Wasser wie nie seit Menschengedenken,'" 183–9.

52 Ibid., 183.

53 In the translated text in ibid., 186.

54 Pomerance provides details of specific damages based on archival documentation
    (ibid., 189–90).

55 Ibid., 190–2.

56 Marx Samuel; Itzig or Isaac Nathan; Horn; Isaac Mendel; Heyman Coppel; Mendele
    Nathan; Benjamin Latzarus; Meyer; Wittib Samue; Simon Nathan. See ibid., 191.

57 In *Die Stadt Mülheim am Rhein*, ed. Bendel, 100ff, also regarding addresses (numbers
    on residences). The locations for Jews in 1770 do not appear to be the same as in 1784.
    Of the five names that appear to be Jews—four are preceded by the demarcation Jew
    and one is Mendel Nathan—three lived Auf der Haubtstraße, one Auf dem wall oder
    Neue Straß, and one Auf der Brücker Gassen.

58 Berger, "Beschreibung der schrecklichen Ueberschwemmung und Eisfahrt wodurch
    . . . ," 122–23; See also Johann Leonard Thelen, "Ausführliche Nachricht von dem
    erschrecklichen Eisgange und den Ueberschwemmungen des Rheines, welche im
    Jahre 1784 die Stadt Köln und die umliegenden Gegenden betroffen . . . ," in *Die Stadt
    Mülheim am Rhein*, ed. Bendel, 465–70, here at 469. The first part of the quote also
    appears in Pomerance, "'Wasser wie nie seit Menschengedenken,'" 182, n. 25.

59 Berger, "Beschreibung der schrecklichen Ueberschwemmung und Eisfahrt wodurch . .
    . ," 138.

60 Ibid., 137.

61 Ibid., 131, 130.

62 Ibid., 136–7.

63 Ibid., 138.

64 Ibid., X.

65 See, for example, Alf Lüdtke, ed., *The History of Everyday Life: Reconstructing
    Historical Experiences and Ways of Life*, trans. William Templer (Princeton: Princeton
    University Press, 1995); Geoff Eley, "Labor History, Social History: Alltagsgeschichte:
    Experience, Culture, and the Politics of the Everyday. A New Direction for German
    Social History?," in *Journal of Modern History* 61, no. 2 (June 1989): 297–343. For
    German Jewish history, see Marion A. Kaplan, ed., *Jewish Daily Life in Germany,
    1618–1945* (Oxford: Oxford University Press, 2005).

66 Klein and Ries, "Zu Struktur und Funktion der jüdischen Oberschicht in Bonn," 301ff.

67 In Swabia Jews and Christians paid their share for building dams to prevent flooding
    in the eighteenth century, see Rolf Kiessling, *Jüdische Geschichte Bayern: Von den
    Anfängen bis in die Gegenwart* (Oldenbourg: De Gruyter, 2019), 331.

Chapter 4

1 Stephen J. Pyne, *Vestal Fire: An Environmental History, Told through Fire, of Europe
   and Europe's Encounter with the World* (Seattle: University of Washington Press, 1997),
   64–6.

2 Ibid., 66–7.

3 See Babylonian Talmud, tractate Shabbat 21b regarding sparks from a hammer or a Hanukkah lamp; also Babylonian Talmud, tractate Bava Kama 6:6.

4 Marie Luisa Allemeyer, "Profane Hazard or Divine Judgement? Coping with Urban Fire in the 17th Century," *Historical Social Research* 32, no. 3 (2007): 145–68, here at 150.

5 Christopher Friedrichs, as cited in ibid., 146.

6 Ibid.

7 George Bankoff, Uwe Lübken, and Jordan Sand, eds., *Flammable Cities: Urban Conflagration and the Making of the Modern World* (Madison: University of Wisconsin Press, 2012), 10ff. Consider the case of Rome, specifically the great fire of 64 and the position of Nero as presented by Tacitus and other writers, or imperial attempts to manage and respond to disasters. Jerry Toner, *Roman Disasters* (Cambridge: Polity Press, 2013), 19, 52. Or consider the case of early modern Russia; see Cathy A. Frierson, "Imperial Russia's Urban Fire Regimes, 1700–1905," in *Flammable Cities*, 103–25, here at 106–08.

8 Johannes Merclius, *Himlische Fewerzeichen, so im grossem lichten Gesicht des Himmels den 30. tag des Monds Januarii dieses 1560. jars auffgangen und erschienen . . .* (Nuremberg: Kreydlein[?], 1560).

9 He also references a range of illnesses, earthquakes, and general misfortunes. While such fire could be terrifying, it was also a sign that the light of redemption through the Son of God was approaching.

10 Ibid., 74a-b. The fires in Wiesbaden were attributed to blasphemy, as well as the sins of foreigners.

11 Allemeyer, "Profane Hazard," 145–6. "Nothing on earth can be stronger/ Than the sighs of pious Christians/ As often a terrible fire's glow/ Extinguishes the dear prayer." 146.

12 Ibid., 148–9.

13 Ibid., 151; Marie Luisa Allemeyer, "'Daß es wohl recht ein Feuer vom Herrn zu nennen gewesen. . .' Zur Wahrnehmung, Deutung und Verarbeitung von Stadtbränden in norddeutschen Schriften des 17. Jahrhunderts," in *Um Himmels Willen. Religion in Katastrophenzeiten*, eds. Manfred Jakubowski-Tiessen and Hartmut Lehmann (Göttingen: Vandenhoeck & Ruprecht, 2003), 201–34 here at 214ff); see also *Verneute Feuer-Ordnung Eines Erbarn Raths allhie zu Nüremberg . . .* (Nuremberg, 1616), which gives particular detail for a variety of communal positions intended to prevent and fight fires.

14 Allemeyer, "Profane Hazard," 153–4; Allemeyer, "'Daß es wohl recht ein Feuer vom Herrn zu nennen gewesen . . . ,'" 217–18. See also Brendan Röder's article on fire prevention in early modern German towns, https://journals.univie.ac.at/index.php/oezg/article/view/7625.

15 Niklaus Bartlome and Erika Flückiger, "Stadtzerstörungen und Wiederaufbau in der mittelalterlichen und frühneuzeitlichen Schweiz," in *Stadtzerstörung und Wiederaufbau: Zerstörungen durch Erdbeben, Feuer und Wasser*, ed. Martin Körner (Bern: P. Haupt, 1999), 1: 123–46, here at 140. For a general overview, see Reinhold Reith, *Umwelt-Geschichte der Frühen Neuzeit* (Munich: Oldenbourg, 2011), 68–9, 89–91.

16 Susanne Pils, "'. . . damit nur an wasser khain menngl erscheine . . .' Vom Umgang der Stadt Wien mit dem Feuer der frühen Neuzeit," in *Stadtzerstörung und Wiederaufbau*, 1: 173–86, here at 176–86.

17 See Bartlome and Flückiger, "Stadtzerstörungen und Wiederaufbau," regarding Chur
in 1574, for example, 132–3.

18 Allemeyer, "Profane Hazard," 156 ff; for an example, see the *Kirchwärder Feuerordnung*
(1673), an excerpt of which is provided in Allemeyer, "'Daß es wohl recht ein Feuer
vom Herrn zu nennen gewesen,'" 221.

19 Allemeyer, "Profane Hazard," 159–60.

20 Ibid., 160–1, 162; Allemeyer, "'Daß es wohl recht ein Feuer vom Herrn zu nennen
gewesen . . . ,'" 229. See also, Jordan Sand and Steven Wills, "Governance, Arson, and
Firefighting in Edo, 1600–1868," in *Flammable Cities*, 44–62, here at 47.

21 See Robert Scribner, "The Mordbrenner Fear in Sixteenth-Century Germany: Political
Paranoia for the Revenge of the Outcast," in *The German Underworld: Deviants and
Outcasts in German History*, ed. Richard J. Evans (New York: Routledge, 1988), 29–56;
Charles Zika, "Heavenly Portents and Divine Anger: The Emotional Intensity of Fire
from the Sky in the Later Sixteenth Century," *Occasion* 13, special issue on Fire Stories
(2022). https://shc.stanford.edu/arcade/publications/occasion/fire-stories/heavenly
-portents-and-divine-anger-emotional-intensity.

22 Bartlome and Flückiger, "Stadtzerstörungen und Wiederaufbau in der
mittelalterlichen und frühneuzeitlichen Schweiz," 136.

23 Ibid., 140–2.

24 Cited in numerous locations, for example, Robert Chazan, *In the Year 1096: The First
Crusade and the Jews* (Philadelphia: Jewish Publication Society, 1996), 6.

25 Gans, *Zemah David*, 139; he also mentioned this incident in the second book of his
chronicle, 393–4.

26 Abraham David, ed., *A Hebrew Chronicle from Prague, c. 1615*, trans. Leon J.
Weinberger with Dena Ordan (Tuscaloosa: University of Alabama Press, 1993), 46–7.
In part, the purpose of such recounting was to serve as a memory for the future.
The Prague chronicler simply explained, "I shall recount the events occurring in
the Exile subsequent to the fifth millennium: the expulsions, miracles, and news
of other occurrences befalling [the Jews] in Prague and the other lands of our long
exile because of our iniquities, to serve as a token of remembrance for us and our
descendants forever" (Ibid., 21). The retelling of specifics, however, might also serve as
something of a communal record.

27 Ber of Bolechow, *The Memoirs of Ber of Bolechow (1723–1805)*, trans. M. Vishnitzer
(Oxford: Oxford University Press, 1922).

28 1729.

29 Ber of Bolechow, *The Memoirs of Ber of Bolechow*, 69–70, 71.

30 Ibid., 71.

31 Ibid., for example, 72, 74.

32 Ibid., 107.

33 Cilli Kasper-Holtkotte, *Die jüdische Gemeinde von Frankfurt/Main in der Frühen
Neuzeit: Familien, Netzwerke und Konflikte eines jüdischen Zentrums* (Berlin:
DeGruyter, 2010), 19.

34 Eoin Bourke, "The Frankfurt Judengasse in Eyewitness Accounts from the
Seventeenth to the Nineteenth Century," in *Ghetto Writing: Traditional and Eastern
Jewry in German-Jewish Literature from Heine to Hilsenrath*, ed. Anne Fuchs and
Florian Krobb (Columbia, SC: Camden House, 1999), 11–24, here 15.

35 See, for example, Edward Fram, *A Window on Their World: The Court Diary of Rabbi
Hayyim Gundersheim, Frankfut am Main, 1773–1794* (Cincinnati: Hebrew Union
College Press, 2012), 162–3, 221ff.

36 Isidor Kracauer, *Die Geschichte der Judengasse in Frankfurt am Main* (Frankfurt am Main, 1906), 334; 337–8, for biographical background.

37 Thomas Carstensen and Wolfgang Henningsen, "'Gaßverbrennner,' Rabbi Cohen: Eine Frankfurter Brandstifter-Legende über die Feuerbrunst vom 14. Januar 1711," *Tribüne: Zeitschrift zum Verständnis des Judentums* 28, no. 109 (1989): 166–71, here at 169. See also Kracauer, *Die Geschichte der Judengasse*, 339.

38 Carstensen and Henningsen, "'Gaßverbrennner,' Rabbi Cohen," 166.

39 Ibid. See also Kracauer, *Geschichte der Judengasse*, 336.

40 In fifteenth-century Regensburg Jews were part of the local fire brigade. See Raphael Straus, *Urkunden und Aktenstücke zur Geschichte der Juden in Regensburg 1453–1739* (Munich: Beck, 1960), nos. 64, 118, 429, 591, 747.

41 Kracauer, *Geschichte der Judengasse*, 335; see also 338 n 3.

42 Ibid., 336.

43 Ibid.

44 Ibid., 337.

45 Carstensen and Henningsen, "'Gaßverbrennner,' Rabbi Cohen," 166.

46 Johann Jacob Schudt, *Jüdische Merckwürdigkeiten* (Frankfurt am Main: Verlegts Samuel Tobias Hocker, 1714), III: 63ff, here 65.

47 Ibid., III: 66.

48 Ibid., III: 72.

49 Ibid., VI: 128–9.

50 *Das unter den Christen vor Zeiten die Juden mit gewohnet haben . . .* (Johann Philipp Gerhard, 1711).

51 Ibid.

52 Kracauer, *Geschichte der Judengasse*, 342.

53 Ibid., 342–3.

54 Ibid., 343.

55 Ibid., 344; a couple of days later, on April 9, the City Council issued an ordinance calling for street lanterns. While unrelated to the Jews, the ordinance does point to a broader concern for safety in the various quarters of the city. As the ordinance itself noted, it was in imitation of similar developments in other cities. Johann Conradin Beyerbach, *Sammlung der Verordnungen der Reichsstadt Frankfurt* (Frankfurt am Main, 1798), V: 1087; see Craig Koslofsky, *Evening's Empire: A History of the Night in Early Modern Europe* (Cambridge: Cambridge University Press, 2011).

56 Kracauer, *Geschichte der Judengasse*, 346.

57 Ibid., 344–6.

58 Beyerbach, *Sammlung der Verordnungen der Reichsstadt Frankfurt*, 1107–8.

59 Ibid., 1099–101; for the Jewish ordinance see 1104–7.

60 Kracauer, *Geschichte der Judengasse*, 347.

61 Ibid., 351.

62 Ibid., 350, 352. Regarding the Bleichgarten, for example, ibid., 356; see also reference in the imperial decree, 72–3.

63 Kracauer, *Geschichte der Judengasse*, 353.

64 Quoted in ibid., 355.

65 Ibid., 341.

66 Ibid., 340.

67 Robert Liberles, *Jews Welcome Coffee: Tradition and Innovation in Early Modern Germany* (Waltham: Brandeis University Press, 2012), 100–1.

68 Ibid., 102–3.

69 Kracauer, *Geschichte der Judengasse*, 358.
70 Ibid., 359.
71 Ibid.
72 Ibid.
73 Ibid.
74 See Christhard Hoffman, "From Heinrich Heine to Isidor Kracauer: The Frankfurt Ghetto in German-Jewish Historical Culture and Historiography," in *The Frankfurt Judengasse: Jewish Life in an Early Modern German City*, eds. Margarete Schlüter, Fritz Backhaus, Gisela Engel, and Robert Liberles (London: Vallentine Mitchell, 2010), 40–58.
75 Ibid., VI: 84; VI: 85; VI: 68.
76 Ibid.
77 Ibid., VI: 87.
78 Ibid., III: 64; III: 69.
79 Ibid., III: 70.
80 Ibid., III: 71.
81 Ibid.
82 Ibid., III: 72.
83 Ibid., 363.
84 Ibid., 366.

Chapter 5

1 Abraham David, *To Come to the Land: Immigration and Settlement in Sixteenth-Century Eretz-Israel* (Tuscaloosa: University of Alabama Press, 1999), 2.
2 Jonathan Israel, *European Jewry in the Age of Mercantilism, 1550–1750*, 3rd edn (Oxford: The Littman Library of Jewish Civilization, 1998 (orig., 1985)).
3 Maurice Eisenbeth, *Le judaïsme nord-africain* (Paris: A. Natason, 1932), 147ff.
4 H.Z. Hirschberg, *A History of the Jews in North Africa*, 2 vols. (Leiden: Brill, 1974–1981), 2: 194.
5 Bernard Lewis, *The Jews of Islam* (London: Routledge, 1984), 151.
6 See Kenan Yildiz, "Istanbul Fires During the Ottoman Period and their Effect on the City's Topography," https://istanbultarihi.ist/393-istanbul-fires-during-the-ottoman-period-and-their-effect-on-the-citys-topography).
7 In his *Mishpat Tzedek*, 3:35.
8 Matt Goldish, *Jewish Questions: Responsa on Sephardic Life in the Early Modern Period* (Princeton: Princeton University Press, 2008), 758–60.
9 There are biblical passages that equate blessing with proper behavior and punishment, often in the form of disasters involving nature, for disobedience. Consider, for example, Deuteronomy 11, 13–18: "And it shall come to pass, if ye shall hearken diligently unto My commandments which I command you this day, to love the LORD your God, and to serve Him with all your heart and with all your soul, that I will give the rain of your land in its season, the former rain and the latter rain, that thou mayest gather in thy corn, and thy wine, and thine oil. And I will give grass in thy fields for thy cattle, and thou shalt eat and be satisfied. Take heed to yourselves, lest your heart be deceived, and ye turn aside, and serve other gods, and worship them; and the anger of the LORD be kindled against you, and He shut up the heaven, so that there shall

be no rain, and the ground shall not yield her fruit; and ye perish quickly from off the good land which the LORD giveth you. Therefore, shall ye lay up these My words in your heart and in your soul."

10 Yaron Ayalon, *Natural Disasters in the Ottoman Empire: Plague, Famine, and Other Misfortunes* (Cambridge: Cambridge University Press, 2015), 59.

11 Marc David Baer, "The Great Fire of 1660 and the Islamization of Christian and Jewish Space in Istanbul," *International Journal of Middle East Studies* 36, no. 2 (May 2004): 159–81, here at 159.

12 Cited in ibid., 172.

13 Cornel Zwierlein, "The Burning of a Modern City? Istanbul as Perceived by the Agents of the Sun Fire Office, 1865–1870," in *Flammable Cities: Urban Conflagration and the Making of the Modern World*, eds. George Bankoff, Uwe Lübken, and Jordan Sand (Madison: University of Wisconsin Press, 2012), 82–102, here at 95.

14 Ayalon, *Natural Disasters in the Ottoman Empire*, 85.

15 Ibid., 86–7.

16 Ibid., 96.

17 Ibid., 103.

18 Ibid., 110.

19 Ben Outhwaite, https://www.lib.cam.ac.uk/genizah-fragments/posts/we-have-seen -mountains-shaking-fatimid-humanitarian-relief-and-earthquake).

20 See 14, 16–17 in Motti Zohar, Amos Salamon and Rehav Rubin, "Reappraised List of Historical Earthquakes that Affected Israel and Its Close Surroundings," *Journal of Seismology* (April 16, 2016): 9–23, https://www.gov.il/BlobFolder/reports/zohar-m -report-2016/en/report_2016_GSI-22-2016-PhD-Thesis-HUJI.pdf).

21 See Julia Phillips Cohen and Sarah Abrevaya Stein, eds., *Sephardi Lives: A Documentary History, 1700–1950* (Stanford: Stanford University Press, 2014), 25–6.

22 Ibid., 25.

23 Ibid., 25–6.

24 Ibid., 26.

25 See Michael Dols, *The Black Death in the Middle East* (Princeton: Princeton University Press, 1977), as well as later, Russell Hopley, "Contagion in Islamic Lands: Responses from Medieval Andalusia and North Africa," *The Journal for Early Modern Cultural Studies* 10, no. 2 (Fall/Winter 2010): 45–64, here at 61, note 23. See also L. I. Conrad, "Epidemic Disease in Formal and Popular Thought in Early Islamic Society," in *Epidemics and Ideas: Ideas in the Historical Perception of Pestilence*, eds. T. Ranger and P. Slack (Cambridge: Cambridge University Press, 1992), 77–99; L. I. Conrad, "'Ta'un and waba': Conceptions of Plague and Pestilence in Early Islam," *Journal of the Economic and Social History of the Orient* 25 (1982): 268–307; and L. I. Conrad, "Arabic Plague Chronologies and Treatises: Social and Historical Factors in the Formation of a Literary Genre," *Studia Islamica* 44 (1981): 51–93.

26 Nükhet Varlik, "Disease and Empire: A History of Plague Epidemics in the Early Modern Ottoman Empire (1453–1600)" (Dissertation, University of Chicago, 2008), 50. The chronicler Kritovoulos suggested that the famous Ottoman policy of repopulation had not only political dimensions but was related to the very real needs to repopulate the capital city after numerous epidemics claimed the lives of numerous residents. (Heath Lowry, "Pushing the Stone Uphill: The Impact of Bubonic Plague on Ottoman Urban Society in the Fifteenth and Sixteenth Centuries," *Osmanli Arastirmalari* 23 (2003): 93–132, 111).

27 Varlik, "Disease and Empire," 47.

28 Ibid., 52–3.

29 In the following seasons/years: winter 1496–97, summer 1497, summer-fall 1500, winter 1500–01, summer 1501, fall 1501, summer 1502, winter 1502–03, summer 1503, winter 1503–04, spring 1510, fall 1512, summer 1513, summer 1514, fall 1514, summer 1516, summer 1518, winter 1518–19, winter-spring 159–20, summer 1520, summer 1522, summer 1523, winter 1523–24, fall 1525, winter 1525–26, summer 1526, fall 1526, winter 1526–27, spring 1527, summer 1527, summer 1529, summer 1530, spring 1532, summer-fall 1532, winter-spring 1533, summer 1533. See Giselle Marien, "The Black Death in Early Ottoman Territories: 1347–1550" (MA thesis, Bilkent University, 2009), 37; see also Varlik, "Disease and Empire," 57.

30 Varlik, "Disease and Empire," 62, 106ff.

31 Ibid., 137.

32 Ibid., 144.

33 In the years: 1611–13, 1620–24, 1627, 1636–37, 1647–49, 1653–56, 1659–66, 1671–80, 1685–95, and 1697 into the early eighteenth century. See ibid., 146.

34 Daniel Panzac, *La peste dans l'empire Ottoman: 1700–1850* (Leuven: Editions Peters, 1985), 198.

35 Panzac, *La peste dans l'empire Ottoman*, 201; see also Alan Mikhail, *Nature and Empire in Ottoman Egypt: An Environmental History* (Cambridge: Cambridge University Press, 2011), 218.

36 William H. McNeill, *Plagues and Peoples* (Garden City, NY: Anchor Press, 1976), 171.

37 Panzac, *La peste dans l'empire Ottoman*, 46. (For details on other areas in the Ottoman Empire, see Dean Phillip Bell, *Plague in the Early Modern World* (London: Routledge, 2019)).

38 Varlik, "Disease and Empire," 158.

39 Ibid., 159; see also Panzac, *La peste dans l'empire Ottoman*, 47.

40 Varlik, "Disease and Empire," 159.

41 Lawrence I. Conrad and Dominik Wujastyk, *Contagion: Perspectives from Pre-Modern Societies* (Aldershot: Ashgate, 2000), xii–xiii; see Birsen Bulmuş, *Plague, Quarantine and Geopolitics in the Ottoman Empire* (Edinburgh: Edinburgh University Press, 2012), 70ff; Dols, *The Black Death in the Middle East*, 9–10, 117.

42 Dols, *The Black Death*, 124.

43 Ibid., 215, 206.

44 Nükhet Varlik, "From 'Bete Noire' to 'le Mal de Constantinople': Plagues, Medicine, and the Early Modern Ottoman State," *Journal of World History* 24, no. 4 (December 2013): 741–70, here at 741–3.

45 Ibid., 748.

46 Bulmuş, *Plague, Quarantine and Geopolitics in the Ottoman Empire*, 70–71; Dols, *The Black Death*, 126–7.

47 Most recently see John J. Curry, "Scholars, Sufis, and Disease: Can Muslim Religious Works Offer Us Novel Insights on Plagues and Epidemics among the Medieval and Early Modern Ottomans?," in *Plague and Contagion in the Islamic Mediterranean*, ed. Nükhet Varlik (Newark: Arc Humanities Press, 2017), 27–55; and Yaron Ayalon, "Religion and Ottoman Society's Responses to Epidemics in the Seventeenth and Eighteenth Centuries," in ibid., 179–97.

48 For a recent reassessment, see Nükhet Varlik, "'Oriental Plague' or Epidemiological Orientalism? Revisiting the Plague Episteme of the Early Modern Mediterranean," in ibid., 57–87.

49 Lowry, "Pushing the Stone Uphill," 129.

50 Dols, *The Black Death*, 23.
51 See John Aberth, *Plagues in World History* (Lanham: Rowman and Littlefield, 2011), 39.
52 Bulmuş, *Plague, Quarantine and Geopolitics in the Ottoman Empire*, 3.
53 Varlik, "Disease and Empire," 188.
54 Ibid., 189.
55 Ibid.
56 Ibid., 179.
57 See Hopley, "Contagion in Islamic Lands," 56–8.
58 Bulmuş, *Plague, Quarantines, and Geopolitics in the Ottoman Empire*, 3.
59 Ibid.
60 Ayalon, *Natural Disasters in the Ottoman Empire*, 13.
61 Ibid., 64.
62 Ibid., 23.
63 Ibid., 45.
64 Ibid., 80.
65 Ibid., 69.
66 Ibid., 24.
67 Ibid., 78.
68 Ibid., 158.
69 Ibid., 70.
70 Ibid., 58.
71 Ibid., 75.
72 Ibid., 83–4.
73 Ibid., 85.
74 Ibid., 86.
75 Ibid., 88.
76 Ibid., 107.
77 Ibid., 77.
78 Yaron Ayalon, *Plagues, Famines, Earthquakes: The Jews of Ottoman Syria and Natural Disasters* (Dissertation, Princeton University, 2009), 147.
79 Ibid.
80 Ibid., 154.
81 Ibid., 153.
82 Ibid., 155.
83 Ibid., 149.
84 Ibid., 228.
85 Ibid., 150.
86 Ibid., 158, 201.
87 Ibid., 204.

Chapter 6

1 Jerry Toner, *Roman Disasters* (Cambridge: Polity Press, 2013), 10.
2 Ibid., 4.
3 Ibid., 7.
4 Ibid., 5.

5 Ibid., 12–13; including economic and religious, 38, 42.

6 Ibid., 13.

7 Oliver-Smith, Anthony, "'What is Disaster?' Anthropological Perspectives on a Persistent Question," in *The Angry Earth: Disaster in Anthropological Perspective*, eds. Oliver-Smith, Anthony and Susanna M. Hoffman (London: Routledge, 2020), 29–44, here at 32.

8 Ibid., 31.

9 Ibid.

10 Ibid., 33.

11 Toner, *Roman Disasters*, 14.

12 Ibid., 24.

13 Ibid., 44–5.

14 Ibid., 43.

15 Ibid., 51.

16 Ibid., 45.

17 Ibid., 56.

18 Ibid., 3.

19 John Robb, "The End of the World (Again)," in *The Power of Nature: Archaeology and Human-Environmental Dynamics*, ed. Monica L. Smith (Denver: University Press of Colorado, 2022), 256–67, here at 258.

20 Toner, *Roman Disasters*, 58–9, 63.

21 Ibid., 72, 75, 78.

22 Ibid., 79, 82.

23 Ibid., 83.

24 Ibid., 91.

25 Ibid., 111–13.

26 Ibid., 87.

27 Emmanuel Levinas, *Ethics and Infinity: Conversations with Philippe Nemo*, trans. Richard A. Cohen (Pittsburgh: Duquesne University Press, 1985 (orig., 1982)), 50.

28 Robb, "The End of the World (Again)," 265.

29 Ibid., 262.

30 Ibid., 264.

31 Ibid., 265.

32 See: *The Anthropocene: Key Issues for the Humanities*. In March 2024, the International Commission on Stratigraphy (ICS) officially rejected the Anthropocene as a new geological epoch. This decision was not due to a denial of humanity's impact on the planet but rather the inability of science to reliably determine the precise starting point of such impact. The ICS acknowledged, however, that in the humanities, social sciences, and various ecological movements, the term "Anthropocene" might be fruitful to name the irreversible influence of humans on the geological and ecological shape of the Earth. https://stratigraphy.org/news/152.

33 Julia Adeney Thomas and Jan Zalasiewicz, "Strata and Three Stories," *RCC Perspectives* no. 3 (2020): 3, 5; see also Daniel R. Headrick, *Humans Versus Nature: A Global Environmental History* (Oxford: Oxford University Press, 2020), 1–2.

34 Michael Northcott, "On Going Gently into the Anthropocene," in *Religion in the Anthropocene*, eds. Celia Deane-Drummond, Sigurd Bergmann, and Markus Vogt (Eugene, OR: Cascade Books, 2017), 19–34, here at 10.

35　Julia Adeney Thomas, Mark Williams, and Jan Zalasiewicz, *The Anthropocene: A Multidisciplinary Approach* (Cambridge: Polity, 2020), vii. See also Headrick, *Humans Versus Nature*, 461.

36　Including rising heat—see Jeff Goodell, *The Heat Will Kill You: Life and Death on a Scorched Planet* (New York: Little, Brown and Company, 2023).

37　See Adeney Thomas, Williams, and Zalasiewicz, *The Anthropocene: A Multidisciplinary Approach*.

38　J.R. McNeill and Peter Engelke, *The Great Acceleration: An Environmental History of the Anthropocene since 1945* (Cambridge, MA: The Belknap Press of Harvard University Press, 2014), 40ff, 56.

39　Ibid., 2, 4; 11, 28. For a helpful general overview, see Michael S. Hogue, *American Immanence: Democracy for an Uncertain World* (New York: Columbia University Press, 2018), 56ff.

40　Adeney Thomas and Zalasiewicz, "Strata and Three Stories," 5.

41　Ibid., 9.

42　Ibid., 6 and Adeney Thomas, Williams, and Zalasiewicz, *The Anthropocene: A Multidisciplinary Approach*, 196.

43　McNeill and Engelke, *The Great Acceleration*, 84–88.

44　Todd LeVasseur and Anna Peterson, eds., *Religion and Ecological Crisis: The "Lynn White Thesis" at Fifty* (London: Routledge, 2017), 10.

45　Michelle Martinez, "Environmental Justice and Detroit's Long Shadow," in *Gonna Trouble the Water: Ecojustice, Water, and Environmental Racism*, ed. Miguel A. De la Torre (Cleveland: The Pilgrim Press, 2021), 70–86, here at 83. See also Peter Frankopan, *The Earth Transformed: An Untold History* (New York: Alfred A. Knopf, 2023), 637, and Hogue, *American Immanence*, 163, where he notes that wealthy nations are responsible for 2/3 of historically cumulative GHG emissions.

46　McNeill and Engelke, *The Great Acceleration*, 65–71.

47　Matthew C. Peros, Jago Cooper, and Frank Oliva, "Hurricanes as Agents of Cultural Change: Integrating Paleotempestology and the Archaeological Record," in *The Power of Nature: Archaeology and Human-Environmental Dynamics*, ed. Monica L. Smith (Denver: University Press of Colorado, 2022), 27–48, here at 28.

48　Ibid., 35.

49　Jordan Pickett, "Earthquakes and Agency in the Roman Mediterranean: Resilience and Transformation," in *The Power of Nature: Archaeology and Human-Environmental Dynamics*, ed. Monica L. Smith (Denver: University Press of Colorado, 2022), 77–98, here at 81.

50　Adeney Thomas, Williams, and Zalasiewicz, *The Anthropocene: A Multidisciplinary Approach*, 136.

51　Ibid., 142. See also Adam Kirsch, *On Settler Colonialism: Ideology, Violence, and Justice* (New York: W.W. Norton & Company, 2024), 64–5, regarding the connection in some ideological circles between different social and political issues and the critique of the Anthropocene, which appears to ascribe culpability to all humans rather than a "minority of colonialists, capitalists, and patriarchs."

52　Adeney Thomas, Williams, and Zalasiewicz, *The Anthropocene: A Multidisciplinary Approach*, 153–4.

53　McNeill and Engelke, *The Great Acceleration*, 152.

54　Adeney Thomas, Williams, and Zalasiewicz, *The Anthropocene: A Multidisciplinary Approach*, 139.

55　Ibid., 141, 158.

56 McNeill and Engelke, *The Great Acceleration*, 153.
57 Thomas, Williams, and Zalasiewicz, *The Anthropocene*, 170.
58 Ibid., 158–9.
59 Ibid., 180, 187.
60 Smith, ed., *The Power of Nature: Archaeology and Human-Environmental Dynamics*, 7.
61 Ibid., 8–9; 12.
62 Ibid., 9.
63 Ibid., 11.
64 Ibid., 10. The question of agency is intriguing in this context. Steven Ammerman, for example, cites the work of Helen Seward regarding agency, in which she argues for a four-point definition that includes: capability of independent motion, some form of subjectivity with some self-awareness as an entity, at least some action toward some purpose, and some kind of directed control over the actions it takes to cause outcomes. (Steven Ammerman, "Animal Agents in the Human Environment," in *The Power of Nature: Archaeology and Human-Environmental Dynamics*, ed. Monica L. Smith (Denver: University Press of Colorado, 2022), 213–32, here at 217.
65 Michael S. Hogue, "Sustainability and Climate Change," *Encyclopedia of Religious Ethics*, 3 vols, ed. William Schweiker (Wiley & Sons Ltd., 2022), 1250–6, here at 1250.
66 Frankopan, *The Earth Transformed*, discusses Thomas Jefferson's identification of weather changes in the late eighteenth century (see 411ff).
67 Susan Neiman, *Left is Not Woke* (Cambridge: Polity, 2023), 23.
68 Alexander J.B. Hampton "Ecology and the Unbuffered Self: Identity, Agency, and Authority in a Time of Pandemic," in *Pandemic, Ecology and Theology* (London: Routledge, 2021), 17–28, here at 17.
69 Ibid.,18.
70 Ibid.,19.
71 Ibid.,18.
72 Ibid., 20.
73 See Amitav Ghosh, *The Great Derangement: Climate Change and the Unthinkable* (Chicago: University of Chicago Press, 2016), 68.
74 Ibid., 123.
75 Neiman, *Left is Not Woke*, 110.
76 See Lois Ann Lorentzen, "Globalization," in *Grounding Religion: A Field Guide to the Study of Religion and Ecology*, eds. Whitney Bauman, Richard Bohannon, and Kevin J. O'Brien, second edn (London: Routledge, 2017), 117–136, here at 117ff.
77 Ibid., 117.
78 Ibid., 118.
79 Ibid., 122.
80 Ibid., 119.
81 Ibid., 118.
82 Adeney Thomas, Williams, and Zalasiewicz, *The Anthropocene: A Multidisciplinary Approach*, 125.
83 Hans Jonas, *The Phenomenon of Life: Toward a Philosophical Biology* (Evanston: Northwestern University Press, 2001 (1966)), 67.
84 Ibid., 71, 73, 74.
85 Jan Zalasiewicz, "Old and New Patterns of the Anthropocene," in Adeney Thomas and Zalasiewicz, "Strata and Three Stories," 32–6.

86 Francis van den Noortgaete, "Reconsidering the Anthropocene as *Milieu*: William Desmond and the Originary Goodness of Being," in *Religion in the Anthropocene*, eds. Celia Deane-Drummond, Sigurd Bergmann and Markus Vogt (Eugene, OR: Cascade Books, 2017), 155–70, here at 167.

87 Kate Crawford, *Atlas of AI: Power, Politics, and the Planetary Costs of Artificial Intelligence* (New Haven: Yale University Press, 2021), 36.

88 Jacob Ward, *The Loop: How Technology is Creating a World Without Choices and How to Fight Back* (New York: Hachette Books, 2022), 16; 116.

89 Ibid., 123–4.

90 Ibid., 64–6.

91 Ibid., 87.

92 Michael S. Hogue, "Theological Ethics and Technological Culture: A Biocultural Approach," *Zygon* 42, no. 1 (March 2007): 77–95, here at 78.

93 Adeney Thomas, Williams, and Zalasiewicz, *The Anthropocene: A Multidisciplinary Approach*, 5.

94 Ibid., 34, 58.

95 The definition and starting point depend potentially on a range of factors and values: Northcott, "On Going Gently into the Anthropocene," 11. Peter Frankopan argues that "By around 3500 BC, the human impact on the environment was not just changing but was becoming so significant that it had itself become a factor in changing ecological habitats of flora and fauna" (Frankopan, *The Earth Transformed*, 79). He notes that "It is striking, though perhaps not surprising, that regions that were vulnerable to changes in weather conditions—above all droughts, but also floods and storms—developed cosmological systems based on 'moralising gods' who used such events to punish, show their displeasure and teach lessons" (87).

96 Adeney Thomas, Williams, and Zalasiewicz, *The Anthropocene: A Multidisciplinary Approach*, 117–19.

97 Jonas, *The Phenomenon of Life*, 86.

98 Adeney Thomas, Williams, and Zalasiewicz, *The Anthropocene: A Multidisciplinary Approach*, x.

99 Headrick, *Humans Versus Nature*, 4, 462ff.

100 Zalasiewicz, "Old and New Patterns of the Anthropocene," 24ff.

101 Ibid., 29–30.

102 Ibid., 20–1.

103 Joshua D. Fisher, *Managing Environmental Conflict* (New York: Columbia University Press, 2022), 34.

104 See Frank Uekötter, *The Vortex: An Environmental History of the Modern World* (Pittsburgh: University of Pittsburgh Press, 2023), 3.

105 Ibid., 9.

106 Ibid., 10, 12, 13.

107 Ibid., 16.

108 Adeney Thomas, Williams, and Zalasiewicz, *The Anthropocene: A Multidisciplinary Approach*, 3.

109 Ibid., 13.

110 Fisher, *Managing Environmental Conflict*, 2.

111 Giorgio Agamben, *Homo Sacer: Sovereign Power and Bare Life*, trans. Daniel Heller-Roazen (Stanford: Stanford University Press, 1998 (orig. 1995)), 6.

112 Fisher, *Managing Environmental Conflict*, 70–1.

113 Ibid., 4.

114 Ibid., 5.
115 Ibid., 35.
116 Ibid., 40; see also 41, 42.
117 Ibid., 45–6.
118 Ibid., 46.
119 Ibid., 52, 60.
120 Ibid., 61.
121 Bruno Latour, *Facing Gaia: Eight Lectures on the New Climate Regime*, trans. Catherine Porter (Cambridge: Polity, 2017), 246.
122 Michael Northcott, "On Going Gently into the Anthropocene," in *Religion in the Anthropocene*, ed. Celia Deane-Drummond, Sigurd Bergmann and Markus Vogt (Eugene, OR: Cascade Books, 2017), 19–34, here at 22. Northcott writes regarding William Ruskin's *Storm Cloud of the Nineteenth Century* that "Ruskin here treated the changes in the weather as a *kairos* event in which humanity was called to moral, spiritual, and social renewal and not only to make technical changes in its positioning of housing or emissions controls on chimneys. Instead of the latter, Ruskin called the industrialists and wealth accumulators who were driving the injustice and pollution of the factory filled cities to recover the old paths of justice and piety, to God, to the land, and to its inhabitants" (23).
123 Ibid., 27.

Chapter 7

1 Kyle Harper, *The Fate of Rome: Climate Disease, & the End of an Empire* (Princeton: Princeton University Press, 2017), 15.
2 Ibid., 55.
3 Lydia Barnett, *After the Flood: Imagining the Global Environment in Early Modern Europe* (Baltimore: Johns Hopkins University Press, 2019), 9.
4 Ibid., 28.
5 Ibid., 31.
6 Ibid., 15.
7 Philip Jenkins, *Climate, Catastrophe, and Faith: How Changes in Climate Drive Religious Upheaval* (Oxford: Oxford University Press, 2021), 13.
8 Ibid., 118, 155.
9 Christof Mauch, "Introduction," in *Natural Disasters, Cultural Responses: Case Studies Toward a Global Environmental History*, eds. Christof Mauch and Christian Pfister (Lanham: Lexington Books, 2009), 1–16, here at 3, 5.
10 See also Christian Pfister, "Learning from Nature-Induced Disasters: Theoretical Considerations and Case Studies from Western Europe," in *Natural Disasters, Cultural Responses*, 17–40, here at 19ff.
11 Mauch, "Introduction," 7, 9.
12 Franz Mauelshagen, "Disaster and Political Culture in Germany since 1500," in *Natural Disasters, Cultural Responses*, 41–75, here at 66.
13 Pfister, "Learning from Nature-Induced Disasters," here at 20.
14 Ibid., 21.

15	Rene Favier and Anne-Marie Garnet-Abisset, "Society and Nature Risks in France, 1500–2000: Changing Historical Perspectives," in *Natural Disasters, Cultural Responses*, 103–36, here at 104.

16	Ibid., 105.

17	George Bankoff, "Cultures of Disaster, Cultures of Coping: Hazard as a Frequent Life Experience in the Philippines," in *Natural Disasters, Cultural Responses*, 265–84, here at 266, 268.

18	Christian Pfister, "Afterword," in *Natural Disasters, Cultural Responses*, 355–9, here at 356.

19	As Vasudha Pande has argued, there is "need for long-term environmental histories that present the relationship between humans and nature as perpetually contingent and changing histories that reveal the adaptive strategies of humans over long-term contexts. However, writing long-term environmental histories requires a new orientation: it entails a flexibility of method; it means moving out of nationalist frames, and integrating diverse historical traditions into interconnected stories." (Vasudha Pande, "Anthropogenic Landscapes of the Central Himalayas," in *At Nature's Edge: The Global Present and Long-Term History*, eds. Gunnel Cederlöf and Mahesh Rangarajan (Oxford: Oxford University Press, 2018), 19–60, here at 21–2).

20	T.R. Shankar Raman, "Expanding Nature Conservation: Considering Wide Landscapes and Deep Histories," in *At Nature's Edge*, 249–67, here at 257.

21	Ibid., 259.

22	Andrew C. Isenberg, "Introduction: A New Environmental History," in *The Oxford Handbook of Environmental History* (Oxford: Oxford University Press 2014), 1–20, here at 4.

23	See Mark Carey, "Beyond Weather: The Culture and Politics of Climate History," in *The Oxford Handbook of Environmental History*, ed. Andrew C. Isenberg, 23–51, here at 24.

24	Ibid., 32, 34.

25	As Sara B. Pritchard notes, "First, environmental history questions the primacy of the sociotechnical within historical and contemporary studies of technology, and integrates nature prominently into their analyses. Second, it pushes us to consider how technology both reflects and mediates human-environment interactions. Finally, environmental historians have refined theories of technical development and change by stressing the ways that technology shapes, but is also shaped by, nonhuman nature" (Sara B. Pritchard, "Toward an Environmental History of Technology," in *The Oxford Handbook of Environmental History*, 227–58, here at 228).

26	Isenberg, "Introduction," 5.

27	See Wolfgang Behringer, *A Cultural History of Climate* (Cambridge: Polity, 2010), for example; or see Isenberg, *The Oxford Handbook of Environmental History*. Izdebski, "The Emergence of Interdisciplinary Environmental History: Bridging the Gap Between the Humanistic and Scientific Approaches to the Late Holocene," preprint version, writes that "the study of past climate is an inherently interdisciplinary undertaking involving a wide range of natural scientific disciplines and historians who try to reconstruct past weather and climate variability based on written sources" (9). He also discusses the limitations on such natural evidence, which can raise new questions for historians that have historical and deep historical relevance and implications (4, 8).

28	Interdisciplinary approaches can help address the multi-temporal nature of climate—see *The Oxford Handbook of Environmental History* and Adam Izdebski, et al., "The

Emergence of Interdisciplinary Environmental History: Bridging the Gap Between the Humanistic and Scientific Approaches to the Late Holocene," preprint version, 10, 48.

29 Isenberg, "Introduction," in *The Oxford Handbook of Environmental History*, 1–20, here at 11.

30 Pritchard, "Toward an Environmental History of Technology," 239.

31 Ibid., 242.

32 Andrew C. Isenberg, "Seas of Grass: Grasslands in World Environmental History," in *The Oxford Handbook of Environmental History*, 133–53, here at 137.

33 Martin Jay, *Songs of Experience: Modern American and European Variations on a Universal Theme* (Berkeley: University of California Press, 2005), 53.

34 Ibid., 290.

35 Jay, *Songs of Experience*, 35.

36 Linda Nash, "Beyond Virgin Soils: Disease as Environmental History," in *The Oxford Handbook of Environmental History*, 76–107, here at 85.

37 Michael Lewis, "And All Was Light?—Science and Environmental History," in *The Oxford Handbook of Environmental History*, 207–26, here at 214; Pritchard, "Toward an Environmental History of Technology," 231.

38 Michael S. Hogue, *American Immanence: Democracy for an Uncertain World* (New York: Columbia University Press, 2018), 5.

39 Ibid., 7

40 Bruno Latour, *Facing Gaia: Eight Lectures on the New Climate Regime*, trans. Catherine Porter (Cambridge: Polity, 2017), 74: "we are now attributing to natural history the terms of human history—tipping points, acceleration, crisis, revolution—and that to speak of human history we are using the words inertia, hysteresis, path dependency, as if humans had taken on the aspect of a passive and immutable nature in order to explain why they are doing nothing against the threat."

41 Ibid., 48–9.

42 Ibid., 69–70.

43 Ibid., 15.

44 Ibid., 36; see also 24.

45 Ibid., 206.

46 Ibid., 285.

47 Ibid., 286.

48 Yosef Hayim Yerushalmi, *Zakhor: Jewish History and Jewish Memory* (Seattle: University of Washington Press, 1982).

49 Latour, *Facing Gaia*, 98–100.

50 Ibid., 139.

51 Philippe Descola, *Beyond Nature and Culture*, trans. Janet Lloyd (Chicago: University of Chicago Press, 2023 (orig., 2005)), 8.

52 Ibid., 66.

53 Ibid., 69.

54 Ibid.

55 Ibid., 8.

56 Ibid., 8.

57 Ibid., 9.

58 Ibid., 5.

59 Ibid., 11.

60 Ibid., 12.

61 Ibid., 30.
62 Ibid., 23.
63 Ibid., 51.
64 Wendell Berry, "Getting Along with Nature," in *The World-Ending Fire: The Essential Wendell Berry* (Berkeley: Counterpoint, 2017), 160.
65 Ibid., 164.
66 Ibid., 159.
67 Wendell Berry, "Two Minds," in *The World-Ending Fire*.
68 Ibid., 181.
69 Ibid., 196.
70 Ibid., 182.
71 See Rita Charon, *Narrative Medicine: Honoring the Stories of Illness* (Oxford: Oxford University Press, 2008).
72 Natan Margalit, *The Pearl and the Flame: A Journey into Jewish Wisdom and Ecological Thinking* (Boulder: Albion-Andalus, 2022), 7.
73 Ibid., 4.
74 Ibid., 5.
75 Ibid., 32.
76 Ibid., 18.
77 Maxwell Boykoff, *Creative (Climate) Communications: Productive Pathways for Science, Policy and Society* (Cambridge: Cambridge University Press, 2019), 52.
78 Ibid., 62.
79 Ibid., 62, 63.
80 Ibid., 96.
81 Ibid., 82.
82 Ibid., 98.
83 Ibid., 91.
84 Ibid., 130, 131, 133.
85 Ibid., 162.
86 Bronislaw Szerszynski, "From the Anthropocene Epoch to a New Axial Age: Using Theory-Fictions to Explore Geo-Spiritual Futures," in *Religion in the Anthropocene*, eds. Celia Deane-Drummond, Sigurd Bergmann, and Markus Vogt (Eugene, OR: Cascade Books, 2017), 35–52, here at 39.
87 Ibid., 40.
88 See, for example, Christopher Schliephake and Evi Zemanek, eds., *Anticipatory Environmental (Hi)Stories from Antiquity to the Anthropocene* (Lanham: Lexington Books, 2023).
89 Boykoff, *Creative (Climate) Communications*, 158.
90 Ibid., 211–12.
91 Stephen M. Gardiner, *A Perfect Moral Storm: The Ethical Tragedy of Climate Change* (Oxford: Oxford University Press, 2011), 34.
92 Ibid., 36.
93 Ibid., 439–40.
94 Reinhart Koselleck, *The Practice of Conceptual History: Timing History, Spacing Concepts*, trans. Todd Samuel Presner and Others (Stanford: Stanford University Press, 2002), 5.

95 Ibid., 45–6.

96 Ibid., 111.

97 Ibid., 120.

98 See also Paul Dragoş Aligică, *Prophecies of Doom and Scenarios of Progress: Herman Kahn, Julian Simon, and the Prospective Imagination* (New York: Continuum International, 2007).

99 Koselleck, *The Practice of Conceptual History*, 132.

100 Ibid., 134.

101 Ibid., 135.

102 Ibid., 53.

103 Roy Scranton, *Learning to Die in the Anthropocene: Reflections on the End of a Civilization* (San Francisco: City Light Books, 2015), 99.

104 Koselleck, *The Practice of Conceptual History*, 146.

105 Alan Lightman, *Einstein's Dreams: A Novel* (New York: Vintage Contemporaries, 1993), 16.

106 Ibid., 29.

107 Willis Jenkins, *The Future of Ethics: Sustainability Social Justice, and Religious Creativity* (Washington DC: Georgetown University Press, 2013), 1.

108 Ibid., 2.

109 Ibid., 3.

110 Ibid., 17.

111 Ibid., 20.

112 Ibid., 17.

113 Dipesh Chakrabarty, "The Climate of History: Four Theses," *Critical Inquiry* 35 (Winter 2009): 197–222, here at 197.

114 Ibid.

115 Ibid., 201.

116 Ibid., 204–6.

117 Dipesh Chakrabarty, *The Climate of History in a Planetary Age* (Chicago: University of Chicago Press, 2021), 5.

118 Chakrabarty, "The Climate of History," 207.

119 Ibid., 211.

120 Ibid., 212.

121 Ibid.

122 Ibid., 220.

123 Ibid., 7.

124 Ibid., 220.

125 Ibid., 221.

126 Ibid., 222.

127 Chakrabarty, *The Climate of History in a Planetary Age*, 8.

128 Ibid., 8–10, 13.

129 Ibid., 49.

130 Ibid., 14–15.

131 Ibid., 15.

132 Ibid., 50.

133 Ibid., 51.

134 Ibid., 58.

Chapter 8

1 Lynn White, Jr., "The Historical Roots of Our Ecological Crisis," *Science* 155 (1967): 1203–7.

2 See David Aberbach, *The Environment and Literature of Moral Dilemmas: From Adam to Michael K* (London: Routledge, 2022), 6. More generally, in the context of Jewish environmental studies, see Manfred Gerstenfeld, "Jewish Environmental Studies: A New Field," *Jewish Political Review* 13, no. 1/2 (Spring 2001): 3–62, here at 6f.

3 Todd LeVasseur and Anna Peterson, "Introduction," in *Religion and Ecological Crisis: The "Lynn White Thesis" at Fifty*, eds. Todd LeVasseur and Anna Peterson (London: Routledge, 2017), 1–17, here at 2.

4 Christopher Cone, "Continuing the Conversation: Applying Lynn White Jr.'s Prescriptions for a Christian Environmental Ethic," in *Religion and Ecological Crisis*, 101–09, here at 101.

5 LeVasseur and Peterson, "Introduction," 12; Elspeth Whitney, "Lynn White Jr.'s 'The Historical Roots of Our Ecological Crisis' after Fifty Years," in *Religion and Ecological Crisis*, 18–32, here at 25. Some point out that stewardship is rather managerial and not entirely helpful in terms of developing new, less hegemonic approaches. See Arianne Conty, *Grounding God: Religious Responses to the Anthropocene* (Albany: SUNY Press, 2023), 44.

6 See the documents on https://climaterepentance.com/the-spiritual-principles/jewish-sources-on-principles/.

7 Michael S. Northcott, "Lynn White Jr. Right and Wrong: The Anti-Ecological Character of Latin Christianity and the Pro-Ecological Turn of Protestantism," in *Religion and Ecological Crisis*, 61–74, here at 67.

8 Mark R. Stoll, "Sinners in the Hands of an Ecologic Crisis: Lynn White's Environmental Jeremiad," in *Religion and Ecological Crisis*, 47–60, here at 56.

9 See Robin Globus Veldman, *The Gospel of Climate Skepticism: Why Evangelical Christians Oppose Action on Climate Change* (Oakland: University of California Press, 2019), 2.

10 Ibid., 4.

11 Ibid., 8.

12 Ibid., 7, 27.

13 Ibid., 20.

14 Ibid., 8, 10.

15 Ibid., 11.

16 Ibid., 48.

17 Ibid., 50–1.

18 Ibid., 59, 61.

19 Ibid., 53.

20 Ibid., 23.

21 Ibid., 132.

22 Ibid., 59.

23 Ibid., 63.

24 Ibid., 97, 101.

25 Ibid., 117.

26 Laurel Kearns, "Climate Change," in *Grounding Religion: A Field Guide to the Study of Religion and Ecology*, eds. Whitney Bauman, Richard Bohannon, and Kevin J. O'Brien, second edn (London: Routledge, 2017), 137–57, here at 145.

27 See Jeremy Benstein, "'One, Walking and Studying . . . ': Nature vs. Torah," *Judaism* 44, no. 2 (1995): 146–68, here at 146; see the discussion in David Abram's work as well.

28 David Vogel, "How Green is Judaism? Exploring Jewish Environmental Ethics," unpublished paper (1999), https://faculty.haas.berkeley.edu/vogel/judaism.pdf, 3 (see also 20–22).

29 Benstein, "'One, Walking and Studying . . . ': Nature vs. Torah," 153–6.

30 7:13.

31 See https://climaterepentance.com/the-spiritual-principles/jewish-sources-on -principles/.

32 Mari Joerstad, *The Hebrew Bible and Environmental Ethics: Humans, Nonhumans, and the Living Landscape* (Cambridge: Cambridge University Press, 2019), 96. Some biblical passages evince a concern with ways in which "privilege of some undermines the livelihood of others" (97–8).

33 Hava Tirosh-Samuelson, *Religion and Environment: The Case of Judaism* (Kitchener: Pandora Press, 2020), 39.

34 Ibid., 44 regarding deep ecology and 45 regarding social ecology.

35 Ibid., 53.

36 Ibid., 70.

37 Ibid., 91.

38 Ibid., 95, 99, 102.

39 See https://climaterepentance.com/the-spiritual-principles/jewish-sources-on -principles/.

40 Tirosh-Samuelson, *Religion and Environment*, 220–1.

41 Jeremy Cohen, *"Be Fertile and Increase, Fill the Earth and Master It": The Ancient and Medieval Career of a Biblical Text* (Ithaca: Cornell University Press, 1989), 5.

42 Ibid., 18.

43 Ibid., 49.

44 Ibid., 58–9.

45 See ibid., 100: Palestinian Targum Pseudo-Jonathan translates "and master it as 'and rule over it with possessions,' hinting that dominion over the earth involves its development with the tools and fruits of human creativity."

46 Ibid., 63.

47 Ibid., 85.

48 Sigurd Bergmann, "Religion at Work within Climate Change: Eight Perceptions about Its Where and How," in *Religion in the Anthropocene*, eds. Celia Deane-Drummond, Sigurd Bergmann, and Markus Vogt (Eugene, OR: Cascade Books, 2017), 67–84, here at 74.

49 Thomas Hieke, "The Covenant in Leviticus 26: A Concept of Admonition and Redemption," in *Covenant in the Persian Period: From Genesis to Chronicles*, eds. Richard J. Bautch and Gary N. Knoppers (University Park: Penn State University Press, 2015), 75–90, here at 80–81.

50 Ibid.

51 Ibid., 81.

52 Ibid., 84.

53 Leslie Davenport, *Emotional Resiliency in the Era of Climate Change: A Clinician's Guide* (London: Jessica Kingsley Publishers, 2017), 23.

54　Ibid., 58ff.

55　Ibid., 44.

56　Ibid., 34.

57　Ibid., 36.

58　Ibid., 40.

59　Ibid., 38.

60　Ibid., 73.

61　Ibid., 74.

62　Ibid., 90.

63　Ibid., 106. See the work of Joanna Macy.

64　See Vogel, "How Green is Judaism?"

65　See Baumgartner, "Transformations of Stewardship in the Anthropocene," 65.

66　Ibid., 54–5.

67　Ibid., 55–6.

68　Emmanuel Levinas, *Ethics and Infinity: Conversations with Philippe Nemo*, trans. Richard A. Cohen (Pittsburgh: Duquesne University Press, 1985 (orig., 1982)), 95.

69　Cited in Shai Held, *Judaism is About Love: Recovering the Heart of Jewish Life* (New York: Farrar, Straus and Giroux, 2024).

70　See Jeremy Benstein, *The Way into Judaism and the Environment* (Woodstock, VT: Jewish Lights Publishing, 2006), 1–2.

71　Ibid., 2–3.

72　Ibid., 8.

73　Ibid., 11.

74　Ibid., 13.

75　Ibid., 21.

76　Ibid., 57.

77　Ibid., 72.

78　Ibid., 59.

79　Ibid., 74.

80　Ibid., 212.

81　Ibid., 213.

82　Joseph B. Soloveitchik's, *The Lonely Man of Faith* (New York: Doubleday, 1992).

83　Alon Goshen-Gottstein, *Covenant & World Religions Irving Greenberg, Jonathan Sacks, and the Quest for Orthodox Pluralism* (London: The Littman Library of Jewish Civilization, 2023), 65.

84　Ibid., 94.

85　Ibid., 199, 221.

86　Ibid., 239.

87　E. L. Allen, "The Hebrew View of Nature," in *Judaism and Environmental Ethics: A Reader*, ed. Martin D. Yaffe (Lanham: Lexington Books, 2001), 80–5, here at 82.

88　Lawrence Troster, "Created in the Image of God: Humanity and Divinity in an Age of Environmentalism," in *Judaism and Environmental Ethics: A Reader*, 172–82, here at 180.

89　Goshen-Gottstein, *Covenant & World Religions*, 16.

90　*Idolatry: A Contemporary Jewish Conversation*, ed. Alon Goshen-Gottstein (Boston: Academic Studies Press, 2023), 34.

91　Shaul Magid, "Idolatry on the Other Side of Morality," in *Idolatry: A Contemporary Jewish Conversation*, 93–124, here at 114.

92　Ibid., 111.

93 Ibid., 122.

94 Eilon Shamir, "Contemporary Idolatry and a Path to Freedom," in *Idolatry: A Contemporary Jewish Conversation*, 151–67, here at 161.

95 Haviva Pedaya, "The Dynamism of Idolatry," in *Idolatry: A Contemporary Jewish Conversation*, 213–31, here at 323ff; 325.

96 Jonathan Wittenberg, "The Idolatry of Humankind," in *Idolatry: A Contemporary Jewish Conversation*, 168–84, here at 168, 170.

97 Ibid., 182.

98 Ibid., 181.

99 Aberbach, *The Environment and Literature of Moral Dilemmas*, 13, 27.

100 Ibid., 20, 27.

101 Ibid., 15.

102 Ibid., 29.

103 Ibid., 41, 54.

104 Ibid., 54, 56, 61.

105 Ibid., 81–2.

106 Ibid., 67.

107 Ibid., 100.

108 See Jeffrey L. Rubenstein, *A History of Sukkot in the Second Temple and Rabbinic Periods* (Atlanta: Brown Judaic Studies, 2020): "R. Akiba cites Zech 14 to prove his view that rainfall depends upon the proper celebration of Sukkot. Although the prophecy ostensibly makes no reference to the water libation, R. Akiba appears to have 'read in' the ritual. He understands that the punishment of the nations results from their having neglected to make the pilgrimage and perform, or at least, bow while the priest performs, the water libation. The punishment is the lack of rain, hence the verse demonstrates the water libation ensures the rain supply" (169–70).

109 Ibid., 178: "Parallel to the temple ceremonies there may have been prayers for rain, either in the official priestly liturgy or later among proto-rabbinic or Pharisaic groups. That R. Eliezer connects 'mention' of rain with the lulav and R. Akiba and R. Yehuda b. Betera connect it with the water libation reveals the nexus of prayer and cult."

110 Christophe Schulte, *Zimzum: God and the Origins of the World* (Philadelphia: University of Pennsylvania Press, 2023 (orig., 2014)), 348.

111 Held, *Judaism is About Love*, 83.

112 Eilon Schwartz, "*Bal Tashchit*: A Jewish Environmental Precept," *Environmental Ethics* 18 (Winter 1997): 355–74, here at 355.

113 Ibid., 336.

114 Ibid., 360–61.

115 Ibid., 360.

116 Ibid., 361, 363); See TB Bava Kamma 91b, Shabbat 140b: "And Rav Ḥisda also said: One who is able to eat barley bread and nevertheless eats wheat bread violates the prohibition against wanton destruction. One who wastes resources is comparable to one who destroys items of value. And Rav Pappa said: One who is able to drink beer and nevertheless drinks wine violates the prohibition against wanton destruction. The Gemara comments: And this is not a correct matter, as the prohibition against destruction of one's body takes precedence. It is preferable for one to care for his body by eating higher quality food than to conserve his money.), and by extension, even obligations that humans have towards the created world (including themselves)" (Sefaria).

117 Ibid., 357–58.

118 Ibid., 359.

119 Ibid., 363.

120 Ibid., 363–64.

121 Ibid., 364, 369, 371.

122 Ibid., 365.

123 Ibid., 371.

124 Ibid., 372.

125 Ibid., 372.

126 Ibid., 372–73.

127 Eilon Schwartz, "Judaism and Nature: Theological and Moral Issues to Consider While Renegotiating a Jewish Relationship to the Natural World," *Judaism* 44, no. 4 (1995): 437–47, here at 437.

128 Ibid., 440: Schwartz references two approaches: "Halacha, on this side of the pole, acts to prevent ecological abuse in a philosophical system that otherwise legitimates it. In short, the Hasidic tradition came dangerously close to turning the world into the sacred, the Mitnagdim dangerously close to removing Divine presence from the world."

129 Laurie Zoloth, *Ethics for the Coming Storm: Climate Change and Jewish Thought* (Oxford: Oxford University Press, 2023), 1.

130 Ibid., 39.

131 Ibid., 58.

132 Ibid., 76ff; 182.

133 Ibid., 201.

134 Willemien Otten, *Thinking Nature and the Nature of Thinking: From Eriugena to Emerson* (Stanford: Stanford University Press, 2020), 13.

135 Ibid., 15.

136 Willis Jenkins, *The Future of Ethics: Sustainability, Social Justice, and Religious Creativity* (Washington DC: Georgetown University Press, 2013), 5.

137 Michael S. Hogue, "Sustainability and Climate Change," in *Encyclopedia of Religious Ethics*, 3 vols, ed. William Schweiker (Hoboken: Wiley & Sons Ltd., 2022), 1250–6, here at 1250–1.

Chapter 9

1 Arthur, Rohan, "Narratives from Indian Seas: Marine Resource Use, Ecosystem Responses, and the Accidents of History," in *At Nature's Edge: The Global Present and Long-Term History*, eds. Gunnel Cederlöf and Mahesh Rangarajan (Oxford: Oxford University Press, 2018), 229–48, here at 232, where he discusses history as a critical lens through which to interpret the functioning of ecological systems.

2 Ibid., 230.

3 Willis Jenkins, "Whose Religion? Which Ecology? Religious Studies in the Environmental Humanities," in *Routledge Handbook of Religion and Ecology*, eds. Willis Jenkins, Mary Evelyn Tucker, and John Grim (London: Routledge, 2017), 22–32, here at 23.

4 Ibid., 28.

5 Mary Evelyn Tucker and John Grim, "The Movement of Religion and Ecology: Emerging Field and Dynamic Force," in *Routledge Handbook of Religion and Ecology*, 3–12, here at 7.

6 Sigurd Bergmann, "Developments in Religion and Ecology," in *Routledge Handbook of Religion and Ecology*, 13–21, here at 15.

7 Ibid.

8 Tucker and Grim, "The Movement of Religion and Ecology," 7.

9 Michael S. Hogue, "Sustainability and Climate Change," in *Encyclopedia of Religious Ethics*, 3 vols, ed. William Schweiker (Wiley & Sons Ltd., 2022), 1250–6, here at 1252.

10 Gretel van Wieren, "Conservation and Restoration," in *Routledge Handbook of Religion and Ecology*, 265–74, here at 271.

11 Avi Sagi, *The Open Canon: On the Meaning of Halakhic Discourse* (London: Continuum, 2007), 40.

12 Ibid., 62–3.

13 Ibid., 64.

14 Ibid., 77.

15 Mark C. Taylor, *After God* (Chicago: University of Chicago Press, 2007), 5.

16 Ibid., 13.

17 Ibid., 26.

18 Ibid., 30.

19 Ibid., 326.

20 Ibid., 356.

21 Ibid., 345.

22 Ibid., 348.

23 Ibid.

24 Ibid., 349.

25 Ibid., 354.

26 Ibid.

27 Julia Watts Belser, *Power, Ethics, and Ecology in Jewish Late Antiquity: Rabbinic Responses to Drought and Disaster* (Cambridge: Cambridge University Press, 2015), 6. Belser writes that "Instead of emphasizing the protective power of merit, Bavli Ta'anit advances an idea I call 'performative perception,' claim that individual interpretative choices have the power to materially shape the course of a person's life" (86).

28 Ibid., 81.

29 Devora Steinmetz, *Why Rain Comes from Above: Explorations in Religious Imagination* (New York: Hadar Press, 2024), 5.

30 Ibid., 22.

31 See Moshe Rosman, *How Jewish is Jewish History?*: 'Since meaning is contingent and unstable, one of the basic principles of postmodern scholarship is that phenomena cannot be said to have an 'essential' nature. "Judaism is . . . "; "Judaism teaches . . . " are the kinds of statements that must always be qualified by placing them in a spatial, temporal, and social context. In a certain place, at a certain time, under certain conditions, "this Judaism was . . . " and "that Judaism taught . . . ." That is, Judaism has been variably constructed depending on the context' (4).

32 Edward Shils, *Tradition* (Chicago: University of Chicago Press, 1981), 16.

33 See the *Encyclopedia Judaica* entry.

34 Babylonian Talmud, Tractate Sotah, 10b, in the name of Rabbi Elazar.

35 3:13; Sefaria Community Translation.

36 Mary Mallon, *Traditioning Disciplines: The Contribution of Cultural Anthropology to Ecclesial Identity* (Eugene, OR: Pickwick Publications, 2010), 68.
37 Ibid., 95.
38 Ibid., 103, citing Möhler.
39 Ibid., 99.
40 Ibid., 241.
41 Ibid., 39.
42 Ibid., 68.
43 Ibid., 245.
44 See Shils, *Tradition*, for a discussion on this issue more generally.
45 Marc B. Shapiro, *Changing the Immutable: How Orthodox Judaism Rewrites Its History* (Oxford: The Littman Library of Jewish Civilization, 2015), 1.
46 Ibid., 10.
47 Ibid., 12.
48 Ibid., 26.
49 Ibid., 25–6.
50 Ibid., 257. See Babylonian Talmud, tractate Eruvin (51a).
51 Chaim Burman, "The Invocation of Mesorah in Contemporary Orthodox Jewish Legal Discourse: Polysemic and Reified Usages," *Journal of Modern Jewish Studies* 20, no. 1 (2001), 22–43, here at 23, 26, 27.
52 Ibid., 29.
53 Ibid., 28.
54 Hans-Georg Gadamer, *Truth and Method*, trans. Joel Weinsheimer and Donald G. Marshall (London: Bloomsbury, 2013 (orig., 1960)).
55 Ibid., 250.
56 Ibid., 281.
57 Ibid., 291. See also Karl Popper's "Towards a Rational Theory of Tradition," in *Conjectures and Refutations: The Growth of Scientific Knowledge* (London: Routledge, 1963), 161–82.
58 Gadamer, *Truth and Method*, 292, 293.
59 Ibid., 293.
60 Ibid., 294.
61 Ibid., 301.
62 Ibid., 302.
63 Ibid., 303.
64 Ibid., 305. Popper notes that a person has to know and understand a tradition before that person can criticize it. See "Towards a Rational Theory of Tradition," 164.
65 Gadamer, *Truth and Method*, 307.
66 Ibid., 315.
67 Ibid., 317.
68 Ibid., 590–1.
69 Anniina Leiviskä, "The Relevance of Hans-Georg Gadamer's Concept of Tradition to the Philosophy of Education," *Educational Theory* 65, no. 5 (2015): 581–600, here at 588.
70 Gadamer, *Truth and Method*, 408.
71 Leiviskä, "The Relevance of Hans-Georg Gadamer's Concept of Tradition to the Philosophy of Education," 589.
72 See Jens Zimmerman, *Hermeneutics: A Very Short History* (Oxford: Oxford University Press, 2015), 134ff.

73 See Terry Eagleton, *Literary Theory: An Introduction* (Minneapolis: University of Minnesota Press, 2008 (orig., 1983)), 63.

74 Gadamer, *Truth and Method*, 310.

75 Ibid., 318.

76 Ibid., 320, 333.

77 Ibid., 322.

78 Eagleton, *Literary Theory*, 62. Richard B. Miller, *Why Study Religion?* (Oxford: Oxford University Press, 2021) writes that "Bush hastens to add that 'meaning is not exclusively located in the text or the sentences that constitute the text: it is the joint project of the text and some larger context.'" (206)

79 Ibid., 62.

80 Gadamer, *Truth and Method*, 362.

81 Ibid., 361.

82 Ibid., 369.

83 Eagleton, *Literary Theory*, 62.

84 Gadamer, *Truth and Method*, 282.

85 Leiviskä, "The Relevance of Hans-Georg Gadamer's Concept of Tradition to the Philosophy of Education," 582.

86 Ibid.

87 Ibid., 595.

88 Ibid.

89 Shils, *Tradition*, 44.

90 Leiviskä, "The Relevance of Hans-Georg Gadamer's Concept of Tradition to the Philosophy of Education," 599.

91 Ibid., 596.

92 Ibid., 600.

93 Barry Holtz, *Textual Knowledge: Teaching the Bible in Theory and Practice* (New York: Jewish Theological Seminary of America, 2003).

94 Ibid., 16; "Of course, one of the pleasures of the Jewish interpretive literature is that there is no one authoritative understanding of the text, going back at least to the time of the classical midrashim. There is a wide range of views found within the tradition" (79).

95 Ibid., 38.

96 Taylor, *After God*, 27.

97 David Abram, *The Spell of the Sensuous: Perception and Language in a More-Than-Human World* (New York: Vintage Books, 2017 (orig. 1996)).

98 Ibid., 36.

99 Ibid., 52.

100 Ibid., 38.

101 Ibid., 39.

102 Ibid., 66.

103 Ibid., 79.

104 Ibid., 80, 85–6.

105 Ibid., 94–95.

106 Ibid., 100.

107 Ibid., 101, 110.

108 Ibid., 111.

109 Ibid., 112.

110 Ibid., 113.

111 Ibid., 139.

112 Ibid., 159.

113 Ibid., 183.

114 Ibid., 185.

115 Ibid., 188.

116 Ibid., 186.

117 Ibid., 192.

118 Ibid., 193.

119 Ibid., 237.

120 Ibid., 194.

121 Ibid.

122 Ibid., 195.

123 Ibid., 196.

124 Ibid., 240.

125 Ibid.

126 Ibid., 242.

127 Ibid., 243.

128 Ibid., 248.

129 Ibid., 249.

130 Ibid., 245.

131 Ibid., 197.

132 Ibid., 198.

133 Ibid., 251.

134 Ibid., 252.

135 Ibid.

136 Ibid., 199, 201.

137 Evan Berry, "The Right Climate: Political Opportunities for Religious Engagement in Climate Policy" in *Climate Politics and the Power of Religion*, ed. Evan Berry (Bloomington: Indiana University Press, 2022), 122–44, here at 126.

138 Berry, *Climate Politics and the Power of Religion*, 7–8.

139 See Jenkins' discussion of Norton, in Willis Jenkins, *Ecologies of Grace: Environmental Ethics and Christian Theology* (Oxford: Oxford University Press, 2008), 37.

140 Ibid., 36.

141 Andrew R. H. Thompson, "Climate Vulnerability as Theological Bridge Concept: Examples from Puerto Rico," in *Climate Politics and the Power of Religion*, 206–29, here at 216.

142 Jenkins, *Ecologies of Grace*, 44.

143 Ibid., 45.

144 Ibid., 46.

145 Ibid., 61, 59.

146 Willis Jenkins, *The Future of Ethics: Sustainability, Social Justice, and Religious Creativity* (Washington DC: Georgetown University Press, 2013), 24.

147 Ibid., 26.

148 Ibid., 33, 36.

149 Ibid., 30, for example.

150 Ibid., 40.

151 Ibid., 42.

152 Ibid., 47–9.

153 Ibid., 50–3.

154 Ibid., 56, 81.

155 Ibid., 111–12.

156 Ibid., 117, 126.

157 Ibid., 136, 139.

158 Ibid., 285, 307, 286.

159 Ibid., 166.

160 Ibid., 176, 180–1.

161 Thomas A. Tweed, *Crossing and Dwelling: A Theory of Religion* (Cambridge, MA: Harvard University Press, 2006), 7.

162 Ibid., 59.

163 Ibid., 62, 64, 71.

164 Ibid., 78.

165 Ibid., 74.

166 Whitney Bauman, Richard Bohannon, and Kevin J. O'Brien, eds., *Grounding Religion: A Field Guide to the Study of Religion and Ecology*, second edn (London: Routledge, 2017); Dave Aftandilian, "Animals," 180–201.

167 Ibid., 182.

Chapter 10

1 Complex systems possess some common properties. Melanie Mitchell, *Complexity: A Guided Tour* (Oxford: Oxford University Press, 2009), 13.

2 Meghan O'Gieblyn, *God, Human, Animal, Machine: Technology, Metaphor, and the Search for Meaning* (New York: Anchor Books, 2021), 87.

3 Ibid., 86.

4 Ibid.

5 See David J. Snowden and Mary E. Boone, "A Leader's Framework for Decision Making," *Harvard Business Review* 85, no. 11 (2007): 68–76, here at 70.

6 See the discussion of the work of Stuart Kauffman in Arianne Conty, *Grounding God: Religious Responses to the Anthropocene* (Albany: SUNY Press, 2023), 47–49.

7 Mitchell, *Complexity*, 38.

8 O'Gieblyn, *God, Human, Animal, Machine*, 33.

9 Ibid., 93.

10 Whitney A. Bauman and Heather Eaton, "Gender and Queer Studies," in *Grounding Religion: A Field Guide to the Study of Religion and Ecology*, eds. Whitney Bauman, Richard Bohannon, and Kevin J. O'Brien, second edn (London: Routledge, 2017), 61–76, here at 68.

11 Ibid., 69.

12 Ibid., 71.

13 Ibid.

14 See Carol Wayne White, "Race and Ethnicity," in *Grounding Religion*, 77–93, here at 85.

15 Ibid., 90.

16 See James Bridle, *Ways of Being: Animals, Plants, Machines: The Search for a Planetary Intelligence* (New York: Picador, 2022), 24.

17 David Harvey, *Justice, Nature & the Geography of Difference* (Oxford: Blackwell, 1996), 10.

18 Ibid., 55.

19 Ibid., 11.

20 Ibid., 78ff.

21 Ibid., 201.

22 Ibid., 201.

23 Laura Novak Winer, "Teaching Who They Are: Understanding Teachers' Connections with Israel and How Those Enter into the Classroom," in *Teaching Israel: Studies of Pedagogy from the Field*, eds. Sivan Zakai and Matt Reingold (Waltham: Brandeis University Press, 2024), 29.

24 Stephen M. Kosslyn and Ben Nelson, eds., *Building the Intentional University: Minerva and the Future of Higher Education* (Cambridge, MA: MIT Press, 2017), 111.

25 Zoë Schlanger, *The Light Eaters: How the Unseen World of Plant Intelligence Offers a New Understanding of Life on Earth* (New York: Harper, 2024), 131.

26 Ibid., 192. Or as James Bridle points out, individuality is linked to the political idea of sovereignty and agency that have defined modernity and are largely Western in orientation, differentiating self and other in fundamental ways. See Bridle, *Ways of Being: Animals, Plants, Machines*, 106.

27 William R. Jordan III, *The Sunflower Forest: Ecological Restoration and the New Communion with Nature* (Berkeley: University of California Press, 2003), 41.

28 Ibid., 44.

29 See the documents on https://climaterepentance.com/the-spiritual-principles/jewish-sources-on-principles/.

30 Harvey, *Justice, Nature & the Geography of Difference*, 261.

31 Ibid., 270.

32 Ibid., 293; Robert S. Emmett and David E. Nye, *The Environmental Humanities: A Critical Introduction* (Cambridge, MA: The MIT Press, 2017), 24.

33 Jordan III, *The Sunflower Forest*.

34 Ibid., 28.

35 Ibid., 29.

36 Ibid., 30.

37 Brian G. Campbell, "The Power of Place," in *Grounding Religion*, 94–113, here at 94–95.

38 Ibid., 95.

39 Emmett and Nye, *The Environmental Humanities*, 27.

40 Campbell, "The Power of Place," 100.

41 Ibid., 101.

42 Ibid., 103–05.

43 Ibid., 102.

44 Campbell, "The Power of Place," 98.

45 Harvey, *Justice, Nature & the Geography of Difference*, 304.

46 Ibid., 306.

47 Ibid., 307.

48 Ibid., 305.

49 Ibid., 306.

50 Ibid., 322.

51 Ibid., 342.

52 See ibid., 353 regarding Habermas as a critic of postmodern and poststructuralist particularisms and a strong proponent of universalist arguments.

53 Ibid., 362.

54 Ibid., 363.

55 Ibid., 357.

56 Ibid., 354.

57 Keren E. Fraiman and Dean P. Bell, "A New Approach to Education and Peoplehood: Diversity as a Key to a Sustainable Model of Peoplehood," in *Peoplehood Education: Goals, Pedagogy, Outcomes* (*The Peoplehood Papers*, vol. 30 (Online: Center for Jewish Peoplehood Education, August 2021). [https://old.jpeoplehood.org/wp-content/uploads/2021/09/Peoplehood-Papers-30-Final.pdf], eds. Shlomi Ravid and Dean P. Bell, 42–50.

58 Timothy Morton, *Ecology Without Nature: Rethinking Environmental Aesthetics* (Cambridge, MA: Harvard University Press, 2007), 49.

59 Ibid., 18.

60 Ibid., 47–9.

61 Ibid., 76.

62 Ibid.

63 Ibid., 138.

64 Ibid., 135.

65 Peter T. Coleman, *The Way Out: How to Overcome Toxic Polarization* (New York: Columbia University Press, 2021), 20, 23.

66 Ibid., 24.

67 Ibid., 38, 39.

68 Ibid., 39.

69 Ibid., 100ff.

70 Ibid., 144.

71 Ibid., 60.

72 Ibid., 61.

73 Ibid., 68.

74 Ibid., 73.

75 Ibid.

76 Ibid., 74. And it appears that competition is not the only driver of change, as we learn from plant behavior: "The most earth-shattering thing that this long-term experiment has taught him is that competition isn't actually all that important. It's surely one driver of change, but it's only one in a profusion of drivers" (Schlanger, *The Light Eaters*, 212).

77 Coleman, *The Way Out*, 77.

78 Ibid., 106.

79 Ibid., 122.

80 Ibid., 126.

81 Ibid., 148, 150.

82 Ibid., 150.

83 Ibid., 155.

84 Ibid., 155.

85 Ibid., 157.

86 Ibid., 164, 165, 167, 170–1.

87 Ibid., 176–7.

88 Ibid., 184.

89 Ibid., 185.

90 Ibid., 190.

91 Ibid., 187.

92 Brian Emerson and Kelly Lewis, *Navigating Polarities: Using Both/And Thinking to Lead Transformation* (Washington DC: Paradoxical Press, 2019), *Navigating Polarities*, 20.

93 Ibid., 21.

94 Ibid., 26, 28.

95 Ibid., 31.

96 Ibid., 45.

97 Ibid., 47.

98 Emmett and Nye, 16.

99 Ibid., 20.

100 See Bridle, *Ways of Being*, 110.

101 Stephanie Wakefield, Kevin Grove, and David Chandler, "Introduction: The Power of Life," in *Resilience in the Anthropocene: Governance and Politics at the End of the World*, eds. David Chandler, Kevin Grove, and Stephanie Wakefield (London: Routledge, 2020), 1–21, here at 3–4.

102 Ibid., 7.

103 Ibid.

104 Ibid., 8.

105 Ibid.

106 Ibid., 9–10.

107 Ibid., 10.

108 See Michael S. Hogue and Dean Phillip Bell, *Interreligious Resilience: Interreligious Leadership for a Pluralistic World* (London: Bloomsbury, 2022); Judith Rodin, *The Resilience Dividend: Being Strong in a World Where Things Go Wrong* (New York: The Rockefeller Foundation, 2014).

109 David Chandler, "The End of Resilience? Rethinking Adaptation in the Anthropocene," in *Resilience in the Anthropocene*, 50–67, here at 52, 57.

110 Ibid., 51.

111 Simon Dalby, "Resilient Earth: Gaia, geopolitics and the Anthropocene," in *Resilience in the Anthropocene*, 22–36, here at 25.

112 Sebastien Nobert, Harold Bellanger Rodriguez, and Xochilt Hernandez Leiva, "Colliding Times: Urgency, Resilience and the Politics of Living with Volcanic Gas Emissions in the Anthropocene," in *Resilience in the Anthropocene*, 68–83, here at 69.

113 Ibid., 80.

114 Bridle, *Ways of Being*, 183.

115 Kian Goh, *Form and Flow: The Spatial Politics of Urban Resilience and Climate Justice* (Cambridge, MA: The MIT Press, 2021), 10.

116 Ibid., 12.

117 Ibid., 175.

118 See Hogue and Bell, *Interreligious Resilience*.

Chapter 11

1 Robert S. Emmett and David E. Nye, *The Environmental Humanities: A Critical Introduction* (Cambridge, MA: The MIT Press, 2017), 59.

2 Ibid., 76.

3 Ibid., 159.

4 Ibid., 129.

5 Ibid., 153.

6 Summarized in Ellen Bernstein, "A Biblical Land Ethic? A Response to Aldo Leopold," in *Ecotheology in the Humanities: An Interdisciplinary Approach to Understanding the Divine and Nature*, ed. Melissa J. Brotton (London: Lexington Books, 2016), 25–51, here at 27.

7 Motti Zohar, "Damage Patterns of Earthquakes in Israel and Its Vicinity: Evaluation According to the Historical Sources" (Doctoral Dissertation, Hebrew University of Jerusalem, 2016), 100.

8 Vuokko Jarva, "Introduction to Narrative for Futures Studies," *Journal of Future Studies* 18, no. 3 (March 2014): 5–26, here at 9, 12, 17.

9 Ibid., 17.

10 Matthew S. Henry, *Hydronarratives: Water, Environmental Justice, and a Just Transition* (Lincoln: University of Nebraska Press, 2022), 6.

11 Ibid., 15, 19; 20.

12 Orly Lobel, *The Equality Machine: Harnessing Digital Technology for a Brighter, More Inclusive Future* (New York: Hachette Book Group, Inc., 2022), 151.

13 Eilon Schwartz, "Environment: Jewish Education as if the Planet Mattered," in *International Handbook of Jewish Education, Part One*, eds. Helena Miller, Lisa D. Grant, and Alex Pomson (Dordrecht: Springer, 2011), 389–406, here at 391.

14 Ibid., 397–8.

15 Ibid., 399–400.

16 Ibid., 401.

17 Ibid., 400.

18 Ibid., 402.

19 Ibid., 403.

20 Ibid., 402.

21 Michael S. Hogue, *American Immanence: Democracy for an Uncertain World* (New York: Columbia University Press, 2018), 181.

22 Ibid., 182.

23 Rebecca A. Martusewicz, Jeff Edmundson, and John Lupinacci, *EcoJustice Education: Toward Diverse, Democratic, and Sustainable Communities*, second edn (New York, London: Routledge, 2015), 13.

24 Ibid., 22, 25, 26.

25 Ibid., 13.

26 Ibid., 10.

27 Ibid., 12.

28 Keren E. Fraiman, "Barriers to Entry: Exploring Educator Reticence for Engaging with the Israeli-Palestinian Conflict," in *Teaching Israel: Studies of Pedagogy from the Field*, eds. Sivan Zakai and Matt Reingold (Waltham: Brandeis University Press, 2024), 229–53, here at 230ff.

29 See Arianne Conty, *Grounding God: Religious Responses to the Anthropocene* (Albany: SUNY Press, 2023), 104–05.

30 See Jarva, "Introduction to Narrative for Futures Studies," 5–6.

31 Stuart Russell and Peter Norvig, *Artificial Intelligence: A Modern Approach*, fourth edn (Harlow, UK: Pearson, 2022), 627.

32 Ruth A. Morgan, *Climate Change and International History: Negotiating Science, Global Change, and Environmental Justice* (London: Bloomsbury Academic, 2024), 173ff.

33   Emmett and Nye, *The Environmental Humanities*, 1.

34   Ibid., 2.

35   Ibid., 7.

36   Ibid., 155.

37   Ibid., 177.

38   Ibid.

39   Ibid., 186.

40   See Hogue, *American Immanence*, who argues that "human moral psychology biases us against seeing, experiencing, and feeling the climate crisis as a moral problem in anything close to the way that we experience very intensely the moral dimensions of interpersonal relations" (68).

41   See https://climaterepentance.com/the-spiritual-principles/jewish-sources-on -principles/.

42   Wendell Berry, *The World-Ending Fire: The Essential Wendell Berry* (Berkeley: Counterpoint, 2017), 54.

43   Berry, "The Agricultural Standard," in *The World-Ending Fire*, 133.

44   Ibid., 135.

45   Ibid., 122.

46   Mike Berners-Lee, *There is No Planet B: A Handbook for the Make or Break Years* (Cambridge: Cambridge University Press, 2019), 163.

47   Jeremy Benstein, *The Way into Judaism and the Environment* (Woodstock, VT: Jewish Lights Publishing, 2006), 142, citing Elie Wiesel.

48   Berry, "Faustian Economics," in *The World-Ending Fire*, 209.

49   Ibid.

50   Ibid., 215.

51   Ibid., 216.

52   Berry, "Feminism, the Body, and the Machine," in *The World-Ending Fire*, 258.

53   Berry, *The World-Ending Fire*, 25.

54   See Hogue, *American Immanence*, 141.

55   Ibid., 85.

56   Ibid., 86.

57   Ulrich Beck, *The Metamorphosis of the World* (Cambridge: Polity Press, 2016), 4.

58   Ibid., 20.

59   Ibid., 85.

60   Ibid., 125.

61   Kian Goh, *Form and Flow: The Spatial Politics of Urban Resilience and Climate Justice* (Cambridge, MA: The MIT Press, 2021), 17.

62   Ibid., 18.

63   Sally Weintrobe, *Psychological Roots of the Climate Crisis: Neoliberal Exceptionalism and the Culture of Uncare* (London: Bloomsbury, 2021), 106.

64   Ibid., 1. She writes that "Neoliberal cultural framing reduces *all* our diverse relationships to just one relationship, that of user-used" (119).

65   Ibid., 13.

66   Ibid., 84.

67   Ibid., 89.

68   Ibid., 137.

69   Ibid., 236.

70   Ibid., 195.

71 Amitv Ghosh, *The Great Derangement: Climate Change and the Unthinkable* (Chicago: University of Chicago Press, 2016), 4–5.

72 See Naomi Oreskes and Erik M. Conway, *Merchants of Doubt: How a Handful of Scientists Obscured the Truth on Issues from Tobacco Smoke to Global Warming* (New York: Bloomsbury, 2010).

73 See Libby Robin and Will Steffen, "History for the Anthropocene," *History Compass* 5, no. 5 (2007): 1694–719, here at 1710). Hogue, *American Immanence*, notes that Dewey held that "'the future is not a mere word' but is a set of perils and possibilities that we, quite literally, knowingly bring to life" (88).

74 David Sedlak, *Water for All: Global Solutions for a Changing Climate* (New Haven: Yale University Press, 2023), 80.

75 See also Jean Axelrod Cahan, ed., *Water Security in the Middle East: Essays in Scientific and Social Cooperation* (London: Anthem Press, 2020), which explores the centrality of water in the Koran (7) as well as the political and military issues associated with water scarcity (4) and different opportunities for cooperation (43, 118, 145–6).

76 Jonathan Safran Foer, *We are the Weather: Saving the Planet Begins at Breakfast* (New York: Picador, 2019), 13.

77 See the work of Hal Hershfield cited in ibid., 19.

78 Ibid.

79 Ibid., 50.

80 Ibid., 51.

81 Jarva, "Introduction to Narrative for Futures Studies," 20.

82 Christopher Ward and Sandra Ruckstuhl, *Water Scarcity, Climate Change and Conflict in the Middle East: Securing Livelihoods, Building Peace* (London: I.B. Tauris, 2020 (2017)), 49.

83 Ibid., 95. See also https://en.wikipedia.org/wiki/Water_Tribunal_of_the_plain_of _Valencia

84 Ward and Ruckstuhl, *Water Scarcity*, 304.

85 Noah J. Toly, *The Gardeners' Dirty Hands: Environmental Politics and Christian Ethics* (Oxford: Oxford University Press, 2019), ix.

86 Ibid., 8.

87 Ibid., 71.

88 Ibid., 64.

89 Ibid., 66.

90 Ibid., xii.

91 James Bridle, *Ways of Being: Animals, Plants, Machines: The Search for a Planetary Intelligence* (New York: Picador, 2022), 208ff.

92 See Paulo Freire, *Pedagogy of the Oppressed* (New York: Bloomsbury, 2000 (orig., 1968)).

Bibliography

Aberbach, David. *The Environment and Literature of Moral Dilemmas: From Adam to Michael K*. London: Routledge, 2022.

Aberth, John. *Plagues in World History*. Lanham: Rowman and Littlefield, 2011.

Abram, David. *The Spell of the Sensuous: Perception and Language in a More-Than-Human World*. NY: Vintage Books, 2017 (orig., 1996).

Adeney Thomas, Julia, Mark Williams, and Jan Zalasiewicz. *The Anthropocene: A Multidisciplinary Approach*. Cambridge: Polity, 2020.

Agamben, Giorgio. *Homo Sacer: Sovereign Power and Bare Life*. Translated by Daniel Heller-Roazen. Stanford: Stanford University Press, 1998 (orig., 1995).

Allemeyer, Marie Luisa. "'Daß es wohl recht ein Feuer vom Herrn zu nennen gewesen . . .' Zur Wahrnehmung, Deutung und Verarbeitung von Stadtbränden in norddeutschen Schriften des 17. Jahrhunderts." In *Um Himmels Willen. Religion in Katastrophenzeiten*, edited by Manfred Jakubowski-Tiessen and Hartmut Lehmann, 201–34. Göttingen: Vandenhoeck & Ruprecht, 2003.

Allemeyer, Marie Luisa. "Profane Hazard or Divine Judgement? Coping with Urban Fire in the 17th Century." *Historical Social Research* 32, no. 3 (2007): 145–68.

Allen, E. L. "The Hebrew View of Nature." In *Judaism and Environmental Ethics: A Reader*, edited by Martin D. Yaffe, 80–4. Lanham: Lexington Books, 2001.

Ammerman, Steven. "Animal Agents in the Human Environment." In *The Power of Nature: Archaeology and Human-Environmental Dynamics*, edited by Monica L. Smith, 213–32. Denver: University Press of Colorado, 2022.

Anoruo, Nancy A. "Doctors Rebuff Unproven and Potentially Dangerous Oleander Chemical Falsely Touted as COVID-19 'Cure.'" *ABC News*, August 19, 2020. https://abcnews.go.com/Health/doctors-rebuff-unproven-potentially-dangerous-oleander-chemical-falsely/story?id=72428650.

Arthur, Rohan. "Narratives from Indian Seas: Marine Resource Use, Ecosystem Responses, and the Accidents of History." In *At Nature's Edge: The Global Present and Long-Term History*, edited by Gunnel Cederlöf and Mahesh Rangarajan, 229–48. Oxford: Oxford University Press, 2018.

Asaria, Zvi. *Die Juden in Köln: Von den Ältesten Zeiten bis zur Gegenwart*. Cologne: J.P. Bachem, 1959.

Axelrod Cahan, Jean, ed. *Water Security in the Middle East: Essays in Scientific and Social Cooperation*. London: Anthem Press, 2020.

Ayalon, Yaron. *Natural Disasters in the Ottoman Empire: Plague, Famine, and Other Misfortunes*. Cambridge: Cambridge University Press, 2015.

Ayalon, Yaron. "Plagues, Famines, Earthquakes: The Jews of Ottoman Syria and Natural Disasters." Dissertation, Princeton University, 2009.

Ayalon, Yaron. "Religion and Ottoman Society's Responses to Epidemics in the Seventeenth and Eighteenth Centuries." In *Plague and Contagion in the Islamic Mediterranean*, edited by Nükhet Varlik, 179–97 (Newark: Arc Humanities Press, 2017).

Backhaus, Fritz, Gisela Engel, Robert Liberles, and Margarete Schlüter, eds. *The Frankfurt Judengasse: Jewish Life in an Early Modern German City*. London: Vallentine Mitchell, 2010.

Baer, Marc David. "The Great Fire of 1660 and the Islamization of Christian and Jewish Space in Istanbul." *International Journal of Middle East Studies* 36, no. 2 (May 2004): 159–81.

Bankoff, George. "Cultures of Disaster, Cultures of Coping: Hazard as a Frequent Life Experience in the Philippines." In *Natural Disasters, Cultural Responses: Case Studies Toward a Global Environmental History*, edited by Christof Mauch and Christian Pfister, 265–84. Lanham: Lexington Books, 2009.

Bankoff, George, Uwe Lübken, and Jordan Sand, eds. *Flammable Cities: Urban Conflagration and the Making of the Modern World*. Madison: University of Wisconsin Press, 2012.

Barnett, Lydia. *After the Flood: Imagining the Global Environment in Early Modern Europe*. Baltimore: Johns Hopkins University Press, 2019.

Barrick, William D. "The Eschatological Significance of Leviticus 26." Paper, 1999. https:// biblicalelearning.org/wp-content/uploads/2022/01/Barrick-Lev26Eschat.pdf.

Bartlome, Niklaus and Erika Flückiger. "Stadtzerstörungen und Wiederaufbau in der mittelalterlichen und frühneuzeitlichen Schweiz." In *Stadtzerstörung und Wiederaufbau: Zerstörungen durch Erdbeben, Feuer und Wasser*, edited by Martin Körner, vol. 1: 123–46. Bern: P. Haupt, 1999.

Bauman, Whitney A. and Heather Eaton. "Gender and Queer Studies." In *Grounding Religion: A Field Guide to the Study of Religion and Ecology*, edited by Whitney Bauman, Richard Bohannon, and Kevin J. O'Brien, second edn, 61–76. London: Routledge, 2017.

Bauman, Whitney, Richard Bohannon, and Kevin J. O'Brien eds. *Grounding Religion: A Field Guide to the Study of Religion and Ecology*, Second edn. London: Routledge, 2017.

Baumgartner, Christopher. "Transformations of Stewardship in the Anthropocene." In *Religion in the Anthropocene*, edited by Celia Deane-Drummond, Sigurd Bergmann, and Markus Vogt, 53–66. Eugene, OR: Cascade Books, 2017.

Beck, Ulrich. *The Metamorphosis of the World*. Cambridge: Polity, 2016.

Behringer, Wolfgang. *A Cultural History of Climate*. Cambridge: Polity, 2010.

Bell, Dean Phillip. "Environmental History and Jewish Studies: Methodological Intersections and Opportunities." *Casden Annual*, edited by Sander Gilman, 187–204. West Lafayette, IN: Purdue University Press, 2022.

Bell, Dean Phillip. "The Great Fire of 1711: Re-Conceptualizing the Jewish Ghetto and Jewish-Christian Relations in Early Modern Frankfurt am Main." In *Archaeologies of Confession: Writing the German Reformation 1517–2017*, edited by Carina Johnson, David Luebke, and Jesse Spohnholz, 193–218. New York: Berghahn, 2017.

Bell, Dean Phillip. *Jewish Identity in Early Modern Germany: Memory, Power and Community*. Aldershot: Ashgate, 2007.

Bell, Dean Phillip. "Learning from Disasters Past: The Case of an Early Seventeenth-Century Plague in Northern Italy and Beyond." *Jewish Social Studies* 26, no. 1 (Fall 2020): 55–66.

Bell, Dean Phillip. "The Little Ice Age and the Jews: Environmental History and the Mercurial Nature of Jewish-Christian Relations in Early Modern Germany." *AJS Review* 32, no. 1 (Spring 2008): 1–27.

Bell, Dean Phillip. "Navigating the Flood Waters: Perspectives on Jewish Life in Early Modern Germany." *Leo Baeck Institute Yearbook* 56 (2011): 29–52.

Bell, Dean Phillip. *Plague in the Early Modern World: A Documentary History*. London: Routledge, 2019.

Bell, Dean Phillip. "The Trembling of the Earth: Jewish Descriptions of Earthquakes in the Early Modern World." In *Studies in Jewish Civilization 20: "'The Mountains Shall Drip Wine': Jews and the Environment,"* edited by Leonard J. Greenspoon et al., 1–20. Omaha: Creighton University Press, 2009.

Bell, Dean Phillip. "Vulnerability in Judaism: Anthropological and Divine Dimensions." In *Exploring Vulnerability*, edited by Heike Springhart and Günter Thomas, 93–106. Göttingen: Vandenhoeck and Ruprecht, 2017.

Belser, Julia Watts. *Power, Ethics, and Ecology in Jewish Late Antiquity: Rabbinic Responses to Drought and Disaster*. Cambridge: Cambridge University Press, 2015.

Benstein, Jeremy. "'One, Walking and Studying…': Nature vs. Torah." *Judaism* 44, no. 2 (1995): 146–68.

Benstein, Jeremy. *The Way into Judaism and the Environment*. Woodstock, VT: Jewish Lights Publishing, 2006.

Bergmann, Sigurd. "Developments in Religion and Ecology." In *Routledge Handbook of Religion and Ecology*, edited by Willis Jenkins, Mary Evelyn Tucker, and John Grim, 13–21. London: Routledge, 2017.

Bergmann, Sigurd. "Religion at Work within Climate Change: Eight Perceptions about Its Where and How." In *Religion in the Anthropocene*, edited by Celia Deane-Drummond, Sigurd Bergmann, and Markus Vogt, 67–84. Eugene, OR: Cascade Books, 2017.

Berners-Lee, Mike. *There is No Planet B: A Handbook for the Make or Break Years*. Cambridge: Cambridge University Press, 2019.

Bernstein, Ellen. "A Biblical Land Ethic? A Response to Aldo Leopold." In *Ecotheology in the Humanities: An Interdisciplinary Approach to Understanding the Divine and Nature*, edited by M. J. Brotton, 25–51. Lanham: Lexington Books, 2016.

Berry, Evan, ed. *Climate Politics and the Power of Religion*. Bloomington: Indiana University Press, 2022.

Berry, Evan. "The Right Climate: Political Opportunities for Religious Engagement in Climate Policy." In *Climate Politics and the Power of Religion*, edited by Evan Berry, 122–44. Bloomington: Indiana University Press, 2022.

Borst, Arno. "Das Erdbeben von 1348: Ein historischer Beitrag zur Katastrophenforschung." *Historische Zeitschrift* 233, no. 3 (1981): 529–69.

Bos, Gerrit. "The Black Death in Hebrew Literature: Abraham Ben Solomon Hen's 'Tractatulus de pestilential." *Jewish Studies Quarterly* 18, no. 1 (March, 2011): 32–63.

Bosch, Hilmer J. and Joyeeta Gupta. "The Tension Between State Ownership and Private Quasi-Property Rights in Water." *Wiley Interdisciplinary Reviews, Water* 10, no. 1 (2023): e1621.

Bourke, Eoin. "The Frankfurt Judengasse in Eyewitness Accounts from the Seventeenth to the Nineteenth Century." In *Ghetto Writing: Traditional and Eastern Jewry in German-Jewish Literature from Heine to Hilsenrath*, edited by Anne Fuchs and Florian Krobb, 11–24. Columbia, SC: Camden House, 1999.

Boykoff, Maxwell. *Creative (Climate) Communications: Productive Pathways for Science, Policy and Society*. Cambridge: Cambridge University Press, 2019.

Breuer, Mordechai. "Modernism and Traditionalism in Sixteenth-Century Jewish Historiography: A Study of David Gans' Tzemah David." In *Jewish Thought in the Sixteenth Century*, edited by Bernard Dov Cooperman, 49–88. Cambridge, MA: Harvard University Press, 1983.

Bridle, James. *Ways of Being: Animals, Plants, Machines: The Search for a Planetary Intelligence*. New York: Picador, 2022.

Brisch, Carl. *Geschichte der Juden in Cöln und Umgebung*, 2 vols. Mühlheim am Rhein: C. Meyer, 1879–82.

Bulmuş, Birsen. *Plague, Quarantine and Geopolitics in the Ottoman Empire*. Edinburgh: Edinburgh University Press, 2012.

Campbell, Brian G. "The Power of Place." In *Grounding Religion: A Field Guide to the Study of Religion and Ecology*, edited by Whitney Bauman, Richard Bohannon, and Kevin J. O'Brien, second edn, 94–113. London: Routledge, 2017.

Carey, Mark. "Beyond Weather: The Culture and Politics of Climate History." In *The Oxford Handbook of Environmental History*, edited by Andrew C. Isenberg, 23–51. Oxford: Oxford University Press, 2014.

Carstensen, Thomas and Wolfgang Henningsen. "'Gaßverbrennner,' Rabbi Cohen: Eine Frankfurter Brandstifter-Legende über die Feuerbrunst vom 14. Januar 1711." *Tribüne: Zeitschrift zum Verständnis des Judentums* 28, no. 109 (1989): 166–71.

Catalano, Abraham. "Olam Hafukh." Ed. Cecil Roth, *Kovetz al Yad* 4, no. 14 (1946): 67–101.

Chakrabarty, Dipesh. "The Climate of History: Four Theses." *Critical Inquiry* 35 (Winter 2009): 197–222.

Chakrabarty, Dipesh. *The Climate of History in a Planetary Age*. Chicago: University of Chicago Press, 2021.

Chandler, David. "The End of Resilience? Rethinking adaptation in the Anthropocene." In *Resilience in the Anthropocene: Governance and Politics at the End of the World*, edited by David Chandler, Kevin Grove, and Stephanie Wakefield, 50–67. London: Routledge, 2020.

Chandler, David, Kevin Grove, and Stephanie Wakefield, eds. *Resilience in the Anthropocene: Governance and Politics at the End of the World*. London: Routledge, 2020.

Charon, Rita. *Narrative Medicine: Honoring the Stories of Illness*. Oxford: Oxford University Press, 2008.

Chazan, Robert. *In the Year 1096: The First Crusade and the Jews*. Philadelphia: Jewish Publication Society, 1996.

Chiu, Remi. *Plague and Music in the Renaissance*. Cambridge: Cambridge University Press, 2017.

Christian, Brian. *The Alignment Problem: Machine Learning and Human Values*. New York: W.W. Norton & Co., 2020.

Coates, Peter. *Nature: Western Attitudes since Ancient Times*. Berkeley: University of California Press, 1998.

Cohen, Jeremy. *"Be Fertile and Increase, Fil the Earth and Master It": The Ancient and Medieval Career of a Biblical Text*. Ithaca: Cornell University Press, 1989.

Cohn, Samuel. "Changing Pathology of Plague." In *Le interazioni fra economia e ambiente biologico nell'Euopa preindustriale, secc. XII–XVIII*, edited by Simonetta Cavaciocchi, 33–56. Florence: Firenze University Press, 2010.

Coleman, Peter T. *The Way Out: How to Overcome Toxic Polarization*. New York: Columbia University Press, 2021.

Cone, Christopher. "Continuing the Conversation: Applying Lynn White Jr.'s Prescriptions for a Christian Environmental Ethic." In *Religion and Ecological Crisis: The "Lynn White Thesis" at Fifty*, edited by Todd LeVasseur and Anna Peterson, 101–09. London: Routledge, 2017.

Conrad, L. I. "Arabic Plague Chronologies and Treatises: Social and Historical Factors in the Formation of a Literary Genre." *Studia Islamica* 44 (1981): 51–93.

Conrad, L. I. "Epidemic Disease in Formal and Popular Thought in Early Islamic Society." In *Epidemics and Ideas: Ideas in the Historical Perception of Pestilence*, edited by T. Ranger and P. Slack, 77–99. Cambridge: Cambridge University Press, 1992.

Conrad, L. I. "'Ta'un and waba:' Conceptions of Plague and Pestilence in Early Islam." *Journal of the Economic and Social History of the Orient* 25 (1982): 268–307.

Conrad, L. I. and Dominik Wuastyk. *Contagion: Perspectives from Pre-Modern Societies.* Aldershot: Ashgate, 2000.

Conty, Arianne. *Grounding God: Religious Responses to the Anthropocene.* Albany: SUNY Press, 2023.

Coomans, Janna. *Community, Urban Health and Environment in the Late Medieval Low Countries.* Cambridge: Cambridge University Press, 2021.

Crawford, Kate. *Atlas of AI: Power, Politics, and the Planetary Costs of Artificial Intelligence.* New Haven: Yale University Press, 2021.

Crown, Alan D. "The World Overturned: The Plague Diary of Abraham Catalano." *Midstream* (January 1973): 65–76.

Curry, John J. "Scholars, Sufis, and Disease: Can Muslim Religious works Offer Us Novel Insights on Plagues and Epidemics among the Medieval and Early Modern Ottomans?" In *Plague and Contagion in the Islamic Mediterranean*, edited by Nükhet Varlik, 27–55. Newark: Arc Humanities Press, 2017.

Dalby, Simon "Resilient Earth: Gaia, Geopolitics and the Anthropocene." In *Resilience in the Anthropocene: Governance and Politics at the End of the World*, edited by David Chandler, Kevin Grove, and Stephanie Wakefield, 22–36. London: Routledge, 2020.

Davenpot, Leslie. *Emotional Resiliency in the Era of Climate Change: A Clinician's Guide.* London: Jessica Kingsley Publishers, 2017.

David, Abraham, ed. *A Hebrew Chronicle from Prague, c. 1615.* Translated by Leon J. Weinberger with Dena Ordan. Tuscaloosa: University of Alabama Press, 1993.

David, Abraham. *To Come to the Land: Immigration and Settlement in Sixteenth-Century Eretz-Israel.* Tuscaloosa: University of Alabama Press, 1999.

Davis, Ellen F. *Scripture, Culture, and Agriculture: An Agrarian Reading of the Bible.* Cambridge: Cambridge University Press, 2009.

de Boer, Jelle Zeilinga and Donald Theodore Sanders. *Earthquakes in Human History: The Far-Reaching Effects of Seismic Disruptions.* Princeton: Princeton University Press, 2005.

De la Torre, Miguel A., ed. *Gonna Trouble the Water: Ecojustice, Water, and Environmental Racism.* Cleveland: The Pilgrim Press, 2021.

del Valle, Carlos, ed. *Los terremotos de Girona de 1427 en la fuente hebrea.* Hebrew text with Spanish translation. Madrid: Aben Ezra, 1996.

Descola, Philippe. *Beyond Nature and Culture.* Translated by Janet Lloyd. Chicago: University of Chicago Press, 2023 (orig., 2005).

Dine, Harper, Traci Arden, and Chelsea Fisher. "Vegetative Agency and Social Memory in Houselots of the Ancient Maya." In *The Power of Nature: Archaeology and Human-Environmental Dynamics*, edited by Monica L. Smith, 137–62. Denver: University Press of Colorado, 2022.

Dols, Michael. *The Black Death in the Middle East.* Princeton: Princeton University Press, 1977.

Eckert, Edward. *The Structures of Plagues and Pestilence in Early Modern Europe: Central Europe, 1560–1640.* Basel: Karger, 1996.

Eidelberg, Shlomo. *Medieval Ashkenazic History: Studies on German Jewry in the Middle Ages*, 2 vols. New York: Sepher-Hermon Press, 1999–2001.

Einbinder, Susan L. "Poetry, Prose and Pestilence: Joseph Concio and Jewish Responses to the 1630 Italian Plague." In *Shirat Dvora: Essays in Honor of Professor Dvora Bregman*, edited by Haviva Ishay, 73–101. Beersheba: Ben-Gurion University of the Negev Press, 2019.

Einbinder, Susan L. *Writing Plague: Jewish Responses to the Great Italian Plague.* Philadelphia: University of Pennsylvania Press, 2022.

Eisenbeth, Maurice. *Le judaïsme nord-africain.* Paris: A. Natason, 1932.

Eley, Geoff. "Labor History, Social History: Alltagsgeschichte: Experience, Culture, and the Politics of the Everyday. A New Direction for German Social History?" *Journal of Modern History* 61, no. 2 (June 1989): 297–343.

Emerson, Brian and Kelly Lewis. *Navigating Polarities: Using Both/And Thinking to Lead Transformation.* Washington DC: Paradoxical Press, 2019.

Emmett, Robert S. and David E. Nye. *The Environmental Humanities: A Critical Introduction.* Cambridge, MA: The MIT Press 2017.

Faruqui, Naser I., Asit K. Biswas, and Murad J. Bino. *Water Management in Islam.* Tokyo: United Nations University, 2001.

Favier, Rene and Anne-Marie Garnet-Abisset. "Society and Nature Risks in France, 1500–2000: Changing Historical Perspectives." In *Natural Disasters, Cultural Responses: Case Studies Toward a Global Environmental History*, edited by Christof Mauch and Christian Pfister, 103–36. Lanham: Lexington Books, 2009.

Fisher, Joshua D. *Managing Environmental Conflict.* New York: Columbia University Press, 2022.

Fleerman, Bastian. *Marginalisierung und Emanzipation: Jüdische Alltagskultur im Herzogtum Berg, 1779–1847.* Neustadt an der Aisch: VDS, Verlagsdruckerei Schmidt, 2007.

Fraiman, Keren E. "Barriers to Entry: Exploring Educator Reticence for Engaging with the Israeli-Palestinian Conflict." In *Teaching Israel: Studies of Pedagogy from the Field*, edited by Sivan Zakai and Matt Reingold, 229–53. Waltham: Brandeis University Press, 2024.

Fram, Edward. *A Window on Their World: The Court Diary of Rabbi Hayyim Gundersheim, Frankfurt am Main, 1773–1794.* Cincinnati: Hebrew Union College Press, 2012.

Frankopan, Peter. *The Earth Transformed: An Untold History.* New York: Alfred A. Knopf, 2023.

Freire, Paulo. *Pedagogy of the Oppressed.* New York: Bloomsbury, 2000 (orig., 1968).

Frierson, Cathy A. "Imperial Russia's Urban Fire Regimes, 1700–1905." In *Flammable Cities: Urban Conflagration and the Making of the Modern World*, edited by George Bankoff, Uwe Lübken, and Jordan Sand, 103–25. Madison: University of Wisconsin Press, 2012.

Gadamer, Hans-Georg. *Truth and Method.* Translated by Joel Weinsheimer and Donald G. Marshall. London: Bloomsbury, 2013 (orig., 1960).

Gans, David. *Zemah David*, edited by Mordechai Breuer. Jerusalem: Y.L. Magnes, Hebrew University of Jerusalem, 1983.

Gardiner, Stephen M. *A Perfect Moral Storm: The Ethical Tragedy of Climate Change.* Oxford: Oxford University Press, 2011.

Georgi, Matthias. "Christlicher Bedrohungsraum und protestantische Identität: Die englische Selbstwahrnehmung in der Debatte um das Erdbeben von Lissabon (1755)." In *Europäische Wahrnehmungen 1650–1850: Interkulturelle Kommunikation über*

Medienereignisse, edited by Joachim Eibach et al., 185–205. Hannover: Wehrhahn, 2008.

Georgi, Matthias. *Heuschrecken, Erdbeben und Kometen: Naturkatastrophen und Naturwissenschaft in der englischen Öffentlichkeit des 18. Jahrhunderts.* Munich: August-Dreesbach-Verlag, 2009.

Georgi, Matthias. "The Lisbon Earthquake and Scientific Knowledge in the British Public Sphere." In *The Lisbon Earthquake of 1755: Representations and Reactions,* edited by Theodore E.D. Braun and John B. Radner, 81–96. Oxford: Voltaire Foundation, 2005.

Gerstenfeld, Manfred. "Jewish Environmental Studies: A New Field." *Jewish Political Review* 13, no. 1/2 (Spring 2001): 3–62.

Ghosh, Amitav. *The Great Derangement: Climate Change and the Unthinkable.* Chicago: University of Chicago Press, 2016.

Glaser, Rüdiger. *Klimageschichte Mitteleuropas: 1000 Jahre Wetter, Klima, Katastrophen.* Darmstadt: Primus, 2001.

Gleiser, Marcelo. *The Dawn of a Mindful Universe: A Manifesto for Humanity's Future.* New York: HarperOne, 2023.

Globus Veldman, Robin. *The Gospel of Climate Skepticism: Why Evangelical Christians Oppose Action on Climate Change.* Oakland: University of California Press, 2019.

Goh, Kian. *Form and Flow: The Spatial Politics of Urban Resilience and Climate Justice.* Cambridge, MA: The MIT Press, 2021.

Goldberg, Sylvie Anne. *Crossing the Jabbok: Illness and Death in Ashkenazi Judaism in Sixteenth- through Nineteenth-Century Prague.* Translated by Carol Cosman. Berkeley: University of California Press, 1996.

Goldish, Matt. *Jewish Questions: Responsa on Sephardic Life in the Early Modern Period.* Princeton: Princeton University Press, 2008.

Goodell, Jeff. *The Heat Will Kill You: Life and Death on a Scorched Planet.* New York: Little, Brown and Company, 2023.

Goshen-Gottstein, Alon. *Covenant & World Religions Irving Greenberg, Jonathan Sacks, and the Quest for Orthodox Pluralism.* London: The Littman Library of Jewish Civilization, 2023.

Goshen-Gottstein, Alon, ed. *Idolatry: A Contemporary Jewish Conversation.* Boston: Academic Studies Press, 2023.

Grübel, Monika and Georg Mölich, eds. *Jüdisches Leben im Rheinland: Vom Mittelalter bis zur Gegenwart.* Cologne: Böhlau, 2005.

Hampton, J. B. Alexander. "Ecology and the Unbuffered Self: Identity, Agency, and Authority in a Time of Pandemic." In *Pandemic, Ecology and Theology,* 17–28. London: Routledge, 2021.

Hampton, J. B. Alexander, ed. *Pandemic, Ecology and Theology.* London: Routledge, 2021.

Harper, Kyle. *The Fate of Rome: Climate Disease & the End of an Empire.* Princeton: Princeton University Press, 2017.

Harvey, David. *Justice, Nature & the Geography of Difference.* Oxford: Blackwell, 1996.

Haverkamp, Alfred. "Die Judenverfolgungen zur Zeit des Schwarzen Todes in Gesellschaftsgefüge deutscher Städte." In *Zur Geschichte der Juden im Deutschland des Späten Mittelalters und der Frühen Neuzeit,* edited by Alfred Haverkamp, 27–93. Stuttgart: A. Hiersemann, 1981.

Headrick, Daniel R. *Humans Versus Nature: A Global Environmental History.* Oxford: Oxford University Press, 2020.

Held, Shai. *Judaism is About Love: Recovering the Heart of Jewish Life*. New York: Farrar, Straus and Giroux, 2024.

Henry, Matthew S. *Hydronarratives: Water, Environmental Justice, and a Just Transition*. Lincoln: University of Nebraska Press, 2022.

Hieke, Thomas. "The Covenant in Leviticus 26: A Concept of Admonition and Redemption." In *Covenant in the Persian Period: From Genesis to Chronicles*, edited by Richard J. Bautch and Gary N. Knoppers, 75–90. University Park: Penn State University Press, 2015.

Hirschberg, H.Z. *A History of the Jews in North Africa*, 2 vols. Leiden: Brill, 1974–81.

Hoffmann, Christhard. "From Heinrich Heine to Isidor Kracauer: The Frankfurt Ghetto in German-Jewish Historical Culture and Historiography." *Jewish Culture and History* 10, no. 2–3 (2008): 45–64.

Hogue, Michael S. *American Immanence: Democracy for an Uncertain World*. New York: Columbia University Press, 2018.

Hogue, Michael S. "Sustainability and Climate Change." In *Encyclopedia of Religious Ethics*, 3 vols, edited by William Schweiker, 1250–6. Wiley & Sons Ltd., 2022.

Hogue, Michael S. "Theological Ethics and Technological Culture: A Biocultural Approach." *Zygon* 42, no. 1 (March 2007): 77–95.

Hogue, Michael S. and Dean Phillip Bell. *Interreligious Resilience: Interreligious Leadership for a Pluralistic World*. London: Bloomsbury, 2022.

Hopley, Russell. "Contagion in Islamic Lands: Responses from Medieval Andalusia and North Africa." *The Journal for Early Modern Cultural Studies* 10, no. 2 (Fall/Winter 2010): 45–64.

Ingram, Robert G. "'The Trembling Earth is God's Herald': Earthquakes, Religion and Public Life in Britain during the 1750s." In *The Lisbon Earthquake of 1755: Representations and Reactions*, edited by Theodore E.D. Braun and John B. Radner, 97–115. Oxford: Voltaire Foundation, 2005.

Isenberg, Andrew C. "Seas of Grass: Grasslands in World Environmental History." In *The Oxford Handbook of Environmental History*, edited by Andrew C. Isenberg, 133–53. Oxford: Oxford University Press, 2014 (2017 edition).

Isenberg, Andrew C., ed. *The Oxford Handbook of Environmental History*. Oxford: Oxford University Press, 2014.

Israel, Jonathan. *European Jewry in the Age of Mercantilism, 1550–1750*, 3rd edn. Oxford: The Littman Library of Jewish Civilization, 1998 (orig., 1985).

Izdebski, Adam, et al. "The Emergence of Interdisciplinary Environmental History: Bridging the Gap Between the Humanistic and Scientific Approaches to the Late Holocene." *Annales: Histoire, Sciences Sociales* 77, no. 2 (2024): 1–48.

Jakubowski-Tiessen. "'Erschreckliche und unerhörte Wasserflut': Wahrnehmung und Deutung der Flutkatastrophe von 1634." In *Um Himmels Willen: Religion in Katastrophen*, edited by Manfred Jakubowski-Tiessen and Hartmut Lehmann, 179–200. Göttingen: Vandenhoeck & Ruprecht, 2003.

Jarva, Vuokko. "Introduction to Narrative for Futures Studies." *Journal of Future Studies* 18, no. 3 (March 2014): 5–26.

Jay, Martin. *Songs of Experience: Modern American and European Variations on a Universal Theme*. Berkeley: University of California Press, 2005.

Jellinek, Adolf, ed. *Märtyrer und Memorbuch: Verzeichniss der Märtyrergemeinden aus den Jahren 1096 und 1349, das alte Memorbuch der Deutzer Gemeinde von 1581 bis 1784 nebst Auszügen aus dem neuen vom 1786 bis 1816*. Vienna: D. Löwy's Buchhandlung, 1881.

Jenkins, Philip. *Climate, Catastrophe, and Faith: How Changes in Climate Drive Religious Upheaval*. Oxford: Oxford University Press, 2021.

Jenkins, Willis. *Ecologies of Grace: Environmental Ethics and Christian Theology*. Oxford: Oxford University Press, 2008.

Jenkins, Willis. *The Future of Ethics: Sustainability Social Justice, and Religious Creativity*. Washington DC: Georgetown University Press, 2013.

Jenkins, Willis. "Whose Religion? Which Ecology? Religious Studies in the Environmental Humanities." In *Routledge Handbook of Religion and Ecology*, edited by Willis Jenkins, Mary Evelyn Tucker, and John Grim, 22–32. London: Routledge, 2017.

Joerstad, Mari. *The Hebrew Bible and Environmental Ethics: Humans, Nonhumans, and the Living Landscape*. Cambridge: Cambridge University Press, 2019.

Jonas, Hans. "Contemporary Problems in Ethics from a Jewish Perspective." In *Judaism and Environmental Ethics: A Reader*, edited by Martin D. Yaffe, 250–63. Lanham: Lexington Books, 2001.

Jonas, Hans. *The Phenomenon of Life: Toward a Philosophical Biology*. Evanston, IL: Northwestern University Press, 2001 (orig., 1966).

Jordan III, William R. *The Sunflower Forest: Ecological Restoration and the New Communion with Nature*. Berkeley: University of California Press, 2003.

Jüdische Geschichte und Kultur in NRW: Ein Handbuch. Compiled by Bruno Reicher. Essen: Klartext, 1993.

Kaiser, Otto. *Die mythische Bedeutung des Meeres in Ägypten, Ugarit und Israel*. Berlin: A Töpelmann, 1962.

Kaplan, Marion A., ed. *Jewish Daily Life in Germany, 1618–1945*. Oxford: Oxford University Press, 2005.

Kasper-Holtkotte, Cili. *Die jüdische Gemeinde von Frankfurt/Main in der Frühen Neuzeit: Familien, Netzwerke und Konflikte eines jüdischen Zentrums*. Berlin: DeGruyter, 2010.

Kearns, Laurel. "Climate Change." In *Grounding Religion: A Field Guide to the Study of Religion and Ecology*, edited by Whitney Bauman, Richard Bohannon, and Kevin J. O'Brien, second edn, 137–57. London: Routledge, 2017.

Kehnel, Annette. *The Green Ages: Medieval Innovations in Sustainability*. Translated by Gesche Ipsen. Waltham: Brandeis University Press, 2024.

Kempe, Michael. "Noah's Flood: The Genesis Story and Natural Disasters in Early Modern Times." *Environment and History* 9 (2003): 151–71.

Kiessling, Rolf. *Jüdische Geschichte Bayern: Von den Anfängen bis in die Gegenwart*. Oldenbourg: De Gruyter, 2019.

Kirsch, Adam. *On Settler Colonialism: Ideology, Violence, and Justice*. New York: W.W. Norton & Company, 2024.

Klein, Birgit and Rotraud Ries. "Zu Struktur und Funktion der jüdischen Oberschicht in Bonn." In *Eine Gesellschaft im Wandel: Alltag und Umwelt im Rheinland des 18. Jahrhunderts*, edited by Frank Günter Zehnder, 289–315. Cologne: DuMont, 1999.

Kober, Adolf. *Cologne*. Translated by Solomon Grayzel. Philadelphia: Jewish Publication Society of America, 1940.

Koselleck, Reinhart. *The Practice of Conceptual History: Timing History, Spacing Concepts*. Translated by Todd Samuel Presner and Others. Stanford: Stanford University Press, 2002.

Koslofsky, Craig. *Evening's Empire: A History of the Night in Early Modern Europe*. Cambridge: Cambridge University Press, 2011.

Kosslyn, Stephen M. and Ben Nelson, eds. *Building the Intentional University: Minerva and the Future of Higher Education*. Cambridge, MA: MIT Press, 2017.

Kracauer, Isidor. *Die Geschichte der Judengasse in Frankfurt am Main*. Frankfurt am Main, 1906.

Laster, Richard, Rabbi David Aronovsky, and Dan Livney. "Water in the Jewish Legal Tradition." In *The Evolution of the Law and Politics of Water*, edited by J.W. Dellapenna and J. Gupta, 53–66. NP: Springer, 2009.

Latour, Bruno. *Facing Gaia: Eight Lectures on the New Climate Regime*. Translated by Catherine Porter. Cambridge: Polity, 2017.

Leibovitz, Joshua. "The Plague in the Roman Ghetto (1656) according to Zahalon and Cardinal Gastaldi." *Korot* 4, no. 3–4 (1967): 155–69.

LeVasseur, Todd and Anna Peterson, eds. *Religion and Ecological Crisis: The "Lynn White Thesis" at Fifty*. London: Routledge, 2017.

Levinas, Emmanuel. *Ethics and Infinity: Conversations with Philippe Nemo*. Translated by Richard A. Cohen. Pittsburgh: Duquesne University Press, 1985 (orig., 1982).

Levy, Ascher. *Die Memoiren des Ascher Levy aus Reichshofen im Elsass (1598–1635)*. Berlin: L. Lamm, 1913.

Lewis, Bernard. *The Jews of Islam*. London: Routledge, 1984.

Lewis, Michael. "And All Was Light?—Science and Environmental History." In *The Oxford Handbook of Environmental History*, edited by Andrew C. Isenberg, 207–26. Oxford: Oxford University Press, 2014.

Liberles, Robert. *Jews Welcome Coffee: Tradition and Innovation in Early Modern Germany*. Waltham: Brandeis University Press, 2012.

Lightman, Alan. *Einstein's Dreams: A Novel*. New York: Vintage Contemporaries, 1993.

Lindemann, Mary. *Medicine and Society in Early Modern Europe*, second edn. Cambridge: Cambridge University Press, 2010.

Lobel, Orly. *The Equality Machine: Harnessing Digital Technology for a Brighter, More Inclusive Future*. New York: Hachette Book Group, Inc., 2022.

von Looz-Corswarem, Clemens. "Zur Entwicklung der Rheinschiffahrt vom Mittelalter bis ins 19. Jahrhundert." In *Düsseldorf und seine Häfen: Zur Verkehrs- und Wirtschaftsgeschichte der Stadt as Anlaß des 100jährigen Hafenjubiläums 1896–1996*, edited by Horst Rademacher, Clemens von Looz-Corswarem, and Annette Fimpler-Philippen, 9–31. Wuppertal: Müller + Busmann, 1996.

Lorentzen, Lois Ann. "Globalization." In *Grounding Religion: A Field Guide to the Study of Religion and Ecology*, edited by Whitney Bauman, Richard Bohannon, and Kevin J. O'Brien, second edn, 117–36. London: Routledge, 2017.

Lowry, Heath. "Pushing the Stone Uphill: The Impact of Bubonic Plague on Ottoman Urban Society in the Fifteenth and Sixteenth Centuries." *Osmanli Arastirmalari* 23 (2003): 93–132.

Lüdtke, Alf, ed. *The History of Everyday Life: Reconstructing Historical Experiences and Ways of Life*. Translated by William Templer. Princeton: Princeton University Press, 1995.

MacKay, Ruth. *Life in a Time of Pestilence: The Great Castilian Plague of 1596–1601*. Cambridge: Cambridge University Press, 2019.

Magid, Shaul. "Idolatry on the Other Side of Morality." In *Idolatry: A Contemporary Jewish Conversation*, edited by Alon Goshen-Gottstein, 93–124. Boston: Academic Studies Press, 2023.

Magnus, Shulamit S. *Jewish Emancipation in a German City: Cologne, 1798–1871*. Stanford: Stanford University Press, 1997.

Margalit, Natan. *The Pearl and the Flame: A Journey into Jewish Wisdom and Ecological Thinking*. Boulder: Albion-Andalus, 2022.

Marien, Giselle. "The Black Death in Early Ottoman Territories: 1347–1550." MA thesis, Bikent University, 2009.

Martinez, Michelle. "Environmental Justice and Detroit's Long Shadow." In *Gonna Trouble the Water: Ecojustice, Water, and Environmental Racism*, edited by Miguel A. De la Torre, 70–86. Cleveland: The Pilgrim Press, 2021.

Martusewicz, Rebecca A., Jeff Edmundson, and John Lupinacci. *EcoJustice Education: Toward Diverse, Democratic, and Sustainable Communities*, Second edn. New York, London: Routledge, 2015.

Mauch, Christof. "Introduction." In *Natural Disasters, Cultural Responses: Case Studies Toward a Global Environmental History*, edited by Christof Mauch and Christian Pfister, 1–16. Lanham: Lexington Books, 2009.

Mauelshagen, Franz. "Disaster and Political Culture in Germany since 1500." In *Natural Disasters, Cultural Responses: Case Studies Toward a Global Environmental History*, edited by Christof Mauch and Christian Pfister, 41–75. Lanham: Lexington Books, 2009.

McNeill, J. R. and Peter Engelke. *The Great Acceleration: An Environmental History of the Anthropocene since 1945*. Cambridge, MA: The Belknap Press of Harvard University Press, 2014.

McNeill, William H. *Plagues and Peoples*. Garden City, NY: Anchor Press, 1976.

Meyer, Michael. *Ideas of Jewish History*. Detroit: Wayne State University Press, 1987.

Mikhail, Alan. *Nature and Empire in Ottoman Egypt: An Environmental History*. Cambridge: Cambridge University Press, 2011.

Mitchell, Melanie. *Complexity: A Guided Tour*. Oxford: Oxford University Press, 2009.

Morgan, Ruth A. *Climate Change and International History: Negotiating Science, Global Change, and Environmental Justice*. London: Bloomsbury Academic, 2024.

Morton, Timothy. *Ecology without Nature: Rethinking Environmental Aesthetics*. Cambridge, MA: Harvard University Press, 2007.

Morton, Timothy. *Hyperobjects: Philosophy and Ecology after the End of the World*. Minneapolis: University of Minnesota Press, 2013.

Nash, Linda. "Beyond Virgin Soils: Disease as Environmental History." In *The Oxford Handbook of Environmental History*, edited by Andrew C. Isenberg, 76–107. Oxford: Oxford University Press, 2014.

Nasr, Seyyed Hossein. *Man and Nature: The Spiritual Crisis of Modern Man*. Chicago: ABC International Group, Inc., 1997.

Neiman, Susan. *Left is Not Woke*. Cambridge: Polity, 2023.

Nobert, Sebastien, Harold Bellanger Rodriguez, and Xochilt Hernandez Leiva. "Colliding Times: Urgency, Resilience and the Politics of Living with Volcanic Gas Emissions in the Anthropocene." In *Resilience in the Anthropocene: Governance and Politics at the End of the World*, edited by David Chandler, Kevin Grove, and Stephanie Wakefield, 68–83. London: Routledge, 2020.

Northcott, Michael S. "Lynn White Jr. Right and Wrong: The Anti-Ecological Character of Latin Christianity and the Pro-Ecological Turn of Protestantism." In *Religion and Ecological Crisis: The "Lynn White Thesis" at Fifty*, edited by Todd LeVasseur and Anna Peterson, 61–74. London: Routledge, 2017.

Northcott, Michael S. "On Going Gently into the Anthropocene." In *Religion in the Anthropocene*, edited by Celia Deane-Drummond, Sigurd Bergmann, and Markus Vogt, 19–34. Eugene, OR: Cascade Books, 2017.

Novak Winer, Laura. "Teaching Who They Are: Understanding Teachers' Connections with Israel and How Those Enter Into the Classroom." In *Teaching Israel: Studies of*

Pedagogy from the Field, edited by Sivan Zakai and Matt Reingold, 283–308. Waltham: Brandeis University Press, 2024.

O'Gieblyn, Meghan. *God, Human, Animal, Machine: Technology, Metaphor, and the Search for Meaning*. New York: Anchor Books, 2021.

Oliver-Smith, Anthony. "'What is Disaster?' Anthropological Perspectives on a Persistent Question." In *The Angry Earth: Disaster in Anthropological Perspective*, edited by Anthony Oliver-Smith and Susanna M. Hoffman, 29–44. London: Routledge, 2020.

Oreskes, Naomi and Erik M. Conway. *Merchants of Doubt: How a Handful of Scientists Obscured the Truth on Issues from Tobacco Smoke to Global Warming*. New York: Bloomsbury, 2010.

Otten, Willemien. *Thinking Nature and the Nature of Thinking: From Eriugena to Emerson*. Stanford: Stanford University Press, 2020.

Outhwaite, Ben. https://www.lib.cam.ac.uk/genizah-fragments/posts/we-have-seen -mountains-shaking-fatimid-humanitarian-relief-and-earthquake.

Pande, Vasudha. "Anthropogenic Landscapes of the Central Himalayas." In *At Nature's Edge: The Global Present and Long-Term History*, edited by Gunnel Cederlöf and Mahesh Rangarajan, 19–60. Oxford: Oxford University Press, 2018.

Panzac, Daniel. *La peste dans l'empire Ottoman: 1700–1850*. Leuven: Editions Peters, 1985.

Pedaya, Haviva. "The Dynamism of Idolatry." In *Idolatry: A Contemporary Jewish Conversation*, edited by Alon Goshen-Gottstein, 213–31. Boston: Academic Studies Press, 2023.

Peros, Matthew C., Jago Cooper, and Frank Oliva. "Hurricanes as Agents of Cultural Change: Integrating Paleotempestology and the Archaeological Record." In *The Power of Nature: Archaeology and Human-Environmental Dynamics*, edited by Monica L. Smith, 27–48. Denver: University Press of Colorado, 2022.

Petuchowski, Jakob J. *The Theology of Haham David Nieto: An Eighteenth-Century Defense of the Jewish Tradition*. New York: Ktav, 1970 (orig., 1954).

Pfister, Christian. "Afterword." In *Natural Disasters, Cultural Responses: Case Studies Toward a Global Environmental History*, edited by Christof Mauch and Christian Pfister, 355–59. Lanham: Lexington Books, 2009.

Pfister, Christian. "Learning from Nature-Induced Disasters: Theoretical Considerations and Case Studies from Western Europe." In *Natural Disasters, Cultural Responses: Case Studies Toward a Global Environmental History*, edited by Christof Mauch and Christian Pfister, 17–40. Lanham: Lexington Books, 2009.

Pfister, Christian. "'The Monster Swallows You:' Disaster Memory and Risk Culture in Western Europe, 1500–2000." *RCC Perspectives* 1 (2011): 1–23.

Phillips Cohen, Julia and Sara Abrevaya Stein, eds. *Sephardi Lives: A Documentary History, 1700–1950*. Stanford: Stanford University Press, 2014.

Pickett, Jordan. "Earthquakes and Agency in the Roman Mediterranean: Resilience and Transformation." In *The Power of Nature: Archaeology and Human-Environmental Dynamics*, edited by Monica L. Smith, 77–98. Denver: University Press of Colorado, 2022.

Pils, Susanne. "'…damit nur an wasser khain menngl erscheine…' Vom Umgang der Stadt Wien mit dem Feuer der frühen Neuzeit." In *Stadtzerstörung und Wiederaufbau: Zerstörungen durch Erdbeben, Feuer und Wasser*, edited by Martin Körner, 173–86. Bern: P. Haupt, 1999.

Pohlig, Matthias. *Zwischen Gelehrsamkeit und konfessioneller Identitätsstiftung: Lutherische Kirchen und Universalgeschichtsschreibung 1546–1617*. Tübingen: Mohr Siebeck, 2007.

Poliwoda, Guido N. *Aus Katastrophen Lernen: Sachsen im Kampf gegen die Fluten der Elbe 1784 bis 1845.* Cologne: Böhlau Verlag, 2007.

Pomerance, Aubrey. "'Wasser wie nie seit Menschengedenken': Eine unbekannte jiddische Quelle zum Rheinhochwasser von 1784." In *Memoria—Wege jüdischen Erinnerns: Festschrift für Michael Brocke zum 65. Geburtstag*, edited by Birgit E. Klein and Christiane E. Müller, 177–92. Berlin: Metropol, 2005.

Pritchard, Sara B. "Toward an Environmental History of Technology." In *The Oxford Handbook of Environmental History*, edited by Andrew C. Isenberg, 227–58. Oxford: Oxford University Press, 2014.

Pullan, Brian. "Plagues and Perceptions of the Poor in Early Modern Italy." In *Epidemics and Ideas: Essays on Historical Perceptions of Pestilence*, edited by Terence Ranger and Paul Slack, 101–23. Cambridge: Cambridge University Press, 1992.

Pyne, Stephen J. *Vestal Fire: An Environmental History, Told through Fire, of Europe and Europe's Encounter with the World.* Seattle: University of Washington Press, 1997.

Radkau, Joachim. *Nature and Power: A Global History of the Environment.* Translated by Thomas Dunlap. Cambridge: Cambridge University Press, 2008.

Raphael, Melissa. "Jewish Feminist Liberation Theology and the Modern Criticism of Idols." In *Idolatry: A Contemporary Jewish Conversation*, edited by Alon Goshen-Gottstein, 25–40. Boston: Academic Studies Press, 2023.

Reith, Reinhold. *Umweltgeschichte der Frühen Neuzeit.* Munich: Oldenbourg, 2011.

Reuter, Fritz. Warmaisa: *1000 Jahre Juden in Worms.* Worms: Verlag Stadtarchiv Worms, 1984.

Rifkind, Isaac. "Kuntres takkanot Prag." *Reshumot* 24 (1926): 345–52.

Robb, John. "The End of the World (Again)." In The *Power of Nature: Archaeology and Human-Environmental Dynamics*, edited by Monica L. Smith, 256–67. Denver: University Press of Colorado, 2022.

Robin, Libby and Will Steffen. "History for the Anthropocene." *History Compass* 5, no. 5 (2007): 1694–719.

Rohr, Christian. "The Danube Floods and Their Human Response and Perception (14th to 17th C)." *History of Meteorology* 2 (2005): 71–86.

Rohr, Christian. "Writing a Catastrophe: Describing and Constructing Disaster Perception in Narrative Sources from the Late Middle Ages." *Historical Social Research* 32 (2007): 88–102.

Roth, Cecil. "Isaac Nieto." In *Encyclopedia Judaica*, edited by Michael Berenbaum and Fred Skolnik, second edn, vol. 15: 261–62. Detroit: Macmillan Reference, 2007.

Rubenstein, Jeffrey L. *A History of Sukkot in the Second Temple and Rabbinic Periods.* Atlanta: Brown Judaic Studies, 2020.

Ruderman, David B. *Jewish Thought and Scientific Discovery in Early Modern Europe.* New Haven: Yale University Press, 1995.

Russell, Stuart and Peter Norvig. *Artificial Intelligence: A Modern Approach*, Fourth edn. London: Pearson, 2022.

Safran Foer, Jonathan. *We are the Weather: Saving the Planet Begins at Breakfast.* New York: Picador, 2019.

Sagi, Avi. *The Open Canon: On the Meaning of Halakhic Discourse.* London: Continuum, 2007.

Sand, Jordan and Steven Wills. "Governance, Arson, and Firefighting in Edo, 1600–1868." In *Flammable Cities: Urban Conflagration and the Making of the Modern World*, edited by George Bankoff, Uwe Lübken, and Jordan Sand, 44–62. Madison: University of Wisconsin Press, 2012.

Savitz, Harry A. "Jacob Zahalon, and His Book 'The Treasure of Life'." *New England Journal of Medicine* 213, no. 4 (July 25, 1935): 167–76.

Schlanger, Zoë. *The Light Eaters: How the Unseen World of Plant Intelligence Offers a New Understanding of Life on Earth.* New York: Harper, 2024.

Schliephake, Christopher and Evi Zemanek, eds. *Anticipatory Environmental (Hi)Stories from Antiquity to the Anthropocene.* Lanham: Lexington Books, 2023.

Schudt, Johann Jacob. *Jüdische Merckwürdigkeiten.* Frankfurt am Main: Verlegts Samuel Tobias Hocker, 1714.

Schulte, Christoph. *Zimzum: God and the Origins of the World.* Philadelphia: University of Pennsylvania Press, 2023 (orig., 2014).

Schwartz, Eilon. "*Bal Tashchit*: A Jewish Environmental Precept." *Environmental Ethics* 18 (Winter 1997): 355–74.

Schwartz, Eilon. "Environment: Jewish Education as if the Planet Mattered." In *International Handbook of Jewish Education, Part One,* edited by Helena Miller, Lisa D. Grant, and Alex Pomson, 389–406. Dordrecht: Springer, 2011.

Schwartz, Eilon. "Judaism and Nature: Theological and Moral Issues to Consider While Renegotiating a Jewish Relationship to the Natural World." *Judaism* 44, no. 4 (1995): 437–47.

Scranton, Roy. *Learning to Die in the Anthropocene: Reflections on the End of a Civilization.* San Francisco: City Light Books, 2015.

Scribner, Robert. "The Mordbrenner Fear in Sixteenth-Century Germany: Political Paranoia for the Revenge of the Outcast." In *The German Underworld: Deviants and Outcasts in German History,* edited by Richard J. Evans, 29–56. New York: Routledge, 1988.

Sedlak, David. *Water for All: Global Solutions for a Changing Climate.* New Haven: Yale University Press, 2023.

Segal, Lester A. *Historical Consciousness and Religious Tradition in Azariah de' Rossi's* Me'or 'Einayim. Philadelphia: Jewish Publication Society, 1989.

Shamir, Eilon. "Contemporary Idolatry and a Path to Freedom." In *Idolatry: A Contemporary Jewish Conversation,* edited by Alon Goshen-Gottstein, 151–67. Boston: Academic Studies Press, 2023.

Shankar Raman, T.R. "Expanding Nature Conservation: Considering Wide Landscapes and Deep Histories." In *At Nature's Edge: The Global Present and Long-Term History,* edited by Gunnel Cederlöf and Mahesh Rangarajan (Oxford: Oxford University Press, 2018), 249–67.

Shoham-Steiner, Ephraim. "Jews and Healing at Medieval Saints' Shrines: Participation, Polemics, and Shared Cultures." *Harvard Theological Review* 103, no. 1 (2010): 111–29.

Smith, Monica L., ed. *The Power of Nature: Archaeology and Human-Environmental Dynamics.* Denver: University Press of Colorado, 2022.

Snowden, David J. and Mary E. Boone. "A Leader's Framework for Decision Making." *Harvard Business Review* 85, no. 11 (2007): 68–76.

Soloveitchik, Joseph B. *The Lonely Man of Faith.* New York: Doubleday, 1992.

Steinmetz, Devora. *Why Rain Comes from Above: Explorations in Religious Imagination.* New York: Hadar Press, 2024.

Stoll, Mark R. "Sinners in the Hands of an Ecologic Crisis: Lynn White's Environmental Jeremiad." In *Religion and Ecological Crisis: The "Lynn White Thesis" at Fifty,* edited by Todd LeVasseur and Anna Peterson, 47–60. London: Routledge, 2017.

Straus, Raphael. *Urkunden und Aktenstücke zur Geschichte der Juden in Regensburg 1453–1739.* Munich: Beck, 1960.

Szerszynski, Bronislaw. "From the Anthropocene Epoch to a New Axial Age: Using Theory-Fictions to Explore Geo-Spiritual Futures." In *Religion in the Anthropocene*, edited by Celia Deane-Drummond, Sigurd Bergmann, and Markus Vogt, 35–52. Eugene, OR: Cascade Books, 2017.

Taylor, Mark. C. *After God*. Chicago: University of Chicago Press, 2007.

Teplitsky, Joshua. "Plague, Passover, and Perspectives on Social Distancing." *Columbia University Libraries*, April. 21, 2020. https://blogs.cul.columbia.edu/rbml/2020/04/21/plague-passover-and-perspectives-on-social-distancing-dr-joshua-teplitsky/.

Thelen, Johann Leonard. "Ausführliche Nachricht von dem erschrecklichen Eisgange und den Ueberschwemmungen des Rheines, welche im Jahre 1784 die Stadt Köln und die umliegenden Gegenden betroffen …" In *Die Stadt Mülheim am Rhein*, edited by Johann Bendel, 465–70. Mülheim am Rhein, 1913.

Thomas, Keith. *Religion and the Decline of Magic*. New York: Charles Scribner's Sons, 1971.

Thompson, Andrew R. H. "Climate Vulnerability as Theological Bridge Concept: Examples from Puerto Rico." In *Climate Politics and the Power of Religion*, edited by Evan Berry, 206–29. Bloomington: Indiana University Press, 2022.

Tirosh-Samuelson, Hava. *Religion and Environment: The Case of Judaism*. Pandora Press, 2020.

Toly, Noah J. *The Gardeners' Dirty Hands: Environmental Politics and Christian Ethics*. Oxford: Oxford University Press, 2019.

Toner, Jerry. *Roman Disasters*. Cambridge: Polity Press, 2013.

Troster, Lawrence. "Created in the Image of God: Humanity and Divinity in an Age of Environmentalism." In *Judaism and Environmental Ethics: A Reader*, edited by Martin D. Yaffe, 172–82. Lanham: Lexington Books, 2001.

Tucker, Mary Evelyn and John Grim. "The Movement of Religion and Ecology: Emerging Field and Dynamic Force." In *Routledge Handbook of Religion and Ecology*, edited by Willis Jenkins, Mary Evelyn Tucker, and John Grim, 3–12. London: Routledge, 2017.

Turniansky, Chava. "Yiddish Song as Historical Source Material: Plague in the Judenstadt of Prague in 1713." In *Jewish History: Essays in Honour of Chimen Abramsky*, edited by. Ada Rapoport-Albert and Steven J. Zipperstein, 189–98. London: P. Halban, 1989.

Tweed, Thomas A. *Crossing and Dwelling: A Theory of Religion*. Cambridge, MA: Harvard University Pres, 2006.

Uekötter, Frank. *The Vortex: An Environmental History of the Modern World*. Pittsburgh: University of Pittsburgh Press, 2023.

van den Noortgaete, Francis. "Reconsidering the Anthropocene as *Milieu*: William Desmond and the Originary Goodness of Being." In *Religion in the Anthropocene*, edited by Celia Deane-Drummond, Sigurd Bergmann, and Markus Vogt, 155–70. Eugene, OR: Cascade Books, 2017.

van Wieren, Gretel. "Conservation and Restoration." In *Routledge Handbook of Religion and Ecology*, edited by. Willis Jenkins, Mary Evelyn Tucker, and John Grim, 265–74. London: Routledge, 2017.

Varlik, Nükhet. "Disease and Empire: A History of Plague Epidemics in the Early Modern Ottoman Empire (1453–1600)." Doctoral Dissertation, University of Chicago, 2008.

Varlik, Nükhet. "From 'Bete Noire' to 'le Mal de Constantinople:' Plagues, Medicine, and the Early Modern Ottoman State." *Journal of World History* 24, no. 4 (December 2013): 741–70.

Varlik, Nükhet. "'Oriental Plague' or Epidemiological Orientalism? Revisiting the Plague Episteme of the Early Modern Mediterranean." In *Plague and Contagion in the Islamic Mediterranean*, 57–87. Newark: Arc Humanities Press, 2017.

Vogel, David . "How Green is Judaism? Exploring Jewish Environmental Ethics." Unpublished Paper, 1999. https://faculty.haas.berkeley.edu/vogel/judaism.pdf.

Ward, Christopher and Sandra Ruckstuhl. *Water Scarcity, Climate Change and Conflict in the Middle East: Securing Livelihoods, Building Peace*. London: I.B. Tauris, 2017.

Ward, Jacob. *The Loop: How Technology is Creating a World Without Choices and How to Fight Back*. New York: Hachette Books, 2022.

Warde, Paul. *Ecology, Economy and State Formation in Early Modern Germany*. Cambridge: Cambridge University Press, 2006.

Warren, Louis. "Owning Nature: Toward an Environmental History of Private Property." In *The Oxford Handbook of Environmental History*, edited by Andrew C. Isenberg, 398–424. Oxford: Oxford University Press, 2014.

Wayne White, Carol. "Race and Ethnicity." In *Grounding Religion: A Field Guide to the Study of Religion and Ecology*, edited by. Whitney Bauman, Richard Bohannon, and Kevin J. O'Brien, second edn, 77–93. London: Routledge, 2017.

Webster, Robert. "The Lisbon Earthquake: John and Charles Wesley Reconsidered." In *The Lisbon Earthquake of 1755: Representations and Reactions*, edited by Theodore E.D. Braun and John B. Radner, 116–26. Oxford: Voltaire Foundation, 2005.

Weinberg, Joanna. "The Voice of God: Jewish and Christian Responses to the Ferrara Earthquake of November 1570." *Italian Studies* 46 (1990–91): 69–81.

Weintrobe, Sally. *Psychological Roots of the Climate Crisis: Neoliberal Exceptionalism and the Culture of Uncare*. London: Bloomsbury, 2021.

White, Jr., Lynn. "The Historical Roots of Our Ecological Crisis." *Science* 155 (1967): 1203–07.

White, Sam. *A Cold Welcome: The Little Ice Age and Europe's Encounter with North America*. Cambridge, MA: Harvard University Press, 2017.

Whitney, Elspeth. "Lynn White Jr.'s 'The Historical Roots of Our Ecological Crisis' after Fifty Years." In *Religion and Ecological Crisis: The "Lynn White Thesis" at Fifty*, edited by Todd LeVasseur and Anna Peterson, 18–32. London: Routledge, 2017.

Wittenberg, Jonathan. "The Idolatry of Humankind." In *Idolatry: A Contemporary Jewish Conversation*, edited by Alon Goshen-Gottstein, 168–84. Boston: Academic Studies Press, 2023.

Wormser Minhagbuch des R. Jousep (Juspa) Schammes. Prepared by Erich Zimmer, 2 vols. Jerusalem: Mifal Torat Chachme Aschkenas, 1988) [Hebrew].

Yaffe, Martin D., ed. *Judaism and Environmental Ethics: A Reader*. Lanham: Lexington Books, 2001.

Yerushalmi, Yosef Hayim. *Zakhor: Jewish History and Jewish Memory*. Seattle: University of Washington Press, 1982.

Yildiz, Kenan. "Istanbul Fires During the Ottoman Period and Their Effect on the City's Topography." https://istanbultarihi.ist/393-istanbul-fires-during-the-ottoman-period -and-their-effect-on-the-citys-topography.

Zaidman-Mauer, Daniella. "'May God Shield us from the Plague.' Vernacular Remedies for the Plague from Moyshe Kalish's Yiddish Self-help Medical Book Seyfer Yerum Moyshe (Amsterdam 1679)." *Zutot*, 19, no. 1 (2022): 144–62.

Zehnder, Günter, ed. *Eine Gesllschaft zwischen Tradition und Wandel: Alltag und Umwelt im Rheinland des 18. Jahrhunderts*. Cologne: DuMont, 1999.

Zika, Charles. "Heavenly Portents and Divine Anger: The Emotional Intensity of Fire From the Sky in the Later Sixteenth Century." *Occasion* 13, special issue on Fire Stories (2022). https://shc.stanford.edu/arcade/publications/occasion/fire-stories/heavenly -portents-and-divine-anger-emotional-intensity.

Zinger, Nimrod. "'Our Hearts and Spirits were Broken': The Medical World from the Perspective of German-Jewish Patients in the Seventeenth and Eighteenth Centuries." *The Leo Baeck Institute Year Book* 54, no. 1 (2009): 59–91.
Zohar, Motti. "Damage Patterns of Earthquakes in Israel and Its Vicinity: Evaluation According to the Historical Sources." Doctoral Dissertation, Hebrew University of Jerusalem, 2016. https://www.gov.il/BlobFolder/reports/zohar-m-report-2016/en/report_2016_GSI-22-2016-PhD-Thesis-HUJI.pdf.
Zohar, Motti, Amos Salamon, and Rehav Rubin. "Reappraised List of Historical Earthquakes that Affected Israel and its Close Surroundings." *Journal of Seismology* (16 April 2016): 9–23.
Zoloth, Laurie. *Ethics for the Coming Storm: Climate Change and Jewish Thought*. Oxford: Oxford University Press, 2023.
Zwierlein, Cornel. "The Burning of a Modern City? Istanbul as Perceived by the Agents of the Sun Fire Office, 1865–1870." In *Flammable Cities: Urban Conflagration and the Making of the Modern World*, edited by George Bankoff, Uwe Lübken, and Jordan Sand, 82–102. Madison: University of Wisconsin Press, 2012.

Index

Abdal Musa   82
Aberbach, David   131
Abraham   52, 53, 61
Abraham bar Joseph Kosman   194 n.31
Abram, David   147–50
acceleration   91
    of Anthropocene   109
    of change   5, 85, 116
    of modernity   116
Adam   121, 124, 129
Adventists   123
Aegean Anatolia   81
Aftandilian, Dave   151
Agamben, Giorgio   103
Agamemnon   33
agency   3, 6, 63, 97, 117, 119, 162, 164,
        205 n.64, 222 n.26
Akiba   132, 215 n.108
Albo, Joseph   138
Aleppo   84, 85
Algiers   76
alphabetic writing   149
American Immanence (Hogue)   226 n.40,
        227 n.73
American immanental theological
        framework   110
Ammerman, Steven   205 n.64
Amsterdam   52, 55, 56
Ancient Near Eastern   31, 45, 46
Anthropocene   1, 2, 4, 45, 93, 95, 103–5,
        107, 109, 116, 118, 135, 136,
        139, 155, 156, 158, 164, 183, 203
        n.32, 204 n.51
    human and nature of humanity   95–7
    acceleration of time and
        complexity   101–3
    globalization   99
    modernity   97–8
    modern self   98–9
    progress   99
    science and technology   100–1
    universal and particular   98
    thinking, writing, and learning   170–4

anthropocentrism   122
anthroscape   97
anticipatory environmental histories   114
anti-Jewish activities   42
Antiquity   17, 33, 60, 169
antisocial postures   97
apocalypse   111, 121
    fatigue   127
    thinking   108, 151
Apollo   33, 188 n.11
aquatic metaphors   151
Archbishop of Mainz   68
Arendt, Hannah   116, 118
Aristotle   15, 16
arson   64
Artificial Intelligence (AI)   100
Asher Levy of Reichshofen   34
atmospheric cover   50
av bet din (head of the court)   24
Averroes   83
awareness, formed   177
Ayalon, Yaron   78, 83, 84

Babylonian reign   19
backloading   115
bad air   34, 37
bal tashchit   133, 134
Bamberg   50, 51
banishment   37
Barnett, Lydia   107
Basel   17
Baucom, Ian   103
Bauman, Whitney A.   157
Bavli Ta'anit   140, 217 n.27
Beck, Ulrich   177
behavioral change   174–9
Bell, Dean Phillip   191 n.68
Belser, Julia Watts   139, 217 n.27
Benedictine abbey   194 n.31
Benstein, Jeremy   124, 128, 129
ben Zakkai, Yoḥanan   62
Berger, J. W.   55, 56
Berners-Lee, Mike   176

Ber of Bolochow   65
Berry, Evan   150
Berry, Wendell   112–13, 175, 176
biblical deluges   107
biblical literature   122
biblical writings   34, 70
binaries   5, 113, 155, 157, 165, 166
binary thinking   86, 87, 92
bin Ibrahim al-Yahudi, Ilyas   82, 83
biological organisms   139
biosphere   161
Black Death   35, 36
Blanchot, Maurice   94
blasphemy   196 n.10
Bohr, Niels   170
Bonn   50–3, 56
Boroditsky, Lera   171
Boykoff, Maxwell   114
bridge building   114
Bridle, James   222 n.26
bubonic plague   30, 41, 80, 83

Cairo   82
Campbell, Brian   159
capitalism   119, 158
capitalist Management   118
Capitalocene   96, 176
carbon credits   173
Carinthia   17
Catalano, Abraham   39–41
Catholic General Vicarius   56
causality   101, 103, 116, 181
causation   6, 142
Chakrabarty, Dipesh   117–19
Chandler, David   164, 165
charity   20, 55, 56
Chewong   112
Chosen People   15
Christian, Brian   174
Christianity   66, 69, 76, 121, 122, 150
Christian rule   75
Christian West   75, 85
Chryses   33, 188 n.11
circle of impact   108
City Council   66–8, 198 n.55
city of Mainz   64
civil ordinance   63
climate change   1, 2, 4, 5, 30, 95, 96, 107,
		110, 114, 115, 117–19, 123, 127,
		128, 135, 150, 151, 169, 172,
		177–80, 182
climate convulsions   108
climate crisis   5, 110, 111, 117, 118, 131,
		138, 177, 179, 181, 226 n.40
climate grief   127
climate skeptics   123
Cohen, Jeremy   125, 126
Cohen, Naphtali   66
Coleman, Peter   139, 161–3
collaboration   3, 5, 57, 72, 104
Cologne   51–4, 56
comets   42
communal boundaries   43, 57
communal/religious improvement   66
community   6, 18, 24, 35, 37, 39, 40, 49,
		55–7, 65–7, 78, 92, 95, 142, 143,
		149, 158, 159, 170–2, 182
	collaboration 179
complexity   6, 85, 101–3, 113, 139, 156,
		162–6, 172, 183
	beyond binaries 157
	change 157–8
	emergence 156–7
	relationships 158–9
	spatial and temporal
		considerations 159–61
complex resilience   165, 166
complex system   102, 155–8, 162
conflict   57, 103, 104, 127, 139, 173, 179
consciousness   5, 144, 149, 156–8
conservatism   146
Constance   35
consumption   1, 4, 97, 125, 134
	culture 131
contagion   34, 37, 81, 82, 84
covenant   31, 32, 46, 86, 94, 121, 126,
		129–30
Covid-19 pandemic   29, 30, 41, 43, 98
Crawford, Kate   100
creation   17, 23, 72, 86, 102, 121, 124,
		125, 130, 135, 144

Dalby, Simon   165
Davenport, Leslie   127
David ben Simon Sougers of Prague   66,
		70, 71
Davidic prophecy   19
de-centering humans   165

decision-making   163, 173
deep ecology   109, 159
deep history   5, 101, 109
Deism   25
de Rossi, Azaria   19–22
Descola, Philippe   112
Design of the Divine Chariot   62
Detroit   96
deus absconditus   23
Deutz   52, 53, 55, 56, 194 n.31
Dewey, John   177, 227 n.73
disasters   30, 59, 72, 93–5, 199 n.9
   historiography of   108–9
   management   3
   natural   2–5, 11, 12, 23, 26, 29, 31, 45,
      51, 58–9, 71–2, 75, 78, 80, 83–4,
      86, 91–3, 96, 107, 108, 122, 126,
      155, 169, 174, 191 n.68
diseases   29, 30, 41–3, 80, 82, 83, 92
divine contraction   132, 133
divine disempowerment   23
divine intervention   21
divine omnipotence   17, 123
divine providence   21, 23
divine punishment   24, 42, 58, 62–4, 66,
      67, 72, 92, 122
divine truth   131
divine wrath   64, 78
   Anger of Heaven 24
domination   121, 125, 126, 135, 155, 176
Duchy of Berg   52
dwelling   151, 160

Eagleton, Terry   145
earthquakes   11, 12, 78–80, 85, 96, 186
      n.30, 191 n.68
   accounts at the edge of
      modernity   22–6
   early modern narratives   19–22
   in Middle Ages   16–19
   understanding sources   12–16
earth system   91, 95–7, 102, 118, 166
Eaton, Heather   157
eco-anxiety   177
eco-authoritarianism   97
ecological crisis   172
ecological debt   165
ecological imperative   132
ecological system   45, 109, 117, 216 n.1

ecology   137, 138, 150
economy of sin   29, 31, 33, 47, 77, 107,
      121
Edirne   81
education   158, 171, 173, 182, 183
Edzard, Esdras   69
Efendi, Ebussund   82
Einstein, Albert   116
Eisenstadt, Moses ben Hayim   36, 37
Elasa   159
Elazar ben Arakh   62
Elazar ben Azariah   175
Elberfeld   56
Eliade, Mircea   149
Eliezer Lezer Oppenheim   70, 192 n.3
emergence   156–7
Emerson, Brian   163
Emmett, Robert   173
empathy burnout   127
engagement   6, 58, 140, 145, 147, 172,
      173, 181
Engelke, Peter   96
Enlightenment   23, 108, 144
   dualism   140
environment   1, 11, 58, 72, 85, 95, 97, 99,
      101, 102, 105, 108–10, 112, 113,
      121, 123–4, 126–8, 131, 133,
      135–7, 155, 157, 169–71
environmental challenges   99, 121, 136,
      180
environmental change   107, 155, 181
environmental concerns   104, 117, 122,
      130, 135, 137, 157, 162, 182
environmental crises   4, 96, 99, 114, 122,
      128, 138, 151, 156, 157, 160,
      171, 180
environmental decision-making   163
environmental degradation   85, 91, 96,
      103, 114, 128, 138, 150, 164,
      173, 178, 180, 182
environmental disaster   50, 131, 157
environmental distress   58
environmental ethics   150
environmental historians   110, 208 n.25
environmental history   4, 58, 85, 108–10,
      114, 119, 208 n.25
environmental humanities   110, 170
environmentalism   121, 123, 125, 133,
      159

environmental pragmatism   150
environmental problems   100, 104, 113,
        122
environmental strategy   176
epidemics   30, 42, 81, 200 n.26
eschatology   137
essentialisms   147
Eternal One   54, 55
ethics   117, 135, 170
Europe   23, 50, 81
evangelical identity   123
evangelicals   123
Eve   121
exceptionalism   131, 177
experience   6, 110, 115, 116, 127, 145

fatalism   82
Favier, Rene   108
Feminist Studies   170
Fez   76
Ficino, Marsilio   191 n.74
"Fiddler on the Roof" conundrum   140
Finkelman, Yoel   143
fire   59, 71, 72, 77–8, 98
    biblical and rabbinic discussions   59–
        62
    in early modern history   62–5
    Great Fire of 1711, Frankfurt Jewish
        Ghetto   65–71
Fishbane, Michael   126
Fisher, Joshua   104
flight from plague   82
flooding   43, 46–8, 50–2, 54, 98, 107, 194
        n.31, 195 n.67
floods   42, 45, 57, 58, 93, 107
    of 1784   50, 56
    in biblical and rabbinic texts and
        thought   46–8
    histories   48–9
forced resettlement   81
fore-meaning   143
Fortuna   107
Foucault, Michel   103–4
fracking   12
Fraiman, Keren   161, 173
Frankfurt am Main   59, 65
Frankfurt City Council   67
Frankfurt ghetto   66, 69
Frankfurt jurisdiction   68

Frankopan, Peter   206 n.95
Freire, Paulo   182
future   113, 115, 116, 197 n.26
    disasters   3, 4, 58, 59
    generations   115, 128, 129, 151, 172, 183
    narratives   179

Gadamer, Hans-Georg   143–7
Gaia   111
Galata   78
Galen   83
Gans, David   21, 22, 64
Garden of Eden   122, 124
Gardner, Stephen   115
Garnet-Abisset, Anne-Marie   108
gemilut hesed (giving of loving-
        kindness)   36
Genesis Rabbah   60
geographic proximity   112
geo-spatial practices   151
Germany   50, 51, 56, 58, 194 n.47
Gerona   18, 19
ghetto   36, 39, 40, 59, 66–9, 71, 72
Ghosh, Amitav   99, 178
globalization   98, 99, 160
Global North   165
Global South   165
global warming   1, 161
glocalization   98
Glückel of Hameln   36
God   19, 24, 26, 46, 126, 129, 156, 186
        n.30, 196 n.9
    anger   12–14, 22, 24, 25, 67, 79
    commandments   31, 175
    control of history   126
    covenant   126
    creation   124, 125
    curative interventions   82
    decision   84
    divine names   82
    fury   62
    image   122, 123
    justice   21
    law   31, 60, 62
    plan   130
    power   14, 15, 48, 130
    punishment for sin   57, 62
    sovereignty   17
    thundering voice   15

wonders 21
wrath 14, 23, 39, 60
Goh, Kian 165
Goshen-Gottstein, Alon 129, 130
Gottlieb, Roger 151
Great Fire of 1711 65–71
Greek medicine 34
Greek Orthodox Christians 77
Greek scribes 150
Green, Arthur 131
Greenberg, Yitz 129
green religious movements 123
greenwashing 127
grief 127
Grove, Kevin 164

Habermas, Jürgen 145, 222 n.52
Haci Bektaş 82
HaCohen, Elijah 80
Haidt, Jonathan 100
Hakham Meir ben Shemtov Melamed 77
halakhah (Jewish law) 138
Halevi, Joseph 52
Hampton, Alexander J. B. 98
Hand of Divine Justice 24
Hanina 133
harmony orientation 162
Harper, Kyle 107
Harvey, David 157, 158, 160, 161
heating 1
Hebraic religiosity 149
Hebrew alphabet 149
Hebrew Bible 3, 31, 32, 46, 51, 60, 126,
 131
 Gen.
 2:15 122
 6 46
 Lev.
 26 31
 Deut.
 11, 13-18 199 n.9
 2 Chron.
 6:28-31 32
 Job
 14:19 47
 22:10-11 47
 Ps.
 18:8 14
 91 32

Isa.
 5:25 14
 24 19
 Ezek.
 20:37 141
 38:18-23 12
 39:1-8 13
Hebrew month
 of Adar 38, 52, 54
 of Elul 54
 of Shevat 54
 of Sivan 39
 of Tevet 52, 70, 79
 of Tishrei 37
Hebrew Prayerbook 131
Hebrew Scriptures 30
Hebrew texts 149
Hebrew vowels 149
Heidegger, Martin 144, 160
Held, Shai 133
Henry, Matthew S. 171
hermeneutics 143, 145
Hewish environmentalism 125
Ḥilfai 125
Hippocrates 83
historians 30, 66, 86, 92, 107, 109, 110,
 116, 208 n.27
historical flood narratives 48
historical horizon 144
historical records 91, 109
history 2, 11, 12, 19, 29–31, 35, 48, 77,
 80, 83, 86, 91, 92, 94, 102, 104,
 108, 109, 112–17, 126, 132, 137,
 142, 147, 149, 155, 157, 163,
 169, 180–2
 of life 118
 role and limits 117–19
Hizir 82
Hogue, Michael S. 97, 101, 110, 135,
 136, 138, 165, 172, 177
Holocene 95, 101
Holtz, Barry 146
Holy Land 31
Holy One of Blessing 192 n.3
holy people 33
Holy Roman Empire 65
Holy Seer of Lublin 176
Homo sapiens 95
human activity 1, 12, 96, 165, 169

human brotherhood   51
human dominance   132, 183
human domination   123
human evildoing   23
human evolution   118
human history   45, 101, 111, 117, 209
      n.40
human-induced climate change   1, 45,
      91, 100, 117
Humanities disciplines   113
humanity   23, 95, 101, 107, 112, 117,
      122, 124, 130, 137, 166, 170, 203
      n.32, 207 n.122
human power   103, 117
human practice   125, 150
human responsibility   127
   for tree   134
human self-restraint   132, 133
human sins   33, 42, 46, 62, 71, 94, 122,
      123
human social development   59
human technology   100
human transgressions   32
Husserl, Edmund   143, 148
hyperobject   1, 161

Ibn Khātima   83
ibn Pakuda, Bahya   17
idolatry   130–1, 159
Iliad   33
indigenous religion   137
indigenous societies   147, 182
industrial civilization   118
industrialism   175
inequities, codify   165
infectious diseases   1, 107
Inquisition   24
intentionality   111, 112, 159
interdisciplinary history   109
internal discord   56
International Commission on Stratigraphy
      (ICS)   203 n.32
invulnerability/resilience   98, 103
Isenberg, Andrew   110
Islam   73, 75, 76, 78, 81, 82, 85
Islamic heartland   82
Islamic thought   82
Islamization   77, 78, 82
   of urban landscape   78

Israeli-Palestinian conflict   173
Israelites   13, 14, 31, 32, 46, 60, 129
Istanbul   66, 77, 81, 82
Izmir   80

Jacob ben Isaac Zahalon   41, 191 n.77
Jarva, Vuokko   170, 179
Jay, Martin   110
Jenkins, Philip   108
Jenkins, Willis   117, 135, 137, 150, 151
Jesuits   23
Jewish communities   4, 20, 36, 39, 41, 49,
      52, 53, 57, 58, 64–9, 76, 84–6,
      143
Jewish Construction Ordinance   67
Jewish Curiosities (*Jüdische
      Merckwürdigkeiten*)   69
Jewish demographics   76
Jewish education   171, 173
Jewish environmental ethics   125
Jewish environmental history   6, 87
Jewish environmentalism   125, 172
Jewish ghetto   41, 59, 65, 66, 69, 191 n.77
Jewish history   2, 4–6, 11, 21, 65, 69, 75,
      111, 181
Jewish law   3, 57, 138
Jewish learning   6
Jewish life   2, 42, 58
   under Islam   75
Jewish machinations   66
Jewish marginalization   56
Jewish neighborhood   77, 80
Jewish prayers   58
Jewish quarter   18, 36, 66–9, 71, 76, 85
Jewish religiosity   17
Jewish settlement   51, 69, 76, 194 n.47
Jewish space   68, 69, 72
Jewish studies   125
Jewish synagogues   51
Jewish texts   57, 127
Jewish trade   68
Jewish writers   57, 58, 66
Jews   2–4, 12, 15, 18, 21, 22, 25, 26, 34,
      36, 37, 39, 41, 49, 51–4, 56–8,
      60, 61, 65–9, 71–3, 75, 85, 111,
      125, 169, 181, 195 n.57, 198 n.55
   under Islam   75
      earthquakes   78–80
      fires   77–8

Jewish demographics   76
  plague   80–4
jinn   81
Joerstad, Mari   124
Jonas, Hans   100, 102, 132
Jordan, William R.   158, 159
Judaism   2–4, 6, 119, 124, 125, 128, 131,
  133, 134, 137, 140, 141, 146,
  147, 152, 181, 182
Judenstadt   36
Judeo-Christian traditions   2, 121, 122,
  124, 181
Juspa   38, 49, 50

kabbalistic intrigues   66
Kahneman, Daniel   100, 163
Kant, Immanuel   150
Kattina   15
Katz, Mordechai   54
kav   133
Kedushat Levi (Levi Yitzhak of
  Berdichev)   174
Kohen, Berman   55
"Kol Elohim" (The Voice of God)   19
Kopenhagen, Simon ben Jacob
  Abraham   52
Korach   47
Koselleck, Reinhart   115, 116
Kosman, Joseph Juspa   52
Kosslyn, Stephen   158
Kritovoulos   200 n.26

Landjudenschaft   52
landscapes   110
language   66, 108, 171
Latour, Bruno   99, 104, 111, 112,
  157
learning process   5, 58, 108, 115, 117,
  137, 146, 150, 166, 173
Leipziger Zeitung   50
Leiviskä, Anniina   146
Leopold, Aldo   159, 170
leprosy   31
Levi bar Ḥiyya   125
Levinas, Emmanuel   94, 127
Levi Yitzhak of Berdichev   174
Lewis, Kelly   163
Lightman, Alan   116
limitlessness   176

linear causality   164
Lisbon earthquake   22–4
literature   57, 114, 116
liturgical "mention"   132
living tradition   142
Lobel, Orly   171
localization   99, 160
London   23, 24
The Lonely Man of Faith
  (Soloveitchik)   129
longe duree   118
long-term environmental histories
  208 n.19
Lovelock, James   111
lovingkindness   48
Lucretius Carus   33
Lunshitz, Solomon Ephraim   37
Lutherans   56

McNeill, J. R.   96
maggefah   31
Magid, Shaul   131
Maimonides   134, 143
Mallon, Colleen Mary   142
Mameluke rule   76
Mannheim   50
manufactured vulnerability   102
Margalit, Natan   113, 114
Martusewicz, Rebecca   172
Masco, Joseph   180
Mauelshagen, Franz   108
medicine   29, 40, 42
medieval Jews   17, 19
Mehler, Judah ben Joseph   52
mellah   76
Mendel Nathan   15, 52, 54, 55, 58,
  195 n.57
Me'or Enayim (de Rossi)   19
Merleau-Ponty, Maurice   148
metamorphosis   177
Meteorologica II (Aristotle)   16
miasma   34
Middle Ages   17, 33, 64
Midrash Bereshit Rabbah   125
midrashic reading   146
modernity   2, 3, 11, 30, 48, 50, 73, 75,
  85, 86, 91, 97–100, 105, 108,
  110–12, 115, 116, 118, 127, 131,
  169, 173, 222 n.26

modernization   115
modern time   115
mohelim (circumcisers)   38
monotheism   124
moralising gods   206 n.95
morality   131–2, 134
Morton, Timothy   1, 161
Moses ben Maimon. *See* Maimonides
Mülheim   51, 53–6, 58
multiple othernesses   161
Muslim group   75
Muslim lands   82

narratives   12, 49, 104, 113–14, 170, 171,
        179
natural disasters   2–5, 11, 12, 23, 26, 29,
        31, 45, 51, 58, 59, 71, 72, 75, 78,
        80, 83, 84, 86, 91–3, 96, 107,
        108, 122, 126, 155, 169, 174, 191
        n.68
natural events   16, 21, 96, 109
natural history   111
Natural History (Pliny)   16
natural systems   97, 178
natural world   107, 113, 123, 124, 131,
        132, 134, 149
nature   2, 5, 11, 17, 23, 25, 29, 85, 91, 96,
        98, 111, 114, 122–5, 134–7, 151,
        159, 163, 171, 177
    and culture   110–13, 157
    writing   113
Navajo   149
necessary beliefs   143
Neiman, Susan   98, 99
Nelson, Ben   158
Nero   196 n.7
Newton, Isaac   150
Nieto, Isaac   24, 25, 191 n.68
Noah   45–8, 61, 130
nonhuman nature   148
non-Jewish accounts   22, 26, 54, 55
non-Jewish quarters   80
non-Jewish sources   21
non-kosher wine   37
Norberg-Schulz, Christian   160
North Africa   76
Northcott, Michael S.   123, 207 n.122
Norvig, Peter   173
Nye, David   174

O'Gieblyn, Meghan   170
Oklahoma   12
ongoing revelation   5
On the Nature of Things (*De Rerum
        Natura*) (Lucretius)   33
ordinance   67, 68, 198 n.55
Otten, Willemien   135
Ottoman Empire   75–7, 81–4
Ottoman Jewry   76
Ottoman lands   76, 81
Ottoman settlement policies   76

Padua   38–40
Pande, Vasudha   208 n.19
particularism   98
Pedaya, Haviva   131
perception   1, 148
perennial revelation   138
performative perception   217 n.27
Pfister, Christian   108, 109
philosophy   19, 117, 170
physicians   41
Pilsen   51
pious behavior   21, 33
Pirkei Avot   141
Pitum Ha-ketoret   39
places   35, 83, 159, 160
plague   29, 30, 42, 43, 80–4
    biblical, rabbinic, and classical
        understanding and
        approaches   30–4
    case in Padua   38–41
    and Jews in historical context   34–8
planetary climate crisis   117
plant intelligence   158
plastics   102
Pliny the Elder   15, 16, 18
Plutarch   19
polarization   101, 161–4, 166
political action   118
political integration   53
pollution   96
Pomerance   195 n.51, 195 n.54
Popper   218 n.64
posthumanism   101
postmodern sensibilities   111
practical environmentalism   123
practice   37, 43, 86, 133–5, 151, 164, 167
Prague   21, 34–7, 64, 65, 70

Prague Gate   51
prayer   25, 32, 39, 52, 215 n.109
preachers   24, 51
premodern events   11
premodern Jewish life   2
premodern Jews   3, 4, 11, 15, 16
premodern Judaism   3, 4, 86
premodern natural disasters   72, 87
premodern religion   155
premodern sensibility   173
Pritchard, Sara B.   208 n.25
prognoses   116
progress   99, 115, 123, 169
property   55, 64, 122, 124, 149
   ownership   132, 140
      rights   57
Protestantism   123
Providence of God   57
Pseudo-Jonathan, Targum   213 n.45
public Bleichgarten   68, 69
Pullan, Brian   35
punishment for sin   19, 26, 36, 47, 57, 62,
      72, 80, 81, 92, 126
Purim   53, 55

quaking   12–15, 17, 18
quarantine   41, 83, 84
queering   157
Queer Studies   170
queer theory   157
questioning   7, 145, 146
Quran   82

rabbinic authority   52
rabbinic court (*bet din*)   39, 77
rabbinic culture   124
rabbinic literature
   Babylonian Talmud   33, 61
      tractate Berakhot
         35a   124
         59a   15
      tractate Chullin
         63b:11   141
      tractate Nedarim
         80b   179
      tractate Pesachim
         54a   62
      tractate Sanhedrin
         107b-108a   47
      tractate Shabbat
         21b   196 n.3
         54b   127
      tractate Sotah
         10b   141
         17a   61
   Leviticus (Vayikra) Rabbah
      4:6   158
      17   47
   Pirkei Avot
      1:1   141
      3:18   175
   Solomon b. Semah   79
rabbinic sources   20, 138
rabbinic writings   3, 15, 124, 139
rabbis   15, 21, 25, 33, 47, 60–2, 66, 125,
      141, 175
Rashi   60
Rational Mind   113
recognition   178
reconstruction   45, 64, 67, 68, 71–2
record keeping   57
recovery   56, 151, 165
redemptive moments   127
Reform Christians   56
Reform Church   54
"The Refuge from Plague and
      Pestilence" (Ilyas bin Ibrahim
      al-Yahudi)   82
Regensburg Jews   198 n.40
relegere   139
religare   139
religion   2, 3, 5, 23–6, 48, 86, 87, 92, 119,
      121–4, 135–9, 155, 164, 180–2
   and environment   126
      covenant   129–30
      fighting idolatry   130–1
      grief   127
      morality and social justice   131–2
      practice   133–5
      repentance   126–7
      responsibility   127–8
      sustainability   128–9
      tzimtzum   132–3
   responses to environmental
         crises   147–50
   as source of environmental
         degradation   150–2
   tradition   140–7

religious climate skeptics　123

religious discourse　72

religious environmentalists　151

repentance　19, 24–6, 31, 32, 49, 51, 63, 121, 126–7

resilience　103, 164–6
　paradigm　107

responsibility　86, 117, 126–8, 131, 151, 172, 180, 183

revelation　15, 124, 138

Rhineland　50

Rhine-Neckar region　50

Rhine River　45, 50, 51, 54, 55

right-leaning religious groups　123

Robb, John　95

Roman Empire　94, 107

Roman law　140

Rosh Hashanah　61

Rubinstein, Jeffrey　132

Ruckstuhl, Sandra　179

Ruderman, David　17

Ruskin, William　207 n.122

Russell, Stuart　173

Sabbath　31, 38, 53, 54, 61, 63, 121, 130, 137, 191

Sacks, Jonathan　122

Safran Foer, Jonathan　178, 179

Sagi, Avi　138

Salonika　77

scapegoating　26, 30, 42, 94

scenario planning　169, 173

Scholem, Gershom　143

Schotten, Samuel　70

Schudt, Johann Jacob　69, 70

Schulte, Christoph　132

Schwartz, Eilon　133, 134, 171, 172, 216 n.128

science　1, 26, 85, 100, 110, 113, 156, 163, 170, 173, 203 n.32

scientific knowledge　12, 81, 148

scientific revolution　22

Scranton, Roy　116

Second Coming of Christ　69

Sedlak, David　178

seismic activity　12

Selâniki Mustafa Efendi　81

self　4, 72, 85, 93, 98–9, 131

self-centeredness　131

selfishness　131

self-organization　156

self-reflection　26, 63, 71

sermons　24, 41, 51

Seward, Helen　205 n.64

Shamir, Eilon　131

Shammash of Worms　38

Shapiro, Marc B.　142, 143

shared identity　172

Shiite Safavid Empire　76

Shils, Edward　140, 146

Shimon bar Yochai　125, 158

Simhat Torah　38

sin　61
　of disloyalty to God　126
　economy of　29, 31, 33, 47, 77, 107, 121
　human　33, 42, 46, 62, 71, 94, 122, 123
　punishment for　19, 26, 36, 47, 57, 62, 72, 80, 81, 92, 126

Sippur bekhi neharot (Tale of the Weeping of the Rivers)　52

Smith, Monica L.　97

Smyrna　81

social action　157, 161

social change　138, 177, 179

social construction　93

social isolation　123

social justice　126, 131–2, 140, 160

Social Psychology　4

sociology　146

Socrates　148

solidarities　172

Solingen　56

Solomon b. Semah　79

Soloveitchik, Joseph B.　129

Son of God　196 n.9

Southern Baptists　123

space　69, 116, 133, 161, 162, 177

spatial metaphors　151

The Spell of the Sensuous: Perception and Language in a More-Than-Human World (Abram)　148

Speyer　64

stability　157, 164

stakeholders　104

Steinmetz, Devorah　140

stewardship　122, 123, 126, 127, 155, 183, 212 n.5

storytelling   113, 114, 170, 171
subordination   124
Sukkot   132, 215 n.108
Sultan Bayezid II   82
sustainability   128–9, 150, 151
Sympathetic Mind   113
synchronization   163
systems   41, 94, 95, 107, 156, 157, 178

Tacitus   196 n.7
Tammuz   65
Tanakh   140
tāʿūn (pestilence)   81
Taylor, Mark   139
technocratic interventions   165
technology   72, 85, 100–1, 110, 122, 208 n.25
temporal dispersion   115
temporality   114–17
Tetragrammaton   149
Third Way   164
Thirteen scrolls   52
tikkun olam   130
time   33, 101–3, 110, 116, 118, 121, 125, 149, 165
Tirosh-Samuelson, Hava   124, 125
Tisha b'Av   77
Toly, Noah   180
Toner, Jerry   93
top-down technologies   165
topsoil   95
Torah   18, 37, 70, 124, 131, 132, 142, 143
Torah scrolls   52, 54, 55
tradition   5, 6, 49, 86, 138, 140–7, 151, 181, 182
Traditioning Disciplines: The Contribution of Cultural Anthropology to Ecclesial Identity (Mallon)   142
transcendental monotheism   100
Troster, Lawrence   130
true beliefs   143
Truth and Method (Gadamer)   143
Tu b'Shevat   150
Turniansky, Chava   36
Tversky, Amos   163
Tweed, Thomas   151
two minds   113
tzelem   130
tzimtzum (contraction)   132–3

Uekötter, Frank   102
Umar   82
uncertainty   41, 42, 45, 85, 86, 104
United Hebrew Congregations of the Commonwealth   122
universalism   98
universality   161
unrestrained capitalism   131
urban ecologies   177
urban planning   84

values   139, 143, 158
Van den Noortgaete, Francis   100
Veldman, Robin Globus   123
Villach   17
virus   171
VITA framework   166
Vogel, David   124
volcanic ash   50
vortex   103

Wakefield, Stephanie   164
Ward, Christopher   179
Ward, Jacob   100
wasteful destruction   4, 133
water   47, 52, 54, 67, 178–80
   libation   215 n.108
Weintrobe, Sally   177
wellbeing   97
Western Christianity   122
Western religious tradition   135
White, Carol Wayne   157
White, Lynn   103, 121, 122, 125, 151
Whitehead, Alfred North   157
wicked   47, 104, 166, 173
Wiesbaden   196 n.10
wildfires   59
wind   16, 19, 149
wisdom   7, 72, 175
Wittenberg, Jonathan   131
Worms   38, 49
writing   21, 22, 26, 39, 57, 71, 84, 86, 100, 107, 109, 122, 134, 148, 149, 158, 170, 182, 208 n.19
Württemberg   189 n.26

Yehoshua ben Karha   159
Yerushalmi, Yosef Hayim   111

Yitzchak   192 n.3
Yohanan ben Samuel   77, 141
Yom Kippur   61
Yonah   141
Yosei   179, 180

Zemah David (Seed of David)   21, 22
Zimzum   132
Zinger, Nimrod   37, 61
Zohar   20
Zoloth, Laurie   134, 135